JACK WORLTON

Proceedings

Supercomputing 88, Volume II:

SCIENCE AND APPLICATIONS

Edited by Joanne L. Martin and Stephen F. Lundstrom

IEEE Computer Society Press

Washington • Los Alamitos • Brussels • Tokyo

IEEE COMPUTER SOCIETY

THE INSTITUTE OF ELECTRICAL AND ELECTRONICS ENGINEERS, INC.

IEEE

The papers in this book comprise the proceedings of the meeting mentioned on the cover and title page. They reflect the authors' opinions and are published as presented and without change, in the interests of timely dissemination. Their inclusion in this publication does not necessarily constitute endorsement by the editors, the IEEE Computer Society Press, or The Institute of Electrical and Electronics Engineers, Inc.

Published by

IEEE Computer Society Press
1730 Massachusetts Avenue, N.W.
Washington, D.C. 20036-1903

About the cover:

The simulated variability of the volume transport streamfunction (in units of 10^6 m^3/sec) is superimposed on the ocean depths (in km), both from a global ocean model which explicitly resolves turbulence. Bright yellow/red regions found near ridge-like features in the bottom topography indicate strongly unstable portions of the clockwise flowing Antarctic Circumpolar Current—the oceanic equivalent of an atmospheric jet stream. To simulate the variability of this grand current of the Southern Ocean required the global model to be run for 500 hours at 430 MFLOPS on a CRAY X-MP/48 at the National Center for Atmospheric Research. Further information is available in the paper by Semtner and Chervin contained in this volume.

IEEE Computer Society Order Number 1923
Library of Congress Catalog Card Number 88-84040
IEEE Order Number 88TH0237-8
ISBN 0-8186-5923-X (microfiche)
ISBN 0-8186-8923-4 (case)

Additional copies may be ordered from:

IEEE Computer Society
Terminal Annex
P.O. Box 4699
Los Angeles, CA 90080

IEEE Service Center
445 Hoes Lane
P.O. Box 1331
Piscataway, NJ 08855-1331

IEEE Computer Society
13, Avenue de l'Aquilon
B-1200 Brussels
BELGIUM

IEEE Computer Society
Ooshima Building
2-19-1 Minami-Aoyama,
Minato-Ku
Tokyo 107 JAPAN

IEEE THE INSTITUTE OF ELECTRICAL AND ELECTRONICS ENGINEERS, INC.

Introduction

The supercomputing industry worldwide is experiencing a period of exciting growth. To provide a forum for the exchange of ideas among participants in this growth, Supercomputing 88 was organized under the auspices of the IEEE Computer Society and ACM SIGARCH. Argonne, Lawrence Livermore, and Los Alamos National Laboratories, NASA Ames Research Center, the National Center for Atmospheric Research, the National Science Foundation, the SIAM Activity Group on Supercomputing, and the Supercomputing Research Center actively supported the creation and organization of the conference.

Three communities participate in this industry: researchers involved in hardware and software engineering activities; managers and staff of supercomputing centers; and, possibly the most important, the computational scientists – also known as users – who depend on supercomputers as a tool to accomplish their individual objectives, whether they are basic research or the development and evaluation of a design. None of these groups can be successful individually. Their combined talents will be required to assure the development of future supercomputer systems that combine the merits of power that can be found in raw hardware with the usability benefits of flexible programming environments.

As much as computer scientists and engineers might dream to the contrary, the drive behind enhancements to supercomputing capabilities comes from the applications that require the power of these advanced systems. Although the absolute definition of the vanguard of supercomputing systems varies over time, with new machines updating and replacing old, there is a ubiquitous set (also dynamic) of applications that requires more than is currently available: more speed, more memory, more network connectivity. These applications have been referred to as the "grand challenges" of computational science and they tend to establish reference points for the development of future systems.

Among the grand challenges facing the scientific community today are computational aerodynamics involving complete aircraft, earth systems science, new areas in chemical engineering, visualization in scientific computing, and the computational aspects of the Human Genome Initiative. The next generation or two of supercomputers may (finally) permit aerodynamicists to solve problems over complete aircraft accurately and in a reasonable amount of time. However, modern aircraft involve complex interactions between external fluid dynamics (flow over surface of wings), the internal fluid dynamics (flow through the jet engines), the structures (wings that flex in response to fluid flow pressures), thermodynamics (change in structural characteristics with change in temperature on the leading edge of wings and in combustion chambers), and chemistry (a function of the mix of air and fuel resulting in significant increase in temperature). Today's supercomputers can only approach the solution of any one of these problems. The combination of these into a single, consistent, multidisciplinary solution is critical to the achievement of future product design objectives, and cannot be accomplished on current systems.

Earth systems science—the subject of the cover of this volume—is rapidly emerging as an area of interest to computational scientists. This area has requirements capable of challenging today's supercomputers. Here the objective is to gain an understanding of the atmosphere, the oceans, and the earth's mantle together with the interactions among these very different regions. Scientific instrumentation in the earth's crust, the oceans, the atmosphere, and space will be in place within a few years and will provide a more complete set of observations about what is happening within the earth system than is available today. Understanding the earth system is expected to involve multidisciplinary models. Rather than predicting what the performance of a particular design would be (as in computational aerodynamics), earth scientists will be searching for an understanding, through their models, that is consistent with the observations made. The challenge clearly involves both complex computational models and the management and consistent coordination of an exceptionally large amount of data.

The chemical engineering community has already discovered the potential benefits of using supercomputers to address some of their more traditional applications, such as the estimation of thermodynamic properties, oil field reservoir engineering, and process modeling and flow sheet simulation. The challenge that exists is for chemical engineers to use supercomputers in an entirely different manner. Optimization of chemical processes needs to benefit from supercomputing capabilities in addition to design, thus augmenting and improving conventional experimental research. New problem areas, solved previously only through heuristic schemes, need to be investigated using the power of supercomputers. Perhaps the most significant trend affecting chemical industries in industrialized nations is the movement of basic industries offshore. The response has been increased emphasis in flexibility, quality, and service rather than on scale. Batch processing is the key to manufacturing small amounts of high value-added products. Unfortunately, batch processing operations are inherently more complex than those encountered in continuously operating plants and heuristics are widely used, primarily because the mathematical formulation of most scheduling problems involves combinatorial optimization problems that are known to be NP-hard. The emergence of supercomputers with sufficient raw power and new approaches to algorithms offers the opportunity to change the basic mode of attack on these scheduling problems.

The Humane Genome Initiative, a national program to ensure international competitiveness in biotechnology, is biology's first "big science" project. The ultimate goal of the initiative is to gain a detailed understanding of the human genome at the molecular level. There is no existing paradigm for the required database, which must become an automated system for data acquisition and knowledge representation, or for the requisite storage and information retrieval technology. It is the opinion of the program's participants that the only hope for understanding the function of complex genomes is to have a sophisticated computer network that brings all relevant data to the desktops of researchers. New methods for reducing very large amounts of data, sometimes only vaguely related, will also be required. Many pattern analysis problems associated with locating biologically significant regions within DNA sequences are at least as difficult as any "classical" signal processing problem that falls into the category of unknown signal with unknown arrival time—with significant noise and spatial warping.

Today's supercomputers are extremely *in*adequate to solve these problems. At Supercomputing 88, grand challenges were addressed as part of thematic track on science and applications that ran throughout the conference. The papers from that track are compiled in this volume of the Proceedings, and are organized into chapters related to the various disciplines. Many of the papers were submitted in response to the call for participation; others were invited by the program committee. All submissions were reviewed by at least two reviewers. Authors were provided the opportunity to revise their papers in response to the comments of the reviewers.

The applications presented in this volume represent some of the most interesting recent uses of supercomputing and reflect the health of this growing industry. We hope that as the Supercomputing Conference grows and matures, applications specialists will continue to be active participants. Their requirements are critical to the development of the field.

Acknowledgments

The Grand Challenges panel at Supercomputing 88 comprised Gregory J. McRae, Chemical Engineering; Victor L. Peterson, Aerodynamics; Thomas G. Marr, Human Genome; Stephen W. Poole, Visualization; and Edward Fredkin, General Application Challenges. Their contributions to the conference are appreciated. We are particularly grateful to Greg McRae, Vic Peterson, and Tom Marr, who provided position papers in their specific areas of interest. These position papers formed the basis of the above discussion of the challenges facing the supercomputing community. We appreciate their sharing of ideas and directions.

We are also very grateful to the reviewers of the papers in this volume, many of whom were drawn from the IEEE Computer Society's Technical Committee on Supercomputer Applications. These reviewers, listed in this volume, provided valuable comments and directions for authors, and worked within very strict time constraints. Their guidance improved the quality of presentation of many of the papers presented here.

Joanne L. Martin *Stephen F. Lundstrom*

Reviewers for the SUPERCOMPUTING '88 Applications Track

Ramesh Agarwal, McDonnell Douglas Research Labs
David Bailey, NASA Ames Research Center
John T. Barton, NASA Ames Research Center
John Bell, Lawrence Livermore National Laboratory
Patrick J. Burns, Colorado State University
Bill Buzbee, National Center for Atmospheric Research
Tony Chan, University of California at Los Angeles
Melvyn Ciment, National Science Foundation
David M. Cohen, University of Iowa
Patricia Comer, The University of Calgary
Sudarshan K. Dhall, University of Oklahoma
David Dixon, E.I. Du Pont de Nemours & Co.
Raymond L. Elliott, Los Alamos National Laboratory
Charlotte F. Fischer, Vanderbilt University
Michael J. Flynn, Stanford University
Myron Ginsberg, General Motors Research Laboratory
Charles Henderson, Cornell Theory Center
Richard S. Hirsh, National Science Foundation
Leah H. Jamieson, Purdue University
Dennis Jespersen, NASA Ames Research Center
Gary Johnson, San Diego Supercomputing Center
Suraj C. Kothari, Iowa State University
Richard Katz, National Center for Atmospheric Research
Harry Jordan, University of Colorado, Boulder
Joseph Lannutti, Florida State University
Patricia Leary, Cornell Theory Center
Robert H. Leary, San Diego Supercomputing Center
Vijay Madisetti, University of California at Berkeley
Orin Marvel, Hughes Aircraft
Greg McRae, Carnegie Mellon University
Paul Messina, California Institute of Technology
Eugene Miya, NASA Ames Research Center
Wayne Pfeiffer, San Diego Supercomputing Center
Daniel V. Pryor, Supercomputing Research Center
John E. Ranelletti, Los Alamos National Laboratory
Ken Stevens, Jr., NASA Ames Research Center
Ahmed Sameh, University of Illinois at Urbana-Champaign
John Santapietro, Lockheed Electronics Co.
Horst Simon, NASA Ames Research Center
Julie M. Swisshelm, NASA Ames Research Center

Supercomputing 88, Volume II: Science and Applications

Table of Contents

Computational Biology and Chemistry

Study of Protein Sequence Comparison Metrics on the Connection Machine CM-2

Eric Lander†
lander%mitwibr.bitnet@mitvma.mit.edu
Whitehead Institute for Biomedical Research
9 Cambridge Center, Cambridge, Massachusetts 02142
and
Harvard University
Cambridge, Massachusetts 02138

Jill P. Mesirov
mesirov@think.com

Washington Taylor IV
wati@think.com
Thinking Machines Corporation,
245 First Street, Cambridge, Massachusetts 02142-1214

Abstract

Software tools have been developed to do rapid large-scale protein sequence comparisons on databases of amino acid sequences, using a data parallel computer architecture. This software enables one to compare a protein against a database of several thousand proteins in the same time required by a conventional computer to do a single protein-protein comparison, thus enabling biologists to find relevant similarities much more quickly, and to evaluate many different comparison metrics in a reasonable period of time. We have used this software to analyze the effectiveness of various scoring metrics in determining sequence similarity, and to generate statistical information about the behavior of these scoring systems under the variation of certain parameters.

1 Introduction

Proteins are the fundamental molecules responsible for building the structures and maintaining the metabolisms of all living organisms. They catalyze biochemical reactions which perform a variety of functions including regulating gene activity, directing the growth of the organism, and converting food into energy. Proteins are essentially linear chains consisting of subunits called amino acids, of which 20 occur frequently in nature. The sequence of amino acids which constitute a protein is referred to as its *primary structure* and can be represented as a sequence of characters in a 20-letter alphabet. This structure is encoded in the DNA of the organism by the *genetic code*: each amino acid is represented by a triplet of DNA base pairs. (Some amino acids are coded for by several distinct DNA codon triplets.) With the development of rapid methods for DNA sequencing [14,16], it has become standard laboratory procedure to determine the DNA sequence encoding any protein of interest and, by applying the genetic code, to translate it into an amino acid sequence.

During synthesis, proteins fold up into complicated 3-dimensional structures to form the geometrical shapes, called *secondary* and *tertiary* structures, needed to carry out their function. Although the folding process is completely dictated by the primary structure of the protein and the laws of physics, it is quite difficult to determine the 3-dimensional shape of a protein given this information alone. The dynamics involved are sufficiently complicated to make a direct calculation of the minimal energy conformation computationally prohibitive for all but the simplest proteins. There is currently much work being done using heuristics based on biochemical knowledge to help direct molecular dynamics simulations on supercomputers, but several more orders of magnitude of computing power are still needed to accurately simulate the folding of a general protein. Other techniques such as X-ray crystallography and Nuclear Magnetic Resonance (NMR) can be used to determine the tertiary structure of

0† Eric Lander was supported in part by National Science Foundation grant #NSF-DCB-8611317 and System Development Foundation grant #SDF612 a protein, but these techniques involve difficult and time consuming laboratory work and computation. Furthermore, there exists no general procedure at all for inferring the function of a protein from its amino acid sequence.

With the exponential increase in the rate of DNA sequencing which has taken place over the past decade, biologists are faced with a growing mass of data about primary protein sequences without a corresponding increase in the amount of information about the functions and tertiary structures of these proteins. If the current plans to sequence the entire human genome become a reality, the database of human protein sequences will increase some 1000-fold in the next decade, thus intensifying the need for an effective computational means of analyzing this information.

One technique that biologists often use to gain information about a newly sequenced protein is to compare the protein's amino acid sequence against those of many known proteins, searching for ones with very similar sequences. From such sequence similarities, it is often possible to infer similarities in the structures or functions of the related proteins [8]. There are two reasons why this correlation makes sense: first, proteins with very similar biochemistry are apt to fold and to act in very similar ways under the laws of physics; second, it is often the case that proteins which have large similar regions are evolutionarily closely related, which often indicates that the proteins perform related functions or catalyze reactions in very similar ways. Comparison searches have been very successful in helping biologists to uncover relationships between apparently unrelated groups of proteins. For instance, several years ago it was discovered that some oncogenes (cancer-causing genes) have a close similarity with proteins such as human growth factors [7]. This observation suggested a likely mechanism by which oncogenes cause uncontrolled cell growth.

Unfortunately, biologists do not have a precise definition of what is meant by sequence similarity or how to measure it, and the methodology underlying the currently performed similarity searches is not well understood. Several biologists have proposed metrics based on biochemical properties of different amino acids, and on evolutionary relationships between them. Since it is fairly time consuming to do large numbers of comparisons on conventional computers, little statistical information has been compiled about the effectiveness of different metrics at measuring sequence similarity. There is a need for a more careful analysis of the space of possible scoring metrics in order to develop systems which are capable of detecting subtle matches between more distantly related proteins.

One of the goals of this project has been to attempt a preliminary exploration of this space. Using the Connection Machine® system [1] CM-2 [2], a massively parallel supercomputer, we have been able to obtain a substantial increase in performance on the algorithms for sequence matching. In particular, we are able to compare an entire database of proteins against itself in about the same time it takes to compare one protein to the database on a conventional computer. Because of this increase in performance we are able to perform the "experiments" necessary to undertake more comprehensive studies of scoring metrics. We can also use the data we produce to study clusters of related proteins.

In Section 2, we describe briefly the precise scoring metrics that are used to measure sequence similarity. In Section 3, we discuss the hardware and software systems used to do our database comparisons and the performance we achieve, and in Section 4 we summarize the results of some of our research on scoring metrics.

2 Measuring Sequence Similarity

How does one measure sequence similarity? One needs to do more than just find the optimal linear alignment of two sequences. Consider, for example, the following amino acid sequences:

```
GDVEKGKKIFIMKCSQ
GCVEKGKIFINWCSQ.
```

[1] Connection Machine is a registered trademark of Thinking Machines Corporation
[2] CM-2 is a trademark of Thinking Machines Corporation

There are two possible good linear alignments for them, i.e.,

```
GDVEKGKKIFIMKCSQ          GDVEKGKKIFIMKCSQ
| |||||                          ||||  |||
GCVEKGKIFINWCSQ            GCVEKGKIFINWCSQ,
```

neither of which is really optimal. In matching up one end of the sequences the matches at the other end are destroyed. In fact, evolution is known to introduce insertions and deletions into protein sequences. Thus, the general strategy for finding the optimal alignment allows the insertion of gaps into either or both of the two sequences.

```
GDVEKGKKIFIMKCSQ
| ||||| |||  |||
GCVEKGK-IFINWCSQ.
```

A score is then determined to correspond with the alignment taking into account the fact that exact matches in the alignment should increase the score to a greater degree than gaps or nonmatching pairs. Thus, a linear score is usually computed by using a scoring function which assigns a value, $D(\alpha, \beta)$, to every matched pair (α, β) of amino acids, and another function, $g(\ell)$, which assigns a value to every gap of length ℓ, and then summing the scores of each pair in the alignment.

In many cases, proteins do not match along their entire primary structures, but rather contain specific regions which are highly similar. Thus, it is often more interesting to find the best matching subsequences of two proteins than to find the best alignment along their entire lengths.

Formally, given two proteins, i.e. two sequences A, B made up of amino acids a_i and b_j respectively,

$$A = (a_1, a_2, \ldots, a_n), \; B = (b_1, b_2, \ldots, b_n),$$

we want to find the subsequences

$$\begin{aligned} A' &= (a_{i_1}, a_{i_2}, \ldots, a_{i_z}), \qquad i_k < i_{k+1} \\ B' &= (b_{j_1}, b_{j_2}, \ldots, b_{j_z}), \qquad j_k < j_{k+1}, \end{aligned}$$

which maximize a comparison function, or score, $C(A', B')$ defined as follows

$$C(A', B') = \sum_{k=1}^{z} D(a_{i_k}, b_{j_k}) + \sum_{k=2}^{z} [g(i_k - i_{k-1} - 1) + g(j_k - j_{k-1} - 1)],$$

where D is a correlation function between amino acids and g is the gap function. If we assume that g is linear, i.e., $g(\ell) = g \cdot \ell$ with $g < 0$, then

$$C(A', B') = \sum_{k=1}^{z} D(a_{i_k}, b_{j_k}) + g \cdot (i_z - i_1 + j_z - j_1 - 2z + 2).$$

Three commonly used scoring metrics are the *Delta* matrix, *Dayhoff* matrix, and the *Properties* matrix. For each scoring system, a symmetric scoring matrix $M(\alpha, \beta)$ is given, which is intended to reflect the similarities between pairs of amino acids. Figure 1 shows the Dayhoff matrix, which is based on observed substitution rates, and the Properties matrix, which is based on the number of biochemical properties (out of a group of 8) shared by a pair of amino acids. The Delta matrix is simply the identity matrix.

DAYHOFF SCORING MATRIX

α \ β	C	S	T	P	A	G	N	D	E	Q	H	R	K	M	I	L	V	F	Y	W
C	20																			
S	8	10																		
T	6	9	11																	
P	5	9	8	14																
A	6	9	9	9	10															
G	5	9	8	7	9	13														
N	4	9	8	7	8	8	10													
D	3	8	8	7	8	9	10	12												
E	3	8	8	7	8	8	9	11	12											
Q	3	7	7	8	8	7	9	10	10	12										
H	5	7	7	8	7	6	10	9	9	11	14									
R	4	8	7	8	6	5	8	7	7	9	10	14								
K	3	8	8	7	7	6	9	8	8	9	8	11	13							
M	3	6	7	6	7	5	6	5	6	7	6	8	8	14						
I	6	7	8	6	7	5	6	6	6	6	6	6	6	10	13					
L	2	5	6	5	6	4	5	4	5	6	6	5	5	12	10	14				
V	6	7	8	7	8	7	6	6	6	6	6	6	6	10	12	10	12			
F	4	5	5	3	4	3	4	2	3	3	6	4	3	8	9	10	7	17		
Y	8	5	5	3	5	3	6	4	4	4	8	4	4	6	7	7	6	15	18	
W	0	6	3	2	2	1	4	1	1	3	5	10	5	4	3	6	2	8	8	25

PROPERTIES SCORING MATRIX

α \ β	A	C	D	E	F	G	H	I	K	L	M	N	P	Q	R	S	T	V	W	Y
A	8																			
C	6	8																		
D	3	3	8																	
E	1	2	6	8																
F	4	5	1	2	8															
G	7	3	2	1	4	8														
H	1	2	2	3	4	1	8													
I	4	5	1	2	5	4	2	8												
K	2	3	3	4	3	2	6	3	8											
L	4	5	1	2	5	4	2	7	3	8										
M	5	6	2	3	6	5	3	6	4	6	8									
N	4	5	5	4	3	4	2	3	3	3	4	8								
P	4	5	3	2	3	4	0	3	1	3	4	5	8							
Q	3	4	4	5	4	3	3	4	4	4	5	6	4	8						
R	1	2	4	5	2	1	5	2	6	2	3	4	2	5	8					
S	5	4	4	3	2	5	1	2	2	2	3	6	4	5	3	8				
T	5	6	4	3	4	5	3	4	4	4	5	6	4	5	3	5	8			
V	5	6	2	1	4	5	1	6	2	6	5	4	4	3	1	3	5	8		
W	3	4	2	3	6	3	5	4	4	4	5	4	2	5	3	3	5	3	8	
Y	3	4	2	3	6	3	5	4	4	4	5	4	2	5	3	3	5	3	7	8

Figure 1: The above two arrays give the entries of the scoring matrix $M(\alpha,\beta)$ for the Dayhoff and Properties Scoring Matrices.

For each of these metrics one must also specify two constants: a bias b and the gap penalty g. The score for a pair of amino acids is then taken to be $D(\alpha,\beta) = M(\alpha,\beta) + b$, while the cost of a gap of length ℓ is taken to be $g \cdot \ell$. For the Dayhoff matrix, $b = -8$ and $g = -6$ are frequently used values. For the Delta matrix, a common choice is $b = -0.5$ and $g = -1$. Thus, a commonly used Delta metric is:

$$D(\alpha,\beta) = \begin{cases} .5 & \text{if } \alpha = \beta \\ -0.5 & \text{if } \alpha \neq \beta \end{cases}$$

$$g(\ell) = -\ell.$$

Given this kind of scoring system one can determine the best scoring pair of subsequences in serial time $O(mn)$ where m and n are the lengths of the two proteins being compared. This is done by using a dynamic programming algorithm [4] which can be described as follows: if we consider the matrix

$$C_{r,s} = \max_{A',B'}\{C(A' = (a_{i_1},\ldots,a_{i_z}), B' = (b_{j_1},\ldots,b_{j_z})) + g\cdot(r - i_z + s - j_z) \\ |i_z \leq r, j_z \leq s\},$$

then it is easy to see that the following recursion relation holds

$$C_{r,s} = \max \begin{cases} 0 \\ C_{r-1,s-1} + D(a_r, b_s) \\ C_{r-1,s} + g \\ C_{r,s-1} + g. \end{cases}$$

Thus, to compute $\max_{A',B'}\{C(A',B')\}$, where A' is a subsequence of A and B' is a subsequence of B, one need only compute $\max C_{r,s}$ where the matrix elements $C_{r,s}$ can be computed inductively in time $O(mn)$. These applications of dynamic programming to molecular biology were developed by [15,17].

3 Parallel Implementation on the CM-2

The dynamic programming algorithm described at the end of the previous section is easy to parallelize [see for example [9]] since, as we see from Figure 2, the diagonals of $C_{r,s}$ are only dependent on previous diagonals. The algorithm requires $n+m-1$ time steps and m processors to compare proteins of length m and n. If the proteins are ordered so that $m \leq n$, then we obtain optimal speedup since

$O(m)O(n) = O(mn)$.

The algorithms for this project were programmed on the Connection Machine system CM-2 data parallel computer [6,10]. The CM-2 is composed of a microsequencer and a maximum of 64K single-bit processing elements. Each processor is associated with 64K bits of RAM. The processors run in SIMD mode; the instruction stream is broadcast by the sequencer. It is possible to deselect any subset of the processors, so that any instruction will only be performed by those processors in the currently selected set. It is also possible to perform indirect memory references on the currently selected set of processors, allowing each processor to simultaneously reference an independent location in a lookup table. We use this feature to evaluate $D(\alpha, \beta)$ for metrics other than the Delta metric. The sequencer is controlled by an external front end machine, usually a SYMBOLICS® Lisp Machine[3], SUN® [4], or VAX® [5]. Parallel extensions of familiar programming languages allow the user to program the front end to do serial computation, with an expanded instruction set providing access to the "data parallel" part of the system. There is a single high-speed floating point unit for every 32 processors which we do not use in this application. The processors are connected in a boolean n-cube topology, however, the communication system is general enough that an arbitrary connection scheme can be imposed by the user. Thus, data can be rapidly exchanged between the memories of different processors as necessary to complete any computation. One very communication-efficient way to configure the machine is as a k dimensional grid, which is automatically superimposed by the system software onto the boolean cube using a multidimensional gray-code mapping. We will deal here with the CM-2 as if the processors were configured in a 1-d grid. In this situation every processor has a unique identifying coordinate denoted by p, such that processor p only communicates with processors $p - 1$ and $p + 1$, where p ranges from 0 to $N - 1$, where N is the number of processors in the CM-2.

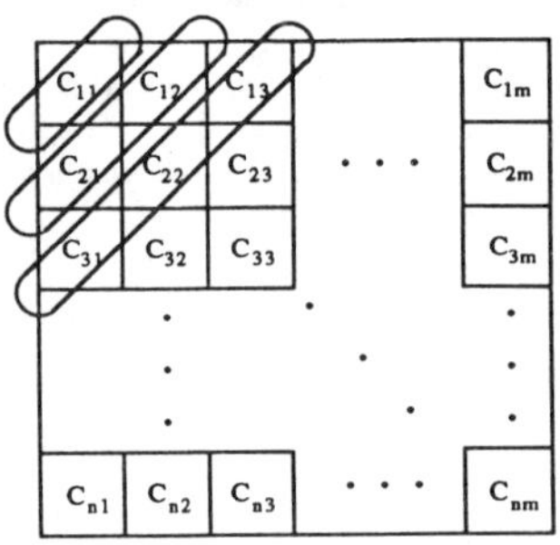

Figure 2: Circled entries on diagonals can be computed in parallel.

The goal of the implementation was to develop software which would calculate the scores between every pair of proteins in a given database according to an arbitrary scoring metric of the kind described above. Because the CM-2 has far more processors than most proteins have amino acids, it is possible to perform the dynamic programming algorithm on many proteins at the same time. Since many individual pairwise comparisons have to be done for a single database search, it is worthwhile to efficiently pack the data so that the overall time spent is minimized. Thus, the proteins in the database are first sorted by length and then partitioned sequentially into sets S_d such that the total number of amino acids in the proteins of each S_d is as large as possible but is less than or equal to the total number of processors available in the CM-2. The proteins in each set S_d are then compared in parallel to the entire database, one protein at a time. Note that, including the symbols used to designate unknowns, there are only 23 distinct amino acid symbols. Thus we represent each as a five bit integer, ranging from 1 to 23.

If M is the total number of such sets S_d, P_k is the kth smallest protein in the database, and K is the total number of proteins in the database, then the basic structure of the program to compare all pairs of proteins is:

[3] Symbolics is a trademark of Symbolics, Inc.
[4] Sun workstation is a registered trademark of Sun Microsystems, Inc.
[5] VAX is a registered trademark of Digital Equipment Corporation

for $d = 1$ **to** M **do**
    set up S_d *on CM-2*
    for $k = 1$ **to** K **do**
        compare in parallel all proteins in S_d *to* P_k
        retrieve results and store on front end

where setting up S_d involves laying out the amino acids in the proteins in S_d in linear fashion into the memory of the processors with the CM-2 configured as a 1-d grid [see Figure 3]; the inner loop which compares S_d to P_k is implemented using the parallelized dynamic programming algorithm. Thus, on each pass through the inner loop, all the proteins in S_d will be compared simultaneously with some protein P_k which we will designate henceforth as a "target" protein. The target protein is injected into the CM-2 one amino acid at a time, and passed along the 1-d grid [see Figure 4]. A more detailed description of the implementation can be found in [12].

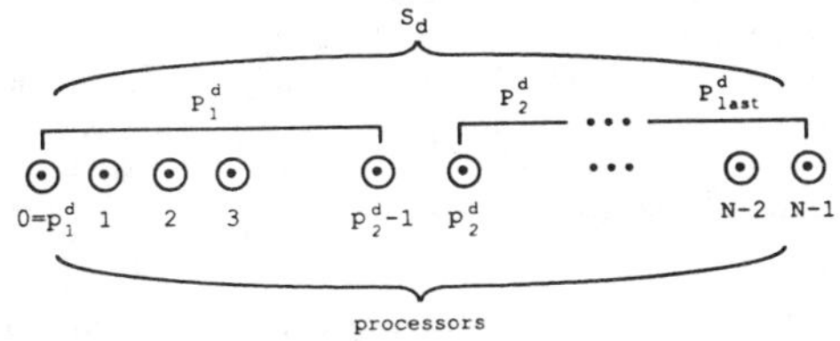

Figure 3: Diagram indicating mapping of amino acids in proteins in S_d onto CM processors. P^d_i is the ith protein in the set S_d. p^d_i is the number of the processor holding the first amino acid in P^d_i.

Since in practice the correlation function D is usually symmetric, in order to compare all pairs of proteins in the database it is only necessary to compare the proteins in S_d to the proteins in all $S_{d'}$ where $d' \geq d$. This is also more efficient than using the proteins in $S_{d''}$ where $d'' \leq d$ as target proteins since we want to use the longer proteins as targets. It is straightforward to show that it is preferable not to have large variations in the lengths of the proteins in a set S_d. This was the motivation for sorting the database before partitioning into sets S_d even though this does not necessarily yield an optimal packing of the proteins into groups of bounded size. [It does, however, come close [11]]. Finally, from Figure 5 it is clear that processors are idle some fraction (less than half) of the time. One might try to reduce the number of cycles in which processors are idle by overlapping comparisons with consecutive target proteins. Although this might give a slight performance improvement, the increased complexity of the inner loop code makes it unclear what, if any, gain would be made.

processors ⟶

pvars ↓	0	1	2	3	4	5	6	7	8	
SD	$P^d_1(1)$	$P^d_1(2)$	$P^d_1(3)$	$P^d_1(4)$	$P^d_2(1)$	$P^d_2(2)$	$P^d_2(3)$	$P^d_2(4)$	$P^d_2(5)$	. . .
H	1	0	0	0	1	0	0	0	0	
TGT_1	$P_k(1)$	0	0	0	$P_k(1)$	0	0	0	0	. . .
TGT_2	$P_k(2)$	$P_k(1)$	0	0	$P_k(2)$	$P_k(1)$	0	0	0	
TGT_3	$P_k(3)$	$P_k(2)$	$P_k(1)$	0	$P_k(3)$	$P_k(2)$	$P_k(1)$	0	0	. . .

Figure 4: Data Layout for the first three iterations of the inner loop for a set of proteins in a typical S_d, where length $(P^d_1) = 4$. $P^d_i(j)$ is the jth amino acid in P^d_i. $P_k(j)$ is the jth amino acid in the target protein P_k. H is a parallel variable used to mark the first amino acid in each protein in S_d.

In addition to information about the score, for analysis purposes, it is often important to know where the best matching subsequence occurs, or how many gaps have been inserted. In fact, the actual implementation is a slightly modified version of the above algorithm which retains this information with little effect on the performance. Another variation penalizes the initiation of a gap more heavily than the continuation of one to mimic more closely the manner in which proteins tend to evolve.

In the current version of the code run on a CM-2 with a 7 Mhz clock, the inner loop takes 600 to 700 μseconds per iteration depending upon the amount of information kept about score and position. This gives us a rate of about 100 million matrix entries per second. Note that the Delta matrix computation does not require any use of indirect addressing and runs significantly faster. The code was run on a database of about 2000 proteins (approximately 600,000 amino acids) comparing all the proteins against the entire database. For the Dayhoff scoring matrix the computation took 2 hours on a 32K processor CM-2; for the Delta matrix the computation took 3 hours on an 8K processor CM-2. We also did a run on a database of about 6300 proteins, which took several days on a 4K CM-2.

Other groups have done similar work on serial machines, with smaller databases. We present some performance figures for their codes with the caveat that, while they are all implementing the same algorithm, there may be differences in the amount of analysis done to the resulting data as well as the extent to which the codes were optimized. Temple Smith (personal communication) and a group at Harvard University ran the algorithm on the complete database when it consisted of about 300 proteins. Their program took 170 minutes on a CRAY-1 to do 44,000 pairwise protein comparisons. Assuming the average length of a protein to be about 300 amino acids, this gives a rate of about 400,000 matrix entries per second.

Jacob Maizel (personal communication) and a group at NIH have also been doing large-scale database comparisons on protein sequences. To compare one protein of 561 amino acid residues against a database of proteins containing a total of 1,683,998 amino acids, their software took 1641.9 seconds running on a single processor of a CRAY XMP. Of this time, about 48% was spent in analyzing the resulting data. Thus, we estimate that they were getting about 1.1 million matrix entries per second on the part of the code which actually did the comparisons.

Rob Jones (personal communication) has been doing related work at USC using SUN computers. On the 1.5 mip SUN 3/50, his software gets 72,000 matrix entries per second, and on the 3 mip SUN 3/280, it gets 139,000 per second.

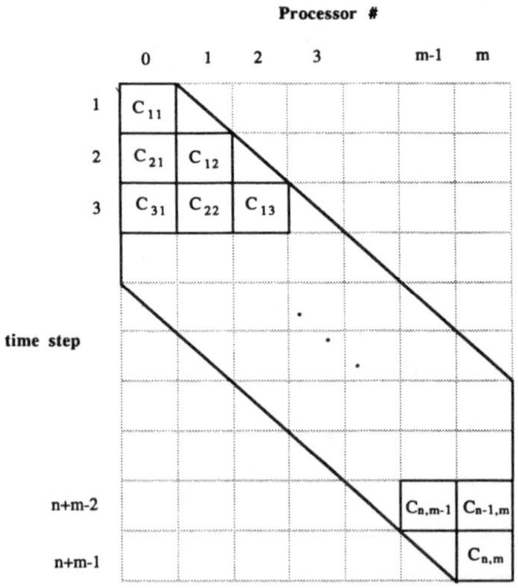

Figure 5: Diagram indicating activity of processor p at time step t. If $1 \le t-p \le n$, then processor p computes $C_{t-p,p+1}$ at step t. Otherwise, the processor is inactive.

4 Results

The software tools described above make it feasible to explore different approaches to detecting protein similarities. The following three topics illustrate some of the studies currently underway.

4.1 Phase transition in lengths of matching regions

As described in Section 2, a scoring system consists of a basic scoring matrix $M(\alpha, \beta)$, a bias b to be added to each entry of M, and a gap penalty g. For a fixed choice of M, the values of b and g govern how closely two subsequences must match in order to receive a high similarity score. For $b \ll 0$ and $g \ll 0$, only perfect matches between sequences would receive positive similarity scores. On the other hand, for b large and $g = 0$, any two sequences could be aligned along their entire length to produce a high similarity score. Thus, the choice of b and g govern the "quality" of matches that will be found.

Given two sequences A and B, let $S_{Delta,b,g}(A,B)$ denote the similarity score for the optimal subsequence alignment of A and B when using the Delta matrix with bias b and gap penalty g. Suppose that A and B are both sequences of length n with characters independently chosen according to some probability distribution P on the alphabet of amino acids. Recently, Waterman et. al. [2,3,19] showed that, depending on the values of b and g, either:

$$\begin{aligned} S_{Delta,b,g}(A,B) &\approx X_{b,g} \cdot n, \quad \text{or} \\ S_{Delta,b,g}(A,B) &\approx Y_{b,g} \cdot log(n), \end{aligned}$$

where $X_{b,g}$ and $Y_{b,g}$ are constants depending on b, g, and the distribution P. They show that the bg-plane is divided into two regions, in which the optimal score is asymptotically proportional to either n or $log(n)$, with a sharp phase transition separating them. In principle, such estimates would allow one to rigorously compute the statistical significance of an interesting alignment.

For a given probability distribution P, however, the proof does not explicitly compute $A_{b,g}$, $B_{b,g}$, or the location of the phase transition in the bg-plane. Also, one lacks explicit error estimates bounding the rate of convergence to the asymptotic behavior. In addition, the corresponding results are not available for arbitrary scoring matrices.

To explore these questions empirically, we selected a set of 200 apparently unrelated proteins approximately 50 amino acids in length. For each of the Delta, Dayhoff, and Properties matrices, all pairwise comparisons were performed for a wide range of values of b and g. Each test of the 19,900 comparisons requires about 30 seconds on a 4096 processor CM-2. For each matrix, the mean scores are tabulated as functions of b and g in Figure 6. In each case, there is a clear region in which the mean score increases rapidly. This confirms Waterman's result for the Delta matrix, and shows that this property appears to hold for the other scoring metrics. To confirm that the result did not depend on any hidden structure within the proteins chosen, we repeated the experiment after randomly permuting the amino acid sequences of the 200 proteins; the locations and shapes of the phase transitions did not change significantly.

Knowledge of the location of the phase transition allows one to select values for the bias and gap penalty which lie in the $log(n)$ region, but are near the phase transition. Such choices will allow the detection of weaker matches between proteins. For some purposes, one may wish to select several different (b, g) pairs from different regions of the $log(n)$ domain in order to discriminate preferentially against gaps or against amino acid substitutions. It is interesting to note that the usual choices for the Dayhoff matrix ($b = -8$ and $g = -6$) lie well within the interior of the $log(n)$ region and thus may demand more stringent matching than is desirable.

4.2 Exploration of properties of a new scoring system.

Various approaches have been used to construct scoring matrices. The use of the Delta matrix presumes

g= \ b=	-0.88	-0.75	-0.63	-0.50	-0.38	-0.25	-0.13	0.00	0.13	0.25	0.38	0.50	0.63	0.75	0.88	1.00
-0.13	7.54	16.14	58.55	244.81	322.33	346.73	358.98	365.62	369.38	372.25	374.19	375.87	377.12	377.98	380.70	384.58
-0.25	6.54	7.54	10.96	16.14	28.71	58.95	150.76	244.31	296.36	322.33	338.04	346.73	362.69	370.86	376.42	381.68
-0.38	6.47	6.81	7.54	10.05	12.20	16.14	23.43	35.40	58.95	113.87	245.05	316.42	348.64	363.21	371.83	378.77
-0.50	6.47	6.54	6.89	7.54	9.83	10.96	12.93	16.14	24.19	43.71	122.70	260.23	327.23	353.94	366.51	375.42
-0.63	6.47	6.50	6.81	6.92	7.54	9.76	10.60	12.80	17.01	26.20	56.65	168.85	296.20	343.40	362.42	373.40
-0.75	6.47	6.47	6.54	6.81	6.93	7.00	9.94	11.21	13.81	19.97	34.23	92.21	254.00	332.04	357.56	371.00
-0.88	6.47	6.47	6.50	6.81	6.89	7.16	7.88	10.91	12.50	16.34	25.89	59.28	195.25	318.96	353.41	368.97
-1.00	6.47	6.47	6.50	6.54	6.81	7.02	7.27	8.43	11.87	14.30	21.66	42.15	141.80	299.36	348.02	365.26
-1.13	6.47	6.47	6.47	6.50	6.81	6.93	7.23	7.68	10.77	13.29	18.71	33.18	98.68	274.22	344.08	364.92
-1.25	6.47	6.47	6.47	6.50	6.54	6.94	7.16	7.68	9.96	11.89	17.17	27.96	75.72	256.65	340.97	364.23
-1.38	6.47	6.47	6.47	6.50	6.50	6.94	7.09	7.63	9.56	11.20	16.25	25.13	64.74	237.92	337.93	363.18
-1.50	6.47	6.47	6.47	6.47	6.50	6.70	6.97	7.54	9.39	10.84	14.99	22.56	55.51	216.93	334.54	362.16

6a: Mean match lengths for Delta Matrix

g= \ b=	-15.00	-14.00	-13.00	-12.00	-11.00	-10.00	-9.00	-8.00	-7.00	-6.00	-5.00
-1.00	2.92	3.51	4.94	8.42	26.66	213.24	353.07	377.99	385.55	388.97	390.69
-2.00	2.27	2.54	3.11	4.27	6.95	20.25	231.30	361.46	379.71	385.70	388.71
-3.00	2.15	2.32	2.86	3.56	5.09	10.20	60.51	338.64	374.86	383.21	386.77
-4.00	2.14	2.26	2.69	3.36	4.53	8.10	31.66	306.89	370.67	381.35	385.10
-5.00	2.09	2.25	2.63	3.26	4.33	7.17	21.37	267.72	366.34	379.52	384.24
-6.00	2.09	2.22	2.62	3.19	4.19	6.79	18.31	216.08	363.15	378.01	383.26
-7.00	2.09	2.21	2.59	3.16	4.14	6.62	16.44	170.29	360.20	377.17	382.32
-8.00	2.09	2.21	2.59	3.15	4.11	6.43	15.46	133.79	357.05	376.34	381.75
-9.00	2.09	2.21	2.59	3.14	4.09	6.36	15.12	109.21	353.70	375.67	381.25
-10.00	2.09	2.21	2.59	3.13	4.08	6.30	14.80	96.42	351.07	374.93	380.94
-11.00	2.09	2.21	2.59	3.13	4.08	6.27	14.57	86.46	349.19	374.48	380.58
-12.00	2.09	2.21	2.58	3.13	4.08	6.26	14.47	79.10	346.55	373.76	380.46
-13.00	2.09	2.21	2.58	3.13	4.07	6.26	14.36	74.85	344.03	373.27	380.14
-14.00	2.09	2.21	2.58	3.13	4.08	6.25	14.28	71.21	342.01	372.98	380.02
-15.00	2.09	2.21	2.58	3.13	4.08	6.25	14.28	65.86	339.40	372.54	379.88

6b: Mean match lengths for Dayhoff Matrix

g= \ b=	-8.00	-7.00	-6.00	-5.00	-4.00	-3.00	-2.00	-1.00	0.00
-1.00	0.00	7.77	26.44	347.62	381.14	388.09	390.92	392.26	393.03
-2.00	0.00	6.73	11.48	143.15	368.42	383.52	388.54	390.56	391.58
-3.00	0.00	6.65	9.55	41.48	355.71	380.43	386.29	388.80	390.20
-4.00	0.00	6.65	9.13	27.24	340.13	378.28	384.69	387.20	388.79
-5.00	0.00	6.65	9.01	23.43	322.24	376.89	383.43	386.23	387.59
-6.00	0.00	6.65	8.95	21.68	302.96	375.30	382.45	385.48	386.66
-7.00	0.00	6.65	8.95	20.76	282.62	374.38	381.99	384.66	385.97
-8.00	0.00	6.65	8.95	20.22	261.25	373.47	381.52	384.20	385.38
-9.00	0.00	6.65	8.95	20.02	245.79	372.48	381.13	383.82	385.08
-10.00	0.00	6.65	8.95	19.98	229.44	371.71	380.97	383.57	384.74
-11.00	0.00	6.65	8.95	19.98	218.85	371.16	380.76	383.37	384.52
-12.00	0.00	6.65	8.95	19.93	206.55	370.59	380.59	383.11	384.26

6c: Mean match lengths for Properties Matrix

Figure 6: Mean lengths of subsequence matches for Delta, Dayhoff, and Properties Matrices, as functions of gap (g) and bias (b). The protein database consisted of fifty (50) proteins with lengths between 192 and 220. The phase transition regions are highlighted in gray.

that important features in proteins will only be conserved by exact matches of amino acids. The Properties matrix is premised on the assumption that a good measure of similarity is proportional to the number of shared biochemical properties between amino acids. The Dayhoff matrix was derived by (1) examining the frequency of different amino acid substitutions found among closely related proteins, separated by an evolutionary distance of about 1 million years, so as to infer the parameters of a random walk on sequence; and (2) extrapolating this walk to describe the substitutions expected among proteins at an evolutionary distance of 250 million years. This presumes that the local random walk is not constrained by "boundaries" when allowed to run over long periods, as well as assuming a typical distance (250 million years) between proteins of interest. Clearly, objections can, and have, been raised to each of these approaches.

Another alternative would be to select a general set of features on which to base a comparison metric, as was done in constructing the Properties matrix, but to choose precise weights so as to increase the signal-to-noise ratio. For example, biochemists generally agree that the following sets of amino acids are similar:

{K,R}	{Q,D,E,N}
{M,C}	{H,Y,F,W}
{P,G}	{A,V,I,L}
{S,T}	

and that interchanging members of a set constitutes a "conservative substitution" from the functional point of view. We therefore defined a Conservative Substitution matrix, in which

$$
\begin{aligned}
D(\alpha, \alpha) &= 1, \\
D(\alpha, \beta) &= c \qquad \text{if } \alpha \text{ and } \beta \text{ are in the same set,} \\
D(\alpha, \beta) &= 0 \qquad \text{otherwise,}
\end{aligned}
$$

where c is a free parameter. By varying c, b, and g, one can search for those values which differentiate most strongly between related and unrelated proteins.

We assembled a database consisting of 71 cytochrome c sequences and 69 ferredoxin sequences taken from different organisms. These are two unrelated proteins involved in electron-transport in mitochondria and chloroplasts, respectively. For a variety of values of c, b and g, we performed all pairwise comparisons. The sum of the mean scores between the two groups of related proteins (cytochrome-cytochrome plus ferredoxin-ferredoxin) divided by the mean score between unrelated proteins (cytochrome-ferredoxin) provides a measure of the selectivity of the scoring system. From the data we have gathered so far, it appears that the values $c \approx .4$, $b \approx -.4$, and $g \approx -.5$ optimally separate these two classes of proteins. We are currently sampling more data points for this pair of protein groups, and repeating these experiments for other classes of proteins, in order to determine whether these parameters are of general use.

4.3 Detection of clusters among proteins

While some striking matches exist between pairs of proteins, many functionally similar proteins exhibit only subtle similarity. Recognizing significant relationships between groups of proteins is an active area of research in molecular biology. The availability of a complete database of all pairwise comparisons among a large set of proteins makes it possible to apply new computational methods to the study of this question. We have begun to develop some algorithms for finding clusters of proteins which have similar regions, using this database. One approach we have used involves putting the results of the database comparisons on a 76,300 node graph, each node corresponding to a protein, with the edges labeled by the score between the corresponding pair of proteins. If we consider the subgraph which contains the best $n\%$ of the edges to any given node, we have a sparse graph with dense clusters tending to indicate groups of highly related proteins. Lander and Arratia [1] have mathematically analyzed the probability distribution of clusters occurring in random graphs, so that it is possible to determine when a cluster of related proteins is statistically significant.

We are still actively involved in research along these lines, so we will not attempt a full presentation of our results here; we merely mention an example of the sort of thing at which we have been looking. Ferredoxins from bacteria and from plants have rather different amino acid sequences. In many cases, the matches are sufficiently weak that if a single bacterial ferredoxin were compared to the database of all known proteins, many of the plant ferredoxins would not be recognized as significantly related to it. While the similar biochemistry of the various ferredoxins leaves no doubt as to their structural, functional and evolutionary relationship, many such situations will probably arise involving proteins of unknown function when sequences of entire genomes are analyzed. We have used simple pointer-jumping schemes to analyze the graph described above for dense clusters. These algorithms successfully recognize the overall ferredoxin group as a cluster, as well as dividing it into the two subgroups consisting of the plant and bacterial versions of the protein.

5 Conclusion

Our implementation of a parallelized version of the dynamic programming algorithm for sequence comparisons has allowed us to do research on several interesting problems in the area of protein sequence analysis. Without the increased performance on these algorithms obtainable on a supercomputer such as the Connection Machine system CM-2 the time to process the data for each of the experiments we performed would have been practically prohibitive.

References

[1] Arratia, R. and Lander, E.S. "The Distribution of Clusters in Random Graphs", manuscript.

[2] Arratia, R. and Waterman, M.S. 1985. "An Erdos-Renyi law with shifts." *Adv. Math* 55, 13-23.

[3] Arratia, R., Gordon, L. and Waterman, M.S. 1986. "An Extreme Value Distribution for Sequence Matching. Ann. Stat." 14, 971-993.

[4] Bellman, Richard. 1957. Dynamic Programming. Princeton University Press. Princeton, NJ.

[5] Collins, J.F. and Coulson, A.F.W. 1984. "Applications of parallel processing algorithms for DNA sequence comparison." *Nucleic Acid Research* 12, 181-192.

[6] *Connection Machine® Model CM-2 Technical Summary* Thinking Machines Corporation. 1987.

[7] Doolittle, R.F., M.W. Hunkapiller, L.E. Hood, S.G. Devare, K.C. Robbins, S.A. Aaronson and H.M. Antoniades. 1983. "Simian Sarcoma Viruses Oncogene v-sis is Derived from the Gene (or Genes) Encoding a Platelet-derived Growth Factor." *Science* 221, 275-276.

[8] Doolittle, Russell F. 1986. Of Urfs and Orfs, A Primer on How to Analyze Derived Amino Acid Sequences. University Science Books. Mill Valley, CA.

[9] Edmiston, Elizabeth and Robert A. Wagner. 1987. *Parallelization of the Dynamic Programming Algorithm for Comparison of Sequences.* Proceedings of the 1987 International Conference on Parallel Processing. Penn State Press. Pennsylvania, PA. 78-80.

[10] Hillis, W. Daniel. 1985. The Connection Machine. MIT Press. Cambridge, MA.

[11] Johnson, D.S. 1973. "Near-Optimal Bin Packing Algorithms." Doctoral Dissertation, Department of Mathematics, Massachusetts Institute of Technology. Cambridge, MA.

[12] Lander, E., Mesirov, J.P., Taylor, W., 1988, "Protein Sequence Comparison on a Data Parallel Computer", Proceedings of the 1988 International Conference on Parallel Processing. Penn State Press. Philadelphia, PA. 257-263.

[13] Lipman, D.J. & W.R. Pearson (1985) "Rapid and Sensitive Protein Similarity Searches." *Science* 227, 1435-1441.

[14] Maxam, A.M. and Gilbert, W. 1977. *Proc. Natl. Acad. Sci. USA* 74, 560-564.

[15] Needleman, S.B. and C.D. Wunsch. 1970. "A General Method Applicable to the Search for Similarities in the Amino Acid Sequences of Two Proteins." *J. Mol. Biol.* 48, 444-453.

[16] Sanger, F., Nicklen, S. and Coulson, A.R. 1977, *Proc. Natl. Acad. Sci. USA* 74, 5463-5467.

[17] Smith, T.F. and Waterman, M.S. 1981. "Identification of common molecular subsequences." *Journal of Molecular Biology* 147, 195-197.

[18] Smith, T.F., Waterman, M.S. and Burks, C. 1985. "The statistical distribution of nucleic acid similarities." *Nucleic Acid Research* 13, 645-656.

[19] Waterman, M.S., L. Gordon, and R. Arratia. 1987. "Phase Transitions in Sequence Matches and Nucleic Acid Structure." *Proc. Natl. Acad. Sci. USA* 84, 1239-1243.

Computational Fluid Dynamics

MULTITASKING A THREE-DIMENSIONAL NAVIER-STOKES ALGORITHM ON THE CRAY-2

Julie M. Swisshelm

NASA Ames Research Center
Moffett Field, CA 94035

A three-dimensional computational aerodynamics algorithm has been multitasked for efficient parallel execution on the Cray-2. This provides a means for examining the multitasking performance of a complete computational fluid dynamics (CFD) application code. An embedded zonal multigrid scheme is used to solve the Reynolds-averaged Navier-Stokes equations for an internal flow model problem. The explicit nature of each component of the method allows a spatial partitioning of the computational domain to achieve a well-balanced task load for multiple-instruction, multiple-data stream (MIMD) computers with vector-processing capability. Experiments have been conducted with both two- and three-dimensional multitasked cases. The best speedup attained by an individual task group was 3.54 on four processors of the Cray-2, while the entire solver yielded a speedup of 2.67 on four processors for the three-dimensional case. The multiprocessing efficiency of various types of computational tasks is examined, performance on two Cray-2s with different memory access speeds is compared, and extrapolation to larger problems is discussed.

INTRODUCTION

In an effort to build ever faster computational engines, computer architects are increasingly incorporating parallelism in their designs. This is driven by the development stage of scalar, or von Neumann, computers, where the technological performance limits of components are being approached [1,2]. To effectively use multiprocessing devices for the numerical simulation of aerodynamic flows, the scientist must understand both the architecture of these machines and the methods by which their parallelism is optimally exploited.

Computational fluid dynamics is one discipline that paces the development of more powerful computers. Flow simulation about a complex aerodynamic configuration, with sufficient resolution for large-eddy simulation of turbulence, would require a several order of magnitude increase in both memory size and computational speed over currently available machines [3]. Improved numerical algorithm performance (generally measured by convergence rate and work per iteration) is one way to attack the problem of reducing the time to solution; another is to obtain the best possible execution rate from the computer hardware. Unfortunately, algorithm performance is often improved by increasing code complexity, while full advantage of parallel architectures is most easily accomplished by using simpler codes. While multiprocessor systems offer increased CPU power, the slow development of parallel-processing software makes peak execution rates fairly difficult to attain for most applications.

The goal of parallel computation is to obtain good performance on the fastest available computer while retaining the ability to solve complex flow problems using the best possible algorithms. The convergence properties of an algorithm remain just as important as speedup factors and Mflop rates of the code. The zonal embedded multigrid scheme for solving the Reynolds-averaged Navier-Stokes equations, an advanced, efficient, and complex numerical algorithm, is, therefore, used in this research to explore the parallel-processing performance of several present-day supercomputers.

EQUATIONS OF MOTION

The nondimensional equations of motion may be written in conservation-law form as

$$q_t = -(F_x + G_y + H_z)$$

where, for the full Navier-Stokes equations,

$$F = f - Re^{-1}p, \quad G = g - Re^{-1}r, \quad H = h - Re^{-1}s,$$

while, for their thin-layer version,

$$F = f, \quad G = g, \quad H = h - Re^{-1}d,$$

and, for the Euler equations,

$$F = f, \quad G = g, \quad H = h.$$

The components of the vector variables in the above equations are given in Reference 4 and will not be included in this report.

Although, for simplicity, the equations of motion are presented here written in Cartesian coordinates, this does not imply any loss of generality. A generalized coordinate transformation is used for the actual calculations. The thin-layer version of the Navier-Stokes equations given above is valid when x and y represent the body-conforming coordinates, so that the viscous terms in the coordinate directions along the body may be neglected. Turbulence is simulated by means of a two-layer algebraic eddy viscosity model due to Baldwin and Lomax [5].

ALGORITHM DESCRIPTION

In order to minimize the cost of simulating complex, three-dimensional viscous flow past a complete aerodynamic configuration, a synergistic approach to the solution algorithm must be taken. Traditionally, the development of CFD schemes proceeds along the following lines. Given some physical phenomenon, for example a flow field, a mathematical model of it is developed (for instance, the Navier-Stokes equations). Then a solution algorithm is devised to solve the mathematical equations numerically, and, finally, that algorithm is implemented on some computer (i.e., a code is written). On advanced-architecture machines, where actual performance is very code-dependent, the need to revise this traditional approach becomes apparent. The interaction among all the development stages of a solution scheme is crucial to achieving the high performance necessary for complex flow simulations. The embedded multigrid algorithm represents such an approach. Incorporated in the solution procedure are: an explicit three-dimensional flow solver, embedded mesh refinements, a model equation hierarchy ranging from the Euler equations through the full Navier-Stokes equations, multigrid convergence acceleration, and vectorization and multitasking for efficient execution on parallel-processing supercomputers.

The flow solver is implemented on a collection of local meshes of varying degrees of fineness embedded in a global coarse mesh. Depending on the flow physics to be resolved in these various regions, either the Euler, thin-layer Navier-Stokes, or the full Navier-Stokes equations are solved. A multigrid convergence acceleration procedure is applied simultaneously to all meshes and all model equations. The entire algorithm is explicit and is designed to perform well on computers consisting of multiple processing units, each having vector-processing capability. Testing of this solution strategy has been successfully carried out and reported in [6]. Additional information regarding the physical model problem used for these tests is also contained in Reference 6.

PARALLEL PROCESSING

In the process of adapting algorithms to parallel-architecture computers, several factors affecting performance must be considered. The effects of load balancing, task granularity and overhead, and residual sequential code all contribute to determining the efficiency with which a code may be parallelized.

To analyze the performance of a computer having two primary speeds of execution, Amdahl [7] developed the model

$$R(f) = \frac{1}{(1 - f)/R_H + f/R_L}$$

where the resulting system rate, $R(f)$, is determined by the fraction of results $(1-f)$ generated at the high rate, R_H, and the remaining fraction, f, generated at the low rate, R_L. For a multiple-processor system, the high rate is simply the number of processors, P, multiplied by the low rate. Amdahl's law is then written

$$R(f) = \frac{R_L}{(1 - f)/P + f}$$

If the execution time, T, is defined as the number of results generated at a given execution rate, and speedup is defined as the ratio of execution time on a single processor (T_1) to that on the multiprocessor system (T_P), then

$$S_P = \frac{T_1}{T_P} = \frac{R(f)}{R_L} = \frac{1}{(1 - f)/P + f}$$

From this relation, it can be seen that the residual sequential code, f, limits possible speedup as P gets large. This equation is illustrated graphically in Figure 1.

Worlton [8] uses Amdahl's law to examine the effects of overhead, granularity, and synchronization requirements. In his interpretation of the model, N, t, t_o, and t_s represent, respectively, the number of tasks between synchronization points, average task execution time (granularity), and task overhead time due to and synchronization for parallel execution. The single-processor execution time is then

$$T_1 = Nt$$

Assuming, for simplicity, that the number of tasks is evenly divisible by the number of processors and the tasks are all equal in length (i.e., assuming a perfect load balance), so that each task takes $(t + t_o)$ time to execute and t_s is required for synchronization, the total parallel execution time is

$$T_P = t_s + \frac{N(t + t_o)}{P}$$

Then the speedup becomes

$$S_P = \frac{T_1}{T_P} = \frac{Nt}{t_s + N(t + t_o) / P}$$

The best possible speedup on P processors is obviously equal to P. (This excludes the case of superlinear speedup, which, while plausible for certain algorithms such as tree searching, doesn't appear to have applicability to the numerical solution of partial differential equations in fluid dynamics.)

Efficiency is defined as

$$E_P = \frac{S_P}{P} = \frac{1}{(t_s P / Nt) + (1 + t_o / t)}$$

so that one hundred percent efficiency is equivalent to the maximum speedup, P, attainable on P processors.

If we neglect synchronization time to examine the relative effects of granularity and overhead size, the equation for efficiency can be rewritten

$$E_P = \frac{1}{(1 + t_o / t)}$$

so that the ratio of overhead to granularity must be very small for good efficiency, or, in other words, task granularity must be much larger than task overhead.

If, on the other hand, we examine the effect of synchronization time while neglecting the task overhead, the equation becomes

$$E_P = \frac{1}{(t_s / Nt + 1)}$$

so that synchronization overhead is minimized by increasing task length.

Several conclusions can be drawn from the above model. The performance of a parallel-processing computer is constrained by the fraction of the work that must be done in sequential mode, which limits the attainable speedup as the number of processors is increased. This fraction of sequential code can result from the mathematical model or the algorithm. Synchronization and task overhead effects can be reduced by increasing the granularity of tasks, while better load balancing is achieved by having the number of tasks be equally divisible by the number of processors and all of equal length.

There are several ways in which an algorithm may be partitioned. Functional decomposition of a problem is appropriate when physical processes are evolving on different length or time scales. An example of this is the parallel coarse-grid scheme, a type of multigrid in which the various grid levels have been decoupled so that they may be computed concurrently. Another functional decomposition can be achieved by distributing each equation of a system of partial differential equations to a different processor. Spatial decomposition is appropriate for flow solvers in which groups of points can be viewed as being independent of one another on a given time level. Line implicit and explicit schemes for solving partial differential equations fall under this category. It may even be possible to formulate temporal decomposition schemes where, as the solver finishes a time step on one part of the grid, the next time step could be started there, while computation of the previous time step is being completed elsewhere in the field. These techniques may be combined to create an optimal partitioning scheme for a particular parallel-processing architecture.

MULTITASKING IMPLEMENTATION AND DISCUSSION

Given that MacCormack's method and the multigrid scheme are both explicit, no drastic algorithmic modifications are necessary to take advantage of parallel processing. In the three-dimensional case, spatial decomposition is the method by which parallelizable tasks are created. (An example of functional decomposition, the parallel coarse grid multigrid scheme, has been derived and tested in two dimensions [9].) The computational domain, a grid with dimensions 129x33x33, is partitioned by planar slices in the lengthwise channel direction, as shown in Figure 2. This direction is chosen so as to preserve vectorization potential in the inner DO loops, which execute along lines parallel to the partition boundaries (the x-direction). Some overhead is introduced to enable flexible task management through variably-sized partitioning. Redundancy is also added to the computational scheme along the partition boundaries. In these regions, the subdomains are overlapped to avoid the need to protect shared data from being updated more than once per time step.

Once the grid has been partitioned into P subdomains, calls to the macrotasking library routines TSKSTART and TSKWAIT are used to spawn and synchronize groups of tasks. The type of computational work done in these groups, for each time cycle of the algorithm, ranges from simply loading values from one matrix into another, to computation-intensive yet identical (and, therefore, SIMD-type) tasks, to heterogeneous (or MIMD-type) tasks. Examples of each type are: loading the solution array into another array to preserve it; the basic MacCormack time step; and the boundary conditions. The performance of each type of computation as well as that of the composite code is measured on the Cray-2.

In place of using a number of TSKSTARTs and TSKWAITs, necessary to manage the synchronization points in the algorithm, it is conjectured that the use of barriers or event posting and waiting could be a more efficient (i.e., lower overhead) implementation of the macrotasking library. Fatoohi [10] has effectively used a two lock barrier in his two-dimensional Navier-Stokes code. Weeks [11], however, has made timing estimates and measurements of the amount of synchronization and overhead incurred by such an alternative implementation and concludes that the performance would improve little, if at all, over the TSKSTART/WAIT approach, so that, considering the added code complexity, such an implementation may not be advisable.

ALTERNATIVES TO MULTITASKING

The software tools provided for Fortran multitasking on the Cray-2 are referred to as the "macrotasking" library subroutine calls, to distinguish them from another Cray implementation of multitasking called "microtasking" (which will be discussed later). Other extensions to Fortran for use on parallel machines have been developed, including the SCHEDULE package by Dongarra and Sorensen [12] and CoFortran by Weeks [13]. (See Appendix for a brief description of the key routines of each.)

The SCHEDULE package [12] is intended to be a short-term solution to the problem of the inavailability of portable multitasking software. Each parallel system currently has its own language or language extensions, so that code developed for parallel execution on one computer must be modified to run on another. SCHEDULE is meant to be usable on any shared-memory multiprocessing system (provided that an interface has been written for that machine). The package has been implemented in the two-dimensional version of the parallel multigrid algorithm discussed above, which had already been macrotasked on both the Cray the X-MP and a Cray-2. Rewriting the parallel-processing management was relatively straightforward except for one major drawback. SCHEDULE had no efficient means of repeating the same set of processes (or the same "task graph") over and over, as is done in an iterative method and in most CFD solvers, so that (at the time this work was carried out) it was not yet sophisticated enough to be useful to the computational aerodynamicist.

CoFortran is another attempt at creating a portable parallel programming language [13]. It consists of a combination of Fortran and Fortran-like concurrent language constructs. Like SCHEDULE, it is intended to be machine-independent, provided that an interface exists on the system to be used. It has been developed to provide the researcher with tools for the parallel solution of computational fluid dynamics problems, and is currently available on the X-MP and may soon be available on the Cray-2. It has not been tested with the algorithm used in this work.

Microtasking shows the most promise for improving the multitasking capabilities of the Cray-2, and its incorporation into the three-dimensional algorithm is planned as soon as it is made available. Instead of using library calls, multitasking is achieved through the use of compiler directives which appear as comment statements and do not affect portability [14]. (Again, refer to the Appendix for more information.) Because of its low overhead, parallelization at a fine-grained level (such as the DO loop level) may be done efficiently. A code which has been macrotasked is easily converted to microtasking and should show improved performance, as has been demonstrated with the two-dimensional version of the multigrid algorithm on the Cray X-MP/48 [9].

CRAY-2 MACROTASKING RESULTS

The three-dimensional embedded zonal grid algorithm has been multitasked and tested on two Cray-2s with different memory-access speeds. Performance comparisons of the two-dimensional code on the Cray X-MP and the Cray-2 have also been carried out. Macrotasking has been implemented in the form of TSKSTARTs and TSKWAITs in the code, partitioned as described above. All performance data was obtained during dedicated time on all machines, and all runs were repeated at least three times to check the consistency of the timing data. To distinguish the various Cray computers, they will be referred to here as Navier (serial number 2013), with a faster (80 nanosecond) memory access time, Stokes (serial number 2002), with the slower (120 nanosecond) memory access, and the X-MP, a Cray X-MP/48 with a 9.5 nanosecond CPU clock cycle.

Results comparing macrotasking performance of the two-dimensional multigrid code on the X-MP and Stokes were reported previously [9] and are summarized in Table I. Note that a speedup of 3.3 was attained on four processors of the X-MP, while the same implementation on Stokes yielded a speedup of less than 2.3 on four processors.

Table II shows the speedups and efficiency of processor utilization for two-, three-, and four-processor 100-time-cycle test cases of the three-dimensional code on both Navier and Stokes. A speedup of 2.67 on four processors, corresponding to 67%

efficiency, is attained on Navier. On two and three processors, efficiencies of 86% and 74% were achieved, respectively. Comparing these results with the results obtained on the slower-memory Stokes indicates that some of the multitasking inefficiencies may be due to memory bank conflicts, that is, contention between processors for access to the 256-Megaword shared memory. A 2.5% to 8% increase in efficiency is observed when using the faster memory Cray-2.

Table III contains information about the best and worst performance of individual task groups. Each set of tasks may be classified (loosely) as one of the following: 1) loading one array into another (no operations); 2) simple computation (add and/or multiply) at all grid points; 3) many computations with unit stride at all points; 4) many computations with nonunit stride; and 5) heterogeneous tasks. Tasks which exhibit both the best and worst performance fall under category 4, indicating that task classification, at least by this scheme and for a complicated CFD problem, is not necessarily a good predictor of multitasking performance. If the tasks are ranked according to unitasked wall clock execution time (a measure of granularity, on a dedicated machine), the better speedups generally correlate with the longer task segments, an indicator that task overhead (or the ratio of overhead to granularity) is slowing down the computation. The tasks are sufficiently complex so as to obscure the presence and extent of memory bank conflicts, so that any conclusions about the effect of memory contention must be drawn from the above comparison of performance on the two Cray-2s. Additional insight might be gained from experiments consisting of identical tasks with different array sizes, which would vary the memory access patterns.

A further investigation to determine the extent of the overhead contribution to poor performance is needed. This could be accomplished by isolating some computation-intensive section of the code and increasing the problem size, thereby increasing the granularity of the tasks, to study performance improvements resulting from reducing the ratio of overhead to granularity. Other synchronization schemes, such as the use of barriers instead of TSKSTARTs and TSKWAITs, should be explored. A more detailed study of task grouping or classification schemes is also warranted. Finally, microtasking merits serious examination to determine its capabilities on the Cray-2. The Cray-2's lack of certain hardware features, important to the X-MP microtasking implementation, may impact its performance.

CONCLUSIONS

A three-dimensional Navier-Stokes algorithm has been multitasked for the Cray-2. Speedups of 1.73, 2.22, and 2.67 over the unitasked code, corresponding to processor utilization efficiencies of 86%, 74%, and 67%, have been obtained from testing on two, three, and four processors, respectively. Speedups as high as 1.90, 2.69, and 3.54 for the same cases have been achieved by the best-performing task groups.

The performance of multitasking in the macrotasking implementation on the Cray-2 presently seems to be inefficient, as is demonstrated by the comparison with X-MP results. Efficiency is impacted by memory bank conflicts, shown by the comparison between the slower- and faster-access memory machines, and by the overhead incurred in the macrotasking library calls.

Several issues merit further attention. The granularity of tasks should be increased by increasing the problem size to study in greater detail the impact of the macrotasking library overhead. Task classification schemes deserve further development. Microtasking, a small-granularity, low-overhead alternative to macrotasking, should be implemented in the code when available.

ACKNOWLEDGEMENTS

The author wishes to thank all who made suggestions to improve this paper, especially her colleagues at NAS and Gary Johnson.

REFERENCES

[1] Kutler, P., Steger, J.L., and Bailey, F.R.: Status of Computational Fluid Dynamics in the United States. AIAA Paper 87-1135-CP, 1987.

[2] Johnson, G.M.: Parallel Processing in Fluid Dynamics. *Applications of Parallel Processing in Fluid Mechanics,* FED - Vol. 47, O. Baysal, ed., ASME, New York, 1987, pp. 1-8.

[3] Peterson, V.L.: Impact of Computers on Aerodynamics Research and Development. *Proceedings of the IEEE,* Vol. 72, No. 1, 1984, pp. 68-79.

[4] Swisshelm, J.M. and Johnson, G.M.: Numerical Simulation of Three-Dimensional Flowfields Using the CYBER 205. *Supercomputing Applications,* R.W. Numrich, ed., Plenum Press, New York, 1985, pp. 179-195.

[5] Baldwin, B.S. and Lomax, H.: Thin-Layer Approximation and Algebraic Model for Separated Turbulent Flows. AIAA Paper 78-257, 1978.

[6] Swisshelm, J.M. and Johnson, G.M.: Development of an Aerodynamics Algorithm for Parallel-Processing Supercomputers. ISC TR 88001, 1987.

[7] Amdahl, G.M.: Validity of the Single Processor Approach to Achieving Large Scale Computing Capabilities. *Proceedings of the American Federation of Information Processing Societies,* Vol. 30, Thompson, Washington, D.C., 1967, pp. 483-485.

[8] Worlton, J.: Toward a Science of Parallel Computation. *Computational Mechanics - Advances and Trends,* AMD Vol. 75, A.K. Noor, ed., ASME, New York, 1987, pp. 23-35.

[9] Johnson, G.M., Swisshelm, J.M., and Kumar, S.P.: Concurrent-Processing Adaptations of a Multiple-Grid Algorithm. AIAA Paper 85-1508, 1985.

[10] Fatoohi, R.: private communication.

[11] Weeks, C.L.: private communication.

[12] Dongarra, J.J. and Sorensen, D.C.: SCHEDULE: An Environment for Developing Transportable Explicitly Parallel Codes in Fortran. Presented at the Third SIAM Conference on Parallel Processing in Scientific Computing, Los Angeles, 1-4 December 1987.

[13] Weeks, C.L.: Concurrent Extensions to the Fortran Language. Presented at the First World Congress on Computational Mechanics, Austin, 22-26 September 1986.

[14] Misegades, K., Krause, L., and Booth, M: Microtasking of Fluid Mechanics Codes on the Cray X-MP. *Applications of Parallel Processing in Fluid Mechanics,* FED - Vol. 47, O. Baysal, ed., ASME, New York, 1987, pp. 19-25.

[15] Dongarra, J.J. and Sorensen, D.C.: SCHEDULE Users Guide. Argonne National Laboratory, preprint.

[16] Cray-2 Multitasking Programmer's Manual. Cray Research, Inc., SN-2026, Mendota Heights, Minnesota, revised June 1987.

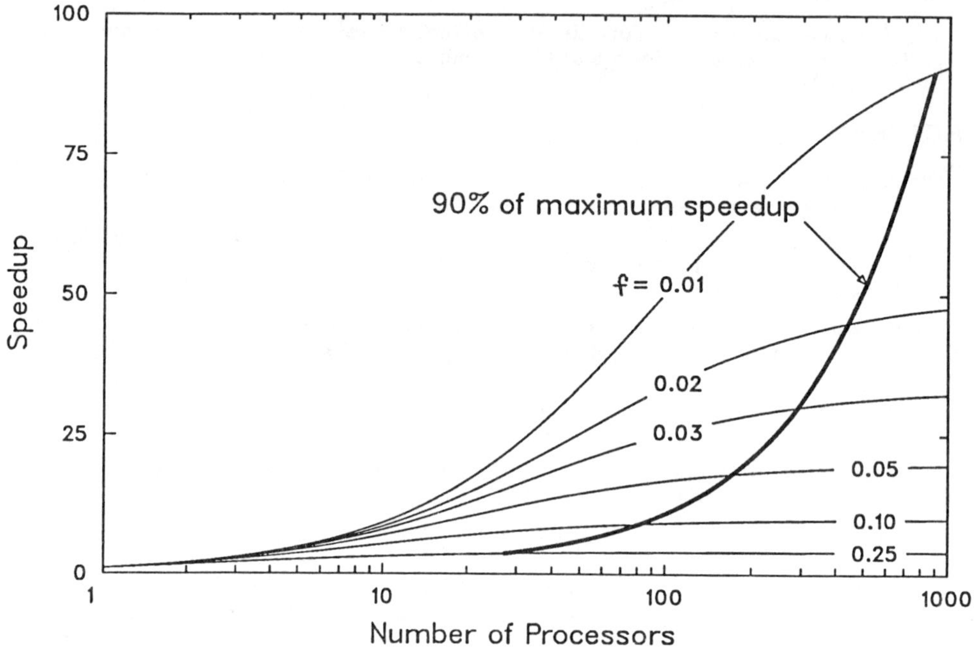

Figure 1. - Amdahl's Law: Effect of Residual Sequential Code on Speedup

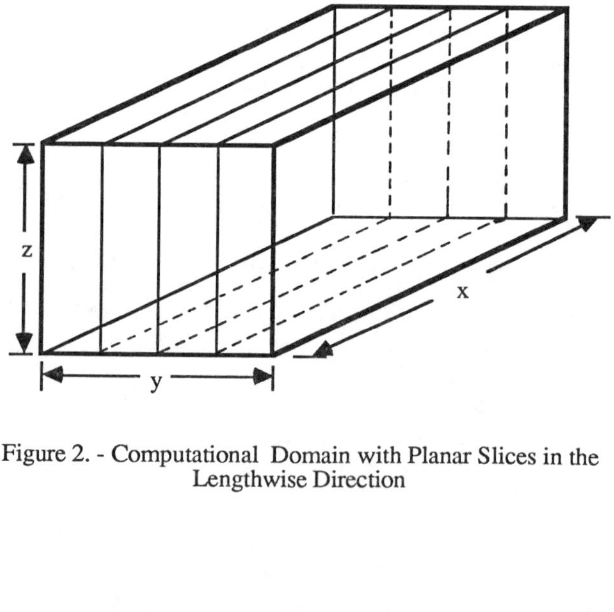

Figure 2. - Computational Domain with Planar Slices in the Lengthwise Direction

Table I. Two-Dimensional Macrotasked Multigridded Scheme Performance

Machine	2 Processors		4 Processors	
	Speedup	Efficiency	Speedup	Efficiency
Cray X-MP	1.87	0.94	3.30	0.83
Cray-2 (Stokes)	1.69	0.84	2.23	0.56

Table II. Three-Dimensional Macrotasked Embedded Multigrid Scheme Performance

Machine	2 Processors		3 Processors		4 Processors	
	Speedup	Efficiency	Speedup	Efficiency	Speedup	Efficiency
Cray-2 (Navier)	1.73	0.86	2.22	0.74	2.67	0.67
Cray-2 (Stokes)	1.69	0.84	2.11	0.70	2.47	0.62

Table III. Best and Worst Performance by Individual Task Groups,
Three-Dimensional Macrotasked Multigridded Scheme
(Sp = speedup, Ef = efficiency)

Machine	Length (secs)	2 Processors		3 Processors		4 Processors	
		Sp	Ef	Sp	Ef	Sp	Ef
Best							
Navier	5.82	1.90	0.95	2.69	0.90	3.54	0.88
Stokes	5.95	1.88	0.94	2.63	0.88	3.40	0.85
Worst							
Navier	0.28	1.50	0.75	1.41	0.47	1.88	0.47
Stokes	0.29	1.48	0.74	1.36	0.45	1.79	0.45

APPENDIX: SCHEDULE, CoFortran, Microtasking, and Macrotasking

SCHEDULE: Fortran extensions [15]

Static Dependency Graph

CALL DEP - assigns data dependencies for each task
CALL PUTQ - puts each task in the queue for execution

Dynamic Spawning

CALL NXTAG - automatically assigns data dependencies and forces the parent process to wait for task completion
CALL SPAWN - puts the process in the execution queue

Low-Level Synchronization

CALL LOCKON - protects code section from concurrent execution
CALL LOCKOFF - marks the end of protected code

CoFortran: Fortran extensions [13]

Concurrency Statements

CoProcess - first statement of concurrent subroutine
CoBegin - begin parallel block of code
CoEnd - end parallel block of code

Synchronization Statements

CoInit - creates CoProcess from the main program
CoStop - signals end of parallel code management in main program
CoStart - starts parallel execution of CoProcess
CoWait - synchronization point in parallel execution

Data Passing

SHARE - share a common block among processes
RELEASE - unshare the common block

Microtasking: Preprocessor directives [14]

CMIC$ MICRO - denotes subroutine to be microtasked
CMIC$ CONTINUE - continue parallel execution at next subroutine level
CMIC$ DO GLOBAL - starts a parallel task for each pass through the following DO-loop
CMIC$ PROCESS - begin control structure (with ALSO PROCESS and END PROCESS), starting a parallel task
CMIC$ ALSO PROCESS - start another parallel task (and end previous task)
CMIC$ END PROCESS - signals the end of parallel tasks and control structure
CMIC$ STOP ALL PROCESS - exit PROCESS or DO GLOBAL without completing

Macrotasking: Fortran extensions [16]

Tuning

CALL TSKTUNE - enables tuning of processor handling

Task Creation

CALL TSKSTART - starts parallel tasks
CALL TSKWAIT - synchronizes parallel tasks

Message Passing

CALL EVPOST - posts an event
CALL EVWAIT - waits for an event to be posted
CALL EVCLEAR - clears (or unposts) an event

Barrier Synchronizaton

CALL BARASGN - creates a barrier for tasks
CALL BARSYNC - registers arrival of task at barrier

Low-Level Synchronization

CALL LOCKON - protects critical region
CALL LOCKOFF - end protection of critical region

THREE-DIMENSIONAL SIMULATION OF UNDEREXPANDED PLUMES USING UPWIND ALGORITHMS

Shigeru Obayashi
NASA Ames Research Center, MS 258-1,
Moffett Field, CA 94035
and
Sharad Gavali
Amdahl Corporation, MS 265,
P.O. Box 3470, Sunnyvale, CA 94088-3470

ABSTRACT: Different numerical techniques have been examined for simulating the underexpanded plumes in supersonic flows. The results revealed that the monotone differentiable limiter is superior to the TVD minmod limiter when the MUSCL approach is used for Roe's upwind scheme. Roe's upwind scheme is found to be superior to the central difference scheme not only for capturing shock waves, but also for capturing shear flows.

INTRODUCTION

It is known that propulsion system plumes can have a significant effect on the aerodynamic characteristics of supersonic and hypersonic vehicles, such as the Space Shuttle. There are experimental difficulties to simulate plume flow fields because the flights are undertaken at high altitude as well as at high speed. In spite of the difficulties in modeling real gas or turbulence effects, computational fluid dynamics (CFD) can provide reliable data and an improved insight into the flow physics. Since only a few data are available experimentally, it is important to achieve solution-to-solution comparisons to show the capability of CFD for simulating such flow fields. The purpose of this study is to examine different numerical techniques for simulating supersonic flow fields with underexpanded plumes using three-dimensional (3-D) Navier-Stokes equations.

Roe's flux-difference upwind scheme is examined against central differencing applied to the inviscid part of the Navier-Stokes equations, since it was reported that the flux-difference splitting leads to a better resolution of flow-field structure [1]. Another key point in this study is the higher-order extension of Roe's scheme. Introducing the MUSCL (monotonic upstream schemes for conservation laws) approach, the minmod limiter based on the TVD (total variation diminishing) concept and the differentiable limiter based on monotonicity concept by Spekreijse [2] will be compared.

Assuming laminar flow with an ideal gas, simulations have been carried out for the Space Shuttle SRB (solid rocket booster) exhaust plume with near flight conditions [3]. The solutions which consists of bow and barrel shock waves and plume slip surface show the characteristics of the different numerical techniques. Amdahl VP 1200 and CRAY-2 supercomputers were used for the 3-D simulations, while the CRAY X-MP was used for the axisymmetric cases.

NUMERICAL ALGORITHMS

A thin-layer Navier-Stokes code has been developed for this study. This code is capable of solving both 3-D and axisymmetric problems. For axisymmetric flows, the number of circumferential grid points is specified to be three, with the two planes to either side of the plane of symmetry being set using the known axisymmetric condition. The source term of the axisymmetric equations are naturally included in the computations through the differencing in the circumferential direction.

The explicit part of the code consists of three different types of schemes. One is a central differencing, another is a partially flux-split upwind scheme, the other is Roe's flux-difference upwind scheme. The partially upwind scheme uses a mixture of Steger-Warming flux splitting in one direction and central differencing in the other two directions [4]. The metric terms are carefully evaluated so as to be valid for both upwind and central differencing [5]. The viscous terms are discretized using the usual second-order central differencing.

The implicit part of the code consists of two different methods. One is the two-factor partially upwind method [4], the other is the LU-ADI method [5]. The current treatment of axisymmetry leads to a vector length of three in the circumferential direction. Since the ADI method can be more efficiently vectorized in the axisymmetric case, only the LU-ADI method is used for the axisymmetric computations. The variable time-stepping technique based on the quantity similar to the CFL number is adapted to accelerate the convergence.

Roe's upwind scheme and MUSCL approach

The thin-layer Navier-Stokes equations written here in the conservation-law form and in the generalized coordinates are given by

$$\partial_\tau \widehat{Q} + \partial_\xi \widehat{F} + \partial_\eta \widehat{G} + \partial_\zeta \widehat{H} = \frac{1}{Re}\partial_\zeta \widehat{H}_v \tag{1}$$

An ideal gas assumption is used. Numerical flux of the inviscid terms due to Roe's upwinding in the locally one-dimensional form [1] can be written, for example in the ξ direction, as

$$\widehat{F}_{j+\frac{1}{2}} = \frac{1}{2}\left(\frac{|\nabla\xi|}{J}\right)_{j+\frac{1}{2}} [F_R + F_L - |A|(Q_R - Q_L)] \tag{2}$$

where A is the Roe-averaged Jacobian matrix and Q_L and Q_R are the state variables to the left and right of the cell interface. The scheme results in the first-order accuracy if $Q_L = Q_j$ and $Q_R = Q_{j+1}$. For highly underexpanded plumes, it is necessary to use the following entropy correction [5] for the absolute value of eigenvalues of the Roe-averaged matrix A when $\lambda_L < 0 < \lambda_R$, $\lambda^{corrected} = \lambda_R - \lambda_L$. Higher-order schemes are constructed from the one-parameter family of interpolation of the primitive variables $q = (\rho, u, v, w, p)^T$:

$$q_L = q_j + \frac{1}{4}[(1-\kappa)\tilde{\nabla}_j + (1+\kappa)\tilde{\Delta}_j]$$

$$q_R = q_{j+1} - \frac{1}{4}[(1+\kappa)\tilde{\nabla}_{j+1} + (1-\kappa)\tilde{\Delta}_{j+1}] \tag{3}$$

where ∇ and Δ are backward and forward differences, respectively, of q which are limited so as to be TVD: $\tilde{\nabla} = \text{minmod}(\nabla, b\Delta)$, $\tilde{\Delta} = \text{minmod}(\Delta, b\nabla)$ where $\text{minmod}(x, y) = \max\{0, \min[x\text{sign}(y), by\text{sign}(x)]\}$ is called the minmod limiter and b is a compression parameter, $b = (3 - \kappa)/(1 - \kappa)$. The third-order discretization, $\kappa = 1/3$, is used in this study.

The alternative approach is to use the differentiable limiter [6] so as to be monotone [2]:

$$q_L = q_j + \frac{s}{4}[(1 - \kappa)\nabla_j + (1 + \kappa)\Delta_j]$$

$$q_R = q_{j+1} - \frac{s}{4}[(1 + \kappa)\nabla_{j+1} + (1 - \kappa)\Delta_{j+1}] \tag{4}$$

with

$$s = \frac{3\nabla\Delta + \epsilon}{2(\Delta - \nabla)^2 + 3\nabla\Delta + \epsilon}$$

where a small constant, ϵ, is added to prevent the division by zero. It should be noted that the differentiability of the limiter guarantees second-order accuracy [2], while the minmod limiter results in first-order accuracy locally at extrema.

Central difference scheme with artificial dissipation

The formulation of central differencing with the artificial dissipation term can be written similarly to Eq. (2) as

$$\widehat{F}_{j+\frac{1}{2}} = \frac{1}{2}[\widehat{F}_j + \widehat{F}_{j+1}] - \epsilon\left(\frac{\sigma}{J}\right)_{j+\frac{1}{2}}\left[(\alpha)_{j+\frac{1}{2}}(Q_{j+1} - Q_j) - \frac{\delta^2 Q_{j+1} - \delta^2 Q_j}{1 + \alpha_{j+1} + \alpha_j}\right] \tag{5}$$

where $\epsilon = 0.1$ in the present study; δ^2 is a central second difference; σ is a spectral radius of the Jacobian matrix, A; and $(\ )_{j+\frac{1}{2}} = [(\ )_{j+1} + (\ )_j]/2$. The parameter α controls the strength of the second-order dissipation

$$\alpha = \left(\frac{3 + 2M_\infty{}^7}{4}\right)\left(\frac{p_{j+1} - 2p_j + p_{j-1}}{p_{j+1} + 2p_j + p_{j-1}}\right) \tag{6}$$

The main difference between Eqs. (5) and (2) is that the central difference scheme, Eq. (5), has only a scalar coefficient for the dissipation term while the upwinding, Eq. (2), has a matrix coefficient [1].

RESULTS

AGARD test case

Because there is a limited amount of data available with which to validate the numerical procedures, a simple AGARD test case was computed for which both experimental [7] and numerical results [5,8] are available. The problem was simplified assuming inviscid flow on the body surface. An upstream condition is specified at a sharp nozzle lip to be the two different supersonic inviscid flows as shown in Fig. 1. The nozzle lip is located at $(x, z) = (0, 1)$ in the computational domain, and $z = 0$ is the plume centerline. The number of grid points used is 121×101. Figure 2 shows the comparison of local Mach number distributions at twice of the body radius where the ratio of nozzle exit over body radii is 0.884.

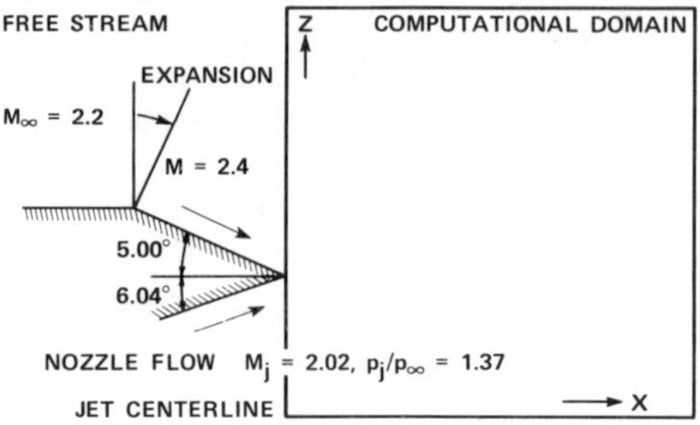

Fig. 1 AGARD test case; $M_\infty = 2.4$, $p_{exit}/p_\infty = 1.37$.

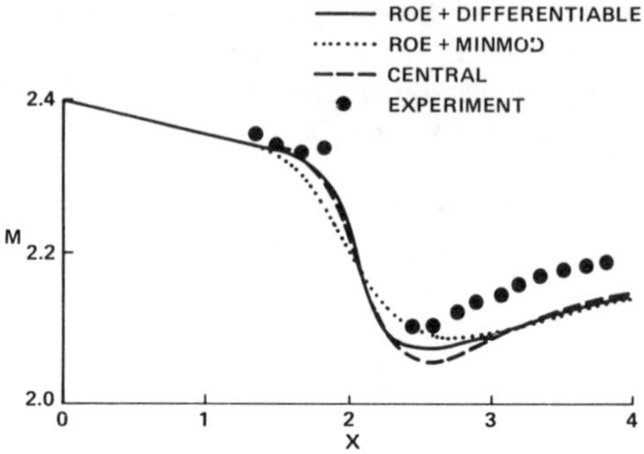

Fig. 2 Comparison of local Mach number distributions at $z = 2.3$ for AGARD test case; $M_\infty = 2.4$, $p_{exit}/p_\infty = 1.37$.

The results demonstrate the basic feature of the different schemes which are Roe's upwind scheme with the differentiable limiter, Roe's with the minmod limiter, and the central difference scheme. It should be noted that even Roe's upwind scheme gives a smeared shock profile because of inclination to the grid line. The use of the differentiable limiter leads to the steepest profile, while the use of the minmod limiter results in the most dissipative profile. The central difference scheme gives a steeper solution than Roe's with the minmod limiter, although it has both an overshoot and undershoot around the shock wave. All three schemes predict the shock location well. The discrepancy with experimental data behind the shock wave is attributed to both the exclusion of the viscous layer in the computation and a disturbance of free stream in the experiment [8].

SRB geometry and flow conditions

Numerical simulations were carried out for the modified SRB geometry shown in Fig. 3. For the axisymmetric case, the two-dimensional grids were used consisting of 127×40 points in the outer flow region and 103×30 points for the nozzle and plume region. The three-dimensional grids were obtained by rotating the two-dimensional grids. Bilateral symmetry was assumed, and 21 grid points were used in the circumferential direction, including two additional points to enforce symmetry. The values on the adjoining boundaries of these grids were found by averaging values at upper and lower grid points taken from both grids.

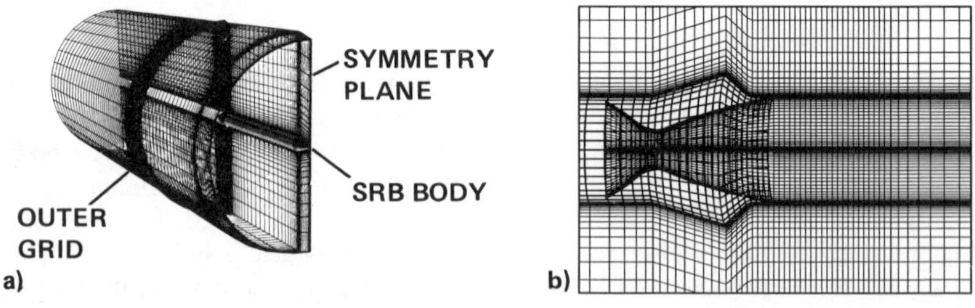

Fig. 3 Modified SRB geometry. a) Overall view. b) Close-up view at nozzle region.

Flow conditions were taken from the flight trajectory (Table 1) [3].

Table 1. Flow Conditions Along the Space Shuttle Flight Trajectory

t (sec)	M_∞	p_∞ (psi)	p_c (psi)	p_c/p_∞	α (deg)	Altitude (ft)
48	1.05	5.55	543.7	97.9	-3.0	24500
64	1.53	2.61	544.7	208.7	-4.2	41980
76	2.03	1.20	576.0	480.0	1.8	57680

The pressure ratio, p_c/p_∞, denotes the chamber pressure over the atmospheric pressure. The chamber temperature was determined as $T_c/T_\infty = 40.0$ so as to be $T_{exit}/T_\infty = 10$ at the nozzle exit, which is close to the results in Ref. 3. The nozzle flow was computed with a specified total pressure and total temperature within the chamber. The mass flow rate was determined through the condition that the throat Mach number was equal to 1.

Axisymmetric plume case

The flow condition corresponding to the $M_\infty = 1.05$ case in Table 1 is used for the axisymmetric test case. First, the entire flow field was computed on the two grids including the SRB body and nozzle using Roe's upwind scheme with the minmod limiter. (See Ref. 5 for the details.) Next, the grid and solution in the downstream region from the nozzle lip were used to adapt the grid based on Mach number distributions, and the flow variables were interpolated on the resulting adapted grid using the SAGE code [9]. By doubling the number of grid points of the resulting grid in both directions, a medium grid is obtained. Again by doubling the number of grid points, a fine grid is obtained. Thus a medium grid uses 127×137 grid points and the fine grid uses 253×273 grid points.

The axisymmetric test case was computed on these grids using the frozen inflow condition at the nozzle exit. Figure 4 shows the grids and the computed solution on the fine grid using Roe's

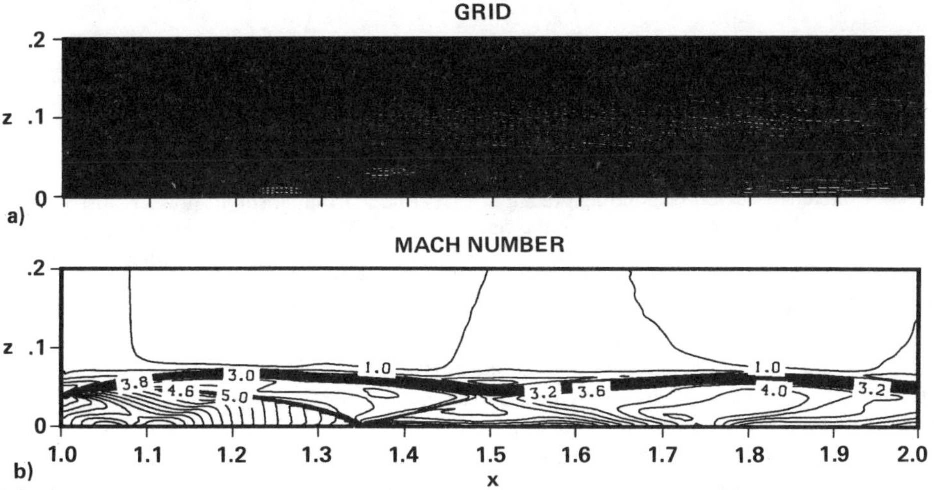

Fig. 4 Close-up view for axisymmetric plume problem; $M_\infty = 1.05$, $p_c/p_\infty = 97.9$, $Re = 8 \times 10^5$. a) Fine grid: 253×273. b) Mach number countour plots using Roe's upwind scheme with the differentiable limiter on the fine grid.

upwind scheme with the differentiable limiter. It should be noted that an additional weak shock pattern which originates from the nozzle curvature can be seen in the primary shock cell that originates from the nozzle lip. The biperiodic structure of the flow field is shown in the pressure distributions along the plume centerline in Fig. 4c. Since the Mach number is close to 1, this periodic structure is physically reasonable.

Figure 5 shows a comparison of different schemes in the pressure distributions along the plume centerline on the medium grid. Since this is a more complicated case than the AGARD test case, the difference of the schemes appears more exaggerated. The use of the minmod limiter appears to result in the most dissipative again, and shows no variation between x = 1.4 to 1.6. The other results show the two peaks there as shown in the fine-grid solution in Fig.4c. Thus the use of the minmod limiter results in a less accurate solution not only locally at extrema, but also globally. The use of the differentiable limiter leads to better accuracy globally as well as locally at extrema compared to the minmod limiter. The central difference scheme gives a comparable solution globally.

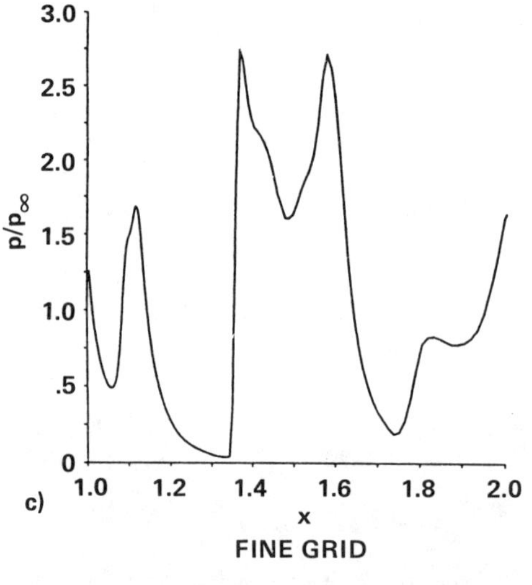

Fig. 4 Concluded. c) Corresponding pressure distributions along plume centerline on the fine grid.

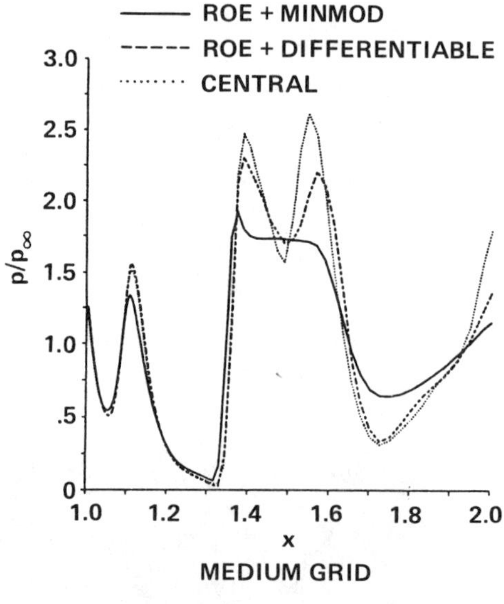

Fig. 5 Comparison of pressure distributions along plume centerline on the medium grid, 127 X 137; $M_\infty = 1.05, p_c/p_\infty = 97.9$, $Re = 8 \times 10^5$.

3-D SRB-plume case

Figures 6 and 7 show the close-up view of the nozzle exit region for the M_∞ = 1.05 case obtained by Roe's upwind scheme with the LU-ADI method (R3D) and the two-factored partially upwind method using Steger-Warming flux splitting in the free-stream direction (F3D), respectively. The MUSCL approach with the minmod limiter was used for both upwind methods because of its robustness for the highly underexpanded plume cases.

Compared with the pressure contour plots obtained by R3D in Fig. 6a, a pressure peak can be found on the plume barrel shock wave near the nozzle lip in the pressure contour plots obtained by F3D in Fig. 7a. This peak corresponds to the temperature oscillations in the plume shear layer as shown in Fig. 7b. However, these contour levels are lower than those in Fig. 6b because of the artificial dissipation produced by Eq. (8). The high temperature at the plume edge originates from the boundary-layer heating on the nozzle wall. The temperature distributions at the back end of the SRB body also differ between the two solutions. Corresponding to the temperature oscillations in the F3D result, it can be found in Fig. 7c that the u-velocity contour plots have higher levels in the plume shear layer throughout the downstream than those in Fig. 6c. Also comparing the boundary layer profiles on the SRB body, the F3D result in Fig. 7c shows more dissipative profiles than the R3D result in Fig. 6c.

The CPU time per grid per time step was 22.7 μsec on an Amdahl VP 1200 computer and 30.6 μsec on a CRAY 2 computer (single processor) for R3D and 66.4 and 95.3 μsec on Amdahl and CRAY computers, respectively, for F3D. The code was completely vectorized on both computers. The convergence was very slow in this study because it took a long time to establish the plume structure and Δt was limited to a small number due to numerical stability. R3D converged about three orders of magnitude after 7000 iterations (7 hours on Amdahl VP 1200 and 10 hours on CRAY 2), while F3D converged about four orders of magnitude in the same number of iterations (20 hours on Amdahl VP 1200 and 30 hours on CRAY 2).

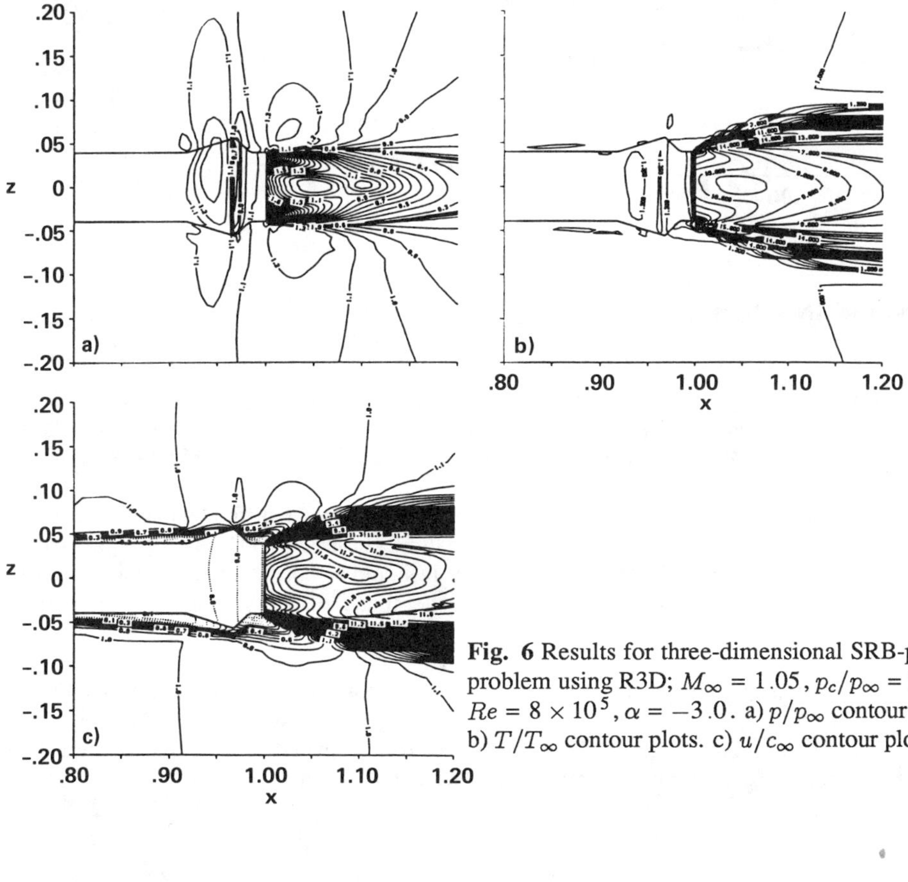

Fig. 6 Results for three-dimensional SRB-plume problem using R3D; $M_\infty = 1.05$, $p_c/p_\infty = 97.9$, $Re = 8 \times 10^5$, $\alpha = -3.0$. a) p/p_∞ contour plots. b) T/T_∞ contour plots. c) u/c_∞ contour plots.

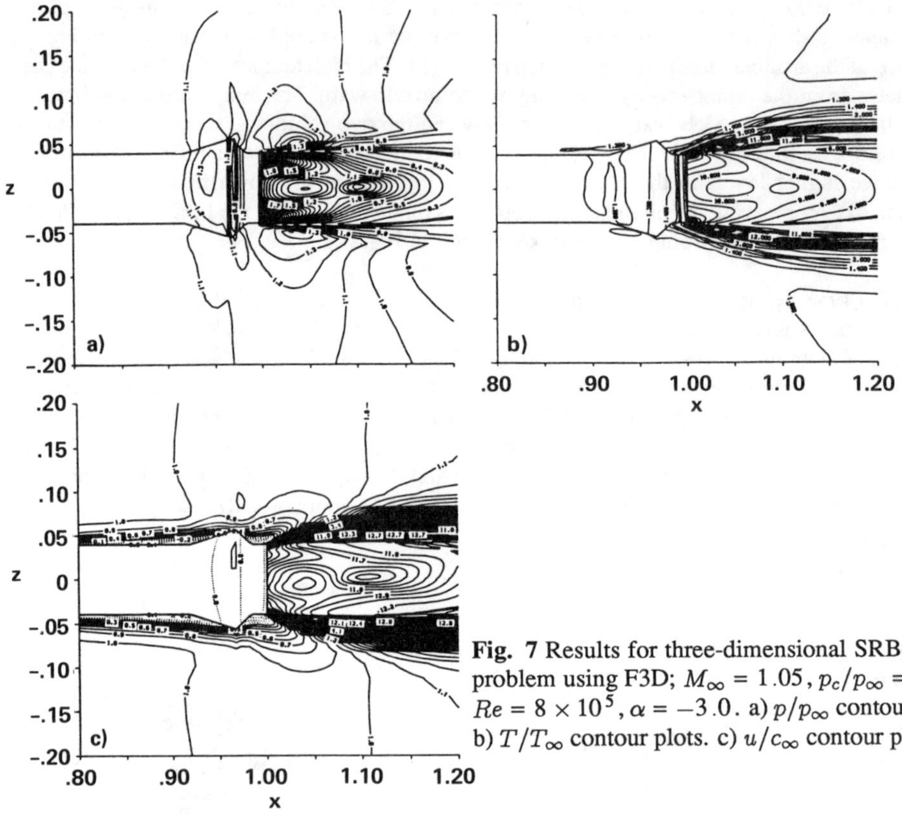

Fig. 7 Results for three-dimensional SRB-plume problem using F3D; $M_\infty = 1.05$, $p_c/p_\infty = 97.9$, $Re = 8 \times 10^5$, $\alpha = -3.0$. a) p/p_∞ contour plots. b) T/T_∞ contour plots. c) u/c_∞ contour plots.

CONCLUDING REMARKS

Numerical simulations for underexpanded plumes have been carried out successfully with different numerical schemes. The results satisfactorily confirm the ability of CFD for simulating the Space Shuttle SRB plumes with pressure and temperature ratios at the flight conditions.

The comparison for the axisymmetric plume case revealed that the differentiable limiter based on monotonicity concept is superior to the minmod limiter based on TVD concept when used for Roe's upwind scheme with the MUSCL approach. It should be noted that the central difference scheme can represent global flow-field structure better than the TVD scheme with the minmod limiter.

The result of Roe's upwind scheme for 3-D SRB-plume case shows the crisp flow-field structure not only for shock waves, but also for boundary layer, compared with that of the central difference scheme. This indicates the advantage of Roe's upwind scheme having the matrix coefficient for artificial dissipation rather than a scalar coefficient.

ACKNOWLEDGMENT

Conducting the present study using a large number of grid points required extensive CPU time. The authors would like to express their gratitude to the Amdahl Corp. in allowing them to use the Amdahl VP 1200.

REFERENCES

1. Vatsa, V. N., Thomas, J. L. and Wedan, B. W., "Navier-Stokes Computations of Prolate Spheroids at Angle of Attack," AIAA Paper 87-2627, Aug. 1987.
2. Spekreijse, S., "Multigrid Solution of Monotone Second-order Discretizations of Hyperbolic Conservation Laws," *Math. Comput.*, Vol. 49, No. 179, July 1987, pp. 135-155.
3. Smith, S. D., "Space Shuttle Solid Rocket Motor (SRM) Exhaust Plume Definitions—Sea Level to SRB Separation," LMSC-HREC TM D496879, Aug. 1976.
4. Buning, P. G., Chiu, I. T., Obayashi, S., Rizk, Y. M. and Steger, J. L., "Numerical Simulation of the Integrated Space Shuttle Vehicle in Ascent," AIAA Paper 88-4359-CP, Aug. 1988.
5. Obayashi, S., "Numerical Simulation of Underexpanded Plumes Using Upwind Algorithms," AIAA Paper 88-4360-CP, Aug. 1988.
6. Koren, B., "Upwind Schemes, Multigrid and Defect Correction for the Steady Navier-Stokes Equations," 11th Intern. Conf. on Numerical Methods in Fluid Dynamics, June 1988. (Proceedings to appear from Springer-Verlag.)
7. AGARD Advisory Report No. 226, "Report of the Working Group on Aerodynamics of Afterbody," June 1986.
8. Venkatapathy, E. and Feiereisen, W. J., "3-D Plume Flow Computations With an Upwind Solver," AIAA Paper 88-3158, July 1988.
9. Davies, C., personal communication. See the following for the reference: Nakahashi, K. and Deiwert, G. S., "A Self-Adaptive-Grid Method with Applications to Airfoil Flow," AIAA Paper 85-1525-CP, July 1985.

A Cellular Automata Simulation of Two-Phase Flow on the CM-2 Connection Machine Computer

Bruce M. Boghosian
Washington Taylor IV
Thinking Machines Corporation,
245 First Street, Cambridge, Massachusetts 02142-1214, U.S.A.

Daniel H. Rothman
Department of Earth, Atmospheric, and Planetary Sciences
Massachusetts Institute of Technology
Cambridge, Massachusetts 02139, U.S.A.

Abstract

A cellular automaton (CA), recently developed by Rothman and Keller [1], simulates the flow of two incompressible, immiscible, viscous fluids in two dimensions. We have simulated this automaton on the CM-2 Connection Machine using a sequence of logical operations and table lookups to determine the new state of a CA site from its old state and those of its neighbors. The logical operations are performed in parallel by each of the Connection Machine processors, while the table lookups use the indirect addressing capabilities among groups of 32 processors.

This paper begins with a general description of CA fluids, including the issue of isotropy, the choice of a rule set, and the averaging procedure used to obtain hydrodynamical quantities. The CM-2 Connection Machine is then described, with emphasis on the indirect addressing capabilities of the machine. Section 2 gives a complete description of the Rothman-Keller model for two-phase flow. Section 3 then describes how the indirect addressing is used in the simulation algorithm, and how a symmetry in the dynamics is used to reduce the size of the lookup tables by a factor of six. Finally, in Section 4, a time sequence of results showing the separation of two immiscible phases from an initially homogenized state is presented.

1 Introduction

1.1 Cellular Automata

Cellular automata (CA) are dynamical systems that are discretized in space, time, and dependent variable. They are becoming increasingly popular as models of physical phenomena [2], and hence there is a great deal of interest in algorithms for their efficient simulation.

The discretization of the dependent variable is what distinguishes CA from, say, finite difference algorithms. It means that CA's can be represented by some (presumably finite) number of bits at every site. The sites are arranged on some sort of regular spatial grid.

The dynamics of the system are then specified by a *rule* that determines what the dependent variable (all the bits at a given site) will be at the next time step as a function of the dependent variable at the same site, as well as at some number of other neighboring sites, at the present time step. This rule is applied *simultaneously* to all the sites on the lattice to evolve it one step in time.

1.2 Lattice Gases

Lattice gases are a class of cellular automata whose coarse-grain averaged behavior obeys the hydrodynamical equations of motion for an incompressible Navier-Stokes fluid [2]. Since the Navier-Stokes equations have been used to model the flow of a wide range of viscous fluids with very different molecular dynamics (e.g. molasses, water and air), it is clear that the exact nature of the molecular dynamics must be largely irrelevant to the flow pattern of the fluid.

We know from the Chapman-Enskog derivation of the Navier-Stokes equation from the Boltzmann equation [3] that the only really indispensable features of the microscopic dynamics of molecules in incompressible fluids are the conservation of mass and momentum. Thus, if we can define dynamics for particles on a lattice that conserve these quantities, then their coarse-grain averaged behavior should be that of a fluid.

One of the first attempts to construct such a model was made by Hardy, de Pazzis, and Pomeau [4] in 1976, and is therefore called the "HPP" lattice gas. It uses a square lattice in two dimensions with four bits per site. These bits can be thought of as indicating the presence (1) or absence (0) of a particle at that site moving east, north, west, or south, respectively. Note that there can be no more than one particle at a given site moving in a given direction at a given time.

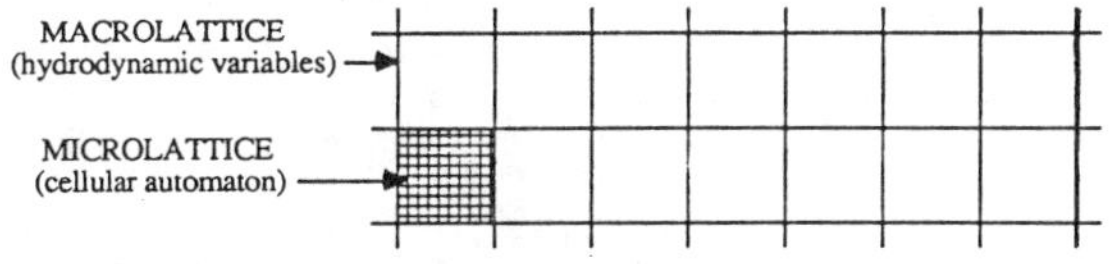

Figure 1: Spatial Averaging

At each time step, the particles first move to the neighboring site on the lattice towards which they are heading, and then they collide in a way that conserves particles and momentum. A moment's thought reveals that the only possible such collision that is nontrivial (i.e. in which the particles actually change direction) is that for which exactly two incoming particles collide head-on and change directions by 90 degrees.

The idea is then to simulate this CA rule on a very large lattice and to coarse-grain average to get results for hydrodynamical quantities, such as fluid velocity. In practice, coarse-grain averaging was done by taking local spatial averages. That is, we partition the lattice into *macrolattice* regions so that one macrolattice point corresponds to many CA sites. Then a hydrodynamical quantity is defined on a macrolattice gridpoint by averaging the velocities of all the particles present on the corresponding CA sites (see Fig. (1)).

Unfortunately the HPP fluid is not *isotropic* [4]. That is, the fluid "knows" that there were two preferred underlying directions, and the bulk flow properties depend upon the angle of orientation with respect to the underlying axes. For example, the drag on a fluid flowing between two parallel plates depends on how the plates are oriented with respect to the lattice axes.

This anisotropy problem was surmounted in an important paper of Frisch, Hasslacher and Pomeau in 1986 [5]. These authors noted that the isotropy of the bulk fluid flow hinged on the symmetry properties of the lattice. In particular, if a fourth rank tensor invariant under the lattice's symmetry group were guaranteed to be isotropic, then the bulk flow would also be isotropic [5]. Invariance under 90 degree rotation is not sufficient to guarantee the isotropy of a fourth rank tensor in two dimensions, and this is why the HPP model did not yield isotropic fluid flow. Invariance under 60 degree rotation *is* sufficient to guarantee such isotropy, however, so the authors proposed a new model which used a triangular lattice in two dimensions.

The resulting model, called the "FHP" lattice gas, was a CA with six bits per site, corresponding to the presence (1) or absence (0) of a particle at that site moving in each of the six lattice directions, respectively. Once again, there can be no more than one particle at a given site moving in a given direction at a given time. All collisions that conserve particles and momentum are allowed.

Extensive simulation (e.g. [6]) has shown that the FHP lattice gas is indeed isotropic, and obeys the incompressible Navier-Stokes equations in two dimensions. Tests have included Poisseuille flow at a variety of Reynolds numbers, in which the drag was measured and found to agree with theory; and flow past a cylinder, in which critical Reynolds numbers for the formation of attached eddies and their subsequent detachment, as well as the Strouhal number as a function of Reynolds number, were measured and found to agree with experiment.

1.3 The CM-2 Connection Machine

The CM-2 Connection Machine® system[1] [7] is a massively data parallel computer with 65536 processors. Each processor has 65536 bits of local memory, so the machine has an overall memory capacity of 536 megabytes. The processors (and their associated memories) are arranged in hardware with 16 to a chip. In addition, every "node," consisting of a pair of chips (32 processors), is supported by floating-point accelerator hardware.

The CM-2 operates in "single-instruction multiple-data" (SIMD) mode; that is, an identical instruction set is broadcast to each processor. It is thus very efficient for tasks that can be solved by simultaneous operation on all of the data present. The CM-2 is furthermore characterized by a very sophisticated communications network linking all of its processors. For all of the above reasons, the CM-2 is very well-suited for many problems in computational physics, including simulations of cellular automata.

The CM-2 Connection Machine system uses a conventional front-end computer. The front-end executes the control structure of programs, issuing commands to the CM-2 processors whenever necessary. Because the front-end could not possibly broadcast instructions directly to the Connection Machine processors as fast as the latter could accept them, high-level instructions are instead sent to a *sequencer* which in turn translates a corresponding packet of *microcode* from a *control store* into many instructions of *nanocode* and broadcasts these to the processors for execution.

For CA research, however, one frequently wants the commands sent to the CM-2 by the sequencer to be very simple logical operations on one-bit fields. A potential problem is that the CM-2 can usually accomplish these in a time short compared with the time it takes the sequencer to accept the high-level instructions and broadcast the corresponding nanocode to the processors. In this circumstance, the communications link between the front-end and the sequencer becomes a bottleneck preventing the achievement of optimal performance. One method of circumventing this difficulty is to prepackage a large number of such logical operations into one single high-level-type command that is kept as microcode in the control store, and, upon execution, gets broken down by the sequencer into very many instructions of nanocode. In other words, this means that the sequencer must be microcoded to achieve optimal performance for CA simulation.

Towards this end, a CA Microcode Compiler has been developed [8]; it generates the necessary microcode for the user, producing a CA updating function that is callable from a high-level language (*LISP). This allows the user access to the full functionality of the CM processors, including the capacity for individual bit operations and for indirect addressing of locally stored lookup tables. This will be described further in Section 3.

Since each processor of the CM-2 has 2^{16} bits of memory, and since each site of a typical CA has far fewer bits than that, it is usually desirable to store many CA sites in each processor. This is an example of a general and powerful technique used on the CM-2, known as *virtual processing.* We make each physical processor simulate some larger number of processors by segmenting the memory of each processor (into CA sites), and applying the rule successively to each site. This is transparent to the high-level language programmer, who inputs the rule as though it were for a single site; the CA Microcode Compiler takes care of the memory segmentation, the communication with neighboring sites, and the sequential application of the instructions to each site.

2 Description of the CA for Two-Phase Flow Simulation

The Rothman-Keller model for two-phase flow begins with a triangular lattice in two dimensions, much like the FHP model. In addition to the possibility of moving in each of the six lattice directions, particles can also be at rest. This gives rise to the possibility of new particle and momentum conserving collisions; for example, two incoming particles that are 180 degrees apart can collide with one at rest to yield three particles emerging 120 degrees apart (see Figure (2)).

[1]Connection Machine is a registered trademark of Thinking Machines Corporation

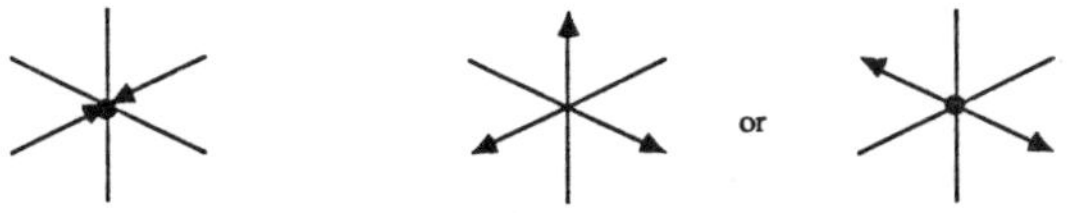

Figure 2: Collision with a Rest Particle

Next we tag the particles with one of two labels, say "red" and "blue," to denote which phase they belong to. We then demand that collisions conserve the number of each type of particle *separately*, as well as the total momentum.

The prescription as given thus far does not uniquely specify the collision rules for the lattice gas. There are incoming configurations for which there are several possible outcomes that conserve red particles, blue particles, and total momentum (see Figure (3)). The strategy is to pick from the possible outcomes only those that preferentially send red particles toward other red particles and blue particles toward other blue particles (this will be made more quantitative momentarily). For example, in Figure (3), result I is better than any of the others in this respect. It is this requirement that gives the two phases cohesion, and creates surface tension at their interface.

Recall that lattice gas updating rules happen in two steps. In the first, or *advection*, step, all particles move from their present site to the site towards which they are headed. In the second, or *collision*, step, the newly arrived particles may collide. In the ordinary FHP model the outcomes of these collisions do not depend on what is at the new neighboring sites, but in the Rothman-Keller model, they do so depend. This means that the total domain of dependence of the CA rule for the Rothman-Keller model is *two* sites in each direction.

To choose from among the various outcomes that conserve both species of particles and total momentum, we define a *color flux* and *color field* at each site. The color flux at lattice position $\mathbf{x}$ is defined to be

$$\mathbf{q}[r(\mathbf{x}), b(\mathbf{x})] \equiv \sum_i \mathbf{c}_i [r_i(\mathbf{x}) - b_i(\mathbf{x})], \tag{1}$$

where the $\mathbf{c}_i$ are unit vectors in each of the six directions,

$$\mathbf{c}_j \equiv -\hat{\mathbf{x}} \sin\left(\frac{2\pi j}{6}\right) + \hat{\mathbf{y}} \cos\left(\frac{2\pi j}{6}\right), \tag{2}$$

and where r_i (b_i) is the number of red (blue) particles moving in direction i (these can be either zero or one, but they cannot both be one at the same time). Note that the color flux can be thought of as the difference between the net red momentum and the net blue momentum at site $\mathbf{x}$.

The color field at lattice position $\mathbf{x}$ is then defined to be

$$\mathbf{f}(\mathbf{x}) \equiv \sum_i \mathbf{c}_i \sum_j [r_j(\mathbf{x} + \mathbf{c}_i) - b_j(\mathbf{x} + \mathbf{c}_i)]. \tag{3}$$

This is simply the (discretized) gradient of the signed (red minus blue) color density. As noted above, it depends on the new neighbors (i.e. the neighbors after the advection step).

The "work" performed by the flux against the field is then defined to be

$$W(r, b) = -\mathbf{f} \cdot \mathbf{q}(r, b). \tag{4}$$

We can now state the full rule for determining collision outcome. Given an incoming state (r, b) after the advection step, then the outgoing state (r', b') is the solution to the minimzation problem

$$W(r', b') = \min_{r'', b''} W(r'', b''), \tag{5}$$

subject to the constraints of red and blue particle conservation

$$\sum_i r_i'' = \sum_i r_i, \qquad \sum_i b_i'' = \sum_i b_i, \tag{6}$$

and total momentum conservation

$$\sum_i \mathbf{c}_i(r_i'' + b_i'') = \sum_i \mathbf{c}_i(r_i + b_i). \tag{7}$$

This optimizaton problem may not have a unique result for a given input configuration, but if it doesn't then we just choose randomly from among the possible results.

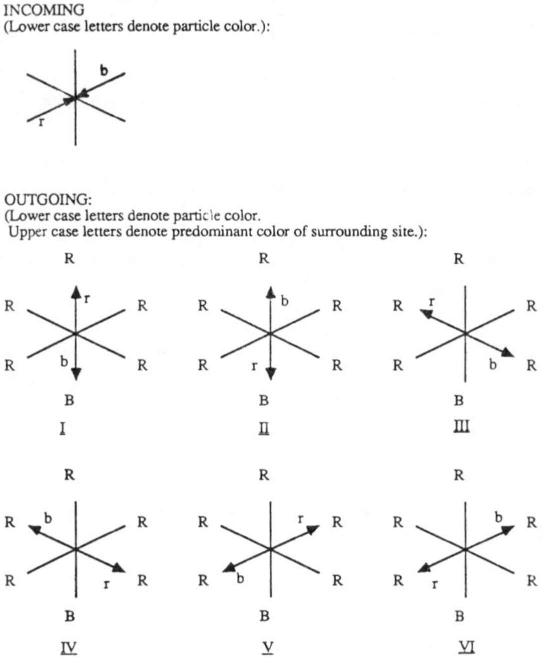

Figure 3: Nonuniqueness of Outcome

For example, return to Fig. (3). A precise determination of the color field would require detailed knowledge of the red and blue populations of all the surrounding sites (see Eq. (3)), and these are not given in the figure. Let us suppose, however, that the color field is simply $\hat{\mathbf{y}}$. This is plausible because the one surrounding site that has a plurality of blue particles is in the negative y direction. Then the color flux and work done for each outcome are listed in the following table. Note that outcome I has the lowest value of W.

Outcome	Color Flux	Work
I	$2\hat{\mathbf{y}}$	-2
II	$-2\hat{\mathbf{y}}$	2
III	$-\sqrt{3}\hat{\mathbf{x}} + \hat{\mathbf{y}}$	-1
IV	$\sqrt{3}\hat{\mathbf{x}} - \hat{\mathbf{y}}$	1
V	$\sqrt{3}\hat{\mathbf{x}} + \hat{\mathbf{y}}$	-1
VI	$-\sqrt{3}\hat{\mathbf{x}} - \hat{\mathbf{y}}$	1

The proof given by Rothman and Keller [1] that this automaton correctly models Navier-Stokes flow with interfacial surface tension is partly theoretical and partly empirical. The theoretical part is the observation that in any region of only red (blue) particles, the CA rule reduces to FHP with a rest particle, and this can be proven to obey the Navier-Stokes equations (e.g. [9] and [10]). Thus, if we are sufficiently distant from an interfacial surface, then we have a Navier-Stokes fluid. By "sufficiently distant" here, we mean a few particle mean free paths (since a mean free path is on the order of a lattice spacing, this means a few lattice spacings).

There are two empirical observations necessary to complete the proof: First, we notice, by simulation, that a homogenized mixture of the two phases *does* indeed separate. This is not a priori obvious;

indeed, it is rather easy to construct other plausible rules for which the two phases do *not* separate. Second, we note that the pressure differential between the inside and the outside of a circular bubble of one phase immersed in the other phase scales as the inverse of the bubble radius; this is the characteristic signature of the presence of interfacial surface tension. This scaling was established over a wide range of bubble radii in the paper by Rothman and Keller [1].

3 Description of the Algorithm

3.1 Description of the Representation

The Cellular Automata Rule Compiler for the CM-2 allows the user to specify CA rules either by logical operations or by lookup tables on Cartesian grids in arbitrary dimensions (up to 16). Since we have a triangular grid, we must first embed it into a Cartesian grid. The technique for doing this is shown in Fig. (4). To go from the triangular grid to the Cartesian grid, we simply shift every other column half a grid spacing. Then alternate columns choose their six neighbors differently (from the eight surrounding neighbors – including diagonals – on the Cartesian grid). This means that we must store a *column parity* bit at each site, so that we will know which six neighbors to choose. Of course, because the CM-2 is a SIMD machine, we always get all eight neighbors everywhere and then apply logical operations using the column parity bit to select the correct six.

At each site we have seven possible particle velocities. Each of these seven velocities can be "populated" by a red particle, a blue particle, or no particle at all. This requires two bits of information per possible particle velocity, or a total of fourteen bits per site. Actually, two bits per velocity is somewhat wasteful, because it is not possible to have both a red and a blue particle populating the same velocity; thus only $\lceil \log_2 3^7 \rceil = 12$ bits are really needed. It was thought preferable to tolerate the waste of two bits per site, rather than hash code down to 12 bits; this is because such hash coding would have to be undone at the beginning of each collision step and done again afterwards, thereby slowing down the updating speed.

Thus, the incoming state in Fig. (3) is encoded into the following fourteen bit string: 00000001000010. This is explained in Fig. (5). Each pair of bits is either 00 (no particle), 01 (red particle), or 10 (blue particle); no pair is allowed to be 11. The first pair refers to the rest particle, and the six subsequent pairs refer to each of the six lattice directions, respectively.

Thus, to do the advection phase, each site communicates with its eight neighbors on the Cartesian grid, and gets the appropriate pair of bits from each of them. It then looks at its parity bit to see which

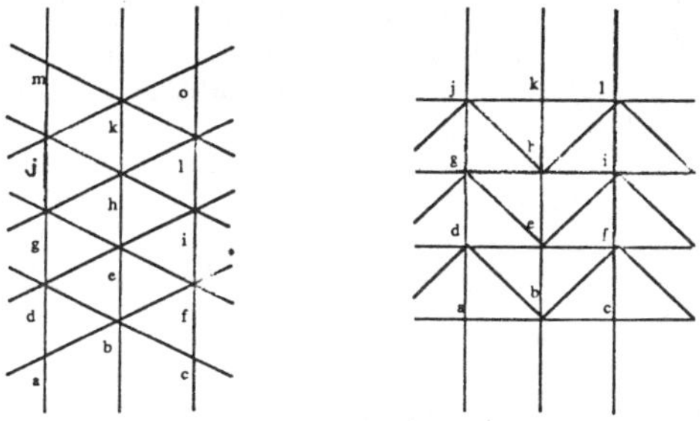

Figure 4: Mapping Triangular Grid to Cartesian Grid

STATE	BIT PAIR
Empty	00
Red	01
Blue	10

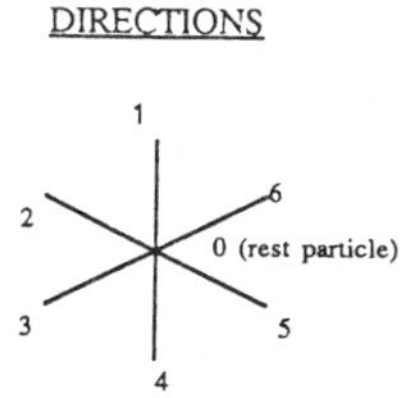

Figure 5: Encoding of Site Configuration into 14 Bit String

ones to keep, and stores them in a new fourteen bit area. It is then ready to get the color density at each site. It does this with a lookup table operation, so we turn to a discussion of how that works.

3.2 Rules for Using the Indirect Lookup Operation

The indirect lookup capability of the CM-2 allows groups of 32 processors (called a "node") to share in the storage of a local lookup table, so that any processor from among them can refer to any entry of the table. It is important to note that there are 2^{11} nodes in a full CM-2, so that the table is replicated in memory this many times. This locality makes a very fast lookup table operation possible.

There are two primary constraints, arising directly from the CM-2 hardware configuration, that govern the use of indirect addressing on the machine: First, data to be referenced must be less than or equal to 32 bits in length. Second, suppose that we want to store N lookup tables for indirect addressing. Denote the length (in bits) of a datum in table i by ℓ_i where $i = 1, \ldots, N$, and denote the number of data in table i by n_i where $i = 1, \ldots, N$. Construct N rectangles of sizes n_i by ℓ_i. Then there is a minimum value of M such that these N rectangles can all be packed into a single rectangle of size M by 32 (with axes aligned). This minimum value of M is the amount of processor memory required by the lookup tables. We shall accept these constraints as postulates throughout the remainder of this paper.

If a lookup table is too long to fit in memory according to the above rules, then there are other means that can be used. For example, consider a table with 2^{20} elements. It can be used as follows: Divide the 20 bit long table index into a 14 bit portion and a 6 bit portion. Now a node consists of all those processors that differ only in the last 5 bits of cube address. The rest of the cube address can thus be referred to as a *node address*. The idea is that the 6 bit portion of the 20 bit index selects a node from among the local group of 64 nodes (those nodes differing only in the last six bits of node address), and the 14 bit portion uses the lookup table at that node. Thus, we are saving storage at the expense of the above-described locality and, hence, of speed. In this work, we can fit the entire lookup table into one node, and so we don't have to resort to this method.

3.3 Use of the Lookup Tables

The next step in the algorithm is to use the lookup table to get the color density at each site. Recall that the color density is defined to be the difference between the number of red particles at a site and the number of blue particles at a site. Each of these can be any number from 0 to 7. In order to get an unsigned integer, we add 7 to the result to get a representation of the color density that can range from 0 to 14 (inclusive); thus we need four more bits per site to store it. So the lookup table for color density is 2^{14} entries long and 4 bits wide.

Next, each site again communicates with its six lattice neighbors to get their color densities. These are needed for the determination of the color field (see Eq. (3)). By unsigned addition and subtraction operations, the six four-bit fields are then combined to get the x and y components of the color field. The x component can be represented by an unsigned integer that varies from 0 to 56, so we need 6 bits to store it; the y component can be represented by an unsigned integer that varies from 0 to 112, so we need 7 bits to store it.

Next we note that the dynamics are completely invariant under rotations by $\pi/6$. This means that we can rotate the entire configuration by $\ell\pi/6$, where ℓ is chosen to make the color field vector point at angle $0 \leq \theta_n < \pi/6$, figure out the result for this *normal form* input configuration, and rotate that result back by $-\ell\pi/6$. This trick reduces the size of the resultant lookup table by a factor of six. We find ℓ and θ_n by a pair of lookup tables both of which take the combined 13 bits of the x and y components of the color field as input; the first returns the number ℓ which can range from 0 to 5, and the second returns θ_n whose unsigned representation can range from 0 to 6. Thus, both of these lookup tables have length 2^{13} and are 3 bits wide.

We now rotate the 14 bit configuration to the normal form. This amounts to a barrel shift by 2ℓ of its last 12 bits. We don't touch the first two bits, because they correspond to the rest particle, and it remains unchanged by the rotation. The factor of two occurs because every *pair* of bits corresponds to one lattice direction. The resulting 14 bits are called the *normal form configuration.*

The set of all normal form configurations can be broken up into 360 separate equivalence classes, distinguished by number of red particles, number of blue particles, and total momentum. Thus, we can pass the 14 bits of normal form configuration to a lookup table to get back 9 bits that uniquely specify this equivalence class. So this table has length 2^{14} and is 9 bits wide.

Now the combination of the 9 bit equivalence class and the 3 bit θ_n determine the final result in normal form. This is accomplished with two more lookup table operations. We first recall that the optimization problem specified in Eqs. (5) through (7) may not have a unique result. In fact, there are anywhere from 1 to 35 possible results. So we feed the above-mentioned 12 bits to a *result-pointer* lookup table that returns a 13 bit pointer to another *result* table. The result-pointer'th element of result table is then the number of results that satisfy Eqs. (5) through (7), and this is followed by the results themselves. Thus, the result-pointer table is 2^{12} elements long and 13 bits wide, while the result table is 2^{13} elements long and 14 bits wide. Instead of randomizing among the tied results, we deterministically cycle through them (of course, the "phase" of these cycles differs from processor to processor); this seems to be adequate, and requires no random number generation.

Finally, we recall that the 14 bit result is still in normal form, and so the bottom 12 bits need to be barrel shifted by -2ℓ to get the final result that is installed in the original 14 bit site storage area. This ends the collision step.

Figure (6) shows how all the above-described lookup tables can be packed into a portion of memory of length 2^{14} (one quarter of the total memory of the CM-2).

To summarize, we have done a total of six lookup table operations to get the final result. We have also done logical operations to determine neighbors from the column parity bit, to do the unsigned additions and subtractions necessary to get the x and y components of the color field, and to do the barrel shifting to and from normal form.

In addition to the 2^{14} bits per processor that go to store the lookup tables, we used 219 additional bits per processor to store intermediate results obtained in the course of an update step. Since there are 64315 user-accessable bits of memory in each CM-2 processor [7], this leaves $64315 - 2^{14} - 219 = 47712$ bits per processor that can be used to store sites. At each site we must store 14 bits for the site representation, 14 more to store the new site representation after the communications step (as described above), one bit of column parity, and four bits to store the color density (as described above). This comes to a total of 33 bits. The total number of sites per processor that we can store is thus approximately $\lfloor 47712/33 \rfloor = 1445$. A full CM-2 has 2^{16} processors so that we can store a total of about 94.7 million

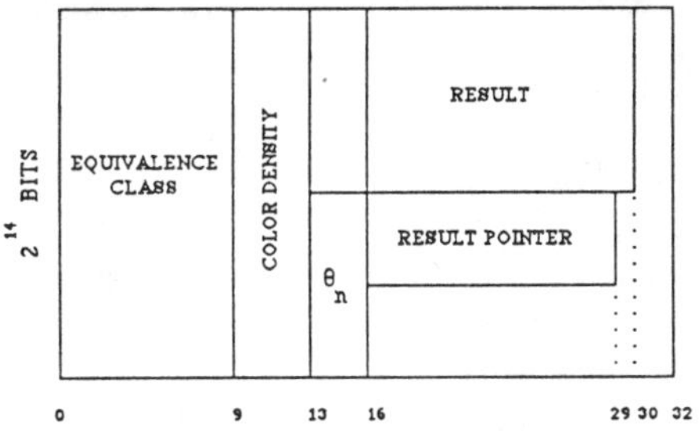

Figure 6: Storage of Lookup Tables

sites (roughly the number in a 9731 by 9731 grid).

It is probably possible to improve this number; in particular, it is known that there are less wasteful techniques of storage than simply double buffering the old and new states. The measured updating rate of our implementation was roughly 100 million site updates per second. So a CM-2 filled to capacity with sites would update all of them in less than one second. This figure might be improved by custom microcoding; in our implementation we did not hand optimize the microcode produced by the CA microcode compiler in any way.

4 Simulation Results

Figures (7) and (8) depict a representative simulation beginning (time step 0) with a random mixture of red and blue particles on a 512 by 512 spatial grid with periodic boundary conditions. In this and the subsequent plots, a site is black if there is a plurality of blue particles, and white otherwise. No averaging has been done to get these plots.

Note that the automaton quickly acts to smooth out all surfaces, producing many bubbles by time step 4000. These move around randomly until they meet and join by cohesion. By time step 60000, most bubbles have joined, and a metastable equilibrium is reached by time step 100000. If the simulation were run for longer times, there would eventually be complete separation.

5 Conclusion

We have described a CA that simulates two-phase flow in some detail, and have explained its implementation on the CM-2 Connection Machine. It used a combination of logical operations and table lookup to update the CA sites. We described the algorithm used in sufficient detail to determine the storage requirements, and we gave a performance figure.

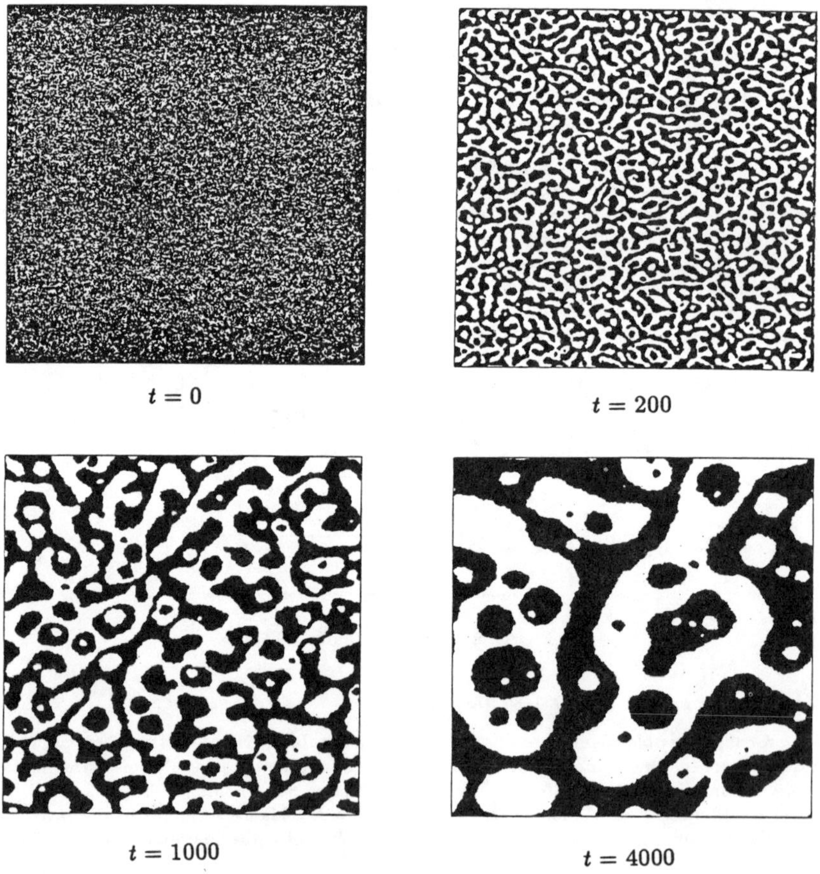

Figure 7: Simulation Results

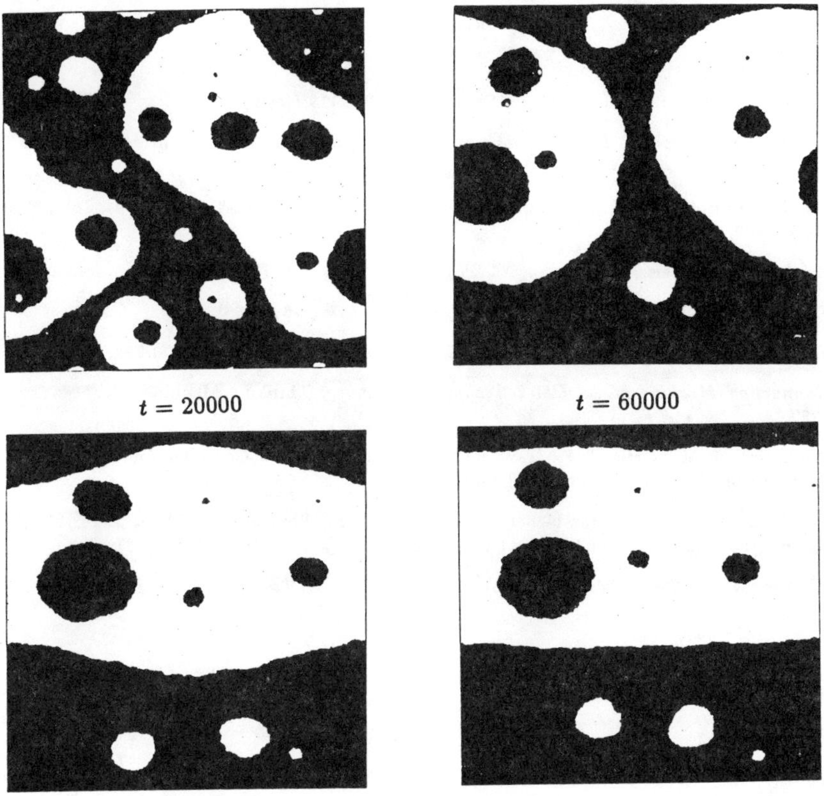

Figure 8: Simulation Results

Extensions of this work will include the study of a variety of two-phase flow phenomena, including the addition of a uniform gravitational field that acts upon the two phases differently. For example, by pulling red particles upwards and blue particles downwards, we can effectively model the flow of two phases with differing gravitational mass per unit volume. By setting up initial conditions with the heavier fluid above the lighter one, we can study the Rayleigh-Taylor instability; by modeling fluids of two different viscosities in a porous medium, we can study the Saffman-Taylor instability; by applying a shearing flow at the interface, we can study the Kelvin-Helmholtz instability; etc.

6 Acknowledgements

We would like to thank Andrew Gunstensen, Jeff Keller, C. David Levermore and Luis Ortiz for helpful suggestions throughout the course of this work. DHR would like to acknowledge support from the sponsors of the MIT Porous Flow Project and the donors of the Petrolium Research Fund, administered by the American Chemical Society.

References

[1] Rothman, D.H. and Keller, J.M., J. Stat. Phys. **52**, 1119 (1988).

[2] Wolfram, S., *Theory and Applications of Cellular Automata,* World Scientific Publishing Co Pte Ltd (1986).

[3] See, for example, Liboff, R. L., *Introduction to the Theory of Kinetic Equations,* John Wiley and Sons, 1969.

[4] Hardy, J., de Pazzis, O., Pomeau, Y., *Phys. Rev. A*, **13**, 5 (1976).

[5] Frisch, U., Hasslacher, B., Pomeau, Y., *Phys. Rev. Lett.*, **56** (1986).

[6] Kadanoff, L.P., McNamara, G.R., Zanetti, G., *Complex Systems*, **1** (1987) 791.

[7] *Connection Machine Model CM-2 Technical Summary,* Thinking Machines Corporation, April, 1987.

[8] Boghosian, B.M., Ortiz, L.F., Taylor IV, W., "A Microcode Compiler for Cellular Automata Research on the CM-2," to be published (1988).

[9] Frisch, U., d'Humières, Hasslacher, B., Lallemand, P., Pomeau, Y., Rivet, J.-P., "Lattice Gas Hydrodynamics in Two and Three Dimensions," *Complex Systems*, **1**, 4 (1987).

[10] Wolfram, S., *J. Stat. Phys.*, *45* (1986) 471.

Spectral Solution of the Incompressible Navier-Stokes Equations on the Connection Machine2

Sherryl Tomboulian *
MassPar Inc., 2940 San Tomas Exprswy, Suite 140, Santa Clara,CA 95051

Craig Streett
Mail Stop 159, NASA Langley Research Center

Michéle Macaraeg
Mail Stop 156, NASA Langley Research Center

This paper addresses the issue of solving the time-dependent incompressible Navier-Stokes equations on the Connection Machine2, for the problem of transition to turbulence of the steady flow in a channel. The spectral algorithm used serially requires $O(N^4)$ *operations; using the massive parallelism of the CM it becomes an* $O(N^2)$ *problem, then solving the equations on an N x N x N grid. Preliminary timings of the code, written in LISP, are included and compared with a corresponding code optimized for the Cray-2 for a 128 x 128 x 101 grid.*

INTRODUCTION

Fast solutions to the Navier-Stokes equations are of enduring interest in computational fluid dynamics. The level of resolution required to accurately simulate the relevant physics of flows involving transition to turbulence may span scales ranging eight orders or magnitude or more. Existing supercomputers still lack the capacity to resolve such problems. In this paper, we examine the possibility of employing massive parallelism towards meeting the ever-increasing computational demands of large-scale fluid dynamic simulations.

The general framework is the time-dependent incompressible Navier-Stokes equations. One of the methods of choice for solving these equations when a high degree of accuracy is required is spectral methods, and we are in the process of examining the feasibility of implementing spectral methods on the Connection Machine2. The particular tensor-product matrix formulation used here involves kernels which are amenable to implementation on this architecture. These basic kernels are presented, along with a spectral algorithm that uses these kernels to solve the Navier-Stokes equations.

MACHINE MODEL

The Connection Machine2 [6,2] is a parallel architecture with 65,000 processors. The machine can be segmented into quarters, and all the work on this paper was done on a 16K processor machine. Each processor has 64K bits of memory, or 2K of single precision floating point numbers. Each subset of 32 processors has a floating point co-processor available.

---

* Research was supported by the National Aeronautics and Space Administration under NASA contract No. NAS1-18107 while the author was in residence at the Institute for Computer Applications in Science and Engineering (ICASE), NASA Langley Research Center, Hampton VA, 23665.

The processors are SIMD (single instruction multiple data), meaning that all the processors must do exactly the same thing at the same time. A serial processor, called the controller, gives the same instructions to the parallel array or processors. As part of the instruction, scalar values can be broadcast. For instance, one could instruct all processors to add '5' to location A in their local memories.

The processors are interconnected in a topology that is hyper-cube like. For the purposes of this paper it is sufficient to consider the machine as arranged as a 128 by 128 toroidal grid of processors, where each processor can communicate with its north, south, east, and west neighbors. A communication facility called the router can also be used for more generalized communication.

NUMERICAL METHOD

In this paper we solve the time-dependent incompressible Navier-Stokes equations:

$$\vec{u}_t + \vec{u}\cdot\nabla\vec{u} = -\nabla P + \nu\nabla^2\vec{u} \tag{1a}$$

$$\nabla\cdot\vec{u} = 0 \tag{1b}$$

The method employed for incremental time solution is a standard splitting method [1]. With $\vec{u}$ representing the three-dimensional velocity vector, we advance the solution from time level 'n' to level 'n+1' via:

$$\vec{u}^{\,*}_t + \vec{u}^{\,n}\cdot\nabla\vec{u}^{\,n} = \nu\nabla^2\vec{u}^{\,*} \tag{2}$$

which solves for the momentum equations without the pressure terms, followed by:

$$\vec{u}^{\,n+1}_t = -\nabla P^{n+1} \tag{3a}$$

$$\nabla\cdot\vec{u}^{\,n+1} = 0 \tag{3b}$$

which solves for the pressure and corrects the velocity to satisfy continuity. This second step is actually carried out in two stages:

$$\nabla^2 P^{n+1} = \nabla\cdot\vec{u}^{\,*} \tag{4a}$$

$$\vec{u}^{\,n+1}_t = -\nabla P^{n+1} \tag{4b}$$

having utilized a backward-Euler time discretization of eq. 3a. The time discretization employed in advancing eq. 2 is a mixed implicit-explicit scheme, with third-order low-storage Runge-Kutta for the nonlinear convection terms, and Crank-Nicholson for the viscous terms.

Spatial discretization is carried out using a spectral collocation method; Fourier series are used in the streamwise and spanwise directions of the channel, with Chebyshev series used in the normal direction between the channel walls. The now-standard matrix method is used for evaluating derivative quantities at the collocation points [1]. That is, the approximate derivatives of a function evaluated at the collocation points may be computed directly by a matrix-vector product; the coefficients of the basis function series need not be explicitly calculated. Formulae for the required Fourier and Chebyshev differentiation matrices are known in closed form [1]. Although at first glance this appears to require N^6 operations to compute the derivative in one direction at each point of an N x N x N three-dimensional grid, the computation can actually be carried out in N^4 operations, using the fact that the discretizations in each coordinate direction are separable. This is known as a tensor-product formulation. Similarly, if the overall discrete differential operator is linear and separable, its characteristic matrices may also be written in tensor product form, and thus the overall operator may be diagonalized in $O(N^4)$ operations [1].

It may be noted that since Fourier discretizations are used in this application, the scheme may be formulated using Fast Fourier Transforms (FFT's) rather than tensor products, with asymptotic work of $O(N^3 \log N)$ rather than $O(N^4)$. We decided, however, to study a general implementation of spectral collocation solution of the Navier-Stokes equations, rather than limit the implementation to the restrictive periodic form. The additions to the time-split scheme to enforce general boundary conditions in all directions are minor [5]. Additionally, for the initial proof-of-concept phase of this project, approximate pressure boundary conditions are used.

KERNEL OPERATIONS

The application we report here is on a 16K CM, with its processors configured as a 128 x 128 toroidally-cyclic grid; we denote processor number by the subscripts 'i,j'. The three-dimensional computational grid is mapped onto the processors in a straightforward manner, with the third direction, the 'z' or 'normal' direction, stored locally in each processor, and denoted by the subscript 'k'. Given the storage requirements of the scheme and the available local memory of each processor, the z-direction is discretized with 101 points, giving an overall mesh of about 1.65 million points.

The bulk of computation in this scheme lies in the tensor product operations. In indical notation, these operations in each of the three directions are defined:

$$T_x(L^x, u) = \sum_{l=1}^{l=N} L^x_{il} u_{ljk} \tag{5a}$$

$$T_y(L^y, u) = \sum_{l=1}^{l=N} L^y_{jl} u_{ilk} \tag{5b}$$

$$T_z(L^z, u) = \sum_{l=1}^{l=N} L^y_{kl} u_{ijl} \tag{5c}$$

The x-direction tensor product is simply a matrix multiply between L^x and each of the k-planes of U. Likewise, the y-direction tensor product is $U(L^y)^T$ for each k-plane. These matrix multiplies are carried out in O(N) operations instead of $O(n^3)$, using the systolic algorithm [3]. This is because all N^2 processors can be used simultaneously. The algorithm works as follows: Before starting the multiply, the first matrix is skewed so that each row in the matrix is shifted over one position for each row down (i.e. the elements in row 3 are shifted 3 places to the right). Similarly, the columns of the second matrix are shifted down for each column over. The multiplication is then performed by shifting each row of the first matrix up one and each column of the second matrix over

$e_n = 0, n = x$ **to** z -- *initialize*

for m= 1 **to** 3 **do:** -- *loop on the three steps of the Runge-Kutta*

for n= x to z **do:** -- *loop over components of*
-- *the momentum equation*

-- *Compute the RHS of the Crank-Nicholson step (eq. 2); the first three terms*
-- *are viscous terms, the next three terms are convection terms, and the last*
-- *is due to the Runge-Kutta scheme.*

$$f_1 = T_x\left(D^{xx}, u_n\right) + T_y\left(D^{yy}, u_n\right) + T_z\left(D^{zz}, u_n\right)$$
$$+ k_m \times \left[u_x \times T_x\left(D^x, u_n\right) + u_y \times T_y\left(D^y, u_n\right) + u_z \times T_z\left(D^z, u_n\right)\right] + e_n$$

$$e_n = d_m^1 e_n + d_m^2 f_1$$ -- *update temporary for Runge-Kutta scheme*

-- *Do tensor-product diagonalization for inversion of viscous operator*
-- *in Crank-Nicholson*

$$f_2 = T_x\left(R^x, T_y\left(R^y, T_z\left(R^z, f_1\right)\right)\right)$$
$$f_3 = C_m \times f_2$$
$$g_n = T_x\left(Q^x, T_y\left(Q^y, T_z\left(Q^z, f_1\right)\right)\right)$$

end (for n) -- *end components loop*

$u_n = g_n, \; n = x$ to z -- *update velocities for next step of Runge-Kutta*

end (for m) -- *end R-K steps loop*

-- *Compute pressure; generate RHS of 4a*

$$g_1 = k_4\left[T_x\left(D^x, u_x\right) + T_y\left(D^y, u_y\right) + T_z\left(D^z, u_z\right)\right]$$

-- *Invert Laplacian by tensor-product diagonalization*

$$g_2 = T_x\left(R^x, T_y\left(R^y, T_z\left(R^z, g_1\right)\right)\right)$$
$$g_3 = C_4 \times g_2$$
$$P = T_x\left(Q^x, T_y\left(Q^y, T_z\left(Q^z, g_3\right)\right)\right)$$

-- *Correct Velocities using eq. 4b*

$$u_n = u_n + k_5\, T_n\left(D^n, P\right), \quad n = x \text{ to } z$$

end (time step)

Figure 1. The Algorithm for one time step

one, multiplying the elements and accumulating the result, then shifting again. This pattern is repeated N times to complete the product. The overall tensor product requires N separate matrix multiplies (one for each k-plane) so the product requires $O(N^2)$ operations.

The summation in the third tensor product is independent of (i,j), so each processor decouples and performs a matrix-vector product. The operator L^z is stored in the CM controller and broadcast element-by-element in the process of computing $T_z(L^z, u)$.

ALGORITHM IMPLEMENTATION

The algorithm consists of applications of the three tensor products defined above (eqs. 5), and direct element-by-element sums (+) and multiplies (×). The velocity variables are denoted u_n, n= x to z, and P for the pressure. D^n and D^{nn} (n= x to z) are used to denote the spectral differentiation operators, first and second derivative respectively, in each of the three directions. These operators are used in the appropriate tensor-product form to compute derivatives of the dependent variables as needed. The characteristic matrices used to diagonalize the implicit operator are denoted as Q^n and R^n (n= x to z), and are also used in the appropriate tensor-product form. In addition, the following quantities are used:

- k_m, m= 1 to 5, are algorithm and case-specific constants.
- d^1_m and d^2_m, m= 1 to 3 are constants from the Runge-Kutta algorithm.
- C_m, m= 1 to 4 is an n x n x n field of constants used in the tensor-product diagonalization process.
- e_n, f_n, and g_n are temporary field arrays, used for clarity of presentation.

The algorithm for one time step is given in Figure1.

COMPLEXITY AND TIMINGS

By using N^2 processors, the overall complexity reduces to $O(N^2)$ instead of $O(N^4)$. Hence, the parallel solution time should clearly be superior to serial solutions. However, one tradeoff with having a large number of processors is that they are not individually as fast as one might like. There is also communications overhead. Timing results are made comparing a CM2 and similar code on a Cray-2. For smaller problems, such as a 32^3 problem, the Cray is significantly faster than the CM. However, as the problem size is increased, the factor of $O(N^2)$ dominates, and the CM becomes more competitive.

The table below shows timing results for the two codes. The Cray achieves better timings, but this result is a somewhat unfair comparison. The Cray results were achieved on 1 processor of a Cray2 using the local memory micro-coded matrix operations provided by the SARL library which achieve peek performance. The CM code is written in *Lisp, a higher level language, and is not particularly well optimized. Nevertheless, the CM does achieve a rate of about 60 Megaflops (counting the multiply and add as 2 instructions).

Cray2 (1 proc) vs CM2 (16K proc)		
solving a (128 x 128 x 101) problem		
operations	Cray2	CM2
direct multiply	0.068	0.015
matrix op T_x	1.41	7.89
matrix op T_y	1.55	7.90
matrix op T_z	1.55	5.70
overall	216.	857.

Table 1 -- Timing Results in Seconds.

It seems obvious that for even larger problems, the CM algorithm will be much faster than the Cray. However, using this method, the 128x128x101 problem is the largest practical problem on a 16K CM2 because of the size of local memories. Using a 65K processor CM2, we estimate that the discretization of a (256×256×101) problem could be solved several times faster than a Cray-2.

CONCLUSIONS

The results obtained from implementing the Navier-Stokes equations were quite encouraging. The Connection machine was slower but still competitive with respect to time with a Cray, while being significantly more cost effective. More spectacular results can be expected with larger versions of the Connection Machine.

There is one final interesting point concerning this work: We have shown the efficient implementation of an implicit time-stepping algorithm utilizing a global discretization scheme on a SIMD parallel-processing machine. This is contrary to the "popular wisdom" which holds that SIMD machines are useful only when nearest-neighbor operations, such as those of an explicit finite-difference scheme, are carried out. The potential exists for this implementation to provide numerical simulations of transition to turbulence in channel flow at resolutions impractical on present supercomputers.

BIBLIOGRAPHY

[1] C. Canuto, M.Y. Hussaini, A. Quarteroni, T.A. Zang, "Spectral Methods in Fluid Dynamics", Springer-Verlag, 1988.

[2] W. Hillis,"The Connection Machine", MIT Press, Cambridge, Mass, 1985.

[3] L. Johnsson,"Dense Matrix Operations on a Torus and a Boolean Cube", Yale Report U/DCS/RR-377, March 85.

[4] R.E. Lynch, J.R. Rice, and D.H. Thomas, "Tensor Product Analysis of Alternating Direction Implicit Methods", J.S.Indust. Appl. Math., Vol. 13m No.4, December 1965

[5] C.L. Streett,"Spectral Methods and their Implementation to Solution of Thermodynamic and Fluid Mechanic Problems", presented at the 6th International Symposium on Finite Element Problems, Antibes, France, June 1986.

[6] L.W. Tucker and G.G. Robertson,"Architecture and Applications of the Connection Machine", to appear in IEEE Trans. on Computers

SUPERCOMPUTER APPLICATIONS IN COMPUTATIONAL FLUID DYNAMICS

Terry L. Holst

Chief, Applied Computational Fluids Branch
NASA Ames Research Center, Moffett Field, California

Abstract: The field of Computational Fluid Dynamics (CFD) involving largescale supercomputer applications is discussed. Formulational and computational requirements for the various governing equations, including the Euler and Navier-Stokes approaches, are examined for typical problems including the viscous flow field solution about a complete aerospace vehicle. Recent computed results and experimental comparisons are given to highlight the presentation. The future of CFD associated with three-dimensional applications is found to be rapidly expanding across a broad front including internal and external flows, and flows across the entire speed regime.

INTRODUCTION

The fields of Computational Fluid Dynamics (CFD) and computer hardware design have been rapidly advancing over the last decade. It is now possible to demonstrate the importance of CFD in the field of aircraft design and performance prediction for general flow conditions including reasonably complete viscous effects. The problem of solving the nonlinear governing system of partial differential equations, the Euler and Navier-Stokes equations, about complex three-dimensional geometries has been undertaken and significant results have already been produced. The purpose of this paper is to describe the current status of CFD applications in this area and to indicate prospects for the future, especially for supercomputer applications involving complex geometries. Computational requirements for producing these results both now and in the future will be addressed.

This paper is divided into several sections as follows: CFD Formulations, where the major governing equations used in CFD are described with special emphasis on the Euler and Navier-Stokes formulations; Example Solutions, including two external and one internal applications; and Concluding Remarks. The first item for discussion is how the various CFD formulations, and in particular, those formulations requiring supercomputers for typical applications, fit into the general CFD hierarchical scheme.

CFD FORMULATIONS

The aforementioned improvements in computer execution speed and main memory capacity achieved in the past several years has made it possible to dramatically expand the field of CFD. This has resulted in significant progress up the hierarchal "ladder" of CFD formulation complexity as shown in Fig. 1. Panel method solutions, which effectively solve the linear Laplace equation using the principle of superposition, have been studied thoroughly during the past three decades. As a result, panel method codes are well established within industry as efficient and reliable design tools for aircraft in the subsonic and supersonic speed regimes.

The next rung on the CFD formulational ladder is occupied by nonlinear potential formulations including the transonic small-disturbance and full potential equations. Both of these formulations have been extensively studied for the past 15 years and except for some grid generation limitations associated with complex geometry applications, these methods are well developed and heavily utilized within the aircraft industry design environment. These nonlinear potential methods extend the range of applicability of CFD to the transonic speed regime and

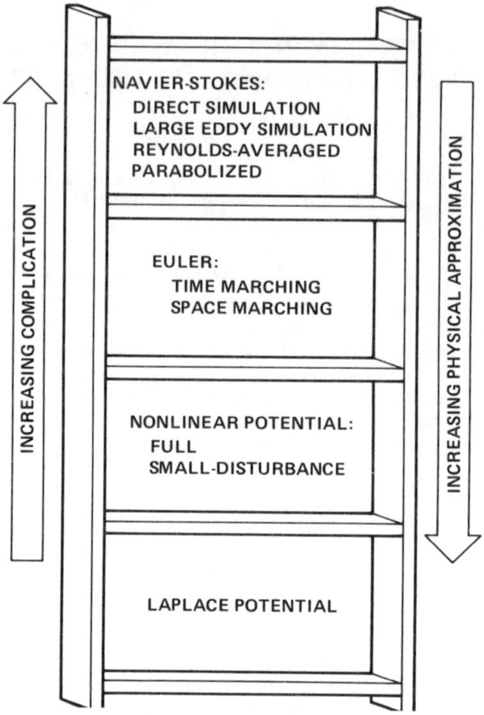

Figure 1. Computational Fluid Dynamics formulational ladder.

therefore have the capability of capturing weak shock waves and wave-drag levels. An appropriate review of this area can be found in [1].

The Euler equation formulation, which occupies the next rung on the CFD formulational ladder, is currently at the center of research in the Aerospace CFD community. New algorithms and applications in three dimensions have proliferated at a very fast rate in the past five years. The various design groups within industry have already started using Euler codes for many applications but significant improvements in code and/or computer efficiency have to be realized before the Euler formulation will be used extensively. The Euler formulation provides better accuracy for strong shock calculations and has the ability to properly track vorticity gradients. These features are important for a variety of advanced flow field situations including vortical aerodynamic studies, strong shock calculations, high angle-of-attack leading-edge flow separation, high-speed blunt body problems, and blast wave studies.

The highest entry on the CFD formulational ladder is occupied by the Navier-Stokes equations. This formulation is the most complex and represents the smallest level of physical approximation. Like the Euler formulation, much work has been completed in the three-dimensional Navier-Stokes area during the past five years. However, the application of typical Navier-Stokes codes in the industry design environment has been slow to evolve. This is largely due to two reasons: First, the Navier-Stokes equations are several times more expensive to solve (at least) than the Euler equations. This is due to more terms in the Navier-Stokes equations; more grid points required to resolve a given problem resulting from viscous effects; and in separated flow cases, more iterations are required to achieve convergence because of the more complicated flow field physics. The second major reason that the Navier-Stokes equations have not been used in design applications is due to the complications of turbulence. To discuss this subject a further breakdown of the Navier-Stokes formulation is required.

The Navier-Stokes equations describe the motion of most fluid flow phenomena including large scale motions associated with the inviscid features of a flow field and small scale motions associated with turbulence. The numerical procedure which directly solves the Navier-Stokes equations and resolves all flow length scales including the smallest turbulent length scales is called direct simulation (DS). When the numerical grid resolution is not fine enough to resolve all length scales problems occur. Because for high Reynolds number flow the range of length scales is so immense, it is not currently possible to simulate this type of flow with schemes based on the DS approach. Thus, the first level of approximation to the Navier-Stokes equations, called Large Eddy Simulation (LES), is introduced. In the LES formulation the Navier-Stokes equations are solved on a grid capable of resolving all length scales except the smallest turbulent length scales, which are associated with the smallest turbulent eddies. Because these smallest eddies tend to be isotropic, they are easier to model than the larger eddies which tend to be random and can vary in nature for different flow conditions. A good review of the DS and LES areas is given in [2].

The LES formulation is still quite expensive and is restricted to problems with limited geometrical complexity and to moderate and low Reynolds numbers. This leads to the Reynolds-averaged Navier-Stokes (RANS) formulation where all turbulent eddies are modeled. The RANS formulation is derived by decomposing all dependent variables, e.g., density, pressure, and velocity components, into two parts, a mean part and an unsteady part. The unsteady part contains the unsteadiness due to high-frequency turbulent fluctuations and the mean part contains the average local flow value for that variable including any low-frequency time variation. After this variable decomposition process the resulting Navier-Stokes equations are time averaged over a time scale which is large in comparison with turbulent fluctuations but small in comparison with mean flow field unsteadiness. As a result of the time-averaging process, certain new terms arising from turbulent eddy correlations remain. These new terms account for the mean or average effect of turbulence and must be modeled. This allows the numerical solution of the Navier-Stokes equations for many applications involving realistic Reynolds numbers on grids that will fit on existing supercomputers.

A comparison of the estimated memory and execution time requirements for several different formulations is given in Fig. 2. An additional horizontal scale indicates the amount of execution time required by a theoretical gigaflop computer, which should be available in the near-term future. The Euler and Navier-Stokes formulations just discussed (DS, LES, and RANS) are all included. Note that several variations of the RANS formulation (steady ideal gas, steady nonequilibrium real gas, and unsteady ideal gas) are presented. Including nonequilibrium real gas effects associated with hypersonic flight or the unsteadiness effects associated with (for example) flight at high angles of attack, may increase the computational costs of a typical steady RANS calculation by an order of magnitude. This additional expense while prohibitive today may not be prohibitive in the near-term future. Additional discussion on the estimated computational costs for various CFD applications can be found in [3,4].

The prospects of computing three-dimensional flows at realistic flight Reynolds numbers using the LES formulation in the near future do not seem bright. As indicated in Fig. 2 the cpu time for such a calculation on a theoretical gigaflop computer would be on the order of one month. The DS picture is even more dismal with cpu times for a single three-dimensional calculation requiring on the order of years. In addition, applications associated with mean flow unsteadiness, real gas effects, or even particularly large Reynolds numbers, could increase these times by orders of magnitude. Hence, it seems that the most appropriate Navier-Stokes formulation for attention in the area of applications involving realistic flight conditions and reasonably complex geometries, is the RANS formulation. The remainder of this paper will describe several CFD applications utilizing the RANS formulation for reasonably complete geometric configurations. For an indepth technical discussion of most of the CFD formulations just discussed, the interested reader is referred to [5].

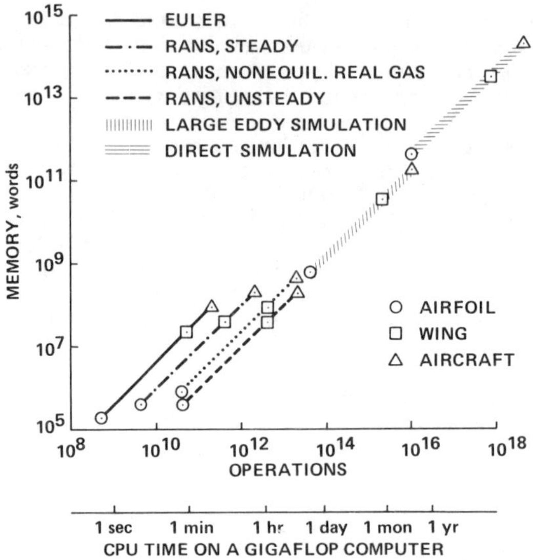

Figure 2. Estimated memory and execution time requirements for several different CFD formulations.

EXAMPLE RANS APPLICATIONS

The first pioneering CFD calculations with the Navier-Stokes formulation started appearing in the early '70s. These first of a kind demonstration calculations were severely limited by computational resources available in this time period, both execution speed and memory. Calculations were generally limited to two spatial dimensions and involved simple geometric shapes, e. g., flat plates, circular cylinders, wedges, or perhaps at most, airfoils. Solutions generally involved turbulent flows with simple algebraic turbulence models (or laminar solutions with no turbulence models). These aspects were required to eliminate the complexity of turbulence and to reduce computational requirements. A good review of early work in this area is given by Peyret and Viviand [6].

Several years after the first two-dimensional Navier-Stokes solutions appeared, three-dimensional simulations were presented, again using algebraic turbulence models (or a laminar flow assumption) and simple geometries. Since then improvements in computers and algorithms have allowed tremendous advances in CFD across a broad front of different applications. These areas are reviewed in two interesting articles by Chapman [7,8] where the entire field of Computational Aerodynamics is reviewed. Pacing items including turbulence modeling, three-dimensional grid generation, algorithm development, and computer speed limitations are discussed; and computational requirements and projected computer capabilities are examined. More recent surveys are presented by Kutler [9] where the same critical pacing items are examined and updated and by Kutler et al. [10] where CFD methods, applications and computer technology are reviewed. To illustrate current CFD capabilities, several recent examples utilizing the RANS formulation are now presented and discussed.

F-16 Simulation

The first example of state-of-the-art RANS technology in a practical application is the numerical simulation of the flow about a complete F-16A aircraft. This was accomplished with a series of flow solutions about several increasingly complete geometrical representations of the F-16A.

This series started with a simple wing-fuselage configuration presented by Reznick and Flores [11] and Flores et al. [12], proceeded with a wing-fuselage-inlet configuration presented by Flores et al. [13], and concluded with the full configuration by Flores and Chaderjian [14]. The geometry in the final simulation consisted of wings, fuselage, inlet, vertical and horizontal tails, and nozzle, and included both sides of the aircraft, that is, sideslip conditions were possible.

This level of geometric complexity was possible because of the zonal grid scheme used in the simulation. The flow field domain was broken into a series of different grid zones, as many as 54 for the sideslip case. One iteration of the solution procedure was performed in each zone followed by appropriate boundary condition implementation. Once all interior and boundary points of each zone were updated, the solution procedure continued to the next iteration until convergence was reached after approximately 2000-5000 iterations. This required about 20-50 hours of cpu time on a Cray XMP/48 computer using a single processor. The sideslip case grid consisted of about one million points and therefore had a total solution database of about eight million words, five dependent variables and the three spatial locations for each grid point. Because of the zonal philosophy and the fact that only one zone was in main memory at a time, the main-memory run-time requirement was under two million words. Without the zonal approach, the run-time memory requirement would have been over 20 million words.

Results from Flores and Chaderjian [14] are presented in Fig. 3 which shows surface pressure contours over the F-16A aircraft for transonic flow conditions at an angle of attack of 6 deg and no sideslip. For this calculation the Baldwin-Lomax [15] tubrulence model was used to simulate turbulent boundary layers on all aircraft surfaces. The jet exhaust is displayed as temperature contours in the jet symmetry plane. The surface pressure contour pattern clearly shows a "lamda" shock system on the upper wing surface, which is typical of transonic swept-wing flow fields. Figure 4 shows comparisons between computed and measured wing surface pressure distributions. For this computation a 0.02 correction in the freestream Mach number was used to improve the comparison [16]. This correction is required to help account for wind tunnel wall effects since the computation was made in free air. Agreement is generally good with the largest disagreement ocurring in the aft shock location near the tip on the wing upper surface.

Space Shuttle Simulation

The next example of RANS technology is the numerical solution of flow about the Space Shuttle in ascent or launch mode [17]. In this simulation the Orbiter, External Tank (ET), and Solid Rocket Boosters (SRB) are all simulated. This represents a different type of simulation difficulty, that associated with multiple, interferring bodies. The RANS equations, with Baldwin-Lomax turbulence model [15], were solved for this configuration using a special type of zonal grid scheme called the Chimera grid scheme. In this approach the grids about each separate body are generated essentially without regard for the other bodies in the flow field. Solutions are obtained, as in the previous case, by completing one iteration in each grid zone followed by boundary condition updates. The interface conditions between the various grid zones are more complicated in this case, relative to the previous one, and involve a general three-dimensional interpolation procedure.

Results from this study are shown in Fig. 5 for a freestream Mach number of 1.05 and an angle of attack of -3 deg. This set of conditions is near the maximum dynamic pressure point in the Space Shuttle launch trajectory. A comparison of computed and wind tunnel surface pressures is presented for the entire configuration looking down on the orbiter. The computed results are displayed in the upper portion of the figure and the wind tunnel results in the lower portion. Note the generally good agreement even though the computation was performed with stings emanating from the aft ends of the orbiter and SRB, while the wind tunnel test had stings emanating from only the SRBs (not shown). This difference was largely motivated by computational convenience and will be removed in future calculations. Other discrepancies are caused by inaccuracies in modelling the attach hardware between the orbiter and the ET, wind tunnel wall interference, other small protuberances, and lack of sufficient grid resoultion.

Figure 3. Computed surface pressure contours on the F-16A aircraft and temperature contours along the jet synmmetry plane, Mach = 0.9, Re = 4.5 million, Flores and Chaderjian [14].

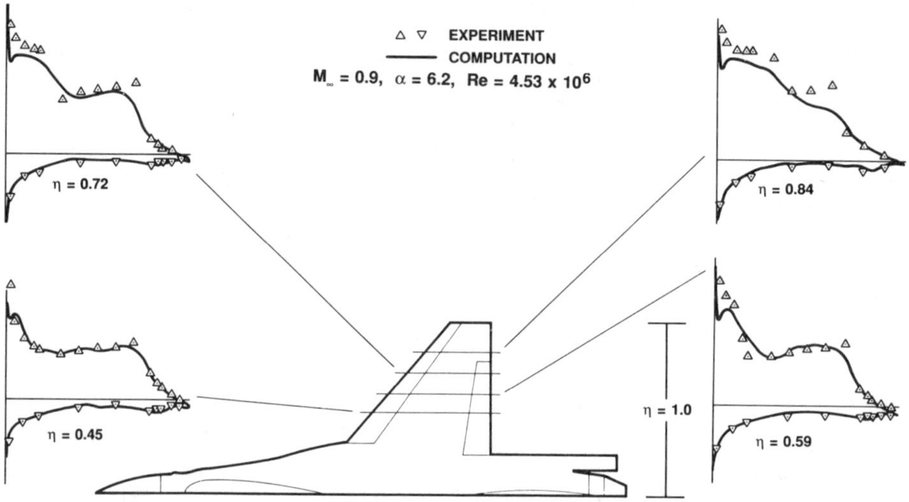

Figure 4. Pressure coefficient comparisons on the F-16A aircraft wing, Mach = 0.9, Re = 4.5 million, Chaderjian and Flores [16].

Figure 6 shows a more quantitative comparison of pressures along the side of the orbiter, indicated by the dashed line. Three sets of results are displayed for two different Mach numbers (1.05 and 0.9) and include computation, wind tunnel, and flight test. The computational results are generally in good agreement with experiment and show smaller disagreements with the two different types of measurements than the disagreements between the two measurements. The largest experimental/computational diagreement appears near the aft portion of the vehicle for the 0.9 Mach number case. This is caused by an inboard-wing control surface deflection, which is included in both the flight and wind tunnel measurements but not in the computation. The deflected control surface is included in the 1.05 Mach number computation, and the three results are in excellent agreement in this vicinity. Thus, CFD simulations are capable of quantitatively discerning relatively small, geometrically-induced flow field perturbations.

The total computer time required for this computation was about 20 hours on a Cray 2 supercomputer using a single processor. The grid consisted of five grid zones and about 750,000 points, which resulted in a total data base of about six million words.

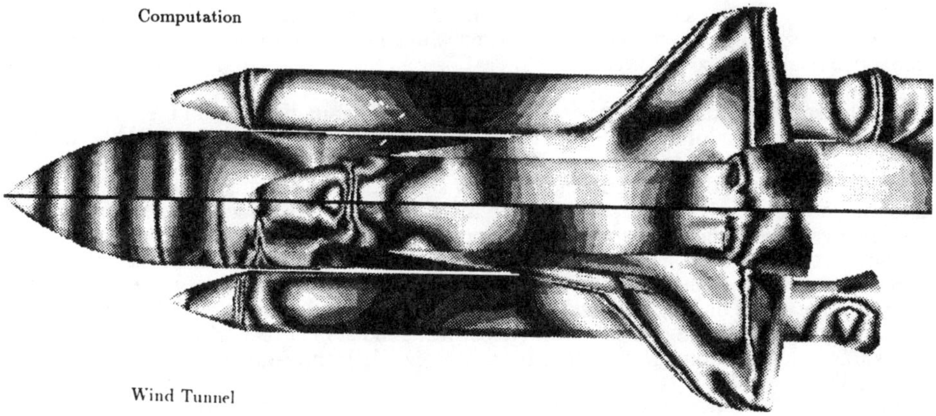

Figure 5. Comparison of pressure coefficient between computation and wind tunnel, Mach = 1.05, Re/ft = 4 million (3% model), [17].

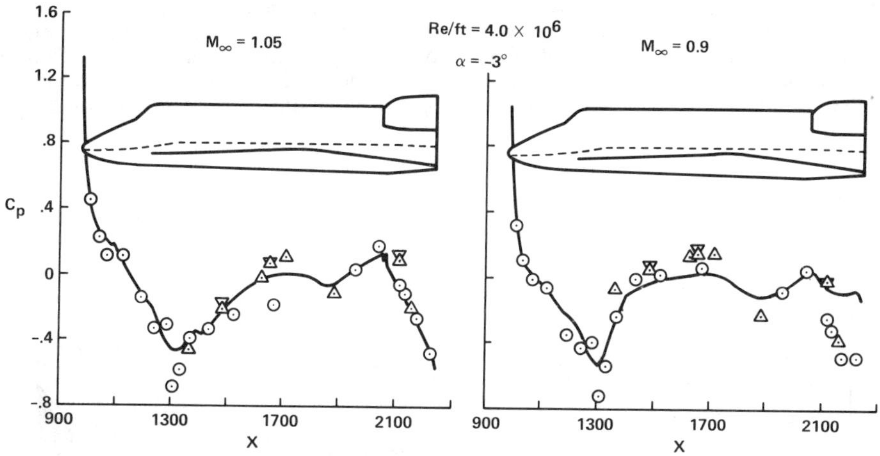

Figure 6. Comparison of pressure coefficient along the Orbiter fuselage just above the wing during Space Shuttle ascent, computation (solid lines), wind tunnel (circular symbols), and flight (triangular symbols), [17].

Turbomachinery Flow Simulation

The last example of recent RANS simulation technology is associated with an internal flow application, in particular, a turbojet engine. Within all turbojet engines are compressors and turbines composed of alternating rows of fixed or "stator" blades and rotating or "rotor" blades. The function of the compressor is to compress the incoming air for optimum combustion, and the function of the turbine is to extract a portion of the energy from the combusted fluid to power the compressor with the result being thrust. These two processes create very interesting and complicated fluid mechanics, which have recently been simulated using the RANS formulation. In particular, the three-dimensional "rotor-stator" combination has been simulated for a typical turbine configuration by Rai [18]. Again in this application a zonal grid system was used to model the complex geometry. Because of the inherently unsteady nature of this problem, the zonal grid system was constructed with an interface surface such that the rotor grid can move relative to the stator grid.

Typical results for a three-dimensional turbine application are displayed in Figs. 7 and 8 for an inlet Mach number of 0.07. Again, this simulation used the standard Baldwin-Lomax turbulence model [15]. In this computation two blades associated with one turbine stage, one rotor and one stator; the inner hub and the outer shroud; and the clearance between the rotor tip and the shroud are all simulated. Multiple rotor and stator blades within the same stage are simulated via periodicity boundary conditions. Figure 7 shows the time-averaged limiting streamlines on the stator pressure side and the rotor suction side. Note the confluence of flow at about 70% of span on the rotor and the flow distribution on the rotor tip. Figure 8 shows time-averaged pressures on the stator and rotor at mid span, both the pressure and suction surfaces. The computed results are compared with experiment and are in excellent agreement. Unsteady pressures are also compared with experiment in [18] and are in good agreement with experiment.

The rotor-stator simulation just discussed is similar to the first two RANS simulations in many ways but differs in one important way -- rotor-stator flows are inherently unsteady. This puts a different light on some of the computational statistics. Because of the requirement for time accuracy, the integration time or number of iterations for this calculation is larger and requires on the order of 100 hours on a single-processor Cray 2 time. The grid used in this simulation involved 200,000 points distributed in five zones. Thus, the data base associated with either a single time step or a time-averaged solution is about 1.6 million words. However, the data base associated with one cycle, which is the time it takes for the rotor to move from one stator to the next stator, is about 3.2 billion words! Even though the entire time-dependent solution does not

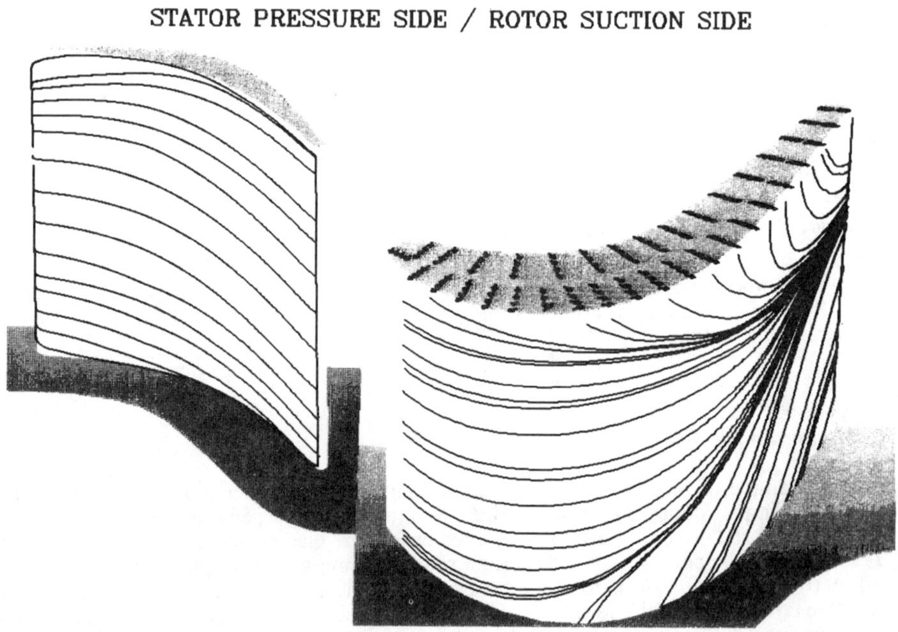

Figure 7. Computed time-averaged limiting streamlines on the pressure side of the stator and the suction side of the rotor, Mach = 0.07, Rai [18].

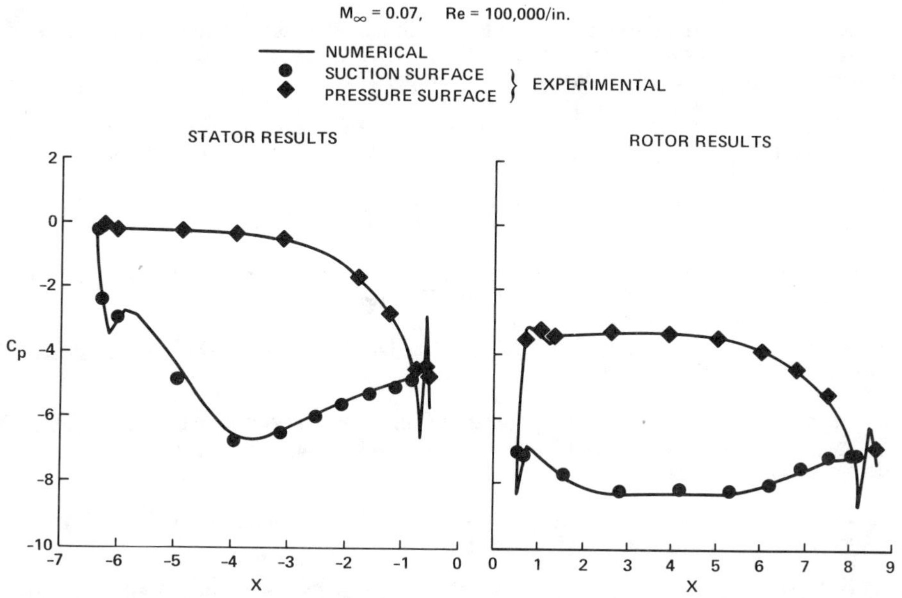

Figure 8. Computed and experimental time-averaged pressures on the stator and rotor blades at midspan, Mach = 0.07, Rai [18].

have to be in main memory at one time, this is the solution size that has to be retained, which is a significant limiting factor for unsteady CFD applications. In addition, the only possible way to understand the full extent of the fluid physics contained in such a solution is through computer graphics. The manipulation of such a large data base for graphical display is another significant problem facing the CFD field. However, with recent and anticipated advances in high-speed graphical work stations, this problem area is currently receiving considerable attention and should allow for the dramatic display of future CFD results.

CONCLUDING REMARKS

The field of Computational Fluid Dynamics has been briefly reviewed with particular emphasis on the Reynolds-averaged Navier-Stokes formulation. Several three-dimensional applications have been presented and discussed to highlight this review. The computational requirements, both execution speed and memory, needed to meet the needs of these applications have also been presented and discussed. Although these requirements are demanding, especially for the more complete formulations and more complex applications, significant progress and utilization of this technology across a broad front of applications is forcast for the next decade.

REFERENCES

1. Holst, T. L., Slooff, J. W., Yosihara, H., and Ballhaus, Jr., W.F., "Applied Computational Transonic Aerodynamics," AGARDograph No. 266, Aug. 1982.

2. Rogallo, R. S. and Moin, P., "Numerical Simulation ofTurbulent Flows," Annual Review of Fluid Mechanics, Vol. 16, 1984, pp. 99-137.

3. Holst, T. L., "Numerical Solution of the Navier-Stokes Equations About Three-Dimensional Configurations--A Survey," Presented at the NASA Conference for Supercomputing in Aerospace, March 10-12, 1987, NASA CP-2454, pp. 281-298.

4. Peterson, V. and Arnold, J., "The Impact of Supercomputers on Experimentation: A View from a National Laboratory," ASEE Annual Conference Proceedings, 1985, pp. 1388-1401.

5. Anderson, D. A., Tannehill, J. C., and Pletcher, R. H., Computational Fluid Mech.and Heat Transfer, Hemisphere Publishing Corp., Washington, 1984.

6. Peyret, R. and Viviand, H., "Computation of Viscous Compressible Flows Based on the Navier-Stokes Equations," AGARDograph No. 212, 1975.

7. Chapman, D. R., "Computational Aerodynamics--Development andOutlook," AIAA J., Vol. 17, No. 12, Dec. 1979, pp. 1293-1313.

8. Chapman, D. R., "Trends and Pacing Items in Computational Aerodynamics," Lecture Notes in Physics, Vol. 141, Eds. Reynolds, W. C. and MacCormack, R., Springer-Verlag, Berlin Heidelberg, Germany, 1981.

9. Kutler, P., "A Perspective of Theoretical and Applied Computational Fluid Dynamics," AIAA J., Vol. 23, No. 3, Mar. 1985, pp. 328-341.

10. Kutler, P., Steger, J. L., and Bailey, F. R., "Status of Computational Fluid Dynamics in the United States," AIAA Paper No. 87-1135-CP, June 1987.

11. Reznick, S. G. and Flores, J., "Strake Generated Vortex Interactions for a Fighter-Like Configuration," AIAA Paper No. 87-0589, Jan. 1987.

12. Flores, J., Reznick, S. G., Holst, T.L., and Gundy, K., "Transonic Navier-Stokes Solutions for a Fighter-Like Configuration," AIAA Paper No. 87-0032, Jan. 1987.

13. Flores, J., Chaderjian, N. M., and Sorenson, R. L., "Simulation of Transonic Viscous Flow over a Fighter-Like Configuration Including Inlet," AIAA Paper No. 87-1199, June 1987.

14. Flores, J. and Chaderjian, N. M., "The Numerical Simulation of Transonic Separated Flow about the Complete F-16A," AIAA Paper No. 88-2506, June 1988.

15. Baldwin, B. S. and Lomax, H., "Thin Layer Approximation and Algebraic Model for Separated Turbulent Flow," AIAA Paper No. 78-257, Jan. 1978.

16. Chaderjian, N. and Flores, J., Private communication, Oct. 1988.

17. NASA Ames Space Shuttle Flow Simulation Group, Buning, P. G., Chiu, I. T., Obayashi, S., Rizk, Y. M., and Steger, J. L., "Numerical Simulation of the Integrated Space Shuttle Vehicle in Ascent," AIAA Paper No. 88-4359, Aug. 1988.

18. Rai, M., "Unsteady Three-Dimensional Navier-Stokes Simulations of Turbine Rotor-Stator Interaction," AIAA Paper No. 87-2058, June 1987.

Supercomputing Efforts on CFD for Nonstationary Flow Analysis at NAL

By

Takayuki Aki

National Aerospace Laboratory

44 - 1, Jindaiji-Higashi 7, Tokyo 182, Japan

Abstract

In this paper, supercomputing efforts on computationl fluid dynamics (CFD) performed at the National Aerospace Laboratory (NAL) are described. The environment supporting supercomputing at NAL is introduced with brief historic retrospection that indicates NAL's continued efforts to obtain supercomputation in CFD discipline over the past decade. The present status of supercomputing efforts including the graphics are also described. To illustrate supercomputing activities in CFD on NS, results obtained from two studies typical of nonstationary flows are discussed. Finally, some requirements on future supercomputation and computers are noted from the present authors' personal point of view.

1. INTRODUCTION

NAL, established in 1955 with its headquarters located at Chofu in the western boundary of the Tokyo metropolitan area, is a fully government supported national research center for the aerospace engineering. NAL has the biggest domestic testing facilities for aerospace studies in the headquarters area, including wind tunnels ranging from low to hypersonic speeds, a flight simulator, and an aeroengine test stand. Among the NAL facilities, the Numerical Simulator System (NS) is significant and is worth introducing here. An outline of NS is given in the next section.

Since its establishment, and because of its mission as the national research center, NAL has sought to develop state-of-the-art technology in all disciplines in aerospace engineering. An enormous amount of energy has been dedicated at NAL to obtain state-of-the-art technology in CFD as well. A very brief historic perspective on this will be given. To display current activities in CFD on NS, two results obtained recently will be presented. Each of the solution procedures used provides an explanation for the need for supercomputing in modern CFD. Although there are many stationary/steady flow analysis results, the presentation here is restricted to analysis results on nonstationary/unsteady flows. A successful application of NAL CFD codes will be reported in a forthcoming paper [1].

Although the importance of graphics in CFD analysis is well recognized, there is still some difficulty in constructing CFD-analysis-oriented graphic display systems. A basic graphics package, absorbing user interface problem which was the main reason for the difficulty, has been developed at NAL. Extended and more flexible packages that can apply directly to the construction of CFD-analysis-oriented graphics systems are available in NS. These efforts to support CFD supercomputation must be included as one of the CFD activities at NAL.

The major purpose for writing the present paper is to introduce the extent of CFD activity at NAL in the past and present not widely known among overseas CFD communities. It is the present author's pleasure if this paper is useful to understand on NAL CFD among overseas CFD scientists.

2. AN OUTLINE OF NS AND CFD ACTIVITIES AT NAL

Figure 1 gives an overview of NS. NS was released to public use in February 1987. The heart of NS is a loosely coupled milti-processor system which is composed of a scalar (M780) and two vector (VP-200 and 400) machines. General descriptions of the architectures of these machines are available from open literature and therefore are not presented here. Instead we should like to point out that development of the VP400 machine at the manufacturer was prompted by the NAL's project to construct NS. The heart computers have been operating at slightly faster clocks than those of the nominal ones without severe troubles since the date of installation. In Fig. 2, frontal views of the VP-200 and 400 main packages respectively are shown.

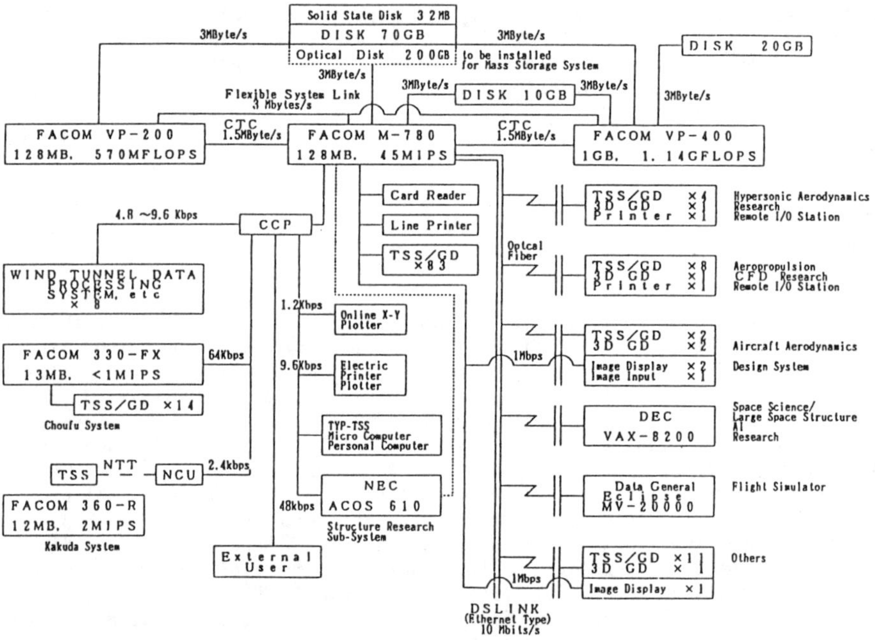

Figure 1 Block diagram of numerical simulater system at NAL.

Main memory in the VP400 consists of 1GB, in which the 0.2GB area is called MSU and loadable for both data and instructions. The remaining 0.7GB(VSU) is used only data storage. However, it is not a simple memory file. The data in the VSU can be treated directly without any explicit data-move instruction, as seen in the sample Fortran program shown in Fig. 3, although special treatments are needed (as in the lines with numbers 1, 2, 3, and 9 enclosed by circle in Fig. 3). As seen on the top of Fig. 1, a magneto-optically read/writ-able disk sytem, which will be installed in late 1988, is controlled by the M780 as the mass storage. Hardware specifica-

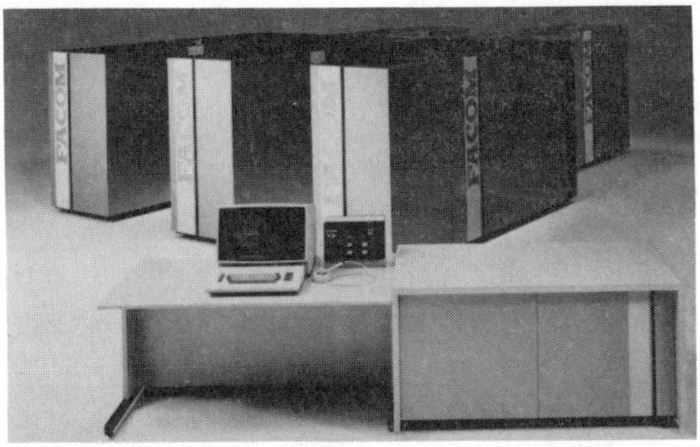

(a)

(b)

Figure 2 Frontal views of VP200 (a) and VP400 (b) processor main packages.

tion of this system will be given elsewhere [2]. The heart computers, the mass storage, and conventional disks, were installed in one building whereas the others shown in Fig. 1 were distributed over several buildings in the headquarters and remote branches areas. Throughout the telecommunication line, the authorized users from outside of NAL can access to NS. No charge is billed CPU time consumption for use by NAL permanent mployees.

In excess of 300 people are included in research work at NAL, of which about 50 have relevance to CFD. About 10 people are active full time in CFD study. A few people (5 below) are active in the international CFD community.

CFD activities on NS show a wide spectrum of fluid dynamics from continuum to rarefied, low to hypersonic speed, laminar to turbulent flows, etc. for both steady and unsteady cases. More than 90 % of available cpu time in the heart computers is consumed by activities from all disciplines of CFD. The majority of the cpu time available on both vector processors is consumed by various analyses on transonic external flows. Super- and hypersonic flow analyses constitute the next major use of the VP200, whereas internal flow analyses are the next major consumer of the VP400.

CFD studies at NAL were initiated in the late sixties when a fully transitorized domestic computer became operational at the headquarters area. Although it was one of the biggest domestic computer systems, every code tested on this system was limitted to research grade due to memory and cpu bottlenecks, which were inevitable for the computers in the second generation.

Efforts to obtain supercomputing were initiated when an internal advisary committee for the NAL computer system had decided in 1974 to install a highly pipelined processor into the central computing facility of NAL. The processor with a model number F230-75 APU was the first domestic supercomputer and was manufactured by

```
//X01P JOB  LARG,NOTIFY=X01                              ①
//     EXEC FORTC1,PARAM='VSU(VSU*)'                     ②

       IMPLICIT  REAL*8  (A-H,X-Z)
       COMMON  /VSU1/  A(4096,4096),B(4096,4096)         ┐
       COMMON  /VSU2/  C(4096,4096),D(4096,4096,3)       ┘ ③
       COMMON  /COM1/  E(4096,4096),F(4096)
       COMMON  /COM2/  G(1000),H(5,5)
       REAL X(100),Y(100)
V      DO  10  I=1,4096
V        DO  10  J=1,4096
V          A(I,J)=B(I,J)+C(I,J)                          ④
V   10 CONTINUE
              :
V      DO  11  I=1,100
V          X(I)=X(I)+Y(I)* A(1,1)                        ┐
V          Y(I)=B(2,2)+F(I)                              ┘ ⑤
V   11 CONTINUE
              :
S      DO  20  I=3,100
S   20     X(I)=X(I-2)+ A(I,1)                           ⑥
              :
V      DO  30  I=1,100                                   ┐
V   30     Y(I)=A(I,2)                                   ├ ⑦
       WRITE(6,*) Y                                      ┘
              :
       CALL SUB(A,B,C,E,4096)                            ┐
              :                                          ├ ⑧
* VOCL TOTAL,VSU(A,B,C)                                  ┘
       SUBROUTINE  SUB(A,B,C,E,N)
       REAL*8  A(N,N),B(N,N),C(N,N),E(N,N)
V      DO  40  J=1,N
V        DO  40  I=1,N
V   40     C(I,J)=B(I,J)*A(I,J)+E(I,J)
       RETURN
       END
//     EXEC LIED1
//*/   EXEC GO1,VSU=ON                                   ⑨
//*/   GOEND
//
```

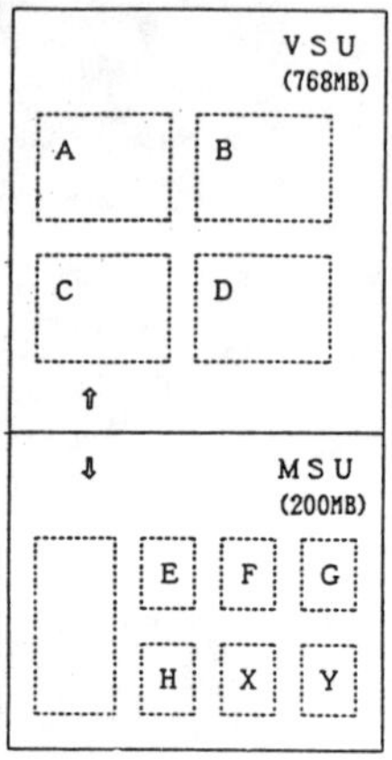

Figure 3 Method to use VSU : a sample Fortran program, and the corresponding memory image (in the enclosure).

Fujitsu Ltd. Almost all the requirements dictated by NAL at that time were realized by Fujitsu. The requirements covered not only those of hardware systems but also system software included the Fortran compiler. Since then NAL and Fujitsu have accmulated a lot of valuable experience on supercomputers and supercomputation. F230-75 APU was set in field operation in 1977. A CFD result obtained on this machine was reported by Matsuno at an AIAA CFD meeting [3].

Since 1983, NAL has been hosting an annual meeting on CFD titled "The NAL Symposium on Aircraft Computational Aerodynamics" which provides an open forum to discuss application methods of CFD on aircraft design as its main theme. In actually, it is an interdisciplinary meeting related to CFD. Papers covering a wide spectrum, such as basic mathematics on computation, architectural practice on a proposed computer, and spacecraft design CFD, are equally welcome.

The importance of graphics in CFD analysis has been long emphasized by many authors, e.g., see [9]. Supercomputer results are unable without graphics to extract key features governing a flow field undr analysis. Unfortunately graphics commercially available today is not standardized in the user interface. In NS, there are several types of graphic devices having such kind of problems. It was impossible to write graphics codes with portability or those which are device-free. To save extraneous labour to CFD analysis, a standardized interface program package which is callable by a Fortran code familiar to CFD analysts and is device-independent was written by a group within the NS [10]. The package has been released to public use in NS. Several application codes also have been released to the public use and updated continuously for widening applicable areas [11]. However, development of intelligent codes as was suggested in [9] is a future theme to be studied.

3. CFD RESULTS

3.1 Shock propagation around 90 deg. smooth bend in two-dimensional channel

Nonstationary shock wave interaction between shock - material surface or shock - shock contains phenomena still not yielding to physically acceptable interpretation, although understanding of it is needed urgently to resolve problems in engineering practice. Shock propagation around a bend in a channel is this kind of problem. For instance, hazard protection in a duct system will not be effective without the knowlege of physical process in the shock propagation. Although the shock propagation around isolated curved surfaces has been studied in detail, the knowledge obtained from the studies does not necessarily lead to understanding of the physical process observable in the bend shock propagation due to the shock - shock interaction arising in middle field across the bend width.

As usual the first step in attacking the problem was initiated by a model flow in two-dimensions. Because of the numerous parameters governing the process, experimental study has been limited to cases with a few sets of the parameters, e.g., see [5]. Complemetary work must be done by numerical simulation. A code to analyze the shock propagation process was written with the specification as follows :

(a) The governing equations to be used are the Euler equations for an ideal compressible flow written in a conservation law form under a surface fitted coordinate transformation in two spactial dmensions;
(b) The numerical scheme to be used is a Total Variation Diminishing (TVD), and implementation is by explicit difference;
(c) Accuracy is the second order in both space and time.

(a) is a conventional technique in modern CFD. If a code was established once for analysis of a flow, it becomes applicable to analyze another flow with minimal work for rewriting boundary treatment routines and generating new grids because these are problem-dependent. (b) is a request to use frontal CFD technique in eighties. A TVD scheme gives a robust code executable at the maximally allowable time step which results a high efficiency in one's computation. Solutions obtainable by TVD scheme show a crisp transition across a shock wave without wasteful oscillation in the solution, which is desirable for high space resolution of a shock wave system. Results shown in the following are those obtained by using the Harten-Yee TVD scheme [5]. A fractional step method of Strang type which presents a simple one to satisfy (b) and (c). was used in implementation.

A grid system which is composed of three sections, each of them is correspondtng to the upstream, the bend itself, and the downstream one respectively, was used. Each section is generated analytically and combined in one to mapp into a rectangular region in the computational space. The number of grid points to be used must be varied depending on region size requiring analysis. The default number of grid point is 4 every degree around the bend itself and 131 across the bend width. When the shock Mach number of the incident or oncoming shock in the upstream channel section exceeds some critical value, local flow behind it becomes supersonic (supersonic shock), otherwise subsonic (subsonic shock). The length of the upstream channel in the subsonic shock case must be taken longer than the supersonic shock case. The downstream channel length can be extendable to 20 times of the bend width at maximum, with constant pitch grid.

The initial conditions to start the computation are set up by assuming arrival of the incident shock at the entrance of the bend without any disturbance on its way to arrive at the initial position. The moving shock relations were used to compute the initial values of flow variables behind the incident shock. The gas state in front of the incident shock is assumed to be rest. A computation was continued up to a prescribed time or to the time the propagating shock front arrived at the downstream end of the given grid by assuming an infinite length of the upstream gas slab.

The boundary conditions to be treated are those at the upstream end and along both walls of the channel. The leftmost grid plane in the computational domain denotes the upstream end, flow variables on this end were kept behind the incident shock for supersonic shock cases and updated at every time increment by using a local characteristic method for subsonic shock cases to protect reflection of unnecessary disturbance from the artificial upstream boundary. On both walls, impermeablity of the fluid through the wall surface is imposed. Grid points on the rightmost or the downstream end need no treatment.

Figures 4 - 5 show time sequence plots of isobaric and isopycnic contours at typical flow conditions. This case was performed on the default grid and with the stability limit of CFL=0.99. Results shown in these figures are in a favorable agreement with experiment [5]. All shock transitions are crisp and osicillation free, and phenomena such as slip and contact discontinuities inherent to this type of shock reflection are captured favorably. Moreover, vortical patterns captured at a later stage of the propagation, which implies an existence of high shear rate in the flow, represent a superior benefit from the TVD scheme.

3.2 Unsteady flow around oscillating airfoil/wing

To evaluate maneuvering characteristics of an aircraft we should analyze an aeroelasticity problem on the aircraft, particularly on lifting elements or wings. Aeroelasticity itself is an interdisciplinary problem between aero- and structural dynamics coupled through boundary conditions for solving respective problems. Boundary conditions for structural analysis are given from analysis results of unsteady flow around a prescribed solid wing. Unsteady flow analysis by experiment often en-

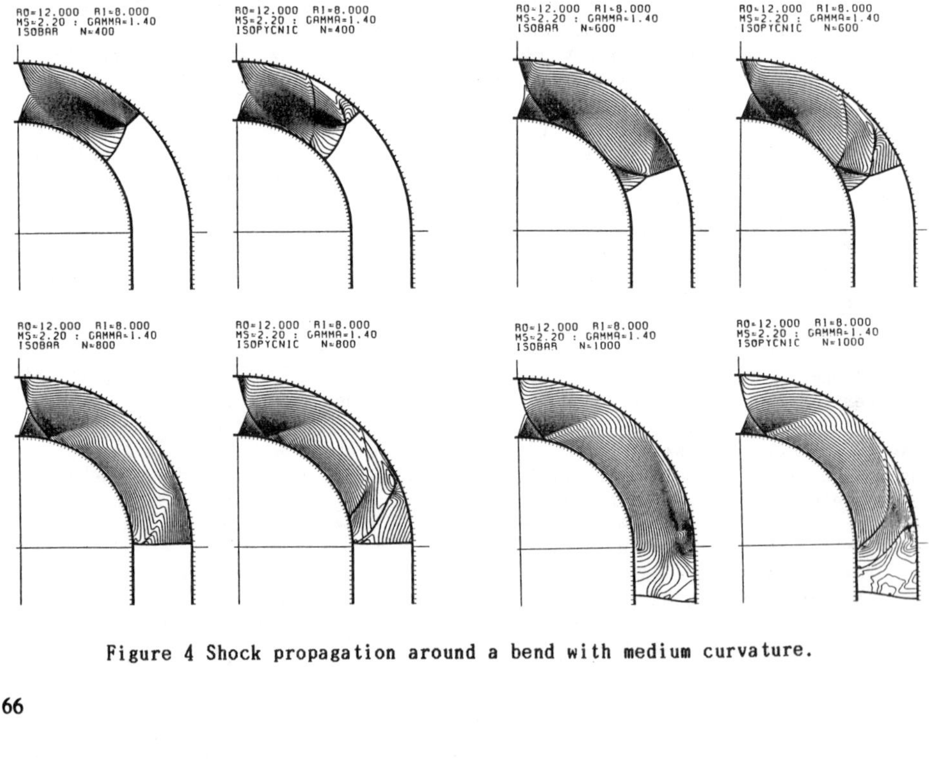

Figure 4 Shock propagation around a bend with medium curvature.

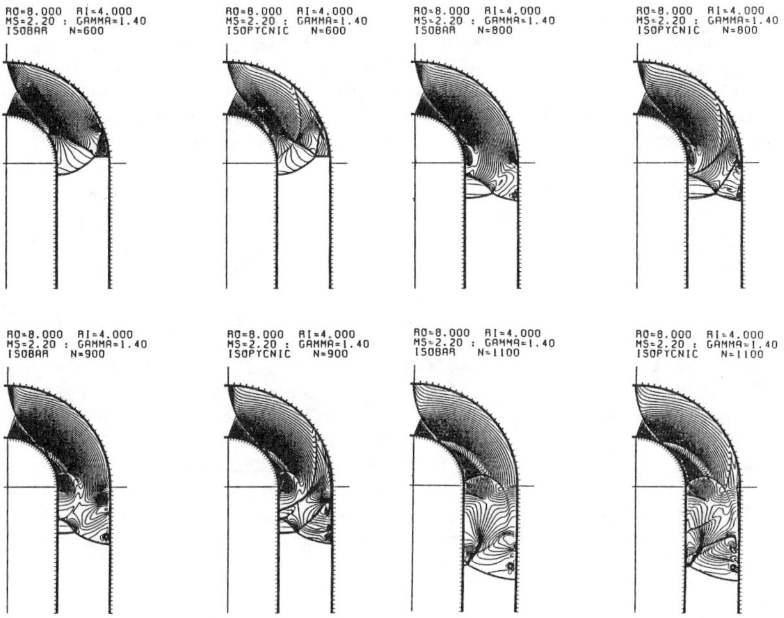

Figure 5 Shock propagation around a bend with small curvature.

conters difficulties in simulating stiffness and mass distribution of the target wing. The difficulties are overcome in numerical simulation without excessive burdens.

Following the analysis codes based on the full-potential equations in the seventies, modern CFD analysis codes based on the Euler and the thin-layer approximated Navier-Stokes equations have been developed by Nakamichi [6, 7]. In the latter flow flow analysis code, a zero equation turbulence model was incorpolated.

The basic numerical scheme used in Nakamich's analysis codes is an Implicit Approximate Factorization (IAF) and it is common to both 2D and 3D codes. The IAF scheme is a well-established algorithm to solve the equations of fluid dynamics for either inviscid or viscous flow. The equations to be solved are written in a conservation law form under a body fitted coordinate transformation. In IAF form, the lefthand of discretized equations is composed of an operators product dimensionally factored and linearized in time. The righthand is composed of the connevction (plus viscous for Navier-Stokes eqs.) flux terms at the present time step. Central difference approximation was applied to the space discretization. To stabilize computation a numerical viscosity is added to the space discretization. The viscosity is of a hybrid type with the second and fourth order terms and affects the second or forth order dissipation to the solution according to the gradient of flow field. The implicit operators in the lefthand may be simplified further by applying a diagonalization technique which enables the block matrix inversion computation to be a scalar one and results in a great deal of reduction in arithmetic operations with a loss of time accuracy. Nakamichi's codes include this option [7].

The grid to be used here is a dynamical one and is generated at every time step which invokes another severe task in computation. A sophisticated dynamical grid generation technique was proposed in [7]. The base method of the grid generation is an algebraic one which enables us to economize generation cost. A dynamical grid is one in which the outer/farther grid planes from an airfoil surface are stationary, whereas inner/nearby grid planes are moving with the surface. The airfoil tionary, whereas inner/nearby grid planes are moving with the surface. The airfoil under elastic deformation can be treated without difficulty by this thnique. The metrics needed are recomputed at every generation.

Initial conditions were obtained from a steady flow solution with the same uniform flow conditions and the grid generated at the mean attitude of the forced oscillation. In other words, this type of unsteady flow analysis necessarily requires steady flow computations. Boundary conditions are imposed at the outmost plane of the outer grid and the innermost plane of the inner grid. The former is the same with the steady flow analysis because the outer grid is stationary. In the latter, the effect of the grid motion should be taken into consideration.

A typical result of a flutter simulation of NACA-64A010 airfoil is shown in Fig. 6. In this simulation, the airfoil was in bending and torsional elastic motions with the prescribed pitching motion, and imitated locally a mode of the elastic motion of a swept back wing whose section is the same with this airfoil. Analyses between flow and elasticity were interactively coupled and computation is repeated to obtain reliability in the solution. Figure 6 is a summary of the Navier-Stokes simulation swept over some range of the elasticity parameter and Mach number, and denotes a flutter boundary of the airfoil under a prescribed motion. One can recognize the transonic dip at Mach number 0.85 above which an increased flutter speed happens (right in Fig. 6). Simulation by the Euler equations gives an unnatural flutter boundary. Reduced flutter frequency diagram summarized in Fig. 6 (left) shows the present result is in favor of the well-known result in the past reseach.

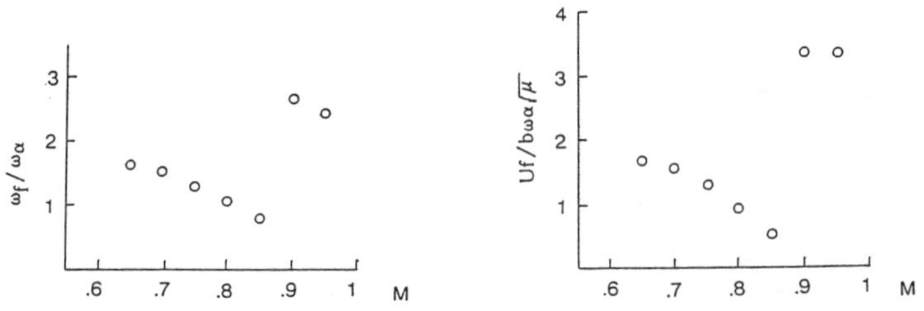

Figure 6 Flutter boundary and frequency on NACA64A010 airfoil.

3D unsteady vicous flow analysis was performed on the LANN wing [8] which is an aeroelastic wing model with experimntal data at high quality. In computation for the wing flow, the classical wing dynamics' theory was used to link flow with structure. In a similar manner in 2D, a 3D dynamical grid was used. By using the mean steady aerodynamic deformation data obtained with the classical wing dynamics' theory, initial conditions to begin unsteady flow computation were obtained. In unsteady flow, the computation was repeated over cycles to establish a steady sinusoidal solution. Transient solutions in the begining (about 3) were discarded because of physial unreality.

In Fig. 7, the computed results of steady/unsteady pressure distribution at three semispan stations are shown with the experimental data which are denoted by circles. In each figure, the result for the elastic oscillation is shown in the righthand whereas that for rigid oscillation in the lefthand and the mean steady real part is shown in the upper. The imaginary part is in the lower. The uniform flow Mach number and frequency are 0.822 and 48Hz, respectively. One can see improvement in the solution by using measured elastic modes compared with that by rigid motion. But agreements in the magnitude of the peaks with the experiment are still insufficient. One plausible reason for the insufficiency of the computational results is a lack of resolution of boundary layer upon the wing due to coarseness of the grid in the simulation. Near the wing tip there occurs severe shock - boundary layer interaction whose resolution needs more grid points. This implies needs for more memory and cpu time for finer resolution than the present one.

The flow model used in both simulations assuming no separated flow around airfoil/wing. For analysis in real flight, effects caused by phenomena such as buffet, stall, etc. should be taken into consideration in the flow model. For analysis including such effects, the approximation in the basic equations and the turbulence model without coupling (the zero equation model does not couple with the basic equations used in the present simulations) should be reconsidered. This implies further needs for memory and cpu time due to increasing number of equations and complexities in computational procedure.

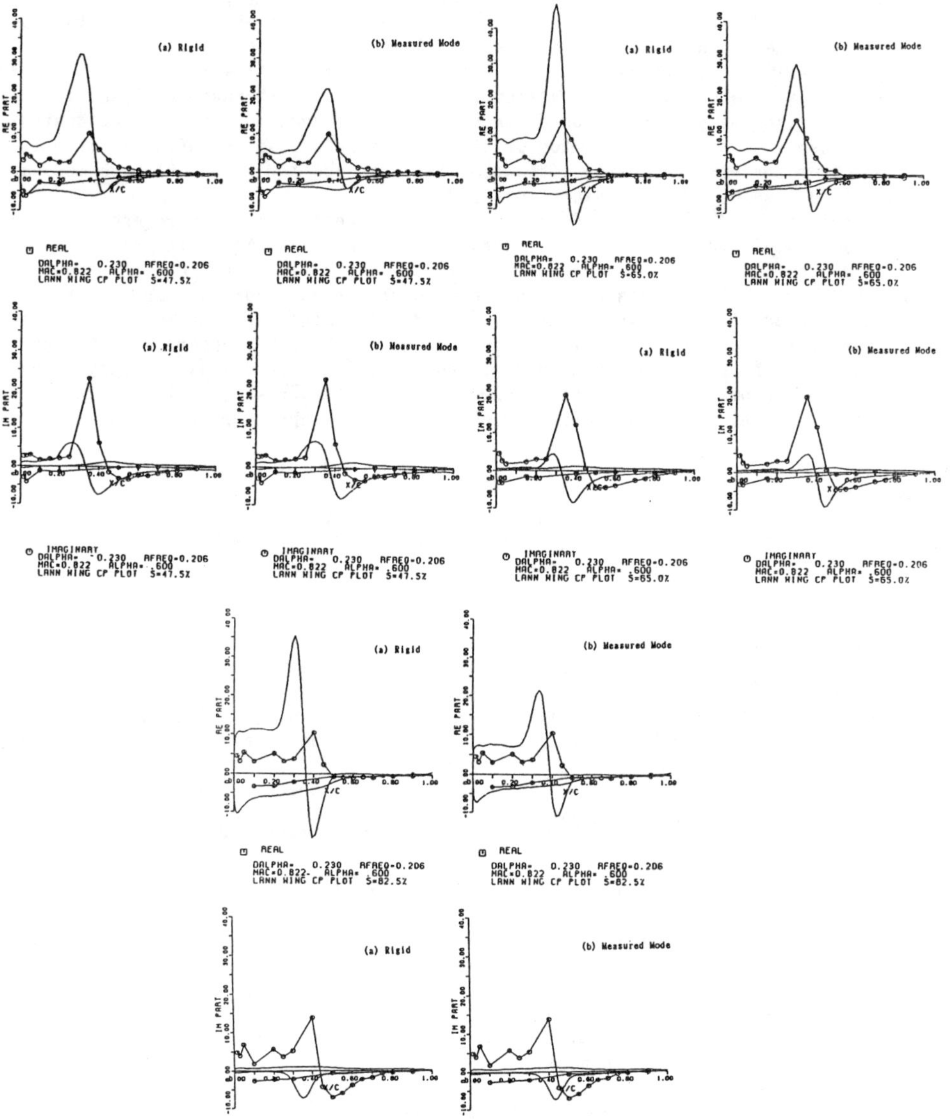

Figure 7 Real and imaginary components of unsteady airload at semi-span stations 47.5 and 65.0, and 82.5 %.

4. CONCLUSIONS

A brief overview of NS constructed at NAL and CFD activities performed on NS was given.

Needs for supercomputing are ceaselessly increasing by demands arising from industrial requirements to survive competition in "high tech" areas. Aerospace engineering is the most in that area. Several projects for aerospace development, which are competitive to those in USA, have been proposed and partly promoted in Japan, too. These demand development of multidisciplinary CFD codes which are able to analyze coupled phenomena in demanded flight, such as the space plane in hypersonic flight. A realistic hypersonic flow analysis needs to solve flow fields coupled with physicochemical processes as encountered in actual flight. The number of the governing equations to analyze such flow becomes large with the number of physicochemical process taken into consideration for obtaining precise evaluation of total effect demanded from engineering design. This fact implies need for enumerably enormous amount of cpu time on supercomputers today.

Algorithm development in modern CFD has been directed toward more precision to capture accurately physics of flow and results in more elaboration in procedure which requires more cpu time. Some methods that drastically reduce cpu time have been proposed for steady flow analysis. They require more memory and are inefficient for nonstationary flow analysis. One may consider the algorithm development is saturating in efficiency. Supercomputation in the future shall be supported by further development in the existing technology of manufacturing supercomputers today or architectural developments in designing supercomputers tomorrow. Activity to survey possible technology and architecture to obtain further supercomputation has been initiated at NAL as a special task.

Acknowlegment

I would like to thank Dr. J.Nakamichi for his support in the preparation of this paper and to express deep gratitude to anonymous reviewers for their recommendaion to the exposition and kind inspection of the first draft.

References

[1] Takanashi, S.,"Numerical Wind Tunnel of NAL," in preparation.
[2] Inoue,Y. and S.Hatayama.,"FACOM 6443 Magnoto-optic Disk Subsystem,"in Supercomputing '88.
[3] Matsuno,K.,"A vector-oriented finite difference scheme for calculating three-dimensional compressible laminar and turbulent boundary layers on practical wing configurations," AIAA paper 81-1020, 1981.
[4] Yee, H.C., "Upwind and Symmetric Shock-Capturing Schemes," NASA TM89464, 1987.
[5] Takayama, K., "Shock Propagation along 90 Degree Bend," Proc. 11 th Intern. Symp.- Shock Tubes and Waves, Eds. B.Ahlborn et al, 1977, Univ. Washigton Press, p.p. 74 - 81.
[6] Nakamichi, J., "Calculations of Unsteady Navier-Stokes Equations Around an Oscillating 3-D wing Using Moving Grid System," AIAA Paper 87-1158, 1987.
[7] Nakamichi, J., "Some Computations of Unsteady Navier-Stokes Flow Around Oscillating airfoil/wing," NAL TR1004T, 1988.
[8] Tijdeman, H., "Investigation of the Transonicn Flow Around Oscillating Airfoils," NLR-TR 77090, 1977.
[9] Kutler, P., "A perspective of computational fluid dynamics," in Proc. 10th Intern. Conf. on Numer. Methods in Fluid Dynamics, Ed. F.G.Zhuang & Y.L.Zhu, Lecture Notes in Pyisics Vol.264, Springer-Verlag, 1986, pp.30-46.
[10] Suematsu, K. and Isobe, T., "Software packages for 3D graphic display," NAL-TM-559, 1986. in Japanese.
[11] Suematsu, K. and Isobe, T., "Computer Graphics for Computational Aerodynamics," in NAL SP-7, 1986, in Japanese.

Computational Physics

Present Status of Computer Simulation at IPP

Yoshihiko Abe

Institute of Plasma Physics, Nagoya University
Furou-chou, Chikusa-ku, Nagoya 464-01, JAPAN

ABSTRACT: It is recognized in general that computer simulations are indispensable to plasma physics and fusion research. The computer center of IPP installed a supercomputer and almost of all computation time is used for simulation studies for plasma. Because the simulations concerning with design of fusion device LHS is increased recently and have many infuluence to needs of computer system, the status of the simulation is reported briefly. Although particle simulation codes are fit to study microscopic phenomenon of plasma, they contain charge assignment part which can not be vectorized because of recurrence of data. We propose a new algorithm to vectorize the charge assignment routine.

INTRODUCTION

In 1957, the Institute of Plasma Physics (IPP) was established at Nagoya University as a central institute for plasma physics and fusion research in Japanese universities. A computer center was added to IPP for common use in this field in 1977. The main objective of the computer center is to support computer simulations of plasma physics. To achieve this purpose, the first supercomputer manufactured in Japan, *VP-100 (32MB)* was installed in December of 1983. The current computer system configuration and network of the computer ceter are shown in Fig. 1. The computer simulations occupy about 98% of the total computation time of *VP-200* which was over 7,286 hours in the last fiscal year. The total computation time of *M-380*s in the last fiscal year was 11,087 hours which was mainly used by others.

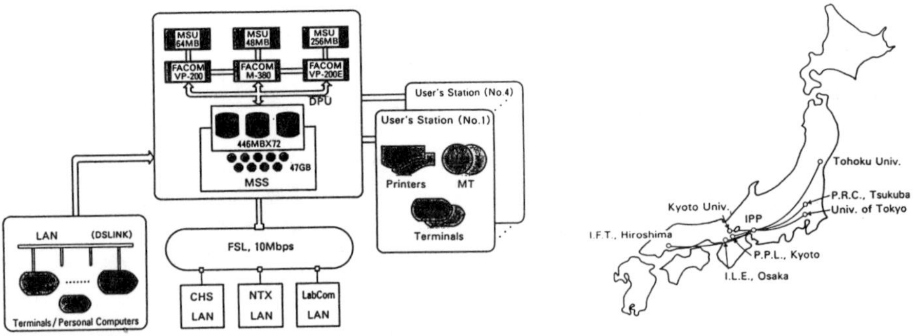

Fig.1 The computer system configuration and the network of IPP computer center (in 1988).

Today, the institute is posed to construct a new large experimental device, *LHS* at Toki city. The institute will be reorganized to centralize the fusion research programs and will also be moved to Toki. Research relating to the *LHS* project is briefly described in section 2. In section 3, we propose a new algorithm to vectorize the charge assignment routine which is the main part of particle simulations.

COMPUTER SIMULATIONS FOR *LHS* PROJECT

LHS is a large helical type device, and experiments using *LHS* are now planned to begin in 1995. Its external appearance is shown in Fig. 2 and the typical magnetic surface is shown in Fig. 3. The main characteristic of *LHS* is stationary operation by adopting superconducting coils. The *LHS* project will be in a state of detailed design until 1990. In designing large Tokamaks such as *JT-60*, *TFTR* and *JET* etc., supercomputers have played important roles, as is well known. It is expected that computer will also play an important role in the design of LHS as in the case of Tokamaks. The following main components of the project are in progress: [1]

- ·magneto-hydrodynamics (MHD) equilibrium and its stability analysis
- ·estimation of realized plasma parameters by transport analysis
- ·improvement of efficiency of NBI and ICRF heating
- ·analysis of confinement of high energy particles
- ·evaluation of boot-strap current by neo-classical theory
- ·evaluation of loss-corn region in velocity space
- ·analysis and design of herical diverter

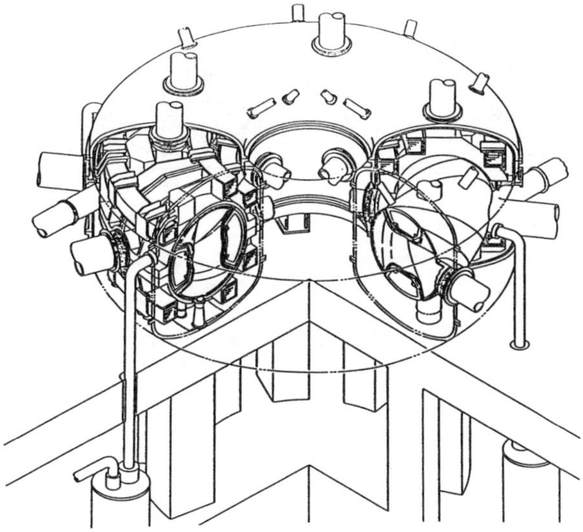

Fig.2 External Appearance of LHS.
Major radius is 4 ~ 5 m. Plasma radius is 50 ~ 60 cm.
Magnetic field is 4 T.

Any of these subjects can not be pushed forward without using a supercomputer, and the supercomputer contributes to the *LHS* project very much. As in almost all cases to analyze Tokamak plasma, two dimensional analysis is possible by using axis-symmetry of device configulation. Since the helical system does not have this kind of symmetry, three dimensional analysis is unavoidable to analyze the plasma. For example, a time dependent three dimensional MHD code is used to analyze finite β effect to the magnetic surface. This simulation needs 10 hours of computation time on the *VP-200E* and a memory region of over *100MB* for each execution. But the researchers emphasize that the available mesh numbers in the current system are quite insufficient, and much higher speed and much bigger memory capacity is indispensable to achieve more reliable results. To correspond to those needs, a reconstruction of the whole computer system will be required in the near future.

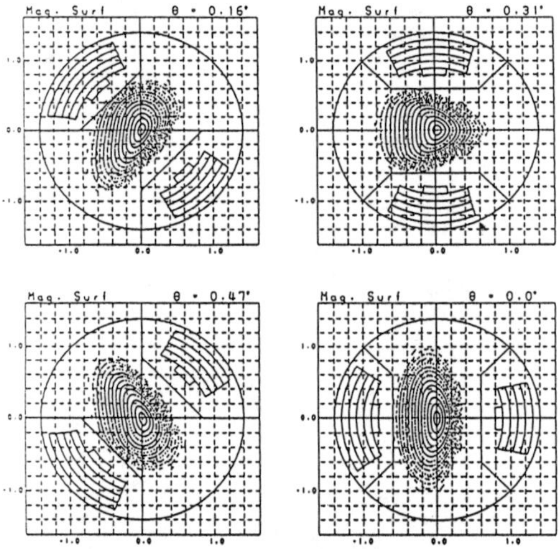

Fig.3 Typical Magnetic Surface of LHS.

VECTORIZATION ALGORITHM FOR PARTICLE CODE

In the particle simulation of plasma [2], since the motion of plasma produces electric and magnetic fields and plasma particles are influenced by the electric and magnetic fields, the motion of the plasma particle has to be solved consistently. Usually, plasma particle simulation consists of the following three steps:

1. Distribution of the charge and current densities are calculated from the positions and velocities of particles.
2. Electric and magnetic fields are obtained from the charge and current distributions.

3. A particle's positions and velocities are changed by the electric and magnetic fields.

By repeating the above three steps, time is advanced in the simulation. Unfortunately, a vector computer can't achieve its full power, since the first step can't be vectorized. A typical program of the first step is as follows:

```
dimension     G(Ng)
do    i = 1, Np
   MESH    = K(i)
   G(MESH) = G(MESH) + D(i)
continue
```

Here, N_p is the total number of particles, N_g is the total number of grid points and $N_p > N_g$. Since the same mesh points are re-used in the loop, the relation between reference and definition of data becomes recurrent. The above loop can not be vectorized and suppresses the total performance of the particle code. The following two vectorization method are known:

·Using a work vector to avoid the overlapping (work vector method) [3] .

·Ordering particles to avoid the overlapping in divided small loops (ordering method).

The efficiency of the ordering method depends on how simple a method is available. But it is difficult to find a faster ordering algorithm than the work vector method. Thus, we adopt the work vector method as a reference against the new method proposed here. Before describing this new algorithm, let's review the characteristics of the work vector method. The work vector method has the following advantages:

·algorithm is simple.

·relatively high performance can be achieved.

On the other hand, this method has the following weak points:

·the region for work space becomes very big for large size problems.

·this contains large numbers of zero-additions for small N_p/N_g.

Because we want to use this method for large size problems, the first weak point is very important to us.

Next, let's consider the case in which the loop in the original program is divided into shorter loops. We select the vector length, L_{vec} to be $L_{vec} \ll N_g$. In the shorter loop, the probability of overlapping preventing vectorization becomes very small, but is not zero. Then we use this property positively. The basic process of our proposal consists of the next three steps:

·divide the very long loop into shorter loops and vectorize each small loop by force,

·detect the overlapping,

·correct error due to overlapping.

It is clear that the frequency of correction must be very low, in order to get good performance by this algorithm. The main part of a program by the proposed algorithm is:

```
            j    = 0
            do    i' = 1, Np, Lvec
*  vectorize next loop by force
                do    i = i', i'+Lvec-1
                    Mesh     = K(i)
                    G(Mesh) = G(Mesh) + D(i)
                    L(Mesh) = i
                continue
*  detect overlapping
                do    i = i', i'+Lvec-1
                    if ( L(K(i)) .ne.  i ) then
                        j       = j +1
                        L'(j) = i
                    endif
                continue
            continue
            Ncorrect = j
```

The second loop in this program is aimed to gather particles which are not counted correctly on the first loop. The complete program is listed in the Appendix. When this algorithm is used, the vector length must be equal to the loop length L_{vec}, i.e. the compiler can not be allowed to divide the loop.

We compared the performance of this algorithm with the work vector method on *VP-200E*. The test case is

$$N_p = 819{,}200, \qquad N_g = 102{,}400.$$

Fig. 4 shows the speed up ratio against scalar calculation for various vector lengths. The performance depends on the overlapping probability which is related to the distribution of particles and grid size N_g. When the particle distribution has a peak, overlapping probability increases and the performance becomes low. We measured for several cases of distributions :

case1: no overlapping and no memory conflict
case2: no overlapping, but distribution is uniformaly random
case3: completely random distribution
case4: normal distribution $\sigma = N_g \times 0.5$, $\times 0.25$, $\times 0.125$.

The best speed up ratio is about 20 in case 1, but this reduces to 15 in case 2. And in case 3, the speed up ratio becomes 11 ~ 12 . Memory conflict has a big influence on performance. Although distribution peaks, i.e., in case 4, the best speed up ratio does not reduce significantly from case 3. The speed up ratios by the work vector method for the same conditions, are shown in the same figure. The upper line corresponds to case 1 and the lower line to case 3. The best speed up ratio of the work vector method is about 11 ~ 12 which is almost equal to the new algorithm. Next, we compare the size of work area for L_{vec} giving the best performance.

work vector method : $N_g \times L_{vec} \sim 102400 \times 64 \sim 25.6MB$

new algorithm : $N_g + 2 \times L_{vec} \sim 102400 + 2048 \sim 0.4MB$

This new algorithm reduces the neccesary working area remarkably.

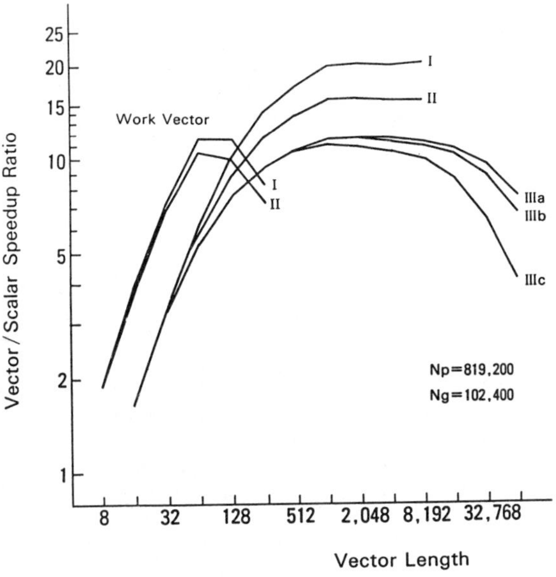

Fig.4 Vector Length vs. Vector/Scalar Speedup Ratio varying particle distributions. This measured on *VP–200E*.
Ⅰ : case 1, Ⅱ : case 2,
Ⅲ a : case 3 and $\sigma = 0.5 \times N_g$ of case 4,
Ⅲ b : $\sigma = 0.25 \times N_g$ of case4, and
Ⅲ c : $\sigma = 0.125 \times N_g$ of case 4.

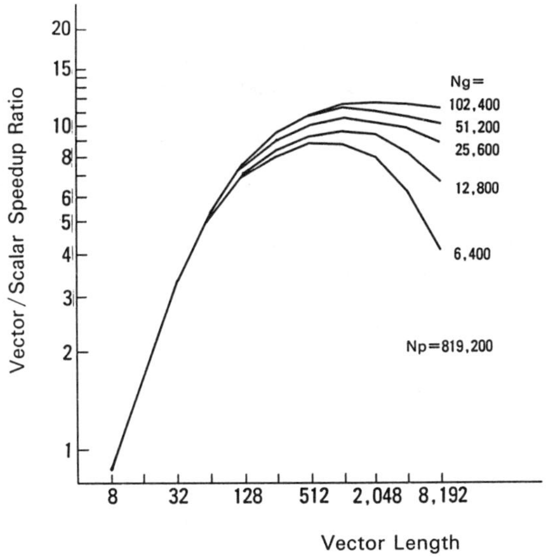

Fig.5 Vector Length vs. Vector/Scalar Speedup Ratio varying grid size N_g. This measured on *VP–200E*. Number of particles N_p = 819,200 is fixed.

Finally, since the overlapping probability increases as N_g decreases, the performance may be reduced by decrease of N_g. The speed up ratio was also measured with varying N_g at fixed N_p = 819,200. The results are shown in Fig. 5. Although the performance decreases as N_g decreases, the change due to N_g is relatively small i.e. this algorithm is also valid for small N_g .

SUMMARY

It is reported that computer simulations using supercomputers play an important role in designing experimental devices similar to the new experimental project *LHS* which will be constructed at Toki. On the other hand, the whole computer system needs to be upgraded in order to achieve more reliable results.
The organization of new computer center, computer system and network, and new basic rule to use the new computer system are now discussed actively among reseachers, who consider that the computer system is expecteed to exceed *10 Gflops* and will be installed at Toki in 1991. A new algorithm to vectorize a charge assignment routine of particle code is proposed. This algorithm achieves about 10 times faster than scalar calculation, and this speedup ratio is almost the same as the work vector method. This method is valuable to three dimensional particle simulation, since this method needs a much smaller working region than the working vector method. This work has been done in collaboration with Prof. K.Nishihara in Osaka University.

REFERENCES

1. *"Large Helical Experimental System Project"* LHS Design Group (IPP, 1988) (in Japanese).
2. for example;
   F.H.Harlow: *"Method in Computational Physics Vol. 3"*, Academic Press.
   R.W.Hockney: *"Computer Simulation using Particels"*, McGraw-Hill.
3. A.Nishiguchi, S.Orii and T.Yabe: *"Vector Calculation of Particle Code"*, J. Comp. Phys. 61, 519-522 (1985).
   S.Orii: *"Fully Vectorizable Particle-Mesh Codes on FACOM VP-100/200"*, International Meeting on Advences in Nuclear Engineering Computational Methods (April 9-11, 1985, Tennessee).
   S.Orii: *"An Accelerating Technique for Particle Model Codes on Vector Computers"*, Joho-Syori (Information Processing) 27 , 1257-1263 (1986) (in Japanese).

APPENDIX 1 A sample program by work vector method.

```
*-----------------------------------------------------------------
*-----    S O U R W V   -------------------------------------------
*-----------------------------------------------------------------
*       to calculate source term (vectorized version: work vector)
*
      subroutine  SourWV ( Np, Ng, G, M, D, Work)
*
      parameter   ( Lvec = 64 )
      real          G(Ng), D(Np), Work(Ng,Lvec)
      integer       M(Np)
*
         do 10,    l = 1, Lvec
            do 10,    Mesh = 1, Ng          clear work area
               Work(Mesh,l) = 0.
   10    continue
*                                           accumulate D(i) into
         do 20,    ii = 1, Np, Lvec         work area temporarily
            do 20,    i = ii, min( ii+Lvec-1, Np)
               l            = i - ii + 1
               Mesh         = M(i)
               Work(Mesh,l) = Work(Mesh,l) + D(i)
   20    continue
*
         do 30,    l = 1, Lvec, 8          accumulate finaly
            do 30,    Mesh = 1, Ng
               G(Mesh) = G(Mesh)
     >                 + Work(Mesh,l  ) + Work(Mesh,l+1)
     >                 + Work(Mesh,l+2) + Work(Mesh,l+3)
     >                 + Work(Mesh,l+4) + Work(Mesh,l+5)
     >                 + Work(Mesh,l+6) + Work(Mesh,l+7)
   30    continue
*
      end
```

APPENDIX 2 A program by the new algorithm.

```
                                                compiler options
*VOCL     TOTAL,NOVREC,VL(1024)                   no recurrsive,
*-----------------------------------------        assign and fix
*-----    S O U R C V   --------------------      vector length
*-----------------------------------------------------------------
*       TO CALCULATE SOURCE TERM (VECTORIZED VERSION)
*
      subroutine  SourcV ( Np, Ng, G, M, D, L)
*
      parameter   ( Lvec = 1024,   Lmin = 10 )
      real          G(Ng), D(Np)
      integer       M(Np), L(Ng), K(2*Lvec)
*
         Nc      = 0                        vectorize by force
         do 60,    ii = 1, Np, Lvec          (by neglecting overlap)
            Iend   = min( ii+Lvec-1, Np)
            do 10,    i = ii, Iend
               Mesh    = M(i)
               G(Mesh) = G(Mesh) + D(i)
               L(Mesh) = i
   10       continue
*
```

compiler option "VL" is a temporal name for convenience, because the native name is not understandable easy.

```
                do 20,     i = ii, Iend
                   Mesh    = M(i)
                   if  ( L(Mesh) .ne. i )    then
                      Nc       = Nc + 1
                      K(Nc)    = i
                   endif
   20           continue
*
```

detect overlap and gather overlapped particle

```
                do 60,    while ( Nc .ge. Lvec )
*
                   Ncc    = 0
                   do 30,    j = 1, Lvec
                      i          = K(j)
                      Mesh       = M(i)
                      G(Mesh) = G(Mesh) + D(i)
                      L(Mesh) = i
   30              continue
*
                   do 40,    j = 1, Lvec
                      i          = K(j)
                      Mesh       = M(i)
                      if   ( L(Mesh) .ne. i )    then
                         Ncc       = Ncc + 1
                         K(Ncc) = i
                      endif
   40              continue
*
                   do 50,    j = Lvec+1, Nc
                      Ncc       = Ncc + 1
                      K(Ncc) = K(j)
   50              continue
*
                   Nc      = Ncc
   60           continue
*
```

if the number of overlapped particle exceeds L_{vec}, repeat the above process.

```
             do 90,    while ( Nc .ge. Lmin )
*
                Ncc    = 0
                do 70,    j = 1, Nc
                   i          = K(j)
                   Mesh       = M(i)
                   G(Mesh) = G(Mesh) + D(i)
                   L(Mesh) = i
   70           continue
*
                do 80,    j = 1, Nc
                   i          = K(j)
                   Mesh       = M(i)
                   if   ( L(Mesh) .ne. i )    then
                      Ncc       = Ncc + 1
                      K(Ncc) = i
                   endif
   80           continue
*
                Nc      = Ncc
   90        continue
*
*VOCL   LOOP,SCALAR
             do 100,    j = 1, Nc
                i          = K(j)
                Mesh       = M(i)
                G(Mesh) = G(Mesh) + D(i)
  100        continue
*
          end
```

compiler options
scalar calulation by force

THE INTERACTION OF COSMIC STRINGS
A STUDY OF RESEARCH AND TEACHING GRAPHICS

Richard A. Matzner

Center for Relativity and Department of Physics
University of Texas at Austin, Austin, Texas 78712

Abstract: The study of large-scale fluid or field theoretical problems requires graphical presentation to make computed results intelligible. I describe here the minimal research tools and ideal state-of-the-art pedagogical tools for such visualization, using research on cosmic strings as an example.

Cosmic strings are putative relics of the very early universe. They trap within themselves primordial high densities (and hence mass densities) and are massive enough that loops a few tens of light-years in length can act as gravitational condensation centers for the formation of galaxies. (For a review, see Vilenkin [1].)

For such a process to succeed, it is necessary that long strings, which are "kinky" and flop around with motions close to the speed of light, break off loops when they self-intersect. This breaking off requires that after two pieces of string collide, the final configuration has exchanged ends: an initial $\times$ before collision looks like $\supset\subset$ after collision.

To determine whether this happens requires an evolution of the full field theory (as a classical field) describing the underlying structure of the string. Following work by Shellard [2], I have computed the probability of partner exchanger [3]. The result is that in every case tested, reconnection occurred, so the astrophysical demand that this take place seems satisfied.

In carrying out this research it became necessary to view the result of 3-dimensional 64^3 field simulation. The day-to-day research used NCAR graphics program EZISOSURF to contour the fields. Single-color frames were captured on a multitasking computer (Amiga 1000) running a Tektronix terminal emulator plus a screensave program. Multiple contours of a single frame were saved and then combined in a multicolor image; these images can be reloaded at about a 3-per-second frame rate to provide a movie capability. Some single contours of such a simultation included here show the interaction and reconnection (with an evanescent loop) of two strings 22.5° from opposite alignment with a collision speed of 0.9c. The strings collide (a) and reconnect (b). The reconnection releases substantial energy (c), which organizes itself into a loop (d) that contracts and self-annihilates (e),(f).

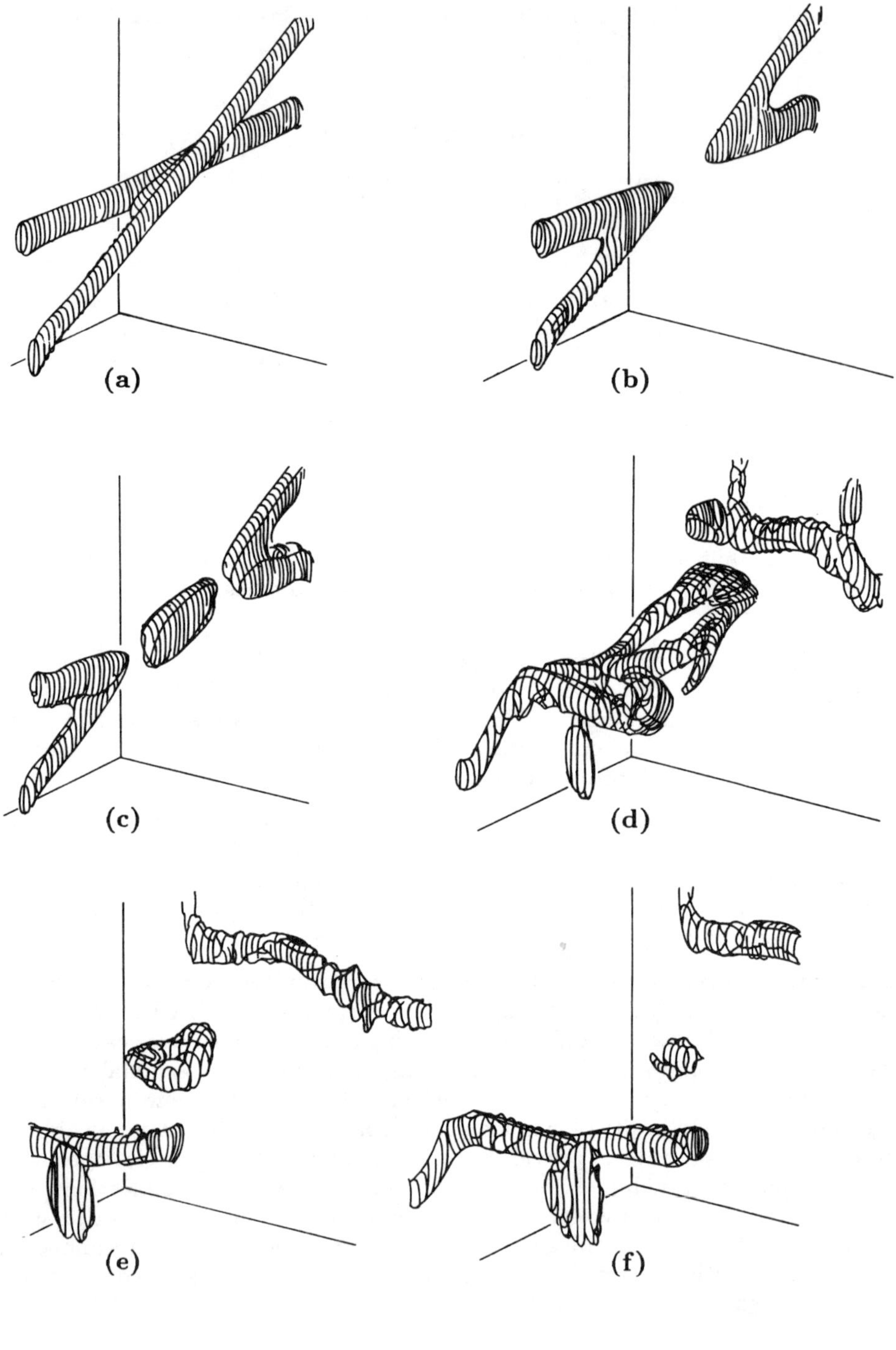
(a)
(b)
(c)
(d)
(e)
(f)

For presentation purposes, a more elaborate teaching video was produced in collaboration with the visualization group at the National Center for Supercomputing Applications, University of Illinois. The eight-minute video combines animation, narration, and high-quality rendered (Wavefront) images of the simulation in one coherent whole. VHS copies of this video may be obtained by sending me a blank video cassette plus return postage.

This work was supported in part by NSF grants PHY8404931 and PHY8806567.

REFERENCES

[1] A. Vilenkin, *Physics Reports* **121**, 263 (1985).

[2] E. P. S. Shellard, *Nuclear Physics,* **B283**, 624 (1987).

[3] R. A. Matzner, *Computers in Physics* **2** No. 5, 51 (1988).

MULTITASKING THE ISING MODEL ON THE ETA10 SUPERCOMPUTER

Dennis W. Duke

Supercomputer Computations Research Institute
and
Department of Physics

Roman Salvador
Daan Sandee

Control Data Corporation
and
Supercomputer Computations Research Institute

Florida State University
Tallahassee, Florida 32306

Abstract: We discuss multitasking various scientific programs on the ETA10 supercomputer. The architecture of the ETA10 is described, especially the features relevant for understanding the multitasking experiments. Next we describe in some detail our strategy for multitasking the Ising model. This strategy will also be useful for a wide class of physical systems which have local interactions. We also summarize our results for solving large, dense, unsymmetric systems of linear equations, i.e. the LINPACK benchmark. Finally, we summarize the multitasking software that will soon be available for general use on the ETA10.

I. ETA10 ARCHITECTURE

The ETA10 is a multiple processor, shared memory supercomputer (see Fig. 1). Each CPU consists of 240 CMOS gate arrays with about 20,000 gates per array. These arrays are mounted on a 16-inch by 22-inch 44 layer printed circuit board. The CPUs can be operated at clock cycles times of about 16-24 nanoseconds (ns) at room temperature and 7-10.5 ns, or even lower, at liquid nitrogen temperature. Cooling the CPUs to lower temperatures would not significantly improve the performance. There are typically either four or eight CPUs on a liquid nitrogen cooled machine, and one or two CPUs on an air cooled machine.

Among the functional units on each ETA10 CPU are a scalar processor and a two-pipeline vector processor. Each vector pipe can output one 64-bit or two 32-bit floating point results per clock cycle. Linked triad (or SAXPY) operations double this rate, so the maximum computation rate is four 64-bit flops per clock cycle per cpu. Like its Cyber 205 predecessor, the ETA10 uses memory-to-memory data motion for its vector operations.

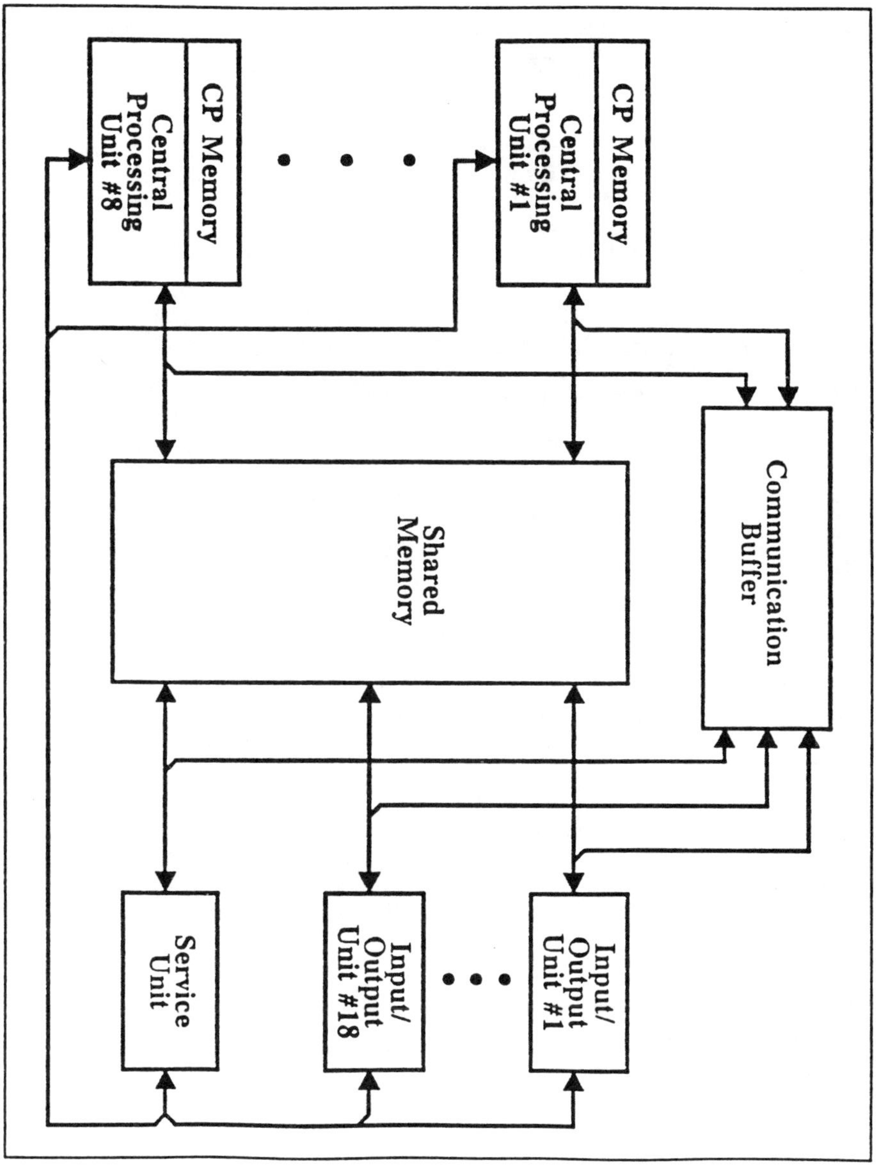

ETA[10] system architecture.

FIGURE 1

Vector lengths can be up to 65,535 elements. The vector startup overhead for the ETA10 is reduced by about a factor of three relative to the Cyber 205, resulting in very high performance on short vector operations.

The memory of the ETA10 is hierarchical. Each CPU has a private central memory of four megawords (32 megabytes). These memories are built from 64 kilobit static rams. However, it is possible to upgrade the CPM to use 256 kbit srams, resulting in CPMs of size 16 megawords (128 megabytes). In fact, a prototype of this memory has been built and tested at ETA, and upgrades for the four FSU processors have been ordered. Delivery is expected in March, 1989.

Each of the central memories is ported to a large shared memory which can range in size from 64 to 256 megawords when built from 256 kilobit dynamic rams, or 256 to 1,024 megawords when built from one megabit drams. In addition, each CPU is also connected to a shared one megaword communications buffer. This memory is used mainly for interprocess communication.

Finally, an ETA10 can have up to 18 I/O units which control disk drives, LCN and/or Hyperchannel connections, ethernet connections for TCP/IP communication, and FCC tape drive controllers.

Especially when discussing multitasking, the memory bandwidths in the ETA10 are important figures of merit. If these bandwidths are too low, the performance of the machine on a multitasked problem can easily be limited by data access times, rather than by computation speed. Fortunately, each ETA10 CPU can read/write to its CPM during vector operations at a rate of three words per clock cycle per pipe. Also, each CPU can transfer data between CPM and SM at a rate of one word per clock cycle, and each transfer can be up to 65,536 words long. Most importantly, it is possible for each of eight CPUs to simultaneously sustain this transfer rate while each CPU is also processing vector data at full speed. These features are exploited to the utmost in the application discussed below.

II. THE ETA10 INSTRUCTION SET

Vector Instructions

High performance programs on the ETA10 make extensive use of a very rich set of vector instructions. These instructions allow the usual vector addition, multiplication, divide, square root, etc. in both 64-bit and 32-bit modes. In addition, logical instructions such as AND, OR, XOR, etc. are also vectorized. Bit vectors can be used as masks to control which elements of a vector stream are actually used, allowing straightforward vectorization of DO loops containing conditionals. Indirect addressing of vectors is accomplished through either compress/expand or gather/scatter instructions.

Finally, a number of vector macro instructions such as dot product, minimum/maximum of a list, sum or product of a list, etc. are also implemented in hardware. In general, most of the vector instructions, including the vector macros, are generated from standard FORTRAN code by either the ETA FORTRAN compiler, FTN200, or the automatic vectorizer, VAST 2.

Shared Memory Instructions

Each SM read or write transfers sequentially stored data between SM and CPM at a rate of one word per clock cycle. The transfers are controlled by various bit fields in a four word transfer request block (TRB). These fields control the direction of the transfer, the starting data addresses in SM and CPM, the length of the transfer, and the size of word transferred (either 32-bit or 64-bit). The TRB also contains certain status and error information pertaining to the transfer. Although individual transfers can not exceed 65,536 words, it is straightforward to chain together TRBs so that very long transfers can be initiated and run with very little attention from the CPU. As mentioned above, once a transfer or sequence of transfers is initiated, the CPU is free to work on other tasks, such as scalar or vector arithmetic. As will be discussed below, we make crucial use of this feature in the multitasking application discussed below.

Communications Buffer Instructions

There are six CB instructions. The first pair simply loads or stores a word between the CPU register file and a CB location. These instructions can form the basis of message passing implementations for multitasking similar to those popular for distributed memory architectures such as the hypercube. The second pair of CB instructions are versions of the bit-branch-and-store operation, and these are used extensively by the operating system. Finally, two extended semaphore instructions are used to implement atomic post and wait operations, useful for task blocking and unblocking, marking critical regions of code, etc. These semaphores are extended, in the sense that the associated counters can be essentially arbitrarily large positive or negative.

The multitasking applications to be described below were performed by modifying the FTN200 compiler to accept the various SM and CB instructions described above in the usual Q8 format for special instructions. This makes it possible to multitask the ETA10 in a relatively friendly environment, but does require a dedicated machine. We can easily control all aspects of the machine through the service units, including reading any memory location in CPM, SM or CB, thus allowing I/O. The only major element of the computer that we cannot use in this way is the disk file system, but we are able to use the disks of the service units (Apollo workstations). Thus, we are running the ETA10 in a manner very similar to that used to run most hypercubes, or other attached processors. In addition, since there are no operating system calls between our applications and the hardware, we achieve very nearly the maximum performance deliverable by the machine.

As will be described below (see Section V), ETA is now providing a Multitasking Library (MTL), which does allow multitasking of the ETA10 in the conventional multi-user environment. For the so-called "coarse grained" applications, i.e. those for which the ratio of communication to computation is small, the MTL will certainly be the method of choice for multitasking the ETA10 in the future. It is still interesting, though, that we have been able to implement a rather simple and easy to use, yet powerful, multitasking environment without any help from the operating system.

III. MULTITASKING THE ISING MODEL

The Ising model[1] is a simple statistical mechanics system of binary (up or down) classical spins that interact via nearest neighbor interactions only. The model consists of a hypercubic lattice with a single spin at each lattice site. In one dimension the model is essentially trivial, while in two dimensions the model is certainly nontrivial but has nevertheless been solved exactly[2]. In higher dimensions no analytic solutions are known and the model must be studied numerically[3].

Apart from its intrinsic physics interest, the Ising model has often served as a prototype application for studying new algorithms and the implementation of various algorithms on new hardware. There is even an informal competition to see who can construct the fastest Ising model program, the largest, etc[4].

The basic computational task of an Ising model simulation is to flip individual spins according to some rule, which usually depends on the state of the neighboring spins (e.g. four in two dimensions) of the object spin. The rule used can be either stochastic, as in Metropolis[5] or heatbath[6] updating, or deterministic, as in microcanonical[7] updating. We have written two independent Ising model simulation programs for multitasking. The program to be described first, MULTI, is a very specialized and extremely fast program that simulates only the two-dimensional Ising model and uses an especially simple updating algorithm known as Q2R[8]. The second program, SPIN, is much more general: the user can choose any dimension from two to ten (or even higher with very simple code changes), and can choose between Metropolis, microcanonical or Q2R updating algorithms. Of course, because it is much more general it does not rival the first program in speed, but for physics purposes the second program is much more useful.

The Ising model, like all nearest neighbor interaction models, can be completely vectorized by the usual red/black or checkerboard data storage strategy. In this scheme, each lattice site is assigned a color (red or black) according to whether that site is located an even or odd number of lattice units from a particular fixed origin on the lattice. Vectors of spins are then composed of spins which have the same color. The reason that this scheme allows vectorization is that the nearest neighbors of a given spin all have the the opposite color of the object spin, thus allowing simultaneous update of all the spins in a vector. Another strategy that is used is to pack 64 spins in a single 64-bit word, thus increasing the speed of the simulation dramatically (a factor of 64 in the Q2R case). In addition, one can choose to associate all the 64 spins in a word with a single lattice or with 64 independent, but smaller, lattices. For our Q2R program we chose the latter case, primarily because it is very easy to control and analyze the statistical fluctuations in that case.

In order to consider both larger lattices and to multitask the programs, it is advantageous to store all the lattice data in SM. The primary programming task is then to manage the data motion between the four CPMs and SM. This leads to the following data movement strategy:

- both the red and black sublattices are imagined as further divided into M 'windows' or slices. In two dimensions, we typically choose a window to contain several columns of spins, such that a single CPM can contain five or six of the windows and such that M is a multiple of the number of CPUs in use during the run. In three dimensions we might let a single plane of spins be a windows, in four dimensions either a plane or a 3D cube of spins be a window, etc.

- we update in turn all M windows of red spins , followed by all M windows of black spins. When using four processors, for example, each processor is responsible for updating exactly one-fourth of the red and black windows. While updating, say, the m-th red window, the responsible processor requires in its memory (essentially) also the m-th window of black spins, which will contain all the neighbors of the red object spins. The amount of computation to be performed during the update will vary depending on the program and algorithm. For the very fast 2D Q2R program (MULTI), exactly eight vector operations per word of spins is required, which means just four clock cycles on the two-pipe CPUs. For the more general program (SPIN), the amount of work depends on the update algorithm and especially upon the lattice dimension, growing rapidly as the dimension increases.

- for the MULTI, the processor performs the following I/O concurrently with computation: while updating the m-th window of red spins, it will write out to SM the contents of the (m-1)-th window of red spins, which it has just finished updating. It then reads in from SM the contents of the (m+1)-th window of both the red and black spins, which will be needed in the next step. This I/O takes just three cycles per word of spins as compared to the four cycles used in the update step, and so is completely overlapped and costs no real wall-clock time, apart from SM transfer initiation which is generally negligible. For SPIN, the ratio of communication time to computation time is very much smaller, particularly in three or more dimensions, and so we make no attempt to overlap the transfers with update computations.

The process described above is illustrated in Fig. 2. It operates with near perfect efficiency in the 2D Q2R case, at least for a modest number of processors. The main source of inefficiency comes from the need to preload a couple of windows at the beginning of the loop over windows, and a corresponding flush to SM at the end of the loop. For problems of interest, these inefficiencies are quite negligible.

The performance we achieve for the 2D Q2R program is 1514 million spin flips per second (megaflips) on a single 10.5 ns ETA10-E CPU, while for a typical large lattice run on four CPUs we obtain a rate of 6037 megaflips, corresponding to an efficiency of 99% (i.e. the speedup is nearly 3.99). On a seven processor run, using the ETA10-E now at the Tokyo Institute of Technology, we obtained a rate of 10,553 megaflips (speedup of 6.92).

The other work most directly comparable to ours is by Herrmann and Zabolitzky[9], using the same 2D Q2R algorithm and the University of Minnesota Cray 2 four processors, 256 megawords of memory, 4.1 ns cycle time). In fact, that work both preceded and motivated our own Q2R work. Herrmann and Zabolitzky obtained a single processor update rate of 1512 megaflips, but the rate using four processors was just 4300 megaflips, corresponding to an efficiency of 71%. This inefficiency is attributed by Herrmann and Zabolitzky to unavoidable memory access contention among the Cray 2 CPUs. Both the Cray 2 rates and our ETA10 rates were obtained on a dedicated, single-user system.

Very recently we have discovered a way to increase the speed of the Q2R algorithm, but performing the update in only six operations, as opposed to the eight as described above [10]. Using this improved method, we now obtain update rates of 1851 and 7380 megaflips on one and four cpus, respectively. This is a speedup of nearly 3.99 still, in spite of the fact that the update operations and the transfer operations now take about equal times of three cycles.

The performance we obtain from the program SPIN is as follows:

cpus	Dimension	Q2R	Microcanonical	Metropolis
1	3	96	87	44
4	3	374	337	173
1	4	69	61	33
4	4	270	238	128
1	10	28	26	14
4	10	110	102	54

Note that the speedups are in all cases about 3.9.

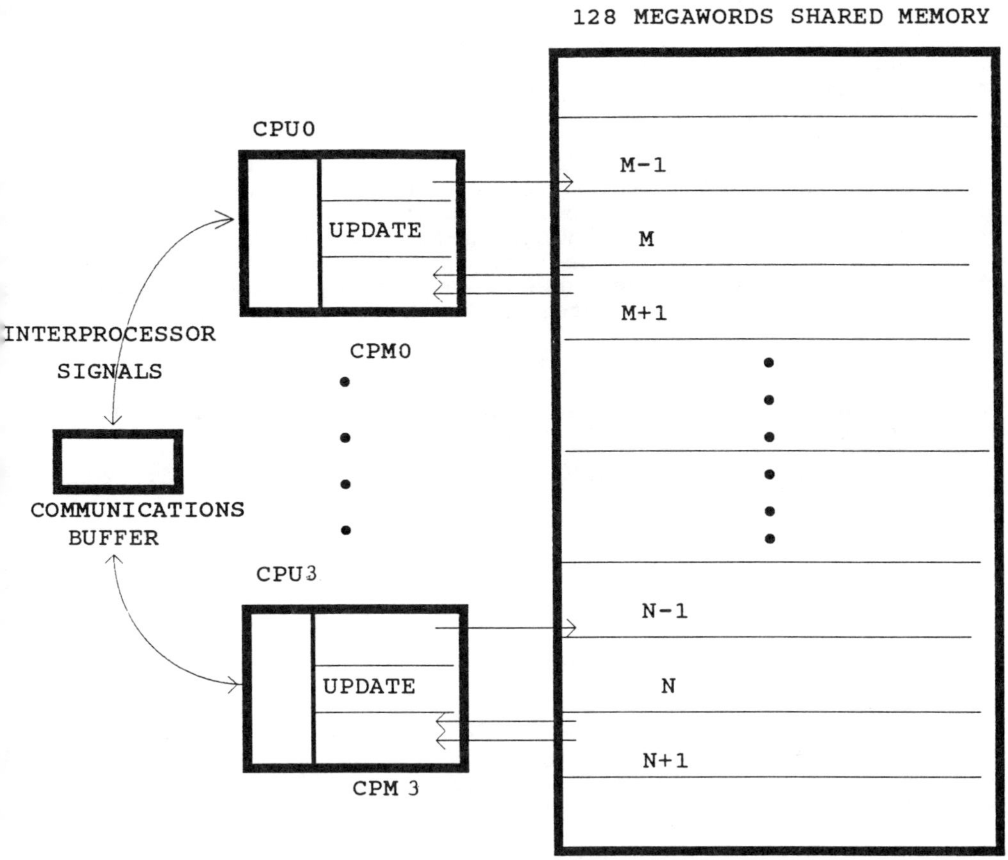

ALL R/W TO SM OVERLAPPED

WITH CPU EXECUTION

FIGURE 2

IV. OTHER MULTITASKING EXPERIMENTS

We also briefly mention results we have obtained multitasking the standard Gaussian elimination algorithm for solving dense, unsymmetrical linear systems. This algorithm is, of course, the basis for the popular LINPACK benchmark[11]. The methods used to multitask these algorithms on the ETA10 are similar to those described for the Ising model above, and are described in more detail elsewhere[11].Our results are presented in the table below, which also contains published results from the Cray 2, the Cray X-MP and the Cray Y-MP, for comparison [12]. All of the eight processor ETA results were obtained on the Tokyo Institute of Technology ETA10 in August, 1988. The authors thank Professor T. Maeno for access to that machine.

RATES IN MEGAFLOPS FOR SOLVING A DENSE 1,000 x 1,000 SYSTEM OF LINEAR EQUATIONS BY GAUSSIAN ELIMINATION

cpus	ETA10-E (64-bit)	ETA10-E (32-bit)	CRAY X-MP (64-bit)	CRAY Y-MP (64-bit)	CRAY 2 (64-bit)
1	323	555	218	308	384
2	632	1076	426	604	741
3	932	1579	626	887	1084
4	1216	2031	822	1159	1406
8	2225	3561	---	2144	----

Very recently, we have succeeded in speeding up the calculations tabulated above, so the our rates for the 64-bit case are now 335, 658, 980, and 1258 megaflops for 1, 2, 3, 4 cpus, respectively. We have not yet had a chance to run the new program on eight cpus.

V. ETA MULTITASKING LIBRARY

The efforts we have described above were begun mainly with the idea of testing whether the various elements of the first delivered ETA hardware would work together to allow multi-tasking. As such, it is clear that the experiments were both valuable and quite successful. We were even pleasantly surprised at the relative ease with which we could create a simple yet friendly software environment for conducting the tests. Nevertheless, routine multitasking by more routine users will require a higher level of system support than we have used. ETA is providing this support through a multitasking library. This library is scheduled for release during 4Q, 1988 and has already been used by the authors in beta test versions internal to ETA[13].

The user will use the MTL in either of two ways:

- by making explicit library calls to a set of subroutines from FORTRAN, or

- by inserting COMMENT card directives into the FORTRAN source code.

In the second case, the compiler will automatically generate the appropriate MTL subroutine calls, with the advantage to the user that the code is still usable in single tasking mode. In any event, the MTL contains the following:

- task control routines for defining, executing, terminating and waiting upon tasks,

- counter control routines for defining, posting, waiting, reading value and setting value for counters or semaphores,

- data buffer and data link control routines for defining various data objects and for doing both synchronous and asynchronous data transfers.

- trace control routines for debugging.

REFERENCES

1. For a thorough review see, e.g. B. M. McCoy and T. T. Wu, The Two Dimensional Ising Model (Harvard U. P., Cambridge, Mass., 1973).

2. L. Onsager, Phys. Rev. 65,117 (1944) and Ref. 1.

3. For a thorough review see Applications of the Monte Carlo Method in Statistical Physics, ed. K. Binder, Springer-Verlag (1984).

4. Dietrich Stauffer, private communication.

5. N. Metropolis, A. W. Rosenbluth, M. N. Rosenbluth, A. H. Teller, and E. Teller, J. Chem. Phys. 21, 1087 (1953).

6. M. Creutz, Phys. Rev. D23, 1815 (1981).

7. M. Creutz, Phys. Rev. Letters 50, 1411 (1983).

8. Y. Pomeau, J. Phys. A17, 415 (1984).

9. H. J. Herrmann and J. G. Zabolitzky, University of Minnesota Supercomputing Institute Report UMSI 87/1 (1987).

10. We thank Phillipe de Forcrand for advising us of the existence, but not the content, of the faster update strategy.

11. D. W. Duke and D. Sandee, Supercomputer '88: Applications, Architecture, Trends, ed. Hans W. Meuer, Mannheim, June 1988.

12. J. J. Dongarra, Argonne National Laboratory Report, May 23, 1988.

13. Multitasking Library User's Guide and Reference, ETA Systems PUB-1120 (1988).

COMPUTER MODELING OF ENGINE KNOCK CHEMISTRY

Charles K. Westbrook and William J. Pitz
Lawrence Livermore National Laboratory
P. O. Box 808
Livermore, California 94550

The development of detailed chemical kinetic reaction mechanisms for analysis of autoignition and knocking of complex hydrocarbon fuels is described. The wide ranges of temperature and pressure which are encountered by end gases in automobile engine combustion chambers result in extreme demands on the reaction mechanisms intended to describe knocking conditions. The reactions and chemical species which are most important in each temperature and pressure regime are discussed, and the validation of these reaction mechanisms through comparison with idealized experimental results is described. The use of these mechanisms is illustrated through comparisons between computed results and experimental data obtained in actual knocking engines.

INTRODUCTION

Computer models of chemical kinetics of autoignition have been used in recent years to help understand the chemical processes which take place in the combustion chamber of an internal combustion engine. In particular, autoignition plays a large role in the problem of engine knock. The degree of kinetic sophistication can vary widely from one model to another, depending on the way in which that model is intended to be integrated into the overall description of the engine combustion problem.

In the past, the most fruitful type of kinetics modeling for autoignition and engine knock was that developed at Shell Thornton Research Centre [1-3], which used a generalized reaction mechanism. The major kinetic processes in the Shell Model are all based on actual reactions observed in the lower temperature oxidation of hydrocarbon fuels. The Shell Model and others based upon it [e.g. 4,5] have been very successful in many cases at helping to describe the dependence of engine knock on engine operating parameters.

A parallel effort over the past several years [6-9] has emphasized a more detailed chemical kinetic modeling approach than that of the Shell Model. Although more costly in terms of development time and requiring much more powerful computational resources, these detailed models promise an improved ability to treat such effects as fuel molecular structure, mixtures of fuels, and the use of fuel additives. In the Shell Model, the global or representative reactions have rates which have to be adjusted for each fuel to be analyzed, a process which requires extensive experimental testing of each fuel. In contrast, a detailed kinetic model uses reaction rate data which are more fundamentally based than those in a more global model. However, these models must be orders of magnitude larger and more complex than global models. Current research, being carried out in moving towards such a goal, is described in this paper, along with some of the accomplishments of this type of approach.

We will also show how this model evolution has been accompanied or in fact driven by ever-increasing computational resources, including hardware (both CPU performance and storage capacity) and development of numerical solution techniques. Growth in the sophistication and complexity of kinetic reaction mechanisms has followed very closely the growth in available computer power and other computational resources.

OVERALL END GAS HISTORY

A typical engine cycle begins when unburned fuel and air are introduced into the combustion chamber. This charge is compressed by the piston and spark-ignited at a time usually close to top-dead-center (TDC). A flame then begins to propagate across the chamber, steadily converting fuel and air to combustion products. The gases which have not yet been consumed (the "end gases") are not chemically inert during this time interval; they are reacting steadily but at rather low rates. Under normal operation, the end gases are eventually consumed by the flame propagating through the engine chamber. However, under extreme conditions of high pressure and/or temperature, it is possible for these end gases to autoignite spontaneously prior to the arrival of the flame. This autoignition produces a rapid pressure rise and involves a significant fraction of the end gas, so that engine knock results. The objective of our current work is to identify the chemical kinetic mechanisms which lead to this autoignition.

Temperature History

During the combustion of the fuel-air mixture in a typical spark ignition engine, the unburned portion of the charge is subjected to a considerable increase in pressure and temperature as a result of compression, both by the engine piston and by the expansion of the burned product gases. Three temperature regimes can be defined which cover the temperature history of the end gas. The first kinetic regime encountered by the end gas is at low temperature. When the intake valve opens, the unburned mixture is at approximately atmospheric temperature (298K) and pressure. As the end gas is compressed by the piston, it spends a large fraction of its time in the temperature range from 450 K to about 800 K; at low engine speeds, the end gases may be in this range for as long as 70 ms. Although the overall rate of combustion is quite slow in this temperature range, the residence time is long enough for some fuel consumption and heat release to occur.

As the temperature of the end gas increases above about 800 - 850 K, the dominant kinetic paths change markedly. At the lowest temperatures, the overall reaction takes place primarily through the formation of various alkylperoxy radicals via addition of molecular oxygen to alkyl radicals, followed by production of alkyl hydroperoxides and other subsequent reactions. At higher temperatures, however, the alkylperoxy radicals become unstable, resulting in a region of negative temperature coefficient. Instead, the combustion becomes controlled by the reactions of the hydroperoxyl radical and hydrogen peroxide.

As the temperature increases further to values above about 1000-1100K, the dominant reaction path changes again, now being controlled by the production of H atoms which then react with molecular oxygen to produce both oxygen atoms and OH radicals. The problem of modeling the chemical kinetics of end gas autoignition is considerably more difficult than modeling the kinetics of most other types of experiments because the end gases spend significant periods of time in all of these temperature regimes, and the kinetic model must be able to describe all of the important reaction paths and rates in each regime. Kinetic models for common hydrocarbon fuels in just one of these regimes can tax current computational resources; covering all three ranges makes this problem even more difficult and demanding.

The history of the end gas temperature as a function of time is illustrated by the solid curve in Fig. 1; we will return later to a discussion of the other curves. In this particular example, the data are from a CFR (Cooperative Fuels Research, the type of engine used to define octane number) engine operating at 600 rpm with a compression ratio of 6.63 [10]. A time of zero corresponds to bottom dead center where the initial temperature is close to room temperature; spark ignition occurs at top dead center (TDC), or 50 msec. From this figure it is clear that the end gas temperature lies between 300 and 600 K for nearly 40 msec, and it exceeds 750 K only after a total elapsed time of 50 msec. The

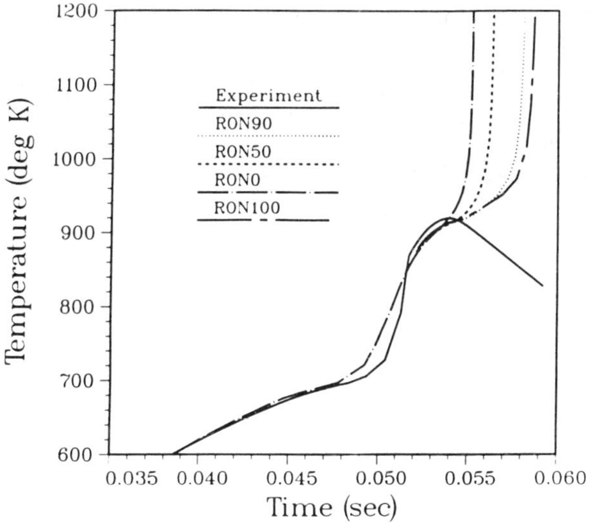

Figure 1. End-gas temperature in a CFR engine operating at 600 RPM. Compression ratio set for 90 Octane Number fuel conditions, solid line represents experimental values, other curves show computed results for various mixtures of iso-octane and n-heptane.

decreasing value of temperature after 53 msec is computed with an assumption that the end gas is not consumed by the flame, but is cooled by the expansion stroke of the piston. Although the reaction rates are small at temperatures below 750 K, there is a considerable amount of time available for reactions to affect the end gas composition and temperature. In contrast, the end gas residence time at temperatures above 750K is considerably shorter, but the reaction rates for the higher temperatures are much faster.

Fuel Structure

Another significant degree of difficulty in modeling the autoignition of typical hydrocarbon fuels under knocking conditions is due to the composition of the fuel itself. Conventional automotive fuel is usually a mixture of different constituents, including saturated and unsaturated straight and branched chain species as well as aromatic and other types of molecular structures. Very few of these species have been described by detailed chemical kinetic reaction mechanisms in any of the temperature and pressure regimes which are important for knock.

In Fig. 2 are shown two isomeric forms of octane, the straight chain molecule n-octane and the branched chain form, iso-octane, also referred to as 2-2-4 trimethyl pentane. Both fuels have the same numbers of C and H atoms, both have very nearly the same heat of reaction, and the burning velocities of flames through mixtures of both fuels with air are very similar. However, the autoignition properties of the two fuels are dramatically different. The octane number of a given fuel is a measure of its autoignition rate and tendency to knock under engine conditions, with a large number indicating good resistance to knock and a small number indicating a tendency to knock. Iso-octane is very knock-resistant; its octane number is equal to 100, and in fact iso-octane is used to define this point of 100 on the octane scale. On the other hand, n-octane has a very high knock tendency, with an octane number less than zero (the similar fuel n-heptane has, by definition, an octane number of exactly zero, and n-octane is slightly more prone to knock than is n-heptane). Therefore, the vast difference in knocking tendency for these fuels can be attributed only to the differences in the structure of the two molecules. Octane ratings in this study are taken from several sources [11,12].

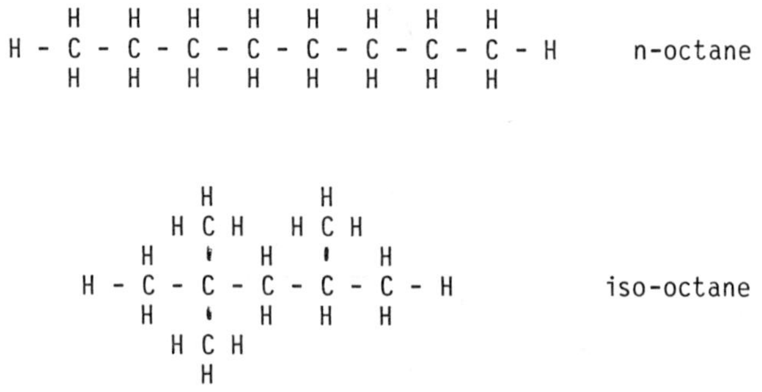

Figure 2
Schematic diagrams for n-octane and iso-octane

Other examples of this same type of trend are shown in Table I. The first five species listed are all isomeric forms of hexane, followed by the related ring compound cyclohexane. Again, the flame temperatures and burning velocities are all very similar, while the octane numbers for the six compounds, as shown in Table I, are dramatically different. Just as observed for the isomers of octane, these differences in autoignition properties for hexane isomers can be attributed directly to their distinct structures. The remainder of Table I summarizes octane ratings for a series of n-alkane fuels, saturated straight-chain molecules all of which have the same general structure but with different chain lengths. The overall conclusion from these data is that fuel size and structure play a major role in determining the octane ratings of hydrocarbon fuels, and it is the intent of our modeling analyses to understand these factors.

	Fuel	Octane number
C_6H_{14}	n-hexane	25
C_6H_{14}	2-methyl pentane	73
C_6H_{14}	3-methyl pentane	74
C_6H_{14}	2-2 dimethyl butane	92
C_6H_{14}	2-3 dimethyl butane	99
C_6H_{12}	cyclohexane	80
C_4H_{10}	n-butane	90
C_4H_{10}	iso-butane	100
C_8H_{18}	n-octane	< 0
C_8H_{18}	iso-octane	100
C_5H_{12}	n-pentane	62
C_7H_{16}	n-heptane	0

Table I. Octane numbers for sample fuels

Comprehensive Reaction Mechanisms

To some extent, any chemical kinetic reaction mechanism is an attempt to simulate the actual reaction history of the reacting gas sample. When these reacting gases encounter a wide range of operating conditions, a great demand is made on the reaction mechanism. Some time ago, Westbrook and Dryer outlined the properties of a so-called "comprehensive" reaction mechanism [13,14], which would be valid over such ranges of operating conditions. The basic idea is that the reaction mechanism should be tested over the entire range of conditions of interest, using experimental data from a variety of separate experiments under disparate conditions. This means that mechanistic simplifications which are valid only within a limited range of conditions cannot be made. Comprehensive mechanisms have been developed for a considerable number of hydrocarbon fuels [15-19].

The modeling of combustion in an internal combustion engine, and in particular the process of autoignition that leads to engine knock, requires a comprehensive reaction mechanism that is even more general than any which has been developed to date. The reaction steps which are dominant between 500 and 800 K are distinctly different from those which are important at higher temperatures and require entirely different elementary reactions and species to be included. Furthermore, the fuel molecules which we would like to consider in a study of engine knock are considerably larger and more complex than those examined in earlier comprehensive reaction mechanisms. In particular, mechanisms for the ignition of fuels such as n-heptane and iso-octane, primary reference fuels for knock rating in automotive engines, are particularly important.

The principal difficulty in modeling the combustion of large, practical fuel molecules in computer simulations is the fact that the models require large amounts of computer time, memory, and extremely sophisticated numerical algorithms. In many ways, our ability to compute the evolution of complex hydrocarbon fuel systems has parallelled the explosive growth in computer resources over the past ten years. This parallel is expected to continue in the near future as we continue to address more and more realistic combustion problems. This trend can be seen by reviewing the past 20 years of kinetics modeling. As recently as 1970, then state-of-the-art reaction mechanisms consisted of only 20 chemical species. During the years following, the sizes of the reaction mechanisms being used in research studies have grown steadily. This growth is illustrated in Fig. 3, showing reaction mechanism size as a function of calendar year. The approximately exponential nature of the curve is evident. Recall that the number of differential equations to be solved in a model is determined by the number of chemical species, not the number of elementary chemical reactions between those species. In addition, the cost of a given model computation is roughly proportional to the square of the number of differential equations, so the overall cost of model calculations has grown far faster than the curve in Fig. 3. In fact, model capabilities have been driven by the explosive growth in computer power, CPU speed, storage capacity, numerical algorithm development, and compiler and system improvements.

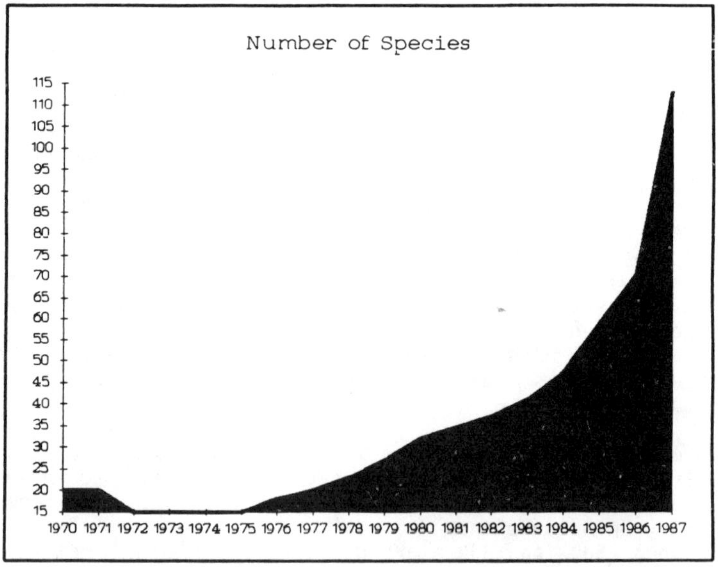

Figure 3. Chronological history of reaction mechanism size in hydrocarbon reaction models from the active kinetics literature.

Knocking Engine

In a typical engine cycle, the reactive end gases are compressed and heated by piston motion and by propagation of a flame after spark ignition. This compression is nearly adiabatic, except for heat transfer to the engine walls. Experimental and modeling investigations into actual engines allow one to address the entire temperature history of the end-gas from 400 K to burnt gas temperatures. Green and coworkers [7-9] investigated engine knock in the Sandia optical research engine, measuring autoignition times of hydrocarbon-air mixtures, primarily with n-butane and iso-butane as fuels. In addition, gas sampling techniques were used to determine species concentration histories in the end gas. Numerical modeling analysis of these engine data have provided considerable insight into end gas chemistry leading to engine knock.

In another study [20], two sets of measured pressure histories from engines were used to develop and test detailed kinetic models. One series of experimental results, provided by Leppard [10] from a CFR engine operating at 600 rpm, gave three different compression ratios corresponding to critical conditions for Research Octane Numbers (RON) of 89.7, 94.3, and 98.3. In the modeling analyses, mixtures of n-heptane and iso-octane followed the prescribed pressure histories, and the times at which autoignition was predicted were compared with experimental results. Heat losses to the engine chamber walls were estimated by means of a Newtonian heat loss term, with the heat loss rate adjusted so that a reference mixture of 90% iso-octane and 10% n-heptane ignited at a time of approximately 22° ATDC, consistent with experimental observation [10].

A representative series of computational results is shown in Fig. 1, giving the end gas temperature histories for five different stoichiometric fuel-air mixtures. Each end gas sample was forced to follow the pressure history in a CFR engine operating at 600 rpm, with a compression ratio of 6.63, corresponding to a RON of 89.7. Spark ignition occurs at TDC, at a time of 0.050 sec, with time measured from BDC. The solid curve already discussed earlier shows the end gas temperature which results from a computation in which only the influence of end gas compression and heat losses are considered, neglecting heat release from reactions. This curve was established by requiring the model to reproduce the experimentally measured pressure history in this engine. The other four curves show computed results for mixtures with octane numbers (RON) of 0, 50, 90, and 100, as indicated by the legend in Fig. 1. All of these reactive end-gas cases produce heat during the period of 0.048-0.052 sec; only one curve is shown in Fig. 1, but this one dot-dash curve applies equally to all four reactive fuel mixtures. These computed results show clearly that the time of autoignition, indicated by the rapid growth in end gas temperature, is a monotonic function of octane number (RON); reducing the octane number results in an earlier autoignition, while increasing the octane number leads to later autoignition.

Careful analysis of the modeling results provides some insight into the specific kinetic processes taking place. Most significant, the production rate of OH radicals decreases with increasing octane number. At a time of approximately 0.054 sec, the OH concentration in the RON50 case is twice that in the RON100 model. The fastest reactions consuming the fuel are its reactions with OH, so this difference in OH level produces a correspondingly large difference in the rate of fuel consumption. Autoignition does not occur until the fuel has been consumed, so enhanced OH production leads directly to advanced autoignition. Also important, the same reactions with OH produce H_2O with a significant release of chemical energy, raising the temperature of the end gases and accelerating the overall rate of autoignition. The OH radicals are themselves the result of decomposition of H_2O_2, produced from reactions of HO_2 with the fuel and from

$$HO_2 + HO_2 = H_2O_2 + O_2 \quad .$$

The largest sensitivity coefficients for ignition of n-heptane and iso-octane at 800K are for conversion of HO_2 radicals to H_2O_2 and the decomposition of H_2O_2 to produce OH+OH.

The kinetic factors responsible for the differences in radical production rates between straight-chain fuels such as n-heptane or n-octane and branched-chain fuels like iso-octane are complex. However, the general principles are quite clear. The initial process of H atom abstraction from the fuel does not depend strongly on fuel structure; iso-octane has one tertiary H atom which is easily abstracted, but it also has 15 primary H atoms which are relatively difficult to abstract, while n-heptane has a large number (10) of secondary H atoms, with abstraction rates somewhat intermediate between primary and tertiary sites. In branched-chain fuels, nearly all of the isomerization pathways which produce OH radicals below 1000K are inhibited because they require the abstraction of primary H atoms with their relatively large energy barriers. In contrast, many paths in the straight-chain fuels involve only secondary H atom sites with much lower energy barriers. These paths, dominated at low and intermediate temperatures by internal H atom abstractions involving R, O_2 and OOROOH radical species, proceed more rapidly when only secondary H atom sites are involved, resulting in an enhanced yield of OH radicals and a more rapid rate of fuel consumption.

SUPERCOMPUTING ISSUES

The chemical kinetic equations for all combustion problems, and for the engine knock analyses described here, consist of large networks of coupled partial differential equations. In most cases these equations are very stiff, meaning that the time scales for different reactions and species can vary by many orders of magnitude. In typical atmospheric pressure problems, the time scales for flame propagation are often microseconds, but the time scales for some fast reactions are ten or more orders of magnitude shorter.

In a conventional methane or methanol reaction mechanism, the number of equations to be solved at each spatial node and each time step (equal to the number of chemical species plus the temperature and perhaps also two or three fluid mechanical variables) is of the order of 30. This is also the number of equations which must be solved at each time step in a spatially homogeneous problem. Even with the limitations provided by stiffness, this type of system of equations is very easy to integrate, using any of a large number of available stiff equation solvers. A typical problem often will require several thousand time steps to arrive at a final result. When a one-dimensional spatial domain is to be considered, for example in a laminar flame or with reactions in a boundary layer, these 30 equations must be multiplied by the number of spatial nodes. This number is often of the order of 30-50 spatial zones, resulting in a total of 1000 or more stiff equations at each time step, and a total of perhaps 10^6 equations to be solved for the entire problem. For two-dimensional problems with the same spatial resolution as the one-dimensional problem, there will be more than $3x10^7$ equations to be solved, with perhaps 10^9 equations in three dimensions.

The number of equations in each dimension must be scaled by the number of chemical species in the given reaction mechanism. In the above example for the simplest hydrocarbon fuels, only 30 species were involved, but the literature data illustrated in Fig. 3 show that this number has been growing rapidly in recent years. The engine knock computations discussed earlier required more than 200 chemical species. For implicit solution techniques such as those employed to solve the stiff chemical kinetic equations of combustion problems, the computational cost can often be scaled approximately with N^2, where N is the number of equations to be solved at each time step. These sets of equations absolutely require supercomputer resources. The results in Fig. 1 required approximately 30 minutes of CPU time on a CRAY-1 computer, together with an assembly language matrix solver and vectorized features of the CRAY-1 computer. A drastically reduced reaction mechanism for such simpler fuels as propane and butane required more than 24 hours of time on a SUN 3/50 computer, using a FORTRAN version of the matrix solver and with no vectorization available.

Further complications are provided by the fact that, for the homogeneous problem, the matrix to be solved has virtually no preordained structure. That is, it is not diagonally dominant, it is not banded, and it is not sparse. For the problem in Fig. 1, the matrix to be solved is approximately 250 x 250, a large problem but not a particularly intimidating problem. Of course, when spatial variations are included, the matrix problem to be solved becomes block-tridiagonal. Each block again has no particular structure, and the overall dimension of the matrix to be inverted is of the order of 200 species and 40 zones or 8000 x 8000. This begins to tax the resources of current supercomputers, and extensions to two and three spatial dimensions are currently impossible.

Computer modeling of the chemical kinetics of hydrocarbon oxidation is a valuable analytical tool in applied physics and chemistry. This technique has demonstrated a wide range of applicability in dealing with laboratory experiments such as flames and shock tubes, but even more important, this technique has been used to study practical, large scale technical problems which impact large sectors of the nation's economy and energy conversion industries.

This technical subfield, depending strongly on the availability of computer hardware and software resources, has grown along with the computer field over the past 10-20 years. Due to the explosive growth in computer powers, chemical kinetics problems which were completely beyond even the formulation stage ten years ago are now routinely being solved. Furthermore, kinetic models can motivate research and technical improvements in practical systems such as automobiles, technical advances which would have been impossible without such modeling tools.

ACKNOWLEDGMENTS

We appreciate the considerable assistance during much of this work from many colleagues, including E. I. Axelsson, K. Brezinsky, N. P. Cernansky, M. Croudace, F. L. Dryer, R. M. Green, P. Jessup, W. Leppard, J. Warnatz, and R. D. Wilk. This work was supported by the U. S. Department of Energy, Division of Energy Conversion and Utilization Technologies and the Office of Basic Energy Sciences, Division of Chemical Sciences. This work was carried out under the auspices of the U. S. Department of Energy by the Lawrence Livermore National Laboratory under contract No. W-7405-Eng-48.

REFERENCES

1. Halstead, M. P., Kirsch, L. J., and Quinn, C. P., Combust. Flame 30, 45 (1977).
2. Cox, R. A., and Cole, J. A., Combust. Flame 60, 109 (1985).
3. Kirsch, L. J., and Quinn, C. P., J. Chim. Phys. 82, 459 (1985).
4. Natarajan, B., and Bracco, F. V., Combust. Flame 57, 179 (1984).
5. Hu, H., and Keck, J. C., SAE paper SAE-872110 (1987).
6. Pitz, W. J., and Westbrook, C. K., Combust. Flame 63, 113 (1986).
7. Cernansky, N. P., Green, R. M., Pitz, W. J., and Westbrook, C. K., Combust. Sci. Technol. 50, 3 (1986).
8. Green, R. M., Parker, C. D., Pitz, W. J., and Westbrook, C. K., SAE paper SAE-870169 (1987).
9. Smith, J. R., Green, R. M., Westbrook, C. K., and Pitz, W. J., Twentieth Symposium (International) on Combustion, p. 91, The Combustion Institute, Pittsburgh (1984).
10. Leppard, W. R., personal communication (1987).
11. Obert, E. F., Internal Combustion Engines and Air Pollution, Harper and Row, New York, pp. 234-235, 1973.
12. "Knocking Characteristics of Pure Hydrocarbons", American Society For Testing Materials", ASTM Special Publication No. 225, 1958.
13. Westbrook, C. K., and Dryer, F. L., Eighteenth Symposium (International) on Combustion, p. 749, The Combustion Institute, Pittsburgh (1981).
14. Westbrook, C. K., and Dryer, F. L., Prog. Energy Combust. Sci. 10, 1 (1984).
15. Westbrook, C. K., and Dryer, F. L., Combust. Sci. Technol. 20, 125 (1979).
16. Westbrook, C. K., Dryer, K. P., and Schug, K. P., Nineteenth Symposium (International) on Combustion, p. 153, The Combustion Institute, Pittsburgh (1983).
17. Westbrook, C. K., and Pitz, W. J., Combust. Sci. Technol. 37, 117 (1984).
18. Pitz, W. J., Westbrook, C. K., Proscia, W. M., and Dryer, F. L., Twentieth Symposium (International) on Combustion, p. 831, The Combustion Institute, Pittsburgh (1985).
19. Miller, J. A., Mitchell, R. E., Smooke, M. D., and Kee, R. J., Nineteenth Symposium (International) on Combustion, p. 181, The Combustion Institute, Pittsburgh (1983).
20. Westbrook, C. K., Warnatz, J., and Pitz, W. J., Twenty-Second Symposium (International) on Combustion, in press (1989).

Computational Mathematics

Finding $95800^4 + 217519^4 + 414560^4 = 422481^4$ on the Connection Machine

Roger E. Frye

Thinking Machines Corporation,
245 First Street, Cambridge, Massachusetts 02142-1214
frye@think.com (617)876-1111

The smallest counterexample to Euler's generalization of Fermat's Last Theorem is $95800^4 + 217519^4 + 414560^4 = 422481^4$. *I explain how this solution was found by exhaustive data parallel search on several Connection Machine systems.*

Keywords: biquadrates, Connection Machine, data parallel algorithms, Diophantine equations, Euler conjecture.

1 INTRODUCTION

Noam Elkies [4] found two solutions to the equation $A^4 + B^4 + C^4 = D^4$ in relatively prime natural numbers A, B, C, and D. The smaller solution was $2682440^4 + 15365639^4 + 18796760^4 = 20615673^4$, and the larger had 71 digit numbers in each term. He used a method of parameterized equations which has very little control over the size of the solution, so that there was a possibility that it was not minimal.

I contacted Elkies about the nature of the problem, and he explained the number theoretic constraints which might be sufficient to make an exhaustive search for a minimal solution feasible on a supercomputer. I implemented his suggestions in Common LISP [12] extended with Zetalisp® [1]LOOP [13] for a Symbolics LISP Machine® [2] front end with calls to Paris [2], for the data parallel Connection Machine® [3] [7] system.

This program was run on several LISP machine/Connection Machine systems for more than 100 front end machine hours, until it found the minimal solution, $95800^4 + 217519^4 + 414560^4 = 422481^4$.

Since then, the search algorithm has been improved and the search range has been extended to 2000000^4 for the right hand side of the equation. No other solutions have been found.

The next section of this paper gives an outline of the history of the problem. Section 3 presents a naive approach to exhaustive search for a minimal solution and develops the mathematical constraints needed to limit the search even for a supercomputer. Section 4 discusses the architecture of the data parallel Connection Machine system. Section 5 presents the parallel algorithm. Section 6 contains timings, final results and open questions.

[1] Zetalisp is a trademark of Symbolics, Inc.
[2] Symbolics is a trademark of Symbolics, Inc.
[3] Connection Machine is a registered trademark of Thinking Machines Corporation

2 HISTORY OF ATTACKS ON EULER'S CONJECTURE

Pierre Fermat is famous for an unproved conjecture that the equation $A^n + B^n = C^n$ has no solution in the natural numbers A, B, C if n is an integer greater than 2. This conjecture is generally, though erroneously, called Fermat's Last Theorem. The "Theorem" has not been proved for all $n > 2$, but the $n = 4$ case was proved by Fermat himself [3] .

In 1769, Leonhard Euler extended Fermat's conjecture:

> It has seemed to many Geometers that this theorem [Fermat's Last "Theorem"] may be generalized. Just as there do not exist two cubes whose sum or difference is a cube, it is certain that it is impossible to exhibit three biquadrates whose sum is a biquadrate, but that at least four biquadrates are needed if their sum is to be a biquadrate, although no one has been able up to the present to assign four such biquadrates. In the same manner it would seem to be impossible to exhibit four fifth powers whose sum is a fifth power, and similarly for higher powers.

The term *biquadrate* may be unfamiliar to modern readers; here it means the fourth power of an integer.

Richard Guy gives this quotation and discusses the problem under the heading **D1** in his list of unsolved problems in number theory [6]. He displays the first assignment of four biquadrates, $30^4 + 120^4 + 272^4 + 315^4 = 353^4$, found by R. Norrie in 1911, and the first counterexample to the conjecture, $27^5 + 84^5 + 110^5 + 133^5 = 144^5$, found by Lander and Parkin in 1966. He also writes

> It has not been proved that $a^4 + b^4 + c^4 = d^4$ has no solution in integers; there is none with $d \leq 222,000$. In fact even $a^4 + b^4 + c^4 = d^2$ is unknown,

The first assertion was the result of an exhaustive search by Lander and Parkin on a CDC 6600® [4] [9]. The second assertion is false. Elkies and Guy have exchanged correspondence about the simple solution,

$$(l \cdot m)^4 + (l \cdot n)^4 + (m \cdot n)^4 = [(l^2 + m^2) \cdot n^2 - (l \cdot m)^2]^2$$

whenever $l^2 + m^2 = n^2$, which was known even to Diophantus[5].

Noam Elkies [4] disproved the $n = 4$ case of Euler's conjecture during the summer of 1987. He combined extensive algebraic manipulation with MACSYMA® [5] and a few hours numeric search on a VAX® [6] to find two particular solutions and to prove that there are an infinite number of solutions to the equation $A^4 + B^4 + C^4 = D^4$ in relatively prime natural numbers A, B, C, and D. I can give only the briefest summary of Elkies's method here. He parameterizes a transformation of the equation with a pair of integers constrained by certain Lemmas. His two solutions are on an elliptic curve with the simplest allowed parameterization, namely $(8, -5)$ in his notation. No other solutions have yet been found with his method, although he has shown that the minimal solution reported here has the fairly small parameterization $(20, -9)$.

The existence of Elkies' solution was the starting point for my search for the minimal solution. I read about his result in a note to *sci.math* on the *USENET* news. My initial attempt at an exhaustive computer search to verify whether his solution was minimal fell so far short of the goal that I began corresponding with him via electronic mail. He explained some of his method and concurred that there was indeed a possibility that it was not minimal. He also explained the constraints which could be applied to speed up the search.

During the Fall of 1988, I implemented his suggestions in a program for a LISP Machine front end to a Connection Machine system. I ran this program over a period of a few weeks on several systems of different sizes and types, and on January 8, 1988, found the minimal solution.

[4]CDC 6600 is a trademark of Control Data Corporation

[5]MACSYMA is a trademark of Symbolics, Inc.

[6]VAX is a trademark of Digital Equipment Corporation

3 NAIVE APPROACH TO EXHAUSTIVE SEARCH

How would you write a program to perform an exhaustive search for a minimal solution to $A^4+B^4+C^4 = D^4$? Here is a very simple sample program in Common LISP with Zetalisp LOOP:

```
(defun naive-search (U)
  "Find solution to A^4 + B^4 + C^4 = D^4 < U^4."
  (loop for D from 1 below U do
    (loop for C from 1 below D do
      (loop for A from 1 to C
            for N = (- (biquad D) (biquad C) (biquad A))
            when (biquadrate-p N) do
              (return-from naive-search (list D C A))))))
```

The program iterates over variables D, C, and A. For each triple, it computes $N = D^4 - C^4 - A^4$. When it finds some N which is a biquadrate, it escapes to the outer level with the identification of the winning values. Details of the definitions of the supporting functions are omitted in order to simplify exposition.

The main problem with this simple program is that it is too slow. It calls the innermost function biquadrate-p about $U^3/6$ times. Even if you had a *super*-supercomputer which could perform the inner loop on 1.0e9 numbers (each up to 75 bits long) in 1 second, then it would take more than 145 days of constant running to find the minimal solution.

This problem is too big just to throw it at a supercomputer; it needs a better algorithm. The required techniques are elementary number theory, and they have long been applied to the related problem of assigning four biquadrates equal to a fifth biquadrate [10,9].

3.1 Modularity Constraints

Consider the fourth powers modulo 5:

N	N^4	$N^4 \bmod 5$
0	0	0
1	1	1
2	16	1
3	81	1
4	256	1

Since the last column contains only zeros and ones, the congruence $a^4 + b^4 + c^4 \equiv d^4$ has only four forms modulo 5:

A^4	+	B^4	+	C^4	$\equiv$	D^4
0	+	0	+	0	$\equiv$	0
0	+	0	+	1	$\equiv$	1
0	+	1	+	0	$\equiv$	1
1	+	0	+	0	$\equiv$	1

The first form may be omitted since all terms are multiples of five and thus are not relatively prime. The last three are the same except for an interchange of variables. As a result D and one other term, say C, must not be multiples of 5, while the other two terms must be multiples of 5. Since A and B are both multiples of 5, the difference $D^4 - C^4$ must be a multiple of $5^4 = 625$.

These constraints may now be combined by considering the possible (D, C) pairs modulo 625. D may take only 500 of the possible 625 residue values. For each value of D, C may take only four values, corresponding to the four complex factors of $D^4 - C^4$. In order for the factor $D - C$ to be congruent to 0 mod 625, C must be congruent to D mod 625. The factor $D + C$ requires $C \equiv -D \bmod 625$. The factor $D + iC$ requires $C \equiv iD \bmod 625 \equiv 182D \bmod 625$, and finally the factor $D - iC$ requires $C \equiv -iD \bmod 625 \equiv 443D \bmod 625$. In the foregoing, I have used the shorthand i and $-i$ for the two residues such that $residue^2 \equiv -1 \bmod 625$.

The modulo 5 constraints reduce the number of (D, C) pairs which must be considered by a factor of $625/500 \cdot 625/4 = 3125/16 \approx 195$.

When you consider the fourth powers modulo 4 and the resulting possible congruences, you have a similar situation. D and one other term must not be even, while the other two terms must be even. There isn't enough freedom of choice to guarantee that C is both not a multiple of 5 and odd. The only improvement on the number of (D, C) pairs is a factor of 2.

Some further improvements can be obtained by considering moduli 9, 13, and 29. Modulus 9 produces only 4 biquadratic residues which can be combined in only 6 congruences of interest. These congruences may may be summarized by the following two rules in which the overline indicates the negative of an assertion:

$$\text{when } D^4 \equiv 0 \bmod 9, \text{ then } \overline{C^4 \equiv 0 \bmod 9}$$

$$\text{when } \overline{D^4 \equiv 0 \bmod 9} \text{ then either } C^4 \equiv 0 \bmod 9$$

$$\text{or } C^4 \equiv D^4 \bmod 9.$$

The modulo 9 constraints reduce the number of (D, C) pairs which must be considered by the fraction $3/9 \cdot 6/9 + 6/9 \cdot (3/9 + 2/9) = 16/27$, so the reduction factor is $27/16 \approx 1.7$.

Modulus 13 may be treated in a similar fashion. The resulting rule is that each D^4 residue excludes one C^4 residue: 0 excludes 0; 1 excludes 3; 3 excludes 9; and 9 excludes 1. The reduction fraction is $1/13 \cdot 1/13 + 3 \cdot (4/13 \cdot 4/13) = 122/169$, so the reduction factor is $169/122 \approx 1.4$.

Finally modulus 29 produces two rules: D^4 can not have residue 0, and every other D^4 residue excludes two C^4 residues: 1 excludes 24 and 25; 7 excludes 1 and 23; 16 excludes 7 and 23; 20 excludes 7 and 16; 23 excludes 1 and 24; 24 excludes 20 and 25; and 25 excludes 16 and 20. The reduction fraction is $1/29 + 7 \cdot (4/29 \cdot 21/29) = 617/841$, so the reduction factor is $841/617 \approx 1.4$.

3.2 Common Factor Constraint

When D and C have a (necessarily odd) prime factor, P, in common, we would like to eliminate them since the quotient pair must have been treated earlier. However, if the sum $A^4 + B^4$ does not also have P as a common factor then the (D, C) pair can not be eliminated. $A^4 + B^4 \equiv 0 \bmod P$ when $B \equiv \sqrt[4]{-1} \bmod P$, and this condition occurs if and only if P is of the form $8K + 1$. See Davenport's introduction to the theory of numbers [3] for a proof.

The modularity constraints have already eliminated the pairs with 3, 5, 13, and 29 as common factors. The list of common factors which remain to be eliminated begins $7, 11, 19, 23, 31, 37, \ldots$ and extends to the largest prime $P < \sqrt{C}$.

The reduction factor for (D, C) pairs eliminated by the common factor constraint is quite small. Nevertheless, every pair which can be eliminated by a simple test like this is important, since these pairs do not have to be matched against the set of A values.

3.3 Prime Factor Constraints

Consider a prime factor P of $A^4 + B^4$. If the factor occurs a multiple of 4 times, then the factor could be common to A and B. On the other hand, if the factor occurs some other number of times, then it can not be common to A and B and must be produced by the sum. Which prime factors can be produced in this manner?

The factor 2 is produced whenever A and B are odd. Odd primes must be of the form $8K + 1$ as we saw in the analysis of common factors in the previous section.

We can apply this information about the prime factors of $A^4 + B^4$ to constrain the (D, C) pairs to be considered. Whenever $D^4 - C^4$ has an odd prime factor which is not of the form $8K + 1$ and which occurs other than a multiple of four times, then that pair should be eliminated.

The reduction factor for (D, C) pairs eliminated by the prime factor constraint is rather hard to calculate. Since $D^4 - C^4$ automatically factors into $(D - C)(D + C)(D^2 - C^2)$, and each factor picks up prime factors more or less independently, the product tends to have many more prime factors than a random number of its size. Empirically, the reduction factor is between 25 and 50.

3.4 Constraints on $A^4 + B^4$

In the previous sections, we discovered several ways in which the numbers produced by the form A^4+B^4 could produce constraints on the (D, C) pairs to be considered. Unfortunately, a reverse application of this method is not as effective, since the form $D^4 - C^4$ is not as limited.

The first constraint is to eliminate the common factor of 5 in A and B. This can be done by dividing $D^4 - C^4$ by 625 before attempting to decompose it into the form $(A^4 + B^4)$.

Let N be the number to be decomposed. The second constraint is to limit $A, B < \sqrt[4]{N}$ rather than to limit $A \leq C$ as was done in the **naive-search** program. In addition to reducing the number of candidates, this constraint eliminates negative candidates.

A third constraint might be that at least one of (A, B) must be even. This would reduce the search space for A by a factor of 2. However, the constraint that one of (A, B) must be at least as large as the other is more powerful, and this constraint is not compatible with the parity constraint. If N is the number to be decomposed, then $N > A^4 \geq B^4$, and the minimum possible value for A would be when A =B, so $2A^4 \geq N$. Therefore $A \geq \sqrt[4]{N/2} = \sqrt[4]{1/2} \cdot \sqrt[4]{N} \approx 0.84\sqrt[4]{N}$. The reduction factor is $1/(1 - \sqrt[4]{1/2}) \approx 6.3$.

Further constraints can be generated for particular residue classes of D and C. For example, one could treat odd and even N separately and apply a parity constraint to the even case. These methods have not been employed since the decomposition into $A^4 + B^4$ does not turn out to be a significant bottleneck in the data parallel program until $D > 1000000$.

Now let's put all of these ideas together into a more reasonable program.

3.5 Constrained Search Program

Even if we combine all of the constraints developed above, the search is likely to take longer than the time a machine can be allocated to the task. Therefore the program should perform the search over some segment of the search space. Furthermore the program separates easily into two passes. In the first pass, it applies constraints to sieve out a set of candidates, and in the second pass, it attempts to decompose each of the candidates. If a decomposition is found, the program returns the decomposition information. Here is a sample LISP program which embodies these ideas:

```
(defun constrained-search (L U)
  "Find solution to A^4 + B^4 + C^4 = D^4
  with L <= D < U."
  (decompose-each (constraint-sieve L U)))
```

This first pass function **constraint-sieve** iterates on the D variable over the values between L and U which are prime with respect to 10. For each D, it iterates on the C variable over the values less than D which are in proper modulo 625 correspondence with D. When a (D, C) pair passes both the set of modularity tests and the common factor and prime-factor tests, then the value $N = (D^4 - C^4)/625$ is put into a list. The lists for each choice of D are appended together and returned as the value of the function. Here is the code for the first pass function:

```
(defun constraint-sieve (L U)
  "Apply modular and factor constraints to D and C.
  Return list of candidates which pass tests."
  (loop for D in (prime-10 L U)
        append
          (loop for C in (good-c-for-d D)
                when (and (mod-ok-p D C)
                          (factor-ok-p D C))
                  collect
                    (/ (- (biquad D) (biquad C))
                       625))))
```

The second pass function **decompose-each** takes the list of candidates generated by the first pass as its argument. It iterates on the variable N over the candidates in the list. For each candidate, it computes the proper limits on A and iterates between them. When it finds an A such that $N - A^4$ is a biquadrate, it escapes to the outer level and returns some information about the winner. If a winner is encountered, another function would be needed to fully identify it. Here is the code for the second pass function:

```
(defun decompose-each (candidates)
  "Attempt to decompose each of the candidates.
  Return successful decomposition."
  (loop with half-root = (biquad-rt 0.5)
        for N in candidates
        for a-limit = (i-biquad-rt N)
        for a-min = (ceiling (* half-root a-limit))
        do
    (loop for A from a-min below a-limit
          when (biquadrate-p (- N (biquad A)))
            do
              (return-from decompose-each (list N A)))))
```

How many candidates can we expect the first pass to produce?

$$U^2/2 \cdot 16/3125 \cdot 1/2 \cdot 16/27 \cdot 122/169 \cdot 617/847 \cdot 1/25 \approx U^2/63000$$

How many A values does the second pass have to scan for the average candidate? Assume that the candidates are evenly distributed below U^4, then the average upper limit on A is about $4/5 \cdot (U^4)^{1/4} = 4U/5$ and only 16% of that range is scanned.

In summary, this program calls the innermost function **biquadrate-p** about $U^2/63000 \cdot 4U/5 \cdot .16 \approx U^3/490000$. Now if you had a supercomputer which could perform the inner loop on 1.0e6 numbers in 1 second, then it would take less than 2 days of constant running to find the minimal solution. This sounds possible. It's time to look at the supercomputer.

4 THE CONNECTION MACHINE ARCHITECTURE

The Connection Machine architecture is a data parallel computing system [1]. A Connection Machine system (CM for short) consists of a set of processors and memories divided into up to four sections of 8192 or 16384 processors and connected through a programmable cross bar switch to up to four external front end computers. The CM-1 Model has 4096 bits of memory per processor, and the CM-2 Model has 65536 bits per processor. Memory is addressable at the bit level and memory fields can be any length. In virtual processing mode, the user sees a larger number of processors, each with a correspondingly smaller memory.

The CM-2 Model has an optional floating point accelerator associated with every 32 processors. It also has optional I/O controllers and framebuffers. The CM-2 may optionally be divided into sections of 4096 processors.

When 65536 processors are operating in parallel, each performing a 32-bit integer addition, the CM-1 operates at about 1000 Mips. (This figure includes all overhead for instruction issuing and decoding.) The CM-2 operates at 2500 Mips. When the CM-2 is equipped with the floating point accelerator, it operates at 2500 MFlops for double precision operands.

The fastest operations such as arithmetic, data manipulation, and data broadcast operations are performed in parallel on all or a selected set of processors and take constant time. Operations which combine the values in selected processors, such as enumeration, rank, scans, and global operations, take time logarithmic in the number of processors. Most of these cooperative operations return a value to the front end computer and thus interrupt instruction pipelines. Operations which move data between processors are slightly more expensive. The most efficient of these operations perform communication between neighbors on a virtual N dimensional grid, while the most general communicate data between any processors and handle collisions. The slowest operations are those which operate entirely on the front end computer or which transmit data serially between individual processors and the front end computer.

The user interacts with one or more ganged sections of the CM through a front end computer, which may be a Symbolics 3600 LISP machine, a DEC VAX 8000 series computer with a BI bus, or a SUN 4 workstation® [7]. The front end provides the program development and execution environment. It issues instructions to one or more microsequencers which operate in parallel and broadcast the lowest level instructions to the data processors.

The high-level languages available for programming the Connection Machine system are Fortran, C*, and *Lisp. These languages are based on well-known standards with minimal extensions to support data parallel constructs. The assembly language for the CM is Paris. This is the target language of the high-level language compilers. Paris functions are available in C and in LISP, and Paris commands may be executed in a UNIX® [8] or LISP environment.

5 PARALLEL IMPLEMENTATION

The implementation of the exhaustive data parallel search on the Connection Machine system is similar in concept to the **constrained-search** program described above in Section 3.5. It is implemented in LISP for the Symbolics Lisp machine front end with calls to Paris for either the CM-1 or the CM-2. The candidates sieved out by the first pass are collected in a list on the front end for the second pass.

[7] Sun workstation is a registered trademark of Sun Microsystems

[8] UNIX is a trademark of AT&T Bell Laboratories

5.1 Parallel Constraint Sieve

The major theme for the first pass is the problem of when to treat the primes in parallel and when to treat the (D, C) pairs in parallel. It isn't possible to extract all of a class of primes from all of the pairs at the same time. The program must iterate either on the primes or on the pairs in order to perform the data parallel operation on the the other type of data. The best efficiency is obtained by iterating over a small amount of data and performing the parallel operation on a large amount of data. We solve the problem by treating a batch of $(D, C]$ pairs in parallel at first, and then when most of the pairs have been sieved out, treating them individually and the primes in parallel.

The modulo 5 and modulo 4 constraints on (D, C) result in a modularity table of 500 residues (D mod 1250) each paired with 4 residues (C mod 625). These 2000 pairs are written to the CM, one per processor and duplicated as many times as there are processors available. In each successive copy, the C mod 625 residues are incremented by 625. This table facilitates loading of (D, C) pairs. Here is a list of the data processor memory fields involved:

Field Name	Field Usage
d-offset-field	Offsets on D from table
c-offset-field	Offsets on C from table
table-flag	Select all table entries
ok-field-flag	Select (D, C) candidates ll
d-field	D
c-field	C
d4-field	D^4
c4-field	C^4

How are a batch of (D, C) pairs loaded into the CM? Say 16384 processors are attached to the front end. There are 8 copies of the modularity table loaded into **d-offset-field** and **c-offset-field**, and **table-flag** is set to 1 in the first $8 \cdot 2000 = 16000$ processors. Say that the first pair in the batch is $(400000, 345000)$. The D values are loaded by broadcasting 400000 to **d-field** and adding **d-offset-field** to it. Similarly, the C values are loaded by broadcasting 345000 to **c-field** and adding **c-offset-field** to it. The next batch will start with $(400000, 350000)$. If the C values get beyond the D values in some processors, then those processors are adjusted.

With the (D, C) pairs arrayed in the processors, the other modularity constraints are easy to perform. The **ok-field-flag** is initialized with the **table-flag**. The modulus is broadcast to a temporary field in all of the selected processors. The residues for each D^4 and each C^4 are calculated in two other temporary fields. Then the particular rules for the different cases are selectively applied to the pairs to which they apply. The result is that some of the processors are deselected and the bit for those processors in **ok-field-flag** is reset to 0.

Common factor restriction begins with the (D, C) pairs in parallel. The first 30 or so primes which are not of the form $8K + 1$ except for 3, 5, 13, and 29 are successively used to divide D and C. All remaining processors which have both residues equal to zero are deselected.

Prime factor restriction also begins with the (D, C) pairs in parallel. The first 30 or so primes which are not of the form $8K + 1$ are successively used on a field containing $N = (D^4 - C^4)/625$. First all fourth powers of the prime are divided out of N. The the residue modulo the prime is calculated. All remaining processors in which this residue is non-zero are deselected.

At this point, we switch to treating the pairs serially and the primes in parallel. We use tables of odd primes whic are computed at initialization time by several iterations of a parallel sieve of Eratosthenes interspersed with communication instructions for packing the results. After the primes have been calculated and packed into memory, it is easy to select those which are not of the form $8K + 1$.

The remaining (D, C) pairs are now matched against the prime number tables. The pairs are enumerated and successively extracted from CM memory into the front end. The application of common factor and prime factor restraints is quite similar to previous descriptions. Each (D, C) pair which passes these two remaining tests, causes the corresponding $(D^4 - C^4)/625$ value to be pushed on a list for the second pass.

5.2 Parallel Decomposition

The primary data structure for the second pass is an array of all of the A^4 values which could be used to decompose any of the candidates in the list of $(D^4 - C^4)/625$ values from the first pass. Each column of the array is a memory field extending over all of the processors. Each row is another memory field. Let U be the maximum value in the list, then the upper limit on A values is $\lfloor \sqrt[4]{U} \rfloor$. Let L be the minimum value in the list, then the minimum A value is $\sqrt[4]{\lceil L/2 \rceil}$. The A values are not stored; they are only used to calculate the A^4 values which are stored in the array.

The program iterates over successive values in the list of candidates. For each candidate N it iterates over the array columns which contain A^4 values which could be used to decompose N. For each column it computes $M = N - A^4$. If $M = (\lfloor \sqrt[4]{M} \rfloor)^4$, then M is a wining biquadrate.

The major theme for the second pass is to avoid checking whether a solution has been found for as long as possible. Solutions are very rare, and it takes time to check. The equality condition indicating a winner is stored as a 1 in a flag field for the winning processor(s). This flag is kept as a logical *OR* of the values for all candidates. At the end of the pass, the flags in all of the processors are combined, and if any of them was a 1, a winner is declared.

If a winner is declared, a modified version of the search program is used to pin it down.

6 TIMINGS, FINAL RESULTS AND OPEN QUESTIONS

Here is some sample output from the first pass of the parallel search program. Explanatory *comments* have been inserted. Many diagnostic outputs which are normally turned off have been switched on in order to show the progress at each stage. With the diagnostics turned off, the program runs much faster than the time stamps would indicate. The pass was run on a 16384 processor CM-1 system. The interval being checked starts with $(D, C) = (500000, 495000)$ and has an upper cutoff limit of $D \leq 501250$.

Initialize the CM.
Cold booting 02/19/1988 05:07:36
Warning: If you are using *Lisp, you must now do *COLD-BOOT.
Initialize one prime number table in the CM.
This output is from an early version with only one table.
Filling CM with primes 02/19/1988 05:07:41
Highest prime found = 180511 02/19/1988 05:07:42
Initialize the (D, C) modularity table in the CM.
Filling CM with modularity table 02/19/1988 05:07:42
8 copies of size 2000 of modularity table fit into CM
Fill the CM with the first batch of (D, C) pairs.
Ensure that $C < D$. For this batch, all of them are.
d-c-c<d leaves 16000 ok entries
Apply modularity constraints.
d-c-mod-9 leaves 9362 ok entries
d-c-mod-13 leaves 6588 ok entries
d-c-mod-29 leaves 4621 ok entries
Apply serial common factor constraints.
Common factors leave 4485 ok entries
Apply serial prime factor constraints.
some-primes leave 391 ok entries
Enumerate remaining pairs. Apply parallel factor constraints.
Checking 391 ok entries
Report total candidates in output list so far.
Now have 87 valid n625
Fill the CM with the second batch of (D, C) pairs.

```
d-c-c<d leaves 13750 ok entries
d-c-mod-9 leaves 8296 ok entries
d-c-mod-13 leaves 5909 ok entries
d-c-mod-29 leaves 4099 ok entries
Common factors leave 3991 ok entries
some-primes leave 303 ok entries
Checking 303 ok entries
Now have 148 valid n625
About to exit, report total number of candidates found.
Now have 148 valid n625 02/19/1988 05:07:59
The function leaves the candidate list in a global variable.
It does not return any value of interest.
NIL
```

The discovery of the minimal solution originally took over 100 hours of running time. This could have been much shorter. Some of the algorithmic short cuts described here had not yet been implemented. Several batches were run multiple times. Some batches were run at inefficient virtual processor ratios, and some were run on very small machines.

Using outputs from partial runs, I estimate that the current algorithm running on a 16384 processor CM-1 would take about 33 hours.

David Plummer [11] has used this program as a model and implemented the search on a network of SYMBOLICS Lisp Machines. He verified the minimal solution in 3300 LISP machine hours.

There are several improvements that could be made to the program. The current method starts the search with (D, C) pairs. Noam Elkies[5] has suggested a method which starts with the pairs $(D + C, D - C)$. This method could be several times faster. A new virtual processor scheme being designed at Thinking Machines should allow better management of variables and result in a speedup.

It would be nice to know how sparsely separated solutions are. Is there no other solution between the minimal one and Elkies' smaller solution?

Another realm of exploration would be to investigate the higher powers of Euler's twice refuted conjecture.

ACKNOWLEDGMENTS

I wish to thank several people who helped with the search for solutions. Without Noam Elkies I would not have known where to start. He very patiently explained the number theory to me, and when I still couldn't understand, Jill Mesirov and Washington Taylor explained it again. Donna Fritzsche found the announcement of the minimal solution waiting on her terminal one morning after a night's run. Roger Locniskar adapted the program as a system exerciser; whenever he repaired a set of memory boards, he would do a final system check and incidentally extend the range of the search by running this program on them. Carmen Crocker put this manuscript in its final form.

References

[1] *Connection Machine Model CM-2 Technical Summary.* Thinking Machines Corporation. Cambridge, MA. 1987.

[2] *Connection Machine Parallel Instruction Set (PARIS): The LISP Implementation.* Thinking Machines Corporation. Cambridge, MA. 1986.

[3] Davenport, H. *The Higher Arithmetic: An Introduction to the Theory of Numbers.* Dover Publications. New York. 1983.

[4] Elkies, Noam D. "On $A^4 + B^4 + C^4 = D^4$." *Mathematics of Computation*, 1988 (to appear).

[5] Elkies, Noam D. Personal communication. January 1988.

[6] Guy, Richard K. *Unsolved Problems in Number Theory.* Springer-Verlag. New York. 1981.

[7] Hillis, W. Daniel. *The Connection Machine.* MIT Press. Cambridge, MA. 1985.

[8] Hillis, W. Daniel, and Guy L. Steele Jr. "Data Parallel Algorithms." *Communications of the ACM.* Vol. 29, No. 12, 1986, pp. 1170-1183.

[9] Lander, L. J., T. R. Parkin and J. L. Selfridge. "A Survey of Equal Sums of Like Powers" *Mathematics of Computation.* Vol. 21, 1967, pp. 446-459.

[10] Leech, John. "On $A^4 + B^4 + C^4 = D^4$" *Proc. Cambridge Philos. Soc.*. Vol. 54, 1958, pp. 554-555.

[11] Plummer, David C. Personal communication. March 1988.

[12] Steele, Guy L. Jr. *Common LISP: The Language.* Digital Press. Burlington, MA. 1984.

[13] *Symbolics Common Lisp: Language Dictionary.* Symbolics, Inc. Cambridge, MA. 1986.

Vectorization of Multiple-Precision Arithmetic Program and 201,326,000 Decimal Digits of π Calculation

Yasumasa Kanada

Computer Centre, University of Tokyo,
Bunkyo-ku Yayoi 2-11-16, Tokyo 113, Japan

More than 200 million decimal places of π were calculated using arithmetic-geometric mean formula independently discovered by Salamin and Brent in 1976. Correctness of the calculation were verified through Borwein's quartic convergent formula developed in 1983. The computation took CPU times of 5 hours 57 minutes for the main calculation and 7 hours 30 minutes for the verification calculation on the HITAC S-820 model 80 supercomputer with 256 Mb of main memory and 3 Gb of high speed semiconductor storage, Extended Storage, for shorten I/O time.

Computation was completed in 27th of January 1988. At that day two programs generated values up to 3×2^{26}, about 201 million. The two results agreed except for the last 21 digits. These results also agree with the 133,554,000 places calculation of π which was done by the author in January 1987. Compare to the record in 1987, 50% more decimal digits were calculated with about 1/6 of CPU time.

Computation was performed with real arithmetic based vectorized Fast Fourier Transform (FFT) multiplier and newly vectorized multiple-precision add, subtract and (single word) constant multiplication programs. Vectorizations for the later cases were realized through first order linear recurrence vector instruction on the S-820. Details of the computation and statistical tests on the first 200 million digits of π-3 are reported.

1. Introduction

Since the epoch-making calculation of π to 100,000 decimals [17], several computations have been performed as in Table 1. The development of new algorithms and programs suited to the calculation of π and new high speed computers with large memory and high speed large semiconductor disk, Extended Storage or Solid State Disk, threw more light on this fascinating number.

There are many arctangent relations for π[9]. However, all these computations until 1981 and verification for 10,000,000 decimal calculation of our previous record[21] used arctangent formulae such as:

$$\pi = 16arctan\frac{1}{5} - 4arctan\frac{1}{239}, \qquad \text{Machin}$$

$$= 24arctan\frac{1}{8} + 8arctan\frac{1}{57} + 4arctan\frac{1}{239}, \qquad \text{Störmer}$$

$$= 48arctan\frac{1}{18} + 32arctan\frac{1}{57} - 20arctan\frac{1}{239}, \qquad \text{Gauss}$$

$$= 32arctan\frac{1}{10} - 4arctan\frac{1}{239} - 16arctan\frac{1}{515}. \qquad \text{Klingenstierna}$$

In 1976, an innovative quadratic convergent formula for the calculation of π was published independently by Salamin [14] and Brent [5]. Later in 1983, quadratic, cubic, quadruple and septet convergent product expansion for π, which are competitive with Salamin's and Brent's formula, were also discovered by two of Borwein[2]. These new formulae are based on the arithmetic-geometric mean, a process whose rapid convergence doubles, triples, quadruples and septates the number of significant digits at each step. The arithmetic-geometric mean is the basis of Gauss' method for the calculation of elliptic integrals. With the help of the elliptic integral relation of Legendre, π can be expressed in terms of the arithmetic-geometric mean and the resulting algorithm retains quadratic, cubic, quartic and septic convergence of the arithmetic-geometric mean process.

The author and Mr. Y. Tamura have calculated π up to more than 200 million decimal places by using the formula of Brent and Salamin and verified through Borwein's quartic convergent algorithm for π. Even for the quartic convergent algorithm, quadratic convergent algorithm of Brent and Salamin is faster through actual FORTRAN programs.

For reducing the computing time, theoretically fast multiple-precision multiplication algorithm was implemented through normal fast Fourier transform (FFA), inverse fast Fourier transform (FFS) and convolution operations[11] as before[19,9,21,8]. And in order to get more speed than before, vectorization schemes to the multiple-precision add, subtract and (single word) constant multiplication were introduced for the first time.

Calculation of 200 million decimal places of π was completed in January 27, 1988 and needed 5 hours 57 minutes of CPU time on a HITAC S-820 model 80 supercomputer at Hitachi Kanagawa Works under a VOS3/HAP/ES 31 bit addressing operating system. Main memory used was about 240 Mb and 2.7 Gb of Extended Storage was also required. If the machine had more memory, CPU time could be reduced and more Extended Storage, calculation decimals could be extended with minor changes in the FORTRAN programs.

The algorithms used in the 200 million place calculation are briefly explained in section 2. Programming in FORTRAN is discussed in section 3. Results of statistical tests and some interesting figures for the 200,000,000 decimals of π appear in section 4.

2. How to Calculate π: Algorithmic Aspects

In this section we briefly explain the algorithms used in the 200 million decimal place calculations.

2.1. The Gauss-Legendre Algorithm: Main Algorithm

The theoretical basis of the Gauss-Legendre algorithm for π is explained in the references [2,5,14]. Here, we summarize the quadratic algorithm for π. (Refer to the references for the details.)

We first define the arithmetic-geometric mean $agm(a_0,b_0)$. Let a_0, b_0 and c_0 be positive numbers satisfying $a_0^2 = b_0^2 + c_0^2$. Define a_n, the sequence of arithmetic means, and b_n, the sequence of geometric means, by

$$a_n = \frac{(a_{n-1} + b_{n-1})}{2}, \quad b_n = (a_{n-1} \times b_{n-1})^{1/2} .$$

Also, define a positive number sequence c_n:

$$c_n^2 = a_n^2 - b_n^2 . \tag{1}$$

Note that, two relations easily follow from these definitions.

$$c_n = \frac{(a_{n-1} - b_{n-1})}{2} = (a_{n-1} - a_n), \quad c_n^2 = 4 \times a_{n+1} \times c_{n+1} . \tag{2}$$

Then, $agm(a_0,b_0)$ is the common limit of the sequences a_n and b_n, namely

$$agm(a_0,b_0) = \lim_{n\to\infty} a_n = \lim_{n\to\infty} b_n .$$

Now, π can be expressed as follows:

$$\pi = \frac{4agm(1,k)agm(1,k')}{1 - \sum_{j=1}^{\infty} 2^j (c_j^2 + c'^2_j)}, \tag{4}$$

where $a_0 = a'_0 = 1$, $b_0 = k$, $b'_0 = k'$ and $k^2 + k'^2 = 1$. It is easier to compute squares of c_j and c'_j by Eq. (2) than to calculate c_j^2 and c'^2_j by Eq. (1).

The symmetric choice of $k = k' = 2^{-1/2}$ is recommendable for the actual calculation and it causes the two sequences of arithmetic-geometric means to coincide. Then, Eq. (3) becomes

$$\pi = \frac{4(agm(1,2^{-1/2}))^2}{1 - \sum_{j=1}^{\infty} 2^{j+1} c_j^2} . \tag{4}$$

After n square root operations in computing $agm = agm(1,2^{-1/2})$, π can be approximated by π_n:

$$\pi_n = \frac{4a_{n+1}^2}{1 - \sum_{j=1}^{n} 2^{j+1} c_j^2} = \frac{a_{n+1}^2}{0.25 - \sum_{j=1}^{n} 2^{j-1} c_j^2} . \tag{5}$$

Then, the absolute value of $\pi - \pi_n$ is bounded as follows (Theorem 2b in reference [14]) :

$$\left| \pi - \pi_n \right| < (\pi^2 \times 2^{n+4} / agm^2) \exp(-\pi \times 2^{n+1}) . \tag{6}$$

Thus, the formula has the quadratic convergence nature. We must note here that all operations and constants in Eq. (4) must be correct up to the required number of digits plus α (20 to 30 as the guard digits for 200 million decimal digits calculation).

Then the sequences of *agm* and *agm* related π are calculated by the following algorithm;

```
A := 1; B := 2^(-1/2); T := 1/4; X := 1;

while A-B>2^(-n) do begin
W := A*B; V := A; A := A+B; A := A/2;
V := V-A; V := V*V; V :=V*X;
T := T-V; B := √W; X := 2*X end;

A := A*B; B := 1/T; A := A*B;
return A .
```

Here, A, B, T, V and W are full-precision variables and X is a double-precision variable. After twenty eight iterations of the main loop, π to 200 million decimal places is to be obtained.

2.2. Borwein's Quartic Convergent Algorithm: Verification Algorithm

Borwein's quartic convergent algorithm is explained as the following scheme:

$$a_0 = 6 - 4 \times \sqrt{2} , \quad y_0 = \sqrt{2} - 1$$

$$y_{k+1} = \frac{1 - (1 - y_k^4)^{1/4}}{1 + (1 + y_k^4)^{1/4}}, \quad a_{k+1} = a_k \times (1 + y_{k+1})^4 - 2^{2k+3} \times y_{k+1} \times (1 + y_{k+1} + y_{k+1}^2),$$

$$\pi \approx \frac{1}{a_k} \quad \text{for large } k .$$

Here, precisions for a_k and y_k must be more than the desired digits. This algorithm is basically the same with that used for the main run of the 29 million decimal calculation done by Dr. D.H. Bailey[1]. Dr. Bailey used the following Borwein's quadratic convergent algorithm for the verification calculation:

$$a_0 = \sqrt{2} , \quad b_0 = 0 , \quad p_0 = 2 + \sqrt{2}$$

$$a_{k+1} = \frac{(\sqrt{a_k} + \frac{1}{\sqrt{a_k}})}{2}, \quad b_{k+1} = \frac{\sqrt{a_k} \times (1 + b_k)}{a_k + b_k}, \quad p_{k+1} = \frac{p_k \times b_{k+1} \times (1 + a_{k+1})}{1 + b_{k+1}},$$

$$\pi \approx p_k \quad \text{for large } k .$$

Here, precisions for a_k, b_k and p_k must be more than the desired digits. It is to be noted that the Gauss-Legendre algorithm is superior to the Borwein's algorithms explained here as in the Table 2.

2.3. Calculation of Reciprocals and Square Roots

As is easily seen from the algorithms explained above, arithmetic operations, reciprocals and square roots must be computed with high efficiency in order to reduce the computing time. Theoretical bases for fast calculation of reciprocals and square roots of multi-precision numbers appear in references [16,12,4,5]. In this subsection we summarize the algorithms used in the actual calculation.

The reciprocal of C is obtained by the Newton iteration for the equation $f(x) = x^{-1} - C \equiv 0$:

$$x_{i+1} = x_i \times (2 - C \times x_i) . \tag{7}$$

A single-, double- or quadruple-precision approximation of $1/C$ is a reasonable selection for x_0, i.e. initial starting value for the Newton iteration.

Square roots of C should be calculated through the multiplication of C and the result obtained by the Newton iteration for the equation $f(x) = x^{-2} - C \equiv 0$:

$$x_{i+1} = \frac{x_i \times (3 - C \times x_i^2)}{2} \,. \tag{8}$$

In this case also, a single-, double- or quadruple-precision approximation of $1/\sqrt{C}$ is a reasonable selection for x_0, initial starting value.

Compare this to the well known Newton iteration for the equation $f(x) = x^2 - C \equiv 0$:

$$x_{i+1} = \frac{(x_i + \frac{C}{x_i})}{2} \,. \tag{9}$$

The iteration of Eq. (8) is better in both computing complexity and in actual calculation than the iteration of Eq. (9). The order of convergence for the iterations of Eq. (7) and Eq. (8) is two. This convergence speed is favorable in the actual calculation. It is to be noted that in these iterations the whole operation need not to be done with full-precision at each step. That is, if k-precision calculation is done at step j, $2k$-precision calculation is sufficient for at step $j+1$.

2.4. Multiple-precision Multiplication

Schönhage-Strassen's algorithm [15], which uses the discrete Fourier transform with modulo $2^n + 1$, could be the key multiple-precision multiplication algorithm for speeding up the π calculation. However, this algorithm is so hard to implement and needs binary to decimal radix conversion for the final result. Dr. Bailey also used discrete Fourier transform but with three prime modulo computation followed by the reconstruction through Chinese Remainder Theorem for his 29 million decimal places calculation[1].

Now, we focused the special scheme which utilizes the fact of "*the Fourier transform of a convolution product is the ordinary product of the Fourier transforms.*"

Let consider the product C of two length n with radix X integers A and B. Note that the radix X need not to be a power of 2.

$$A = \sum_{i=0}^{2n-1} a_i X^i \,, B = \sum_{i=0}^{2n-1} b_i X^i \,,$$

where $0 \le a_i < X, 0 \le b_i < X$ for $0 \le i < n-1$, $0 < a_{n-1} < X, 0 < b_{n-1} < X$ and $a_i = b_i = 0$, for $i < 0, n \le i$.

Then,

$$C \equiv A \cdot B = (\sum_{i=0}^{2n-1} a_i X^i) \cdot (\sum_{j=0}^{2n-1} b_j X^j) = \sum_{i=0}^{2n-1} X^i (\sum_{j=0}^{2n-1} a_j b_{i-j}) \equiv \sum_{i=0}^{2n-1} c_i X^i$$

Thus,

$$c_i = \sum_{j=0}^{2n-1} a_j b_{i-j}, \quad \text{for } i = 0, \cdots, 2n-2, \text{ and } c_{2n-1} = 0.$$

If $\omega = exp(2\pi i/2n)$ is a $2n$th root of unity, the one-dimensional Fourier transform of the sequences of complex numbers $(a_0, a_1, \cdots, a_{2n-1})$, $(b_0, b_1, \cdots, b_{2n-1})$ and $(c_0, c_1, \cdots, c_{2n-1})$ are defined as the sequences of $(\hat{a}_0, \hat{a}_1, \cdots, \hat{a}_{2n-1})$, $(\hat{b}_0, \hat{b}_1, \cdots, \hat{b}_{2n-1})$ and $(\hat{c}_0, \hat{c}_1, \cdots, \hat{c}_{2n-1})$, respectively. Here,

$$\hat{a}_l = \sum_{i=0}^{2n-1} a_i \omega^{il}, \hat{b}_l = \sum_{i=0}^{2n-1} b_i \omega^{il}, \hat{c}_l = \sum_{i=0}^{2n-1} c_i \omega^{il}, \quad \text{for } 0 \le l \le 2n-1 \,.$$

Then, $(\hat{a}_0\hat{b}_0, \hat{a}_1\hat{b}_1, \cdots, \hat{a}_{2n-1}\hat{b}_{2n-1})$ is equal to $(\hat{c}_0, \hat{c}_1, \cdots, \hat{c}_{2n-1})$ as the followings:

$$\hat{a}_k\hat{b}_k = (\sum_{i=0}^{2n-1} a_i \omega^{ki}) (\sum_{j=0}^{2n-1} b_j \omega^{kj}) = \sum_{i=0}^{2n-1} \sum_{j=0}^{2n-1} a_i b_j \omega^{k(i+j)} = \sum_{l=0}^{2n-1} (\sum_{j=0}^{2n-1} a_j b_{l-j}) \omega^{kl} = \sum_{l=0}^{2n-1} c_l \omega^{kl}$$

In these discussions, radix X might be an any number. However, ω must be a complex number, namely *floating point real* arithmetic operations are needed in the process of Fourier transformation. If and only if all the *floating point real* arithmetic operations are performed exactly, this scheme should give the correct result as discussed in page 290-295 of reference[11]. Compared to the discrete Fourier transform based multiplier, *floating point real* arithmetic operations based Fourier transform seems ideal and dangerous, but attractive as for the actual multiple-precision multiplication method.

The reasons are:

1) The speed of double precision floating point operations is faster than integer operations in the available machine, especially for supercomputers. And in general, the number of bits obtainable in one double precision floating point instruction is longer than that obtainable in one single integer instruction.

2) Conversion from binary results to decimal results needs other techniques and coding. (Simple is best. Schönhage-Strassen's discrete FFT algorithm is the binary data multiplier.)

3) A qualified high-speed FFT routine was available as a library. (Qualified programming improves the reliability of the program. If we adopt Schönhage-Strassen's discrete FFT algorithm, we have to code for it.)

4) Chinese remainder based discrete FFT algorithm is not so fast as far as the Dr. Y. Ushiro's experiment in 1983[20] is concerned. (He showed the inferiority of Chinese remainder based discrete FFT to us prior to the Dr. Bailey's experiment[1]. We needed a faster multiple-precision multiplier.)

Followings are the algorithm used in our calculation. Here, let consider the multiplication of two $m \times 2^n$ bit ($= m \times (\log_{10}2) \times 2^n$ decimal digit) integers A and B through our schemes.

Step 1: Prepare two 2×2^n entry double precision floating point array.

Step 2: Convert both of $m \times 2^n$ bit integers into double precision floating point numbers. (The first half of 2×2^n entry contains information for $m \times 2^n$ bit, namely, m bit information per one double precision floating point array entry.)

Step 3: Initialize to double precision floating point zero for the second half of 2×2^n entry.

Step 4: Apply 2^{n+1} point normal Fourier transform, say FFA, operations to A and B giving A' and B', respectively.

Step 5: Do the convolution product operations between A' and B' giving new 2×2^n entry double precision array C'.

Step 6: Apply 2^{n+1} point inverse Fourier transform, say FFS, operations to C' giving C. (Now, C is the double precision floating point array of 2×2^n entry. If operations FFA, FFS and convolution product are performed in infinite precision, each entry of C should be the exact double precision floating point representation for integer with maximum value of $2^n \times (2^m-1)^2$. However, these representation are slightly deviated from exact integer in the actual operation. Because, infinite precision operations are impossible to perform.)

Step 7: Convert each entry of C (let it to be x) into integer representation. (Conversion should be done with IDNINT operation in FORTRAN. (IDNINT(x) = IDINT(x+0.5D0).) If absolute value of $(x-DFLOAT(IDNINT(x)))$ is near to 0.5D0, the multiplication is considered to be incorrect. We don't know that criterion of 0.45D0 is sufficient or not. However criterion of 0.2D0, for example, was sufficient enough in the actual multiplication.)

Step 8: Normalize C under the suitable base. The base of 2^m or $10^{m(\log_{10}2)}$ is better for binary or decimal representation. Final result is the result of multiplication between A and B.

According to the theoretical and experimental analysis of error in FFT [6,10], FFT attains rather stable error behavior. Theoretically roughly speaking, 2^l point FFT attains $l\ log(l)$ bits error at the maximum (worst case). This means that FFA and the convolution product followed by FFS would acquire $2\ l\ log(l)$ bits error at the maximum, even if the trigonometric functions at coefficients for the butterfly operation are calculated exactly.

Available mantissa bits are 56 for double-precision floating point data of the Japanese supercomputers. (CRAY and ETA machines adopt 48 bit mantissa representation for the floating point numbers.) Then, the following equation must be satisfied for the worst case;

$$\textit{bits available in the calculation} \geq (\textit{guard bits} \text{ for } \textit{FFA} \text{ and } \textit{FFS operations}) + (\textit{necessary bits} \text{ for } \textit{preserving the results})$$

$$56 \geq 2\,(n+1)\,log\,(n+1) + log\,(2^n \times (2^m - 1)^2)\,.$$

Here n is an integer. Thus, even for $m = 1$,

$$n \leq 7\,.$$

The analysis suggests a maximum n of 7. However, the maximum n depends on the method of programming, errors in trigonometric function calculations, value of m, *etc.* (There is another error analysis for the *floating point real* FFT multiplier in reference[11] which specifies the radix X in our explanation to be the power of 2.)

The error analysis for the actual calculation is hard. Then, we have checked the availability of the FFT multiplier based on the above schemes through actual programs. We monitored the deviations from integer values after the stage of conversion to integer representation as explained in Step 7 of the above explanation. The monitoring secures a maximum n of 24, for the condition of one data point, a double word, holds 3 decimals at the maximum (m is about 10) on the first half of 2×2^{24} data points and zero on the second half of 2×2^{24} data points. Then we decided that the maximum length of multiplicand to be multiplied in-core is 3×2^{24} decimal places (about 50 million decimals) in the actual multiplication.

For multiplying 3×2^{26} decimal places numbers (multiple-precision data for 200 million decimal places), we used the classical $O(n^2)$ algorithm, e.g. school boy method, for the data of $2^{26}/2^{24} = 2^2 = 4$ units with base of $2^{24} \times 1{,}000$! It is possible to realize multiple-precision multiplier all through FFT, not through school boy method. In order to do so, we must write extra program for out-of-core version of FFT. We preferred to utilize the reliability of the numerical libraries.

2.5. Vectorization of Multiple-Precision Add, Subtract and (Single Word) Constant Multiplication

For the programs of multiple-precision add, subtract and (single word) constant multiplier, time consuming process is releasing the "borrow or carry."

If the machine has special instruction for vectorizing first order linear recurrence relation of the following, the process of releasing the borrow or carry could be vectorized. (Now, all of the Japanese supercomputers are equipped with such instructions.)

```
      DO 10 I = ...
10    A(I) = B(I) * A(I-1) + C(I)
```

Here, vector A has a nature of first order linear recurrence relation. The following program which were extracted form the source codes of the actual run will explain how to rewrite the program for multiple-precision adder. Same strategies can be applied to the multiple-precision routines for subtract and (single word) constant multiplication.

```
C integer*4 -- MA, MB, ICY(=carry), ICW(=work), IONE8(=base=10**6)
C real*8 -- Y(=work), Z(=carry), CY(=work), CW(=work)
C real*8 -- ONED8=DFLOAT(IONE8), ONEDM8=1.DO/ONED8, HLFDM8=.5D0*ONEDM8

      DO 10 J=NDA,1,-1                          DO 10 J=NDA,2,-1
        ICW=MA(J)+MB(J)+ICY                       Y(J)=MA(J)+MB(J)
        IF( ICW.GE.IONE8 ) THEN                   Z(J-1)=Y(J)*ONEDM8+Z(J)*ONEDM8
          MA(J)=ICW-IONE8                         Z(J)=DINT(Z(J)+HLFDM8)
          ICY=1                            10   CONTINUE
        ELSE                        ==>           Z(1)=DINT(Z(J)+HLFDM8)
          MA(J)=ICW                             DO 11 J=NDA,2,-1
          ICY=0                                   MA(J)=Y(J)+Z(J)-Z(J-1)*ONED8
        END IF                             11   CONTINUE
10    CONTINUE                                    CW=DFLOAT(MA(1)+MB(1))+Z(1)
                                                  CY=DINT(CW*ONEDM8+HLFDM8)
                                                  MA(1)=CW-CY*ONED8
```

3. How to Calculate π: Programming Aspects

The actual programs, written in FORTRAN, consisted of 3426 (main) and 3642 (verification) lines of source code with comment lines. The numbers of program units are 59 (main) and 64 (verification). In this section we briefly overview the actual programming.

About the half of the sub-programs are routines related to multiple-precision multiplication. Others are routines for addition, subtraction, reciprocal operations, square root operations, file I/O operations, *etc.*

The HITAC S-820 model 80 is a so called 2nd generation supercomputer in Japan. The machine is single processor model and has theoretical peak performance of 3Gflops. Maximum attachable main memory size is 512 Mb and Extended Storage size is 12 Gb. FFT routines, FFA and FFS, are carefully selected from the non-vectorized FORTRAN numerical library which was provided by the Hitachi and source codes were slightly modified by myself for the vectorization.

3.1. Layout of Storage

As explained in section 2, we used a *floating point real* FFT whose accuracy is secured under the conditions of

(1) 2^{24+1} point double-precision *floating point real* FFT,

(2) maximum number at each entry point for the first half entry is non negative number and must be bounded by 1,000,

(3) the second half entry contains zero.

These conditions allow in-core multiplication of numbers with $2^{24} \times 3$ (= 50,331,648) decimals. If we want more decimals to be calculated in-core (on main memory), we must reduce the above conditions, e.g.

(1) 2^{24+1} points -> 2^{29+1} points,

(2) maximum number at each entry point of 1,000 -> 100.

These new conditions would allow numbers of up to $2^{29} \times 2$ (= 1,073,741,824) decimals to be manipulated in-core. (We did not check the validity of these conditions through actual run. Our examples are only for explanation!) However, currently available maximum memory size prevent such higher precision calculations in-core. In order to run with such ideal conditions, at least 8 GB of main memory should be available. Now, the cases with 2^{17+1} points or 2^{18+1} points and maximum number at each entry point of 10,000 were applied for the previous our π calculations including 133 million decimals record. The increase of in-core operable FFT points is the major factor for the speed-up to the π calculation.

It was impossible to obtain 200 million decimal places through in-core operations because of available main memory size. Therefore we introduced the user controlled virtual memory scheme for saving high precision constants of $1/\sqrt{2}$, $\sqrt{2}$, π, and several working storage with compression factor of 6 decimals / 4 bytes. (Integer representation was used for saving storages on the extended storage. For FFT, a 3 decimals / 8 bytes scheme - double precision floating point representation - was needed as explained.) These schemes needed about 240 Mb of main memory for the working storage, input and output (I/O) buffer, object codes, *etc.* As for the extended storage size, 13.5 Mb / 1 million decimal places was needed.

3.2. Optimization for Speedup

We have employed several optimization schemes:

1) Multiplication by 1 -> normal copy operation.
2) Multiplication by 2 -> normal addition operation.
3) Deletion of unnecessary FFA and FFS operations.
4) Reuse of internal iteration results.

For 1) and 2), explanation is simple enough. In the following two subsections, we explain the details of 3) and 4).

3.2.1. How to Delete FFA and FFS Operations

As explained in section 2.4, the school boy method was employed for multiple-precision multiplication (for data length longer than in-core operable length). Now as for an example of 4×4 school boy method, let consider the simple case of 2×2. That corresponds to the multiplication of two integers, both with a length of 3×2^{25} and in-core operable length of 3×2^{24}. Without optimization, each $2^{24} \times 1{,}000$ decimal based multiplication needs eight FFA for input and four FFS for output as follows;

$$(A_1 \times BASE + A_2) \times (B_1 \times BASE + B_2)$$
$$= (FFS\ of\ (FFA\ of\ A_1 \cdot FFA\ of\ B_1)) \times BASE^2$$
$$+((FFS\ of\ (FFA\ of\ A_1 \cdot FFA\ of\ B_2)) + (FFS\ of\ (FFA\ of\ A_2 \cdot FFA\ of\ B_1))) \times BASE$$

$+(FFS\ of\ (FFA\ of\ A_2 \cdot FFA\ of\ B_2))\ ,$

where $\cdot$ is the convolution product for the Fourier transformed data, + is the vector-wise addition and BASE is $2^{24} \times 1{,}000$.

There are very many FFA and FFS operations. These operations can be reduced a lot by the following schemes:

1) First apply FFA operations to A_1, A_2, B_1 and B_2. Let the results be A_1', A_2', B_1' and B_2', respectively.

2) Now $(A_1' \cdot B_2' + A_2' \cdot B_1')$ preserve information in the sense explained in section 2.4.

3) Then, the linearity of FFS operation satisfies the following equation:

$$\begin{aligned}
&(A_1 \times BASE + A_2) \times (B_1 \times BASE + B_2) \\
&= (FFS\ of\ (A_1' \cdot B_1')) \times BASE^2 + (FFS\ of\ (A_1' \cdot B_2' + A_2' \cdot B_1')) \times BASE \\
&\quad + (FFS\ of\ (A_2' \cdot B_2'))\ .
\end{aligned}$$

According to the results of CPU time profile analysis for 33 million decimal places calculation, multiplication occupies 90% of CPU time. (Here, CPU time does not contain the time for input and output operations.) Thus, this optimization is rather efficient when the length of multiplicand becomes long. (In this case, FFA operations was reduced from 8 to 4 and FFS operations was reduced from 4 to 3.)

3.2.2. Reuse of Internal Iteration Results

Newton's iteration for square roots and reciprocals has second order convergence nature. This implies that internal iteration results at the calculation of the half-length precision of π can be the initial value for the iteration at the calculation of the full-length precision of π. (And this selection is the best selection for reducing CPU time.) According to measurements of CPU time, this scheme reduced the CPU time 10-20% for the 16 or 33 million decimal places calculation.

If we utilize this fact, we can reduce the computation time probably by 10-20%. To do so, however, we had to prepare the permanent storage of about 1.5 Gb. This was completely impossible at the time of actual run. For the history of π calculation, we had saved the internal iteration results from the calculation of 16 million decimal places (data size is around 100 Mb). That data helped for the calculation of 32 million decimal places of π substantially. And also for the calculation of 16 million decimal places of π, we had utilized the internal iteration results from the calculation of 8 million decimal places.

4. Statistical Analysis of 200,000,000 Decimals of π

In order to analyze the statistics of 200,000,000 decimals of π, we used the same statistical tests as Pathria[13], except that the number of digits expanded from 100,000 to 200,000,000. In this section we briefly show the statistical data and some interesting figures from the 200,000,000 decimals of π. Now, the 200,000,000-th decimal number of $\pi - 3$ is 9.

4.1. Results of Statistical tests

Five kinds of statistical tests were performed. These are the frequency test, the serial tests, the Poker hand test, the gap test and the five-digit sum test. We have reproduced only the results of frequency test in the Table 3. The other results are to be published through the reference[7].

4.2. Some Interesting Figures

Analysis of digit sequences for 200,000,000 decimal places of $\pi - 3$ gives some interesting figures;

1) A longest descending sequence of 2109876543 appears (from 26,160,634) only once. The next longest descending sequence is 876543210 (from 2,747,956) only. The next longest descending sequence of length 8 appears 9 times.

2) The longest ascending sequence is 901234567 which appears from 197,090,144. The next longest ascending sequence is 23456789 (from 995,998), 89012345 (from 33,064,267, 39,202,678, 62,632,993 and 78,340,559), 90123456 (from 35,105,378, 44,994,887, 98,647,533 and 127,883,114), 56789012 (from 100,800,812 and 139,825,562), 67890123 (from 102,197,548, 135,721,079 and 178,278,161), 01234567 (from 112,099,767), 78901234 (from

119,172,322, 122,016,838, 182,288,028 and 195,692,744), 12345678 (from 186,557,266) and 45678901 (from 194,981,709). The next longest ascending sequence of length 7 appears 170 times.

3) A sequence of maximum multiplicity (of 9) appears 3 times. These are 7 (from 24,658,601), 6 (from 45,681,781) and 8 (from 46,663,520). The next longest sequence of multiplicity (of 8) appears 16 times.

4) The longest sequence of 27182818 appears from 73,154,827, 143,361,474 and 183,026,622. The next longest sequence of 2718281 appears 22 times.

5) The longest sequence of 14142135 appears from 52,638, 10,505,872 and 143,965,527. The next longest sequence of 1414213 appears from 13,816,189, 40,122,589, 72,670,122, 87,067,359, 104,717,213, 115,301,872, 145,035,762, 147,685,125, 155,299,021, 165,871,476, 166,005,277, 166,491,213 and 191,208,533. The next longest sequence of 141421 appears 169 times.

6) The longest sequence of 31415926 appears 2 times. These are from 50,366,472 and 157,060,182. The next longest sequence of 3141592 appears 7 times.

5. Conclusion

Details of 201,326,000 decimal digits of π calculation and some results of statistical tests on 200,000,000 decimals of π are presented. The original program is written in FORTRAN 77 and heavily utilizes floating point operations. Multiple-precision add, subtract and constant multiplication programs were also vectorized through linear recurrence special instruction. Programs do not depend on the scheme of round-off and cut-off to the results for the floating point operations. Then, not only round-off machine, e.g. supercomputers of CRAY Inc. and ETA systems, but also cut-off machine, e.g. Japanese supercomputers, can generate correct π digits. The program calls few system specific subroutines, e.g. CLOCK, TIME, but adaptation to the new machine is easy. In order to get speed, available main memory size is crucial and shorten elapsed time, availability of high speed I/O devices is also crucial. Thus, the π calculation program based on the scheme explained here can be a good benchmark program for the supercomputer.

We have programmed the fast multiple-precision multiplication through a *floating point real* FFT package, which was available as one of the program libraries. This means that half a hundred lines of code is sufficient for the fast multiple-precision multiplication. (A few lines of array declaration, one line for calling the FFA routine, a few lines of convolution products, one line for calling the FFS routine and a few lines of normalization under a suitable base.) These schemes would be of benefit to other high-precision constant and function calculations. And another scheme, high utilization of floating point operations in the processing of integers, is also favorable for the integer calculation, especially to number crunchers.

As the Table 1 shows, it took 12 years for extending the length of known π value from 100,000 to 1,000,000, 10 years from 1,000,000 to 10,000,000 and 4 years from 10,000,000 to the order of 100,000,000. When can we unveil the digits after 1,000,000,000, how and by whom?

6. Acknowledgments

The author would like to express my thanks to Mr. Yoshiaki Tamura for his collaboration with me and to Dr. Kazunori Miyoshi for utilizing his statistical analysis program for π. Thanks are also due to Mr. Akihiko Shibata for his information concerning the history of π calculation. I also thank to Hitachi Co. for giving me a chance to extend the length of π value.

Calculated by	Machine used	Date	Precision (calculated)	declared	correct	Time (check)	Formula (check)
Reitwiesner et al.	ENIAC	1949	(2040)		2037	~70h (~70h)	M(M)
Nicholson & Jeenel	NORC	1954	(3093)		3092	13m (13m)	M(M)
Felton	Pegasus	1957	(10021)		7480	33h (33h)	K(G)
Genuys	IBM 704	1958	(10000)		10000	1h 40m (1h 40m)	M(M)
Felton	Pegasus	"	(10021)		10020	33h (33h)	K(G)
Guilloud	IBM 704	1959	(16167)		16167	4.3h (4.3h)	M(M)
Shanks & Wrench	IBM 7090	1961	(100265)		100265	8h 43m (4h 22m)	S(G)
Guilloud & Filliatre	IBM 7030	1966	(250000)		250000	41h 55m (24h 35m)	G(S)
Guilloud & Dichampt	CDC 6600	1967	(500000)		500000	28h 10m (16h 35m)	G(S)
Guilloud & Bouyer	CDC 7600	1973	(1001250)		1001250	23h 18m (13h 40m)	G(S)
Miyoshi & Kanada	FACOM M-200	1981	(2000040)	2000000	2000036	137.3h (143.3h)	K(M)
Guilloud	x	1981-82	(x)	2000050	2000050	x (x)	x
Tamura	MELCOM 900II	1982	(2097152)		2097144	7h 14m (2h 21m)	L(L)
Tamura & Kanada	HITAC M-280H	"	(4194304)		4194288	2h 21m (6h 52m)	L(L)
Tamura & Kanada	"	"	(8388608)		8388576	6h 52m (< 30h)	L(L)
Kanada, Yoshino & Tamura	"	1983	(16777216)		16777206	< 30h (6h 36m)	L(L)
Ushiro & Kanada	HITAC S-810/20	1983 Oct.	(10013400)	10000000	10013395	< 24h (< 30h)	G(L)
Gosper	Symbolics 3670	1985 Oct.	(>=17526200)		17526200	x (28h)	R(B4)
Bailey	CRAY-2	1986 Jan.	(29360128)	29360000	29360111	28h (40h)	B4(B2)
Kanada & Tamura	HITAC S-810/20	1986 Sep.	(33554432)	33554000	33554414	6h 36m (23h)	L(L)
Kanada & Tamura	HITAC S-810/20	1986 Oct.	(67108864)		67108839	23h (35h 15m)	L(L)
Kanada, Tamura, Kubo etc.	NEC SX-2	1987 Jan.	(134214728)	133554000	134214700	35h 15m (48h 2m)	L(B4)
Kanada & Tamura	HITAC S-820/80	1988 Jan.	(201326572)	201326000	201326551	5h 57m (7h 30m)	L(B4)

Table 1. Historical records of the calculation of π performed on electronic computers. M, K, G, S, L, R, B4 and B2 are the formulae of Machin, Klingenstierna, Gauss, Störmer, and Gauss-Legendre, formula explained in the reference[3], Borwein's quartic convergent, Borwein's quadratic convergent, respectively. Symbol 'x' means 'unknown'. Check time means the additional time for the calculated value checking. This information was basically obtained from Mr. Shibata[18].

Type of operation	Brent et. al.	Borwein's quartic	Borwein's quadratic
$X^{1/2}$ *or* $X^{1/4}$	n	n	n
×	2n+2	5n	6n
reciprocal	1	n+1	2n
+,−	3n+1	6n	3n

Table 2. Comparison of basic, time consuming, operations in the three historically important algorithms for π calculation. Here n is a number of iterations. In order to compare with fare, both side columns numbers should be doubled.

Digit	0	1	2	3	4	5	6	7	8	9	χ^2
100	8	8	12	11	10	8	9	8	12	14	4.20
200	19	20	24	19	22	20	16	12	25	23	6.80
500	45	59	54	50	53	50	48	36	53	52	6.88
1k	93	116	103	102	93	97	94	95	101	106	4.74
2k	182	212	207	188	195	205	200	197	202	212	4.34
5k	466	532	496	459	508	525	513	488	492	521	10.77
10K	968	1026	1021	974	1012	1046	1021	970	948	1014	9.32
20K	1954	1997	1986	1986	2043	2082	2017	1953	1962	2020	7.72
50K	5033	5055	4867	4947	5011	5052	5018	4977	5030	5010	5.86
100K	9999	10137	9908	10025	9971	10026	10029	10025	9978	9902	4.09
200K	20104	20063	19892	20010	19874	20199	19898	20163	19956	19841	7.31
500K	49915	49984	49753	50000	50357	50235	49824	50230	49911	49791	7.73
1M	99959	99758	100026	100229	100230	100359	99548	99800	99985	100106	5.51
2M	199792	199535	200077	200141	200083	200521	199403	200310	199447	200691	9.00
4M	399419	399463	399822	399913	400792	400032	399032	400650	400183	400694	7.92
5M	499620	499898	499508	499933	500544	500025	498758	500880	499880	500954	7.88
8M	799111	800110	799788	800234	800202	800154	798885	800560	800638	800318	3.79
10M	999440	999333	1000306	999964	1001093	1000466	999337	1000207	999814	1000040	2.78
15M	1500081	1499675	1501044	1499917	1501166	1500417	1498447	1499584	1500435	1499234	4.07
20M	2001162	1999832	2001409	1999343	2001106	2000125	1999269	1998404	1999720	1999630	4.17
25M	2500496	2499915	2500707	2499313	2502826	2500139	2499603	2498290	2499189	2499522	5.28
30M	2999157	3000554	3000969	2999222	3002593	2999997	2999548	2998175	2999592	3000193	4.34
50M	4999632	5002220	5000573	4998630	5004009	4999797	4998017	4998895	4998494	4999733	6.17
80M	7998807	8002788	8001828	7997656	8003525	7996500	7998165	7999389	8000308	8001034	5.95
100M	9999922	10002475	10001092	9998442	10003863	9993478	9999417	9999610	10002180	9999521	7.27
150M	14998689	15001880	15001586	14999130	15003829	14993562	14998434	14999462	15001416	15002012	4.90
200M	19997437	20003774	20002185	20001410	19999846	19993031	19999161	20000287	20002307	20000562	4.13

Table 3. Summary of frequency for the first 200,000,000 digits of π - 3 and corresponding χ^2 values.

References

1. Bailey, D.H., "The Computation of πi to 29,360,000 Decimal Digits Using Borwein's Quartically Convergent Algorithm," *Math. Comp.*, vol. 50, no. 181, pp. 66-88, Jan. 1988.
2. Borwein, J.M. and Borwein, P.B., *Pi and the AGM - A study in Analytic Number Theory and Computational Complexity,* A Wiley-Interscience Publication, New York, 1987.
3. Borwein, J.M. and Borwein, P.B., "Ramanujan and Pi," *Scientific American*, vol. 258, pp. 66-73, Feb. 1988.
4. Brent, R.P., "Fast Multiple-Precision Evaluation of Elementary Functions," *J. ACM.*, vol. 23, no. 2, pp. 242-251, April 1976.
5. Brent, R.P., "Multiple-Precision Zero-Finding Methods and the Complexity of Elementary Function Evaluation," in *Analytic Computational Complexity*, ed. Traub, J.F., pp. 151-176, Academic Press, New York, 1976.
6. Gentleman, W.M. and Sande, G., "Fast Fourier Transforms - For Fun and Profit," *AFIPS Conf. Proc. FJCC*, vol. 29, pp. 563-578, Spartan Books, San Francisco, Calif., November 1966.
7. Kanada, Y., "Statistical Analysis of π up to 200,000,000 Decimal Places," CCUT-TR-88-02, in preparation, Computer Centre, University of Tokyo, Bunkyo-ku, Yayoi 2-11-16, Tokyo 113, Japan, Nov. 1988.
8. Tamura, Y., Yoshino, S., Ushiro, Y. and Kanada, Y., "Circular Constant - It's High Speed Calculation Method and Statistics -," in *Proceedings Programming Symposium, in Japanese*, Information Processing Society of Japan, Jan. 1984.
9. Tamura, Y. and Kanada, Y., "Calculation of π to 4,194,293 Decimals Based on the Gauss-Legendre Algorithm," CCUT-TR-83-01, Computer Centre, University of Tokyo, Bunkyo-ku, Yayoi 2-11-16, Tokyo 113, Japan, May 1983.
10. Kaneko, T. and Liu, B., "Accumulation of Round-Off Error in Fast Fourier Transforms," *J. ACM.*, vol. 17, no. 4, pp. 637-654, Oct. 1970.
11. Knuth, D.E., *The Art of Computer Programming, Vol. 2: Seminumerical Algorithms,* Addison-Wesley, Reading, Mass., 1981.
12. Laasonen, P., "On the Iterative Solution of the Matrix Equation A X^2 - I = 0," *Math. Tables and Other Aids to Comp.*, vol. 12, pp. 109-116, 1958.
13. Pathria, R.K., "A Statistical Study of Randomness Among the First 10,000 Digits of π," *Math. Comp.*, vol. 16, pp. 188-197, 1962.
14. Salamin, E., "Computation of π Using Arithmetic-Geometric Mean," *Math. Comp.*, vol. 30, no. 135, pp. 565-570, July 1976.
15. Schönhage, A. and Strassen, V., "Schnelle Multiplikation Grosser Zahlen," *Computing*, vol. 7, pp. 281-292, 1971.
16. Schutz, G., "Iterative Berechnung der Reziproken Matrix," *Z. Angew. Math. Mech.*, vol. 13, pp. 57-59, 1933.
17. Shanks, D. and Wrench, Jr. W., "Calculation of π to 100,000 Decimals," *Math. Comp.*, vol. 16, pp. 76-79, 1962.
18. Shibata, A., 1982-1983. Private communications
19. Tamura, Y., "Calculation of π to 2 Million Decimals Using Legendre-Gauss' Relation," Proceeding of the International Latitude Observatory of Mizusawa No.22 (in Japanese) in press, Internal Latitude Observatory of Mizusawa, Hoshigaoka-cho 2-12, Mizusawa City, 023 Iwate Prefecture, Japan, 1983.
20. Ushiro, Y., "Calculation of Multiple-Precision Numbers through Vectorizing Processor," in *Numerical Calculation Workshop, in Japanese*, Information Processing Society of Japan, 26-28 May. 1983.
21. Kanada, Y., Tamura, Y., Yoshino, S. and Ushiro, Y., "Calculation of π to 10,013,395 Decimal Places Based on the Gauss-Legendre Algorithm and Gauss Arctangent Relation," CCUT-TR-84-01, Computer Centre, University of Tokyo, Bunkyo-ku, Yayoi 2-11-16, Tokyo 113, Japan, Dec 1983.

ON BLOCK HOUSEHOLDER ALGORITHMS FOR THE REDUCTION OF A MATRIX TO HESSENBERG FORM

Augustin A. Dubrulle
IBM Scientific Center
1530 Page Mill Road
Palo Alto CA 94304

ABSTRACT: This paper presents a block algorithm for the Householder reduction of a matrix to Hessenberg form using the Bischof-Van Loan expression of a product of elementary matrices. Results of performance measurements on an IBM 3090 VF include a comparison with an alternate formulation considered for LAPACK.

0. INTRODUCTION

The advent of super-computers has prompted much recent reshaping of numerical algorithms for efficiency, notably in the area of matrix computations [1, 3-6]. In the design of algorithms for high-speed machines, the minimization of data traffic between memory and arithmetic units has become a performance objective as important as the minimization of arithmetic operations. An answer to this challenge is provided by the use of block algorithms that trade some extra arithmetic for substantial savings in memory updates and allow for the use of very effective extensions of the Basic Linear Algebra Subprograms [5, 11] tuned for specific architectures (see for example IBM's ESSL package [13-14]).

This paper discusses block formulations of the Householder reduction of a matrix to Hessenberg form, and reports some relative performance measurements conducted with an IBM 3090 VF, using one processor. Section 1 outlines the relevant features of the IBM 3090 VF and the VS FORTRAN Version 2 Release 3 vectorizing compiler. The block formulations of products of elementary matrices are summarized in Section 2. Algorithms for the reduction to Hessenberg form are described in Section 3, one akin to a LAPACK design [6], another explicitly based on a Bischof-Van Loan form of the product of Householder matrices [1]. Section 4 summarizes some empirical observations on the relationship between block size and processing efficiency. Sample performance measurements are reported in the Appendix for long-precision computations with pseudo-random matrices. The mathematical notation is from [2].

1. COMPUTING ENVIRONMENT

The central processors of the IBM 3090 VF include vector and scalar arithmetic units fed by a cache. The operands of vector floating-point instructions can be memory sections of μ elements, vector registers of same capacity, and scalar registers. The results are returned in vector registers. The register capacity or section size μ is a model-dependent power of two. Because of the hierarchical memory, best efficiency is achieved in those numerical computations for which data references follow a unit-stride pattern. Hence, matrix algorithms designed for FORTRAN are preferably expressed in terms of vector operations on columns successively fetched in natural order (for more details, see [7]). In the following, programming constructs pertinent to the FORTRAN implementation of block methods are briefly discussed.

The vectorizing FORTRAN compiler usually generates the obvious machine vector operations from programming constructs representing simple combinations of

scalar products	$\sigma \leftarrow \mathbf{x}^T \mathbf{y}$,
elementary linear combinations	$\mathbf{x} \leftarrow \mathbf{x} + \alpha \mathbf{y}$.

As the hardware can perform the above operations on vectors of dimension μ , compiler translations involve a "sectioning": entities recognized as vectors in a FORTRAN sequence containing DO statements are consistently partitioned in "sections" of dimension μ (one section possibly being smaller) and the prescribed computations are expressed in terms of hardware operations on these sections. For illustration, consider the code representing an elementary linear combination:

```
      do 20 i = 1 , n
20    x(i) = x(i) + α * y(i)
```

The FORTRAN representation of machine operation would approximately be

```
      do 20 is = 1 , n , μ
        do 10 i = is , min (n , is + μ - 1)
10      x ( i ) = x ( i ) + α * y ( i )
20    continue
```

where loop " *do* 10 ", actually replaced by vector instructions, is the operation on a pair of corresponding sections of **x** and **y**, while loop " *do* 20 " represents the sectioning operation.
In the presence of nested loops, the compiler performs an analysis of the computations and decides which loop will be "vectorized" based on mutual variable dependences and time estimates of loop overhead, hardware intructions, and operand retrieval and storage. Conceptually, the vectorization of a loop consists of its replacement by the appropriate sectioning loop, and the insertion of a loop at the innermost level for the computation on individual sections, actually representing vector instructions. In the process, depending on the constructs of the original code, very efficient vector operation can be obtained.
This general principle is illustrated by the code for the transformation of a vector by a matrix, $\mathbf{y} = \mathbf{A}\,\mathbf{x}$, $\mathbf{A} \in \mathbb{R}^{m \times n}$,

```
      do 50 i = 1 , m
      s = 0
        do 30 j = 1 , n                                  (1.1)
30      s = s + x ( j ) * a ( i , j )
50    y ( i ) = s
```

The corresponding code describing machine operation is displayed below. Its innermost loop " *do* 20 " is executed in a single vector instruction.

```
      do 50 is = 1 , m , μ
         do 10 i = is,  min ( n , is + μ − 1)
10       reg ( i ) = 0
         do 30 j = 1 , n
            do 20 i = is,  min ( n , is + μ − 1)                    (1.2)
20          reg ( i ) = reg ( i ) + x ( j ) * a ( i , j )
30       continue
         do 40 i = is,  min ( n , is + μ − 1)
40       y ( i ) = reg ( i )
50    continue
```

This translation deserves a few comments. First, note that whereas code (1.1) prescribes scalar products in which the stride for the matrix elements is the (large) first dimension of the array, code (1.2) forms elementary linear combinations of unit-stride sections of the columns of the matrix. Second, the scalar variable s of (1.1) has been replaced by **reg**, a machine vector register accommodating up to μ elements, which allows the computation of each section of **y** to be executed in only n vector instructions for computation proper ("*do* 30") and one for storage ("*do* 40"). In short, the compiler is clever enough to recognize s as a temporary variable and to replace it by another more efficient for vector operation. This approach extends to the matrix product $\mathbf{C} = \mathbf{A}\,\mathbf{B}$, $\mathbf{A} \in \mathbb{R}^{\ell \times m}$ and $\mathbf{B} \in \mathbb{R}^{m \times n}$, as follows:

```
      do 50 i = 1 , ℓ
        do 40 j = 1 , n
        s = 0
           do 30 k = 1 , m
30         s = s + b ( k , j ) * a ( i , k )
40      c ( i , j ) = s
50    continue
```

Optimum vector translation, illustrated by code (1.2), is possible only if, roughly speaking, there is enough independence between loop levels to allow for loop interchange. A simple example for which this condition is not satisfied is provided by the multiplication of a vector by a lower-triangular matrix. There, a dependence between loop parameters prevents a construct similar to code (1.1) to produce an efficient compiler translation, and makes the formulation below much preferable for cache usage when the matrix is large (the notation is the same as above, with $m = n$):

```
      do 10 i = 1 , n
10    y ( i ) = 0
      do 50 j = 1 , n
         do 30 i = j , n
30       y( i ) = y( i ) + x ( j ) * a ( i , j )
50    continue
```

It must be noted, however, that this construct is computationally less efficient than the matrix-vector multiplication (1.1), as each inner elementary linear combination "*do* 30" requires a copy to storage explicitly prescribed by the code.

Consider now the operation $\mathbf{y}^T = \mathbf{x}^T \mathbf{A}$, and its natural FORTRAN implementation below:

```
      do 50 j = 1 , n
      s = 0
        do 30 i = 1 , m
30      s = s + x ( i ) * a ( i ,j )
50    y (j) = s
```

The latest version of the compiler (VS FORTRAN Version 2 Release 3) usually vectorizes the outer loop " *do* 50 " to activate the register-based elementary linear combination at the core of code (1.2). This translation essentially builds the result as a linear combination of the rows of the matrix, and implies a stride equal to the first dimension of the matrix array. If the matrix is nearly contained in the cache, this translation produces the most efficient vector computation of **y**. If it is not, performance can be seriously impaired by cache misses, and it is appropriate to request vectorization for the innermost loop " *do* 30 " by using a compiler directive [10] , as illustrated below ("directive:" is the trigger word).

```
      do 50 j = 1 , n
      s = 0
c     directive: prefer vector
        do 30 i = 1 , m                                    (1.3)
30      s = s + x ( i ) * a ( i ,j )
50    y (j) = s
```

The translation of this code produces unit-stride computations of scalar products, suitable for larger matrices, but somewhat less efficient than the register-based computation (1.2). As block methods are intended for large matrices, their implementations will use code (1.3) where applicable.

Additional performance gains for basic matrix operations can be achieved with FORTRAN code tailored to machine architecture [12]. Such techniques were not used here for algorithm clarity, and because of their explicit dependence on machine parameters.

Finally, best vector operation with the 3090 VF is obtained for matrix algorithms that call on the Basic Linear Algebra Subprograms (BLAS) of the IBM Engineering and Scientific Subroutine Library (ESSL Release 2) described in [13-14]. This library includes three levels of BLAS for vector-to-vector, matrix-to-vector, and matrix-to-matrix operations, implemented in assembler code for optimum use of the machine's architecture. The measurements reported in the Appendix exemplify the effect of tuned level-3 BLAS on the performance of block methods, and supports the general design of LAPACK [3].

2. PRODUCTS OF ELEMENTARY MATRICES

This section summarizes the algorithms leading to the Bischof-Van Loan expressions [1] of a product of elementary matrices

$$\Phi_\ell = \mathbf{T}_\ell \mathbf{T}_{\ell-1} \ \cdots \ \mathbf{T}_1 \,, \qquad \mathbf{T}_j = \mathbf{I} + \mathbf{u}_j \mathbf{v}_j^T \,, \qquad \mathbf{u}_j \,,\ \mathbf{v}_j \in \mathbb{R}^n \,, \tag{2.1}$$

as a rank-ℓ modification of the identity matrix.

The postulated formulation is evident when $\ell = 1$. A little algebra with low values of ℓ quickly reveals two possible forms:

$$\mathbf{\Phi}_\ell = \mathbf{I} + \mathbf{X}_\ell \mathbf{V}_\ell^T, \tag{2.2}$$

and

$$\mathbf{\Phi}_\ell = \mathbf{I} + \mathbf{U}_\ell \mathbf{Y}_\ell^T, \tag{2.3}$$

where

$$\mathbf{U}_\ell = \sum_{i=1}^{\ell} \mathbf{u}_i \mathbf{e}_i^T, \qquad \mathbf{V}_\ell = \sum_{i=1}^{\ell} \mathbf{v}_i \mathbf{e}_i^T,$$

and $\mathbf{X}_\ell$ and $\mathbf{Y}_\ell$ are matrices derived from both $\mathbf{U}_\ell$ and $\mathbf{V}_\ell$.
A combination of equation (2.1) in the form

$$\mathbf{\Phi}_k = \mathbf{T}_k(\mathbf{I} + \mathbf{X}_{k-1} \mathbf{V}_{k-1}^T)$$

with equation (2.2) yields the constructive definition of $\mathbf{X}_k$:

$$\mathbf{X}_k = \mathbf{T}_k \mathbf{X}_{k-1} + \mathbf{u}_k \mathbf{e}_k^T, \qquad k = 2, \ldots, \ell, \qquad \mathbf{X}_1 = \mathbf{U}_1 . \tag{2.4}$$

A similar approach applied to formula (2.3) leads to

$$\mathbf{Y}_k = \mathbf{Y}_{k-1} + (\mathbf{\Phi}_{k-1}^T \mathbf{v}_k) \mathbf{e}_k^T, \qquad k = 2, \ldots ; \ell, \qquad \mathbf{Y}_1 = \mathbf{V}_1 . \tag{2.5}$$

The error analysis in [1] shows that algorithms based on formulations (2.2) and (2.4), or (2.3) and (2.5), are numerically stable when the elementary matrices (2.1) are Householder reflectors, characterized by

$$\mathbf{u}_j = -2 \, \| \mathbf{v}_j \|_2^{-2} \, \mathbf{v}_j .$$

The usefulness of the forms (2.2) and (2.3) is related to the use of supercomputers, for which the time spent in storing the result of an elementary arithmetic operation is practically the same as the time taken by that operation. In such a context, in spite of the extra work implied in the construction of $\mathbf{X}_\ell$ or $\mathbf{Y}_\ell$, the application of a single block transformation (2.2) or (2.3) to a matrix can be more economical of computing time than k successive multiplications by elementary matrices requiring much memory traffic for operand retrieval and storage of intermediate results. Moreover, natural implementations using tuned level-3 BLAS easily allow for additional computing efficiency.
The parameter ℓ determines the amount of computation needed to form $\mathbf{X}_\ell$ or $\mathbf{Y}_\ell$ and thereby controls the performance gain. Its optimum value depends on n and on both system and program characteristics, as we shall see in later sections. Obviously, a block version of a numerical algorithm requires extra storage for a few arrays of size $n \times \ell$, but without much inconvenience, as the optimal values of ℓ are generally modest.
Note that formulations (2.2) and (2.3) generalize the transformations described in [4], and that the above derivations can be extended to the complex case without difficulty.

For simplicity, formulas (2.2) and (2.3) will be referred to as the X and Y forms of $\mathbf{\Phi}_k$. The same designation applies to the corresponding block algorithms discussed in later sections.

3. REDUCTION OF A MATRIX TO UPPER-HESSENBERG FORM

Given $\mathbf{A} \in \mathbb{R}^{n \times n}$, its Hessenberg form $\mathbf{A}^{(n-2)}$ is obtained by successive Householder similarity transformations

$$\begin{aligned} \mathbf{A}^{(0)} &= \mathbf{A}\,, \\ \mathbf{A}^{(k)} &= (\mathbf{I} + \mathbf{u}_k \mathbf{v}_k^T)\,\mathbf{A}^{(k-1)}(\mathbf{I} + \mathbf{v}_k \mathbf{u}_k^T)\,, \qquad k = 1, \ldots, n-2\,, \end{aligned} \tag{3.1}$$

where $\mathbf{u}_k$ and $\mathbf{v}_k$ are defined so that (see, for example, [9]):

$$\mathbf{a}_k^{(k)} = (\mathbf{I} + \mathbf{u}_k \mathbf{v}_k^T)\,\mathbf{a}_k^{(k-1)}\,, \qquad \mathbf{e}_i^T \mathbf{a}_k^{(k)} = 0\,, \qquad i = k+2, \ldots, n\,. \tag{3.2}$$

The above equations generate straightforward FORTRAN implementations denoted HS (for scalar operation) and HV (for vector operation), which will provide a reference for comparative performance measurements. These routines make efficient use of the compiler and system features, along the lines sketched in Section 1. The storage organization follows the customary pattern whereby the nontrivial elements of the Hessenberg matrix and the significant components of the successive $\mathbf{u}_k$ vectors overwrite the original matrix in its array (the storage of the set $\{\mathbf{u}_k\}$ is "free"). The scaling constants producing $\{\mathbf{v}_k\}$ from $\{\mathbf{u}_k\}$ are stored in a separate array of $n-2$ cells. This scheme is used in all the implementations discussed in this paper.

The recurrence defined by formulas (3.1) and (3.2) reveals the main difficulty inherent in the construction of block methods for similarity transformations. In contrast with matrix triangularization [1, 8] , the definition of the kth Householder reflector actually depends on the previous transformations of the whole matrix, and not on transformations of $\mathbf{a}_k$ alone. This makes the block form of similarity transformations fairly complex, but not much more in principle than scalar "left-looking" unit-stride algorithms performing the same function.

To simplify matters, the following derivations will be restricted to the reduction of the leading ℓ columns of a matrix, and the associated transformation of the $n-\ell$ trailing columns (the whole process can be seen as a succession of such operations applied to submatrices). Two block forms of this computation will be discussed, one considered for LAPACK in [6], the other directly derived from the formulations of Section 2.

By simple expansion of the second of equations (3.1), one gets

$$\begin{aligned} \mathbf{A}^{(k)} &= \mathbf{A}^{(k-1)} + \mathbf{u}_k \mathbf{p}_k^T + \mathbf{q}_k \mathbf{u}_k^T\,, \\ \mathbf{p}_k &= \mathbf{A}^{(k-1)T} \mathbf{v}_k + \sigma_k \mathbf{u}_k\,, \\ \mathbf{q}_k &= \mathbf{A}^{(k-1)} \mathbf{v}_k + \sigma_k \mathbf{u}_k\,, \\ \sigma_k &= \frac{1}{2} \mathbf{v}_k^T \mathbf{A}^{(k-1)} \mathbf{v}_k\,. \end{aligned}$$

This formulation is well-known for its applicability to the symmetric case (see, for example, [9]).

A similar derivation for nonsymmetric matrices yields the equivalent and simpler expression

$$\begin{aligned}
\mathbf{A}^{(k)} &= \mathbf{A}^{(k-1)} + \mathbf{u}_k \mathbf{p}_k^T + \mathbf{q}_k \mathbf{u}_k^T , \\
\mathbf{q}_k &= \mathbf{A}^{(k-1)} \mathbf{v}_k , \\
\mathbf{p}_k &= \mathbf{A}^{(k-1)T} \mathbf{v}_k + (\mathbf{q}_k^T \mathbf{v}_k) \mathbf{u}_k .
\end{aligned} \tag{3.3}$$

From the first of equations (3.3), a block form of the transformation is immediate:

$$\mathbf{A}^{(k)} = \mathbf{A} + \mathbf{U}_k \mathbf{P}_k^T + \mathbf{Q}_k \mathbf{U}_k^T , \tag{3.4}$$

where

$$\mathbf{P}_k = \sum_{j=1}^{k} \mathbf{p}_j \mathbf{e}_j^T , \qquad \mathbf{Q}_k = \sum_{j=1}^{k} \mathbf{q}_j \mathbf{e}_j^T .$$

Equations (3.3) and (3.4) actually describe a LAPACK-like algorithm, for which $\mathbf{u}_k$ and $\mathbf{v}_k$ are defined through equations (3.2) by

$$\mathbf{a}_k^{(k-1)} = \mathbf{a}_k + \mathbf{U}_{k-1} (\mathbf{P}_{k-1}^T \mathbf{e}_k) + \mathbf{Q}_{k-1} (\mathbf{U}_{k-1}^T \mathbf{e}_k) ,$$

and where the reduction of the leading ℓ columns includes the computation (3.3) of $\mathbf{p}_k$ and $\mathbf{q}_k$, $k = 1, \dots , \ell$, to produce $\mathbf{P}_\ell$ and $\mathbf{Q}_\ell$. There, the identity

$$\mathbf{A}^{(k-1)} = \mathbf{A} + \mathbf{U}_{k-1} \mathbf{P}_{k-1}^T + \mathbf{Q}_{k-1} \mathbf{U}_{k-1}^T$$

is used without actual computation of $\mathbf{A}^{(k-1)}$. The block update of the trailing columns of the matrix is then performed according to the equation

$$\mathbf{A}^{(\ell)} = \mathbf{A} + \mathbf{U}_\ell \mathbf{P}_\ell^T + \mathbf{Q}_\ell \mathbf{U}_\ell^T . \tag{3.5}$$

An all-FORTRAN implementation HL of this algorithm delivers the substantial performance gains displayed in the Appendix. Further enhancements are obtained from a version HLBLAS calling upon ESSL level-3 BLAS for the matrix updates (3.5). These routines use two $n \times \ell$ arrays of ancillary storage to hold the pair $\mathbf{P}_k$ and $\mathbf{Q}_k$ of each block step.

As shown below, the LAPACK algorithm is essentially a special application of the Y form of the product of Householder matrices, where the Y matrices are not explicitly computed. Using the notation of Section 2, one has

$$\begin{aligned}
\mathbf{A}^{(k)} &= (\mathbf{I} + \mathbf{U}_k \mathbf{Y}_k^T) \mathbf{A} (\mathbf{I} + \mathbf{Y}_k \mathbf{U}_k^T) , \\
&= \mathbf{A} + \mathbf{U}_k (\mathbf{A}^T \mathbf{Y}_k + \mathbf{U}_k \mathbf{Y}_k^T \mathbf{A}^T \mathbf{Y}_k)^T + (\mathbf{A} \mathbf{Y}_k) \mathbf{U}_k^T
\end{aligned}$$

where the parentheses in the second equation isolate the expressions of $\mathbf{P}_k$ and $\mathbf{Q}_k$ in terms of $\mathbf{U}_k$ and $\mathbf{Y}_k$.

Good as they are, the performance gains obtained from HL still were found a little disappointing, based on past experience with other Householder block computations (see, for example, the triangularization in [8]). This prompted the exploration of alternate schemes, among which a "plain" X formulation of the reduction was the most obvious choice. This algorithm is derived below.

Assume that the leading $k-1$ columns have been reduced to Hessenberg form, $k \leq l < n$, and that the matrices $\mathbf{X}_{k-1}$ and $\mathbf{V}_{k-1}$ have been generated in the process. Conceptually, a matrix

$$\mathbf{A}^{(k-1)} = (\mathbf{I} + \mathbf{X}_{k-1}\mathbf{V}_{k-1}^T)\,\mathbf{A}\,(\mathbf{I} + \mathbf{V}_{k-1}\mathbf{X}_{k-1}^T), \tag{3.6}$$

can be associated with this stage of the process. Its kth column alone determines the kth reflector of the reduction, and can be computed as

$$\begin{aligned} \mathbf{a}_k^{(k-1)} &= (\mathbf{I} + \mathbf{X}_{k-1}\mathbf{V}_{k-1}^T)(\mathbf{a}_k + \mathbf{W}_{k-1}\mathbf{X}_{k-1}^T\mathbf{e}_k), \\ \mathbf{W}_{k-1} &= \mathbf{A}\,\mathbf{V}_{k-1}, \end{aligned} \tag{3.7}$$

by post-multiplication of equation (3.6) by $\mathbf{e}_k$. Through equations (3.2), $\mathbf{a}_k^{(k-1)}$ produces the vectors $\mathbf{u}_k$ and $\mathbf{v}_k$, and column k of the Hessenberg matrix. $\mathbf{X}_k$ and $\mathbf{V}_k$ are then obtained by

$$\mathbf{X}_k = (\mathbf{I} + \mathbf{u}_k\mathbf{v}_k^T)\,\mathbf{X}_{k-1} + \mathbf{u}_k\mathbf{e}_k^T, \qquad \mathbf{V}_k = \mathbf{V}_{k-1} + \mathbf{v}_k\mathbf{e}_k^T.$$

$\mathbf{W}_k$, introduced in the second of equations (3.7), can be constructed step-wise by forming

$$\mathbf{W}_k = \mathbf{W}_{k-1} + \mathbf{A}\,\mathbf{v}_k\mathbf{e}_k^T, \qquad k = 2, \dots, n, \qquad \mathbf{W}_1 = \mathbf{A}\,\mathbf{v}_1\mathbf{e}_1^T.$$

Starting with equations (3.7), the above defines a procedure for the reduction of the first ℓ columns of $\mathbf{A}$ to Hessenberg form and the computation of $\mathbf{X}_\ell$ and $\mathbf{V}_\ell$. The $n-\ell$ trailing columns of the matrix are then transformed according to

$$\mathbf{A}^{(\ell)} = (\mathbf{I} + \mathbf{X}_\ell\mathbf{V}_\ell^T)(\mathbf{A} + \mathbf{W}_\ell\mathbf{X}_\ell^T), \tag{3.8}$$

derived from equation (3.6) and the second of equations (3.7).

The performance gains obtained from an all-FORTRAN implementation HX of this algorithm are shown in the Appendix, together with those delivered by an HXBLAS version calling on ESSL level-3 BLAS for the matrix updates (3.8). They are noticeably superior to the gains from HL and HLBLAS for the same requirements of ancillary storage. Similar results should be expected from the corresponding implementations of a "plain" Y formulation.

In addition to inferior performance, HL has another drawback. Although it is essentially a Y algorithm, the underlying Y matrices are not available for the efficient block computation of the product of all the transformations leading to the Hessenberg form (e.g., as a first step in the computation of eigenvectors). By contrast, the product of the transformations can be incorporated in Algorithm HX with the full performance benefits of block operation by taking at each block step the contribution of the corresponding X matrix.

The above observations strongly suggest that algorithms based on Bischof-Van Loan formulations (Algorithms HX, HXBLAS, or their Y counterparts) should be preferred for the machine considered here.

4. BLOCK SIZE AND PERFORMANCE GAINS

Experiments with the above methods show that the values of ℓ producing best performance lie in intervals the bounds of which are dependent on the algorithm used, the matrix order, system characteristics, and program parameters (e.g., FORTRAN first dimension of two-dimensional arrays). The "optimum" values of ℓ displayed in the Appendix correspond approximately to the left bounds of such intervals, determined experimentally for best performance and economy of ancillary storage. These values are generally modest, increase with matrix order, and appear to have an asymptotic limit. To keep things simple, matrix orders and leading dimensions of the associated FORTRAN arrays were made to coincide in all experiments.

While no obstacle seems to stand in the way of the analytic estimation of the optimum value of ℓ for a given matrix order, efforts in that direction have produced disappointing results, and have generated more questions than answers. For example, it is *a priori* questionable that best performance should be achieved with constant block size throughout the reduction. Other considerations, however, indicate that further significant improvements might be hard to obtain. Note, for example, the best gain produced by Algorithm HXBLAS for matrices of order 700 in the Appendix. Assuming that this gain is measured for a reasonably efficient scalar algorithm HS, its value is remarkably high (near 7) when compared to the limit speed-up 8.1 attained in the ESSL library for matrix multiplication [14].

In the absence of reliable algorithms for the estimation of the optimum block size, it is somewhat comforting that substantial gains can still be obtained even when ℓ is far from its optimum value. For example, a fixed value $\ell = 6$ yields satisfactory gains with algorithm HX for matrix orders ranging from 100 to 700 (Appendix B), still better than the best results produced by HL. Hence, in computations with large matrices, the use of HX with blocks markedly smaller than optimum can realize a good compromise between performance and use of ancillary storage when the latter must be managed with parsimony. It is even conceivable that such an approach would advantageously compete with algorithms based on the compact representation of products of Householder matrices [17] for the same memory requirements.

It can be noted that the optimum block sizes for HX are larger than those for HL. This should not be surprising, as some of the matrix-vector operations required in HL for the construction of $\mathbf{P}_\ell$ and $\mathbf{Q}_\ell$ are replaced in HX by matrix-matrix operations embedded in the matrix updates (3.8). The net result is that the computational overhead inherent in the use of block methods is performed more efficiently in HX, allowing for larger blocks.

5. CONCLUSION

The computing efficiency obtained from high-performance machines with block methods is generally impressive, and especially so when the basic matrix operations are carried out with tuned level-3 BLAS. The key element to "squeezing the most" out of block algorithms is the determination of the optimum block size, requiring the modelling of a combination of algorithm and system characteristics. This problem seemingly remains to be solved, but experiments show that substantial performance gains can still be obtained for block dimensions far from optimum.

The algorithms based on the straightforward application of the Bischof-Van Loan formulations consistently appear to produce the best performance in all experiments conducted with the IBM 3090 VF. It is likely that such a behavior should be observed with other machines, but this conjecture remains to be tested. The algorithmic derivations presented in this paper are general enough to apply to other computational schemes based on similarity transformations, including those for the solution of the Hessenberg eigenvalue problem (QR).

6. REFERENCES

1. C. Bischof and C. Van Loan (1987), "The WY representation for Products of Householder Matrices", SIAM J. Sci. Stat. Comp., Vol. 8, No.1.
2. E. Bodewig (1959), Matrix Calculus, North-Holland Publishing Company, Amsterdam.
3. J. Demmel, J.J. Dongarra, J. DuCroz, A. Greenbaum, S. Hammarling, and D. Sorensen (1987), "Prospectus for the Development of a Linear Algebra Library for High-Performance Computers", Tech. Memo. No. 97, Math. and Comp. Sci. Div., Argonne National Laboratory.
4. J.J. Dongarra, L. Kaufman, and S. Hammarling (1986), "Squeezing the Most out of Eigenvalue Solvers on High-Performance Computers", Lin. Alg. and its Appl., Vol. 77, pp. 113-136.
5. J.J. Dongarra, J. DuCroz, I. Duff, and S. Hammarling (1987a), "A Proposal for a Set of Level-3 Basic Linear Algebra Subprograms", Tech. Memo. no. 88, Math. and Comp. Sci. Division, Argonne National Laboratory.
6. J.J. Dongarra, S. Hammarling, and D. Sorensen (1987b), "Block Reduction of Matrices to Condensed Forms for Eigenvalue Computations", LAPACK Working Note #2, Tech. Memo. no. 99, Math. and Comp. Sci. Division, Argonne National Laboratory.
7. A.A. Dubrulle, H.G. Kolsky, and R.G. Scarborough (1985), "How to Write Good Vectorizable FORTRAN", Technical Report G320-3478, IBM Scientific Center, Palo Alto CA.
8. A.A. Dubrulle (1988), "On Block Householder Algorithms", Technical Report G320-3515, IBM Scientific Center, Palo Alto CA.
9. G.H. Golub and C.F. Van Loan (1983), Matrix Computations, the Johns Hopkins University Press, Baltimore MD.
10. IBM (1988), VS FORTRAN Version 2 Release 3, Programming Guide SC26-4222-3.
11. C. Lawson, R. Hanson, D. Kincaid, and R. Krogh (1979), "Basic Linear Algebra Subprograms for FORTRAN Usage", ACM Trans. Math. Soft., Vol. 5, pp. 308-323.
12. B. Liu and N. Strother (1988), "Programming in VS FORTRAN on the IBM 3090 for Maximum Vector Performance", Computer, Vol. 21, No. 6.

13. J. McComb, D. Kapple, and S. Schmidt (1987a), "Engineering and Scientific Subroutine Library (ESSL)", TR 21.1058, IBM Data Systems Division, Kingston NY.
14. J. McComb, D. Kapple, and S. Schmidt (1987b), "Engineering and Scientific Subroutine Library Release 2 -- Performance on the IBM 3090 VF", TR 21.1059, IBM Data Systems Division, Kingston NY.
15. A. Padegs, B.B. Moore, R.M. Smith, and W. Buchholz (1988), "The IBM System/370 Vector Architecture: Design Considerations", IEEE Trans. Comp., Vol. 37, No. 5.
16. R.G. Scarborough and H.G. Kolsky (1986), "A Vectorizing FORTRAN Compiler", IBM J. Res. Dev., Vol. 30, No. 2.
17. R. Schreiber and C. Van Loan (1987), "A Storage-Efficient WY Representation for Products of Householder Transformations", Tech. Rep. CS-87-864, Cornell University.

APPENDIX: PERFORMANCE GAINS WITH THE IBM 3090 VF

For each algorithm, the performance gains (speed-ups) below were measured with reference to the execution times of Algorithm HS (scalar operation) and Algorithm HV (vector operation).

Optimum block size for HL

n	ℓ	HV	HL	HX	HLBLAS	HXBLAS
100	6	3.2 1.0	3.3 1.0	3.3 1.0	3.9 1.2	4.1 1.3
200	10	3.4 1.0	4.1 1.2	4.4 1.3	4.9 1.4	5.3 1.6
300	10	3.5 1.0	4.5 1.3	4.8 1.4	5.3 1.5	5.7 1.6
400	12	3.6 1.0	4.7 1.3	5.3 1.5	5.7 1.6	6.3 1.8
500	12	3.6 1.0	4.8 1.3	5.5 1.5	5.9 1.6	6.6 1.8
600	12	3.6 1.0	4.9 1.4	5.6 1.6	6.0 1.7	6.7 1.9
700	12	3.6 1.0	4.9 1.4	5.6 1.6	6.0 1.7	6.7 1.9

Optimum block size for HX

n	ℓ	*HV*	*HL*	*HX*	*HLBLAS*	*HXBLAS*
100	12	3.2	3.1	3.4	3.6	4.1
		1.0	1.0	1.1	1.1	1.3
200	14	3.4	4.0	4.5	4.7	5.3
		1.0	1.2	1.3	1.4	1.6
300	16	3.5	4.4	5.0	5.3	5.9
		1.0	1.3	1.4	1.5	1.7
400	16	3.6	4.6	5.3	5.6	6.4
		1.0	1.3	1.5	1.6	1.8
500	16	3.6	4.7	5.5	5.9	6.7
		1.0	1.3	1.5	1.6	1.9
600	16	3.6	4.9	5.6	6.0	6.8
		1.0	1.4	1.6	1.7	1.9
700	16	3.6	4.7	5.6	5.9	6.8
		1.0	1.3	1.6	1.6	1.9

Fixed small block size

n	ℓ	*HV*	*HL*	*HX*	*HLBLAS*	*HXBLAS*
100	6	3.2	3.3	3.3	3.9	4.1
		1.0	1.0	1.0	1.2	1.3
200	6	3.4	4.0	4.1	4.7	4.8
		1.0	1.2	1.2	1.4	1.4
300	6	3.5	4.2	4.4	4.9	5.1
		1.0	1.2	1.3	1.4	1.5
400	6	3.6	4.4	4.7	5.3	5.5
		1.0	1.2	1.3	1.5	1.6
500	6	3.6	4.5	4.9	5.5	5.7
		1.0	1.2	1.3	1.5	1.6
600	6	3.6	4.5	4.9	5.5	5.8
		1.0	1.2	1.4	1.5	1.6
700	6	3.6	4.6	5.0	5.5	5.8
		1.0	1.3	1.4	1.5	1.6

ADAPTATION OF THE ISODATA CLUSTERING ALGORITHM FOR VECTOR SUPERCOMPUTER EXECUTION[1]

Gregory A. Riccardi
Peter H. Schow[2]

Department of Computer Science
and
Supercomputer Computations Research Institute
Florida State University
Tallahassee, FL 32306

Cluster Analysis is an interdisciplinary study which involves the grouping of similar objects based on their measured attributes. The purpose of a Cluster Analysis is to investigate the structure and organization of the objects being studied. Described here in detail is the adaptation of the ISODATA clustering algorithm for vector supercomputer execution. On the CYBER 205, this new algorithm runs 30 times faster than the original algorithm on the CYBER 205 using full automatic vectorization and 300 times faster than a VAX 11/780. The major source of improvement over automatic vectorization is achieved by reorganizing the data structures used by the program. The new algorithm will yield increased performance on any vector computer.

INTRODUCTION

The field of Cluster Analysis involves partitioning a set of objects into groups such that objects within each group are similar in some respect. The objective of a Cluster Analysis is to find groups whose members are as alike as possible to each other. The resultant groups or "clusters" can be used to analyze and interpret the structure of the entire set of objects. Important applications of Cluster Analysis occur in the fields of pattern recognition, biology, zoology, and medicine [5].

Cluster Analysis is a new field that has emerged in the last two and a half decades. Its development has been greatly motivated by the advancement and availability of digital computers. The ISODATA[3] procedure, developed by Ball and Hall [1], is a technique for performing a cluster analysis on a given set of input objects.

---

[1]This research is supported in part by the Florida State University through time granted on its Cyber 205 supercomputer and by U.S. Department of Energy contract no. DE-FC05-85ER250000. Electronic mail addresses: `riccardi@nu.cs.fsu.edu` and `schow@burroughs-dev-2.arpa`.

[2]Current address Unisys Corporation, 445 Devon Park Drive, Wayne, PA 19087.

[3]ISODATA stands for "*I*terative *S*elf-*O*rganizing *D*ata *A*nalysis *T*echnique (plus an extra *A*).

In this study, the ISODATA algorithm is implemented on the CYBER 205 supercomputer by re-structuring the computations to use vector instructions wherever possible. An important factor of this process is the arrangement of data in memory.

THE ISODATA ALGORITHM

There are many different methods of performing a Cluster Analysis on a set of data objects. One method, called *partitional* clustering, divides the input data into one partition containing one or more groups. The goal of partitional clustering is to divide a given set of n patterns into exactly C disjoint sets, where $C \ll n$ [2]. The ISODATA algorithm is a member of this class of clustering methods. By performing such a clustering on a collection of objects being studied, natural groupings can be revealed that weren't evident before. Furthermore, after a clustering has been done on a set of "training" data, the newly established clusters can be used to classify additional objects.

Data Description

Objects being classified or inspected are often described by measurements of the objects' attributes and features. On a computer, an objects' measured features can be represented numerically in a *feature vector.* If an object has n measured features, the feature vector, $\mathbf{F}$, for the object can be given as:

$$\mathbf{F} = (x_1, x_2, \ldots, x_n)^T$$

where x_i numerically describes an attribute of the object and T indicates transpose. Feature vectors can be thought of as points in n-dimensional Euclidean space and can be plotted on a graph if they are two or three dimensional. Most practical clustering problems, however, involve objects with more than three attributes and make the associated feature vectors difficult to visualize. If there are k objects, each with n features, an $k \times n$ *pattern matrix* P can be used to describe the group of objects where P_{ij} denotes the jth measured feature for the ith object. Each row represents an object while each column represents a feature.

Criterion Functions

As mentioned previously, partitional clustering methods attempt to form groups from the input data objects. More specifically, they try to partition a set of n feature vectors into exactly C disjoint groups, where n and C are specified by the investigator. To assign feature vectors to these disjoint groups (or clusters), a criterion function is used to determine which cluster they best belong to. The criterion function often involves minimizing a performance index that is based on similarities between patterns. The similarity between two feature vectors can be measured with a distance function that decreases as the vectors resemble each other more, and increases as they tend to be less alike. Since feature vectors can be considered as points in n-dimensional space, the Euclidean distance function is often used to measure the similarity between them. In other words, the closer two feature vectors are to each other in Euclidean space, the more similar they are. The Euclidean distance metric is used here but other metrics may be more suitable, depending on the application.

K-means type algorithms

The K-means family of clustering algorithms Macqueen [3] uses the "square error" criterion as a performance index when assigning feature vectors to clusters. In square-error partitioning, the sum of the squared Euclidean distances between each cluster center and its members is minimized. This is accomplished by first calculating the geometric center of each cluster. If a cluster S has N members, the geometric center is simply the mean vector, $\mathbf{m}$, of all feature vectors assigned to S.

K-means algorithms usually begin with a given set of feature vectors, a fixed number of desired clusters, and an arbitrarily chosen set of cluster centers. They then iteratively attempt to make the current cluster configuration better by minimizing the criterion function. Each iteration is comprised of two steps: assigning the feature vectors to clusters and updating each of the clusters based on the new assignments. The algorithm terminates when a stopping criterion is met. One common stopping criterion involves comparing the calculated cluster centers between two successive iterations. If the cluster centers haven't changed between update steps, the algorithm has converged and execution can be terminated. Since convergence is not always guaranteed [3], a maximum iteration count is usually supplied by the investigator to avoid infinite looping. The output of the algorithm consists of a set of cluster centers and an assignment of each input feature vector to one of the clusters.

The ISODATA algorithm

The ISODATA clustering algorithm is a modified K-means algorithm that uses a set of heuristics to guide the clustering process. Many of the steps in the algorithm have been incorporated as a result of experience gained through experimentation [6]. Unlike the standard K-means routine, ISODATA permits cluster splitting and merging. When a cluster gets too many members, it can be split. Likewise, clusters that have too few members can be coalesced to form a larger cluster. Execution of the ISODATA algorithm is governed by a number of user specified parameters which allows its execution to be tuned for different sets of input feature vectors.

The ISODATA algorithm specification used here is given by Tou and Gonzalez [6]. Input to the algorithm consists of:

1. A set of N feature vectors, $\{\mathbf{x}_1, \mathbf{x}_2, \ldots, \mathbf{x}_N\}$. Each feature vector, $\mathbf{x}_i$ must have the same number of components. The input feature vectors are also called the *sample vectors* or *samples.*

2. Six parameters which control the number of clusters desired, cluster splitting and merging, and the maximum number of iterations that will be permitted.

3. A set of N_c initial cluster centers, $\{\mathbf{z}_1, \mathbf{z}_2, \ldots, \mathbf{z}_{N_c}\}$. These are usually chosen arbitrarily and are sometimes just simply taken from the first N_c feature vectors.

The ISODATA algorithm is summarized below.

ISO1 [*Initialization*] The control parameters are specified and the initial cluster centers are assigned.

ISO2 [*Distribution of Feature Vectors*] The input feature vectors are assigned to clusters based on the criterion function. This step marks the beginning of a new iteration. If the current iteration count exceeds the user specified count, the algorithm terminates.

ISO3 [*Cluster updating*] Clusters with too few members are removed. The centers for the remaining clusters are recalculated since the feature vector assignments were changed in Step ISO1. Cluster statistical information is also calculated in this step, for use in later steps.

ISO4 [*Sequencing*] Depending on the current iteration number and the number of existing clusters, the next step executed is either Step ISO5 (cluster splitting) or Step ISO6 (cluster lumping).

ISO5 [*Cluster splitting*] Determine which clusters, if any, are eligible for splitting and split them. If splitting took place, go to Step ISO2 and start the next iteration.

ISO6 [*Cluster lumping*] Determine if any clusters can be lumped, lump them according to the user specified parameters, and go to Step ISO2.

CYBER 205 IMPLEMENTATION

The CYBER 205 is a uniprocessor system that was first available in 1981. Characteristics of the target CYBER 205 used in this study include a scalar processing unit with a 20 nanosecond (ns) clock, two vector pipelines, and a bit-addressable memory consisting of four million 64-bit words.

Data Structures and Storage

Each existing cluster has an associated vector $\mathbf{z}$ of length n (the number of feature vector attributes) which contains the cluster center. The center vectors are stored in a fixed-size table called the cluster center table. The table is dimensioned at $MAXCENT \times n$, where $MAXCENT$ is a program constant which represents the maximum number of clusters allowed. A linked list is maintained to tie the active cluster centers together. A bit vector is used to indicate which center vector slots are in use.

The sample table holds the input feature vectors and can be considered an $m \times n$ table, where m is the number of feature vectors and n is the number of attributes. Since memory contiguity for operands of vector instructions is important, the sample table is arranged in *attribute order* so that vector operations involving the table are performed efficiently. By attribute order, we mean that the attributes are grouped together in memory. If we let $\vec{A}_i$ denote the attribute group $x_{1i}, x_{2i}, \ldots, x_{mi}$. the storage of the attribute vectors in memory is arranged contiguously as: $\vec{A}_1, \vec{A}_2, \ldots, \vec{A}_n$.

Implementation Strategy

Using a flow analysis of a scalar ISODATA program, it was determined that most of the processing time was spent in Steps ISO2 and ISO3 (distribution of samples and cluster updating). For this reason, most of the optimization effort was directed towards improving these sections in the supercomputer ISODATA program.

Where program code is mentioned, the names of vector variables and functions are in capital letters with an arrow above them (*e.g.* $\overrightarrow{\text{VECTOR}}$) and scalar variables are written in lower case (*e.g.* index). Individual elements of a vector are written as $\overrightarrow{\text{VECTOR}}(i)$.

We have included a description of the new code for cluster updating. A description of the distribution of samples (step ISO2) can be found in [4].

Cluster Updating

In the previous step, the input feature vector samples were distributed among the clusters. Because the number of samples assigned to each cluster may have changed since the previous iteration, the cluster center vectors have to be re-computed. Other cluster statistical information must also be updated. This information is used in later steps to determine if cluster splitting or lumping should take place. Finally, clusters whose number of assigned samples is less than the threshold value must be removed. Figure 1 is the main part of the algorithm for updating the cluster centers. The vector functions VCOUNT, VCOMPRESS, VSUM and VSQRT are used.

Removal of Unwanted Clusters

The ISODATA algorithm permits the removal of a cluster if the number of samples assigned to it is less than a threshold parameter θ_n. If θ_n is given as zero, no cluster removal will be done.

```
BELONG⃗ := (MEMBER⃗ = i)
count := VCOUNT (BELONG⃗)
if (count < θ_n) then
  call REMOVE (i)
else
  sigmax, ndim := −1
  SUM⃗ := 0
  for j := 1 to n loop
     MEMBVEC⃗ := VCOMPRESS (A⃗_j, BELONG⃗)
     center := VSUM (MEMBVEC⃗)/count
     Z⃗ (i, j) := center
     TEMP⃗ := (A⃗_j − center)^2
     zsigma := sqrt((VSUM (TEMP⃗)/count))
     if (zsigma > sigmax) then sigmax := zsigma
     end if
     SUM⃗ := SUM⃗ + TEMP⃗
  end for
  SUM⃗ := VSQRT(SUM⃗)
  AVGDIST⃗ (i) := VSUM (SUM⃗)/count
end if
```

FIGURE 1. Partial cluster update algorithm for the cluster center i.

Using the membership vector from the previous step, the number of samples assigned to each cluster is computed by using a hardware function that counts the number of 1's in a bit vector. If the number is below the specified threshold, the cluster is removed.

The Cluster Centers

In updating the cluster centers, each center vector is computed by using the equation

$$\mathbf{z}_j = \frac{1}{N_j} \sum_{\mathbf{x} \in S_j} \mathbf{x}, \quad j = 1, 2, \ldots, N_c$$

where N_j is the number of samples assigned in cluster j. By using the bit vector $\overrightarrow{\text{BELONG}}$ from the previous step to "gather" members of a cluster, the center can be easily calculated for each cluster.

The Average Distance Vector and the Overall Distance

The average distance vector, $\overrightarrow{\text{AVGDIST}}$, measures the average distance between a cluster center and its members. This vector has N_c elements, one for each cluster, and is computed by the following:

$$\overrightarrow{\text{AVGDIST}}\,(j) = \tfrac{1}{N_j} \textstyle\sum_{\mathbf{x} \in S_j} \|\mathbf{x} - \mathbf{z}_j\|, \quad j = 1, 2, \ldots, N_c$$

The overall distance is a scalar value and is simply the summation of each member of the average distance vector.

Using the gathered cluster members and the member count, the cluster members are gathered and summed. The summation is done by using a hardware instruction which adds selected members of a vector. This instruction is also used to produce the overall distance value.

The Standard Deviation Vector

For each cluster, a standard deviation vector is calculated that is used to measure the distribution of cluster members around the cluster center. This information is used in the cluster splitting stage and is normally calculated only if splitting is to be done. In this implementation, however, the information to calculate the standard deviation vector is readily available in the cluster update step and it is more efficient to compute it at this stage. Although a vector of length n is calculated for each cluster, only the maximum component and the dimension of this component for each vector is needed.

The standard deviation vector for cluster j, σ_j is defined as

$$\sigma_j = (\sigma_{1j}, \sigma_{2j}, \ldots, \sigma_{nj})^T; \quad j = 1, 2, \ldots, N_c$$

Each element of this vector, σ_{ij}, is given as

$$\sigma_{ij} = \sqrt{\tfrac{1}{N_j} \textstyle\sum_{\mathbf{x} \in S_j} (x_{ik} - z_{ij})^2}, \quad i = 1, 2, \ldots, n; \quad j = 1, 2, \ldots, N_c$$

where n is the number of attributes per feature vector, x_{ik} is the ith component of the kth feature vector, z_{ik} is the ith component of $\mathbf{z}_j$, and N_j is the number of feature vectors assigned to cluster j.

Each cluster member is subtracted from the cluster center and the the sum is maintained for each cluster and dimension. While computing this information, the maximum value and the dimension of this value are maintained. At the end of the calculation for a cluster, the maximum value and the dimension are saved.

RESULTS

In order to evaluate the improvements due to explicit vectorization, we ran the original program on a lightly loaded Vax 11/780. The tests of the original program on the CYBER 205 were made using the automatic vectorizers which were available at FSU. The automatic vectorizers were not able to find the data reorganization which was required to utilize the vector architecture. This section presents the performance of the new and original programs on a variety of test cases.

Table 1 shows the timings for one call to the vectorized distribution of samples procedure using a variety of input data sizes. Scalar timings on the CYBER 205 and a DEC VAX 780 are shown for comparison purposes. As can be seen, the vectorized CYBER 205 version is 40 to 50 times faster than the scalar version. Note that in actual ISODATA runs, many calls of the distribution of samples procedure are required.

Table 2 shows the timings for one call to the vectorized cluster update procedure using the same datasets as in the *DISTRIB* timings. This procedure runs about 10 times faster than the corresponding scalar version.

As a comparison of general program performance, the vectorized ISODATA program was run using six different input datasets with different parameters. The parameters were chosen to insure that some cluster splitting and lumping would be done. The timings for these runs are shown in Table 3.

CONCLUSIONS AND FUTURE DIRECTIONS

Explicit vectorization is very important to achieving high performance on vector supercomputers. The programmer must carefully consider the organization of data in memory. The physical memory structure must support fast access to the data. This principle holds for all forms of parallelism, not just that which is supported by vector supercomputers.

The tests of explicit vectorization reported in this paper were made using the CYBER 205 computer and use machine dependent code. The transformations which were made, however, are machine independent. In order to execute the vectorized code on a Cray supercomputer, one would need to translate into the proper explicit vector syntax which is supported on the Cray. Similar performance gains will be found for this program on any vector computer.

The ISODATA clustering algorithm is well-suited for execution on pipelined vector-processing computers. Except for very small sized sets of input feature vectors, the performance benefits gained are well worth the effort of vectorizing the ISODATA program.

The vectorized ISODATA algorithm discussed here should easily migrate to the ETA-10, which is the successor product of the CYBER 205. Since the ETA-10 has multiple processors, further performance benefits will be investigated by identifying portions of the code that can be rewritten as parallel subtasks

Table 1. *DISTRIB* timings for various sample sizes

	CPU time in seconds		
Sample Size	*CYBER 205 (vector)*	*CYBER 205 (scalar)*	*VAX 780*
500 × 10	0.001944	0.0317810	0.42
20000 × 10	0.035028	1.2712760	16.99
60000 × 10	0.102823	3.8010520	49.56
500 × 100	0.017540	0.0500120	3.17
5000 × 100	0.085792	0.5010600	31.52
20000 × 100	0.314445	2.0082580	132.53
100 × 500	0.056618	0.0499340	3.51
1000 × 500	0.123691	0.2603340	36.12
3500 × 500	0.313296	0.9110860	125.47
500 × 1000	0.173170	0.2300530	36.69
1000 × 1000	0.247096	0.4601970	75.55
2000 × 1000	0.397205	0.9202390	147.02

Table 2. *ADJUST* timings for various sample sizes

	CPU time in seconds		
Sample Size	*CYBER 205 (vector)*	*CYBER 205 (scalar)*	*VAX 780*
500 × 10	0.002574	0.0187990	0.21
20000 × 10	0.026291	0.7363820	16.86
60000 × 10	0.074892	2.2028800	78.27
500 × 100	0.023502	0.0458350	0.86
5000 × 100	0.071347	0.4308750	8.46
20000 × 100	0.231613	1.7181350	46.38
100 × 500	0.095174	0.0457850	0.99
1000 × 500	0.142325	0.3164950	9.47
3500 × 500	0.274474	1.0716020	31.82
500 × 1000	0.232928	0.3153300	8.74
1000 × 1000	0.285153	0.6027700	18.29
2000 × 1000	0.389378	1.1739910	36.49

Table 3. Timings from test case runs.

Size	*Iterations*	*VAX 780*	*CYBER 205 (vector)*	*CYBER 205 (scalar)*
500×3	5	0.75	0.003975	0.147589
1000×3	5	2.58	0.011849	0.346090
5000×8	10	14.46	0.105181	3.395927
5000×20	10	27.90	0.252921	4.194992
10000×3	8	11.02	0.074947	5.456444
10000×30	15	124.26	1.192004	8.397792

BIBLIOGRAPHY

1. Ball,G. H., Hall,D. J. [1967] "A Clustering Technique for Summarizing Multivariate Data," *Behavorial Science,* **12**, 153–155.
2. Dubes, R. and Jain, A. K. "Clustering Methods in Exploratory Data Analysis," *Advances in Computers, Volume 19.* Academic Press, 1980.
3. Macqueen, J. B. [1967] "Some methods for classification and analysis of multivariate observations," *Proceedings of the 5th Symposium of Math., Stat., and Probability*, Volume 1, Berkeley, CA.
4. Schow and Riccardi, "Adaptation of the ISODATA Clustering Algorithm for Vector Supercomputer Execution", FSU Supercomputer Computation Research Institute Technical Report FSU-SCRI-88-32.
5. Scoltock, J [1982]. "A Survey of the Literature of Cluster Analysis," *The Computer Journal,* **25**, No. 1, 130–133.
6. Tou, J. and Gonzales, R. *Pattern Recognition Principles*, Addison-Wesley, Reading, MA., 1974.

Novel Applications

MULTI-ISSUE COALITIONS IN THE CONGRESS

JACOB O. STAMPEN and JOHN R. DAVIS
University of Wisconsin - Madison
Legislative Studies Project[1]
Wisconsin Center for Education Research
1025 West Johnson Street
Madison, WI 53706

ABSTRACT

This study explores voting alignments in six U.S. Senates between 1959 and 1981. Our thesis is that the Senate is organized by four recurring "multi-issue" coalitions that combine in various ways to form larger "voting" coalitions. The four-coalition hypothesis was tested with the use of complete-link hierarchical clustering [1] on a matrix of senators over contested bills. The significance of clustering into four rather than some other number of groups was established by computing gamma goodness-of-fit statistics for each possible clustering, a computation that was practical only with the aid of a supercomputer. Beyond the basic clustering result, descriptive statistics were used to measure membership consistency over time. Membership in the four coalitions persisted even across Senates spanning the supposed "Reagan Realignment." This finding and others support our conclusion that the multi-issue coalition is the appropriate unit in roll-call analysis.

This study investigates relationships between two kinds of coalitions in the Congress, multi-issue coalitions and larger, policy determining, voting coalitions. We present evidence showing that the former are the basic components of the latter, and from this develop an empirical foundation for mid-level theories, using multi-issue coalitions as the unit of analysis. We argue that use of this unit will help integrate the results of several separate efforts in coalition research, including studies focusing on individuals and the formal modeling of Congress as a whole. To support this argument, we employ a supercomputer and a cluster analysis program, which make it possible to interpret more of the data in cluster analysis output than was possible in earlier studies.

---

[1] We appreciate the helpful comments of Roger H. Davidson, Frank B. Baker, W. Lee Hansen and the anonymous referees. We also thank Albert L. Divine for preparing Figure 2 and Deborah M. Stewart for editorial assistance. This research was supported by grants from the University of Wisconsin-Madison Research Committee, the Wisconsin Center for Education Research, the National Center for Postsecondary Governance and Finance, and from allocations of computer time from the San Diego Supercomputer Center, the Cornell National Supercomputer Facility, and New York University. An earlier version of this paper was presented at the annual meeting of the American Political Science Association, Washington, DC (September 1-4, 1988).

LITERATURE

Coalitions, caucuses, and factions fitting Hinckley's [6] definition of Congressional coalitions as,

> mixed motive actors (individuals or groups) who work with initial resources (means by which actors can influence the behavior of others) and the rules of the game (formal and informal as in constitutional law or legislative norms)

have been identified in studies focusing on: 1) interaction between legislators and issues; 2) dimensions of voting behavior; and 3) dimensions of issue treatment.

The first category includes several types of observed and empirically verified coalitions. At the highest level, above the level of party, is the voting coalition. A voting coalition forms when intra- or interparty coalitions join forces to determine policy. The long observed Conservative Coalition composed of Republicans and Southern Democrats [9] is an example of an interparty voting coalition. Another kind is the intra party or "party unity" coalition which forms when major elements of either the Democratic or Republican parties vote together.

The subparty elements of voting coalitions have been noted by both journalists and scholars observing the Congress. In fact, in recent years it has become fashionable for journalists to use insect names to refer to Yellow Jacket Republicans, Gypsy Moth Republicans, and Boll Weevil Democrats [4]. Others call these Party Concern Caucuses which sometimes exist without formal organization, but at other times overlap established groups observed by Hammond, Stevens and Mulhollan [5], namely the Democratic Study Group (liberal Democrat), the Conservative Democratic Forum (conservative Democrat), or the (moderate) Republican Gypsy Moths. Empirical evidence also supports the existence of these groups. For example, Stampen and Reeves [14] labeled these groups multi-issue coalitions (a term we henceforth use) in a study that reproduced the Yellow Jackets, Gypsy Moths and Boll Weevils and added a fourth group, the liberal Democrat (Honey Bees).

Coalitions derived from empirical studies focusing on overall determinants of voting have received a great deal of attention in recent years. These are essentially byproducts of efforts to identify the number of dimensions explaining either voting behavior or issue treatment. Those focusing on voting behavior generally argue that the major political parties are of secondary importance to the ideological coalitions. That is, most of the variance in voting is explained by unidimensionally arrayed "liberal" and "conservative" coalitions [13, 7, 11]. Clausen [3] on the other hand, argues that "different alignments (or policy dimensions) form as policy content changes," and that these spawn issue-specific coalitions. Each of the three conceptions of coalitions represent separate streams of research which have yet to be reconciled. We strongly suspect that all three will ultimately blend together and reinforce one another. This study focuses on multi-issue coalitions and how they combine to form larger voting coalitions in order to determine policy. As our analysis will later show, multi-issue coalitions routinely function as basic components of voting coalitions and, in this respect, behave much like the principal units of analysis in coalitional studies in multiparty settings [2] namely parliamentary political parties.

The neglect of multi-issue coalitions may explain one of the principal problems of congressional roll call studies, namely the exclusion of politics as a result of focus on the wrong unit of analysis. Typically, the individual member's ideology, background and constituency are studied to predict individual votes [8, 3, 13]. Such an approach, however, excludes most of the politics of the process of building a voting coalition if, as our research shows, the primary political question is whether a particular multi-issue coalition will join a voting coalition, rather than whether a certain individual will join. In other words, the past studies focused on a unit of analysis that is smaller than the unit of action. Obviously, there are pressures on particular members on particular issues, but these pressures and their effects are significant only after voting coalitions have been organized.

There of course have been many studies focusing on the two major political parties, and our study adds to them since, as we will show later, what we call multi-issue coalitions are for the most part subgroups of the Republican and Democratic parties. However, studies in which American political parties are the unit of analysis also obscure political action affecting the formation of voting coalitions by focusing on a unit of analysis that is larger than the political groupings actually available for coalescence.

This common focus on individuals and parties obscures the process of political bargaining in Congress as well as in the American system in general. Unlike research on individual voting decisions in Congress, our research shows the persistence of a particular constellation of political forces in the persistence of the four coalitions that we define, even across supposed realignments such as that associated with the Reagan landslide. These multi-issue coalitions are not distant from the detailed workings of American politics as are the major political parties in studies that make party the focus; rather, they are supported by precisely the same political forces that other studies have found to be basic in American public opinion and in state and local politics.

METHOD

The basic hypothesis of this research is that the Senate is organized into a small number of multi-issue coalitions below the level of party. A second hypothesis is that these basic groups persist as recognizable groups across Senates, even spanning the Reagan realignment. Initially, the number was hypothesized to be four to correspond to groups that had been identified by Stampen and Reeves [14]. In testing our hypotheses we employed a cluster analysis program capable of establishing goodness-of-fit [1] to identify objectively the basic voting alignments in the Senates of six Congresses spanning the years from 1959 to 1981. These include the Senates of the 86th (1959-61), 87th (1961-63), 91st (1969-71), 92nd (1971-73), 96th (1979-81) and 97th (1981-83) Congresses.[2]

---

[2] Data for this study was obtained from the Interuniversity Consortium for Political and Social Research at the University of Michigan.

Analysis proceeded in three stages. First, we used the Baker and Hubert cluster analysis program on a matrix of senators over highly contested bills, i.e., those on which at least 25% of the senators voted against the majority,[3] to examine the voting records of individual senators, and to identify the number of basic alignments within each Senate. Second, we used the conservative 75 percent voting together rule, defining cohesive coalitions, to identify the number of times each individual group joined with others to form voting coalitions. Finally, we compared our results with those of studies finding similar numbers of similar groups in Congress or the electorate.

Cluster Analysis Procedures

Cluster analysis was chosen to test for the existence of groupings in the Senate between the individual member and the voting coalition. It seemed the most appropriate technique since it avoids the chief methodological limitations of earlier studies in that it requires no a priori grouping of cases into categories and no determination of the "polarity" of a vote (i.e., whether a certain vote is in support of or in opposition to a particular issue). With cluster analysis, the purpose is to find the meaningful categories into which the observations can be grouped, and it matters only whether two senators agreed with each other rather than whether senators fit within one or another predetermined category.

The cluster analysis performed here is the complete link hierarchical method using an algorithm and computer implementation from Baker and Hubert [1]. First, the similarity between each pair of senators is calculated, in terms of a standardized city-block metric. With actual and paired yes votes coded as +1, actual and paired no votes as -1, and abstentions, absences, etc. as 0, this is simply the standardized sum of the arithmetic differences between the votes on each bill of the two senators. The algorithm requires that the similarities next be rank ordered. Then subsets are formed as homogeneously as possible putting the most similar senators together. In the complete link method, subsets receive a diameter corresponding to the highest proximity of a pair in it. It is the diameters of actual and potential subsets that are compared at each step to form new, larger subsets.

While the basic clustering result is achieved via a mechanical rather than a statistical process, it is possible to assess whether the clustering hierarchy gives a reasonable representation of the data using the gamma statistic for testing the agreement between two rank orders. Here the test is for the agreement between the original rank order of the proximity values of pairs of senators, and the rank order of the level in the hierarchy of clusters at which a particular pair first belongs to a single subset [1, p. 93]. Footnote 5 below presents these gamma values for each of the six Senates. All were significant at the .001 level. It is reasonable, therefore, to accept the basic clustering result as a representation of the structure of the data. It seems much more important, however, that the results meet the test of face validity. That is, well-known liberals are clustered together into the same group and well-known conservatives are

---

[3] Number of highly contested bills by Congress: 86th (253), 87th (287), 91th (391), 92nd (566), 96th (653), 97th (580).

clustered together in a different group (e.g., Kennedy and Pell in one and Helms and Laxalt in another).

What is more important for this study than an additional verification of the validity of the hierarchical structure is the selection of the point in the hierarchy at which the most significant grouping can be found. Baker and Hubert have developed an "index of partition adequacy" also based on the gamma statistic. The algorithm compares the original proximity rankings to the rankings of pairs according to whether the pair is yet contained in the same subset. The calculation of these gamma values for each level of hierarchy is very computation-intensive; the task of performing this calculation is what forced the use of supercomputers in this study.[4] The values of this gamma index normally will decline from the level at which only the two most similarly voting members of the Senate are combined into a group and proceed from there until all members are in a single group (i.e., as increasingly dissimilar senators are combined into larger groups). A significant deviation from the pattern of decline points to the most significant grouping, much as a "stress elbow" in multidimensional scaling locates the most appropriate dimensionality [1, p.10]. Essentially, this method is testing the null hypothesis of no structure in the data (i.e., the proximity values are just random numbers).

FINDINGS

1. What are the basic coalitions in the six U.S. Senates? Is membership consistent, and are the coalitions themselves stable over time?

Recall that the first hypothesis of this research is that the Senate is organized into a small number of multi-issue coalitions below the level of party. Initially, the number was hypothesized to be four to correspond to groups identified by journalists and others. Most concisely, the results of the cluster analysis and calculation of the goodness-of-fit statistics support this hypothesis in each of the six Senates that were analyzed. The number of groups found to be most significant ranged from 4 to 11. However, as will be discussed later in connection with Table 1, when the membership of the groups in each of the six are analyzed together, the basic hypothesis is supported. This is because many of the groupings result from the splitting apart of the basic four groups rather than the springing up of an entirely new grouping. The reasons for this splitting, of course, will be an important subject of later research.

The results of the cluster analyses can be seen most clearly in the dendogram that comprises Figure 1. What the cluster analysis did was to create sets of clusters corresponding to different possible groupings of members. The first of these groupings can be seen by tracing a line across the bottom of the diagram directly above the coalitional labels. At that

---

[4] The computation of all of these gamma statistics for one Senate required between 40 and 60 minutes of Cray X-MP cpu time at the NSF-funded San Diego Supercomputer Center. The amount of time that would be required for the same calculation for one House of Representatives would be a great deal more, perhaps as much as 20 hours.

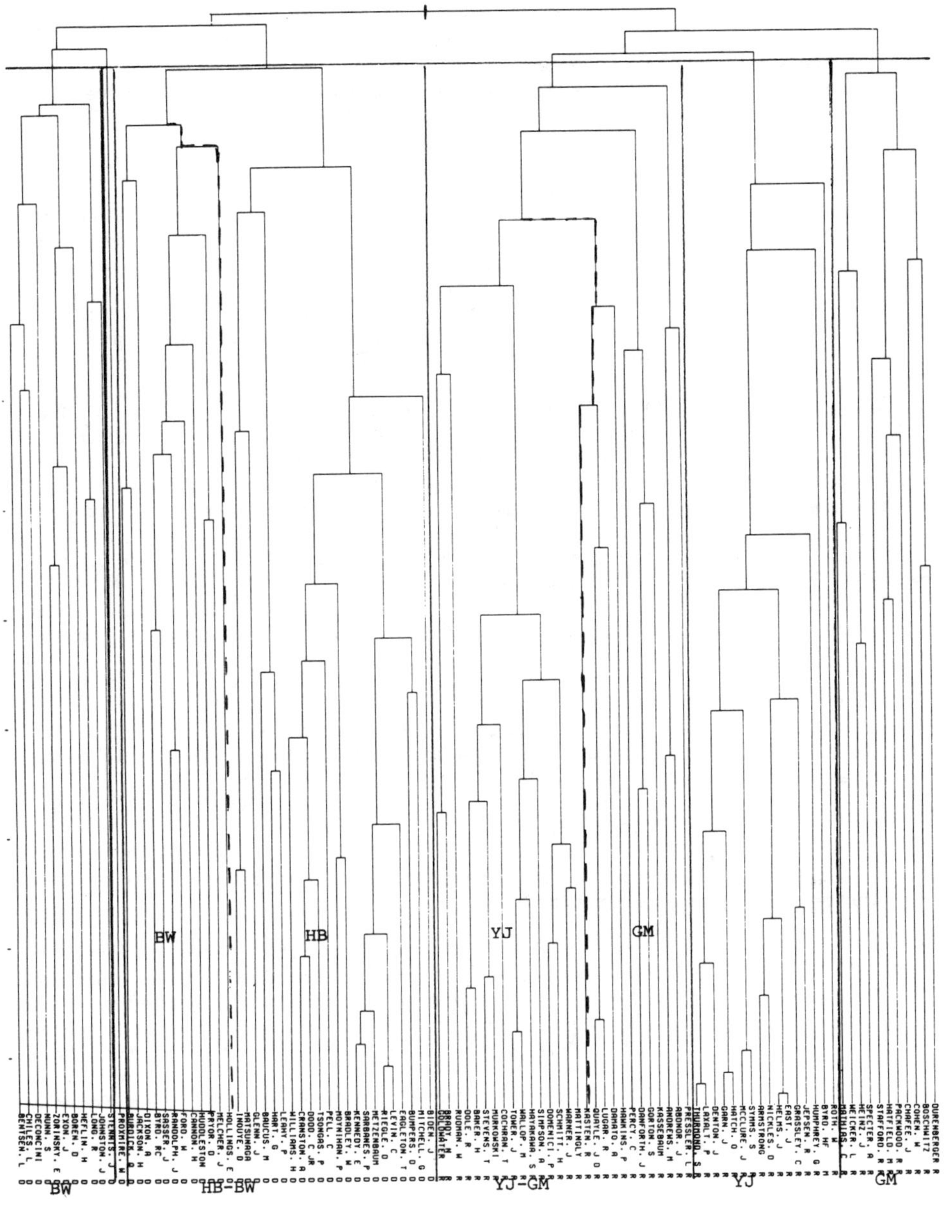

Figure 1
Dendrogram of the 97th Senate

level for the 86th Senate with 103 members there are 102 groups, 101 single members and one pair composed of the two most similar members. Moving up the diagram slightly, one can draw a line that will show 101 groups, with 100 individual members and 2 pairs of very similar members. At the very top there is just one group composed of all of the members.

The results of the cluster analyses as depicted in the dendogram can be used in two ways. Alone, examination of the changes from level to level show relationships within the groups at any level. This examination depends chiefly on noticing whether the members of a group, at whatever level, came together relatively early or late (i.e., whether the members of one group are more or less unified in their voting than the members of other groups at the same level). Together with the gamma goodness-of-fit statistics showing the most significant level of the diagrams, the membership of each of the groups at that level can be determined.[5]

On the dendogram in Figure 1, heavy vertical lines have been drawn indicating the most significant grouping and dividing the dendogram into segments corresponding to those groups. The bottom of each segment has been marked with a label derived from the names of the four groups originally hypothesized to be found in these Senates. As noted earlier, this study is not the first to apply cluster analysis to roll call data, but it is the first to be able to calculate which level of grouping from the cluster analysis is the most significant statistically.

Even without the statistical analysis, the groupings indicated in Figure 1 have a certain face validity. It is hardly necessary to look at the similarity matrices to know that Senator Hubert Humphrey belongs in the Honey Bee group, or that Goldwater is a Yellow Jacket, Javits a Gypsy Moth, or Cannon, Stennis, and Robert Byrd are various kinds of Boll Weevils. What this face validity permits is the attachment of the appropriate labels to groups and the observation that, when one of the four basic clusters splits, it splits into groups that will always maintain their identities as derivative from the parent group.

2. Is there a pattern in relationships among coalitions, and how does the pattern change over time?

The six dendograms in Figure 2 show that, although the number changes over time, multi-issue coalitions always represent combinations of the same four core elements, all of which are sometimes unified, but splintered at other times. For example in the 86th Congress, the Yellow Jackets, Honey Bees, and Gypsy Moths were united, whereas the Boll Weevils were split into three separate coalitions, two on the majority Democratic side and one on the Republican side. In the 87th Senate (1961-63), which followed the Kennedy-Johnson election, the situation was quite different. Except for the Yellow Jackets, all of the core groups were splintered. The previously unified Honey Bees and Gypsy Moths divided into separate coalitions, and nearly all

---

[5] The gammas for the basic clustering results were .759, .741, .668, .660, .692, .772, for the six Senates respectively. Each of these results is significantly different from what would be obtained with a dataset that was random or had no group structure at the 10% level of significance. The methodology of this significance test, the tables of standard deviates derived by monte carlo methods, and the large sample approximation used here, are given in [1, p. 99].

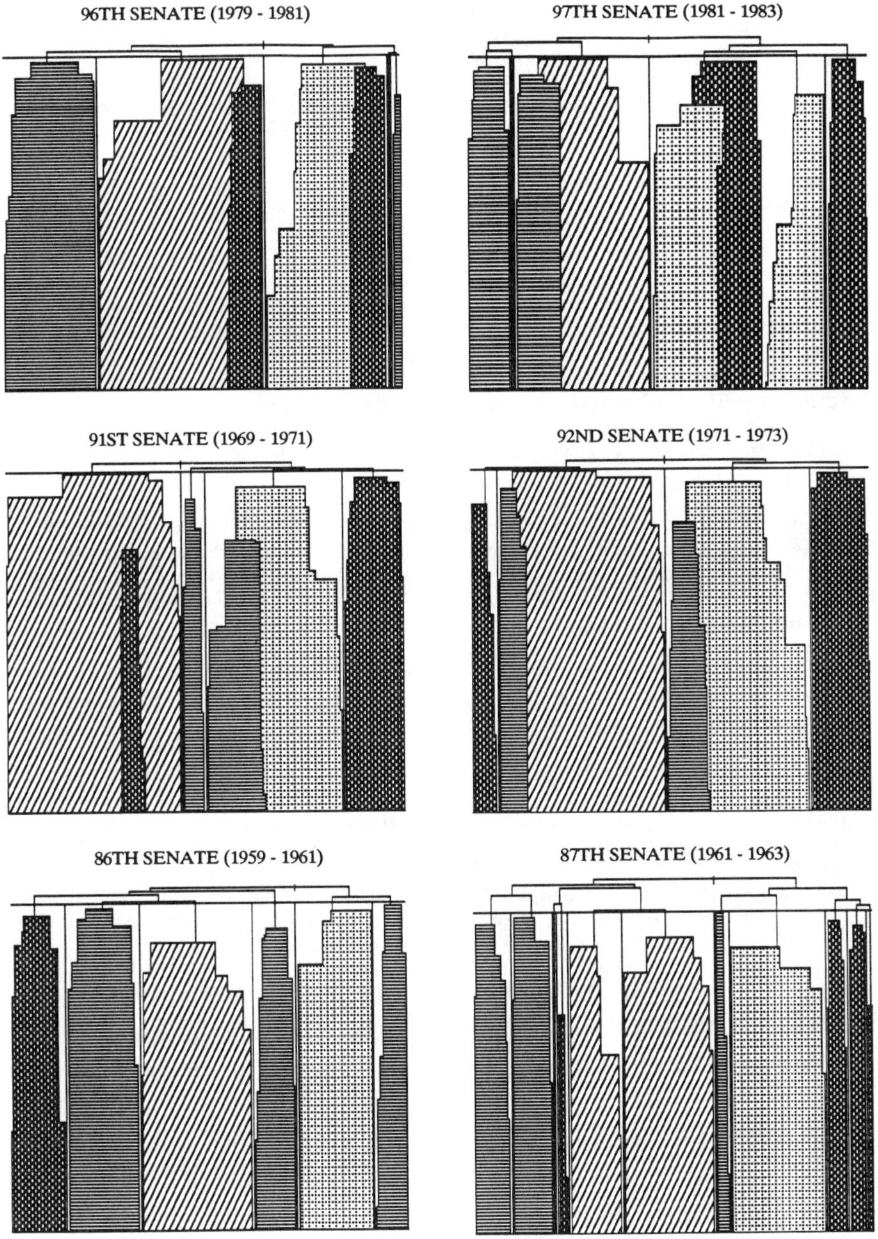

Figure 2. Voting Alignments in Six Senates

of the Gypsy Moths shifted from the Democrat to Republican side. The Boll Weevils, on the other hand, remained in three groups, two on the Democratic side and one on the Republican side.

This pattern of unifying and splintering continued in the later Congresses. However, there was added complexity in that subelements of the Gypsy Moths and Boll Weevils joined Honey Bees and Yellow Jackets to form separate multi-issue coalitions. This happened in five of the Congresses. In the 91st Congress (1969-71), in which Democrats held majorities in both houses but the President was Republican (Nixon), the Boll Weevils were mainly on the Republican side, whereas in the 92nd Congress (1971-73) they were on both sides, as were the Gypsy Moths in both of these Congresses. The Boll Weevils were more unified in the 96th Congress (1979-81), under the Carter Administration, than in any other of the six. However, in the 97th (1981-83), they splintered into two groups, while Gypsy Moths shifted from being split between the majority Republican and Democrat sides to the Republican side after the 1980 election of President Reagan.

3. How do these alignments compare as appropriate units of analysis with political parties or individuals?

In only one of the six Congresses, the Reagan 97th, did party lines clearly divide the Congress. In all the others, Republicans and Democrats combined with one another. Thus, even if the Reagan landslide temporarily unified political parties, it is hard to believe that party is the appropriate unit in Congressional analyses, since the change between the 96th and 97th Congresses is accounted for by movements of multi-issue coalitions similar to those occurring between earlier pairs of Congresses. Also, as we will see later, more party unity in the 97th Congress did not prevent the formation of numerous interparty voting coalitions.

Neither does it seem plausible that individuals constitute the appropriate unit of analysis. If they did, we would expect to find instability in the composition of core groups caused by individual senators moving from one group to another over time. However, as can be seen in Table 1, which shows the membership consistency of senior members of the Senate, this rarely occurred. In fact, it is remarkable how rarely individuals changed core group affiliations. Among the few who did, change typically occurred when subelements of each multi-issue coalition realigned. Only one senator, William Proxmire of Wisconsin, was truly independent. The cluster analysis identified him as a single member coalition in three of the six Senates (86th, 96th, 97th) and as a Honey Bee in the other three. Thus, multi-issue coalitions appear to be the appropriate units of analysis, since they reflect a continuous and ever present recombining of the same four core elements.

The argument that there are basically four multi-issue coalitions can be stated even more clearly by considering the support available for the second hypothesis of this study, that the basic groups persist as recognizable groups. Table 1 shows that senators consistently voted together within a particular multi-issue coalition or within the same subset in Congress after Congress. This pattern is observed even in moving from the 92nd and 96th to the 97th Congresses, spanning the supposed Reagan realignment. Equally important, the persistence of the basic groups also demonstrates the validity of the basic grouping within each of the Senates. Of course, the voting choices of particular multi-issue coalitions, and the cohesiveness of a particular coalition, or its ability to act as a group,

Table 1

Multi-issue Coalition Affiliations of Senior Senators

Member ID		Party	86th	87th	91st	92nd	96th	97th
				HONEY BEES				
1252	Burdick	D	GM	HB	HB-GM	HB-BW	HB-GM	HB-BW
4851	Jackson	D	HB	HB	HB-GM	HB-BW	HB-GM	HB-BW
10147	Williams	D	HB	HB	HB-GM	HB-BW	HB-GM	HB-BW
10605	Matsanuga	D					HB-GM	HB-BW
10808	Kennedys	D			HB-GM	HB-BW	HB-GM	HB-BW
10818	Pell	D		HB	HB-GM	HB-BW	HB-GM	HB-BW
11049	Reigle	D					HB-GM	HB-BW
12103	Cranston	D			HB-GM	HB-BW	HB-GM	HB-BW
12104	Eagleton	D			HB-GM	HB-BW	HB-GM	HB-BW
13039	Sarbanes	D					HB-GM	HB-BW
14073	Metzenbaum	D					HB-GM	HB-BW
				BOLL WEEVILS				
660	Bentsen	D				HB-BW	BW	BW
1366	Byrd, R.	D	BW1	HB	BW	HB-BW	BW	HB-BW
1482	Cannon	D	BW1	BW2	BW	HB-BW	BW	HB-BW
5767	Long, R.	D		BW2	YJ-BW	YJ-BW	BW	BW
7722	Randolph	D	BW1	HB1	HB	HB-BW	BW	HB-BW
8883	Stennis	D	BW3	BW3	YJ-BW	YJ-BW	BW	BW
11204	Hollings	D			BW	HB-BW	BW	HB-BW
13101	Chiles	D				HB-BW	BW	BW
				GYPSY MOTHS				
10535	Mathias	R			HB-GM	GM	HB-GM	GM
11203	Hatfield	R			HB-GM	GM	HB-GM	GM
11205	Percy	R			GM	GM	HB-GM	YJ-GM
12107	Packwood	R			GM	GM	HB-GM	GM
12032	Weicker	R				GM	HB-GM	GM
12109	Stevens	D-R			GM	GM	YJ-GM	YJ-GM
13050	Heinz	R					HB-GM	GM
				YELLOW JACKETS				
3658	Goldwater	R	YJ	YJ	YJ-BW	YJ-BW	YJ-GM	YJ-GM
9369	Thurmond	D-R	BW3	BW1	YJ-BW	YJ-BW	YJ-GM	YJ
10802	Byrd, H	D-I			YJ-BW	YJ-BW	BW	YJ
10513	Dole	R			YJ-BW	YJ-BW	YJ-GM	YJ-GM
10823	Tower	R		YJ	YJ-BW	YJ-BW	YJ-GM	YJ-GM
11029	McClure	R					YJ-GM	YJ
11200	Baker	R			YJ-BW	YJ-BW	YJ-GM	YJ-GM
14002	Armstrong	R					YJ-GM	YJ
14077	Laxalt	R					YJ-GM	YJ
14103	Domencini	R					YJ-GM	YJ-GM
14105	Helms	R					YJ-GM	YJ
				INDEPENDENT				
7638	Proxmire	D	HB	I	HB-GM	HB-BW	I	I

may be the real content of such a realignment as far as the Congress is concerned.

4. Do the observed multi-issue coalitions function as basic components of the larger voting coalitions?

In the Republican controlled Senate of the 97th Congress, one or more multi-issue coalitions voted as a block (i.e., at least 75% of members voted together on a given bill). Yellow Jackets (15 members) block voted most frequently (455 times), followed by the separate Yellow Jacket - Gypsy Moth coalition (28 members) which voted as a block 418 times. The Gypsy Moths (11 members) and the Honey Bee - Boll Weevils (34 members) voted together 341 and 360 times respectively, and the Boll Weevils (12 members) voted together least frequently (337 times).

Table 2 shows the frequency of various types of voting coalitions in the 97th Senate. The column headings at the top of the table identify the multi-issue coalitions, and the two columns on the far right indicate the number of times these combined to form winning or losing voting coalitions. In the rows at the top of the table we see several types of intraparty coalitions. A voting coalition uniting all Republicans appears in the first row and in the far right columns we see that this resulted in a winning coalition 141 times and in a losing coalition only two times. The next row shows that another Republican voting coalition which, lacking support from the Gypsy Moths, won 77 times but lost 21 times. On the following two rows, we see other combinations of Republicans voting together less frequently. Next, we see that the minority party voting coalition (i.e., Boll Weevil and Honey Bee - Boll Weevil Democrats) formed winning coalitions 32 times and losing ones 89 times. All together, intraparty voting coalitions won 281 times (48% of winning coalitions) and lost 112 times (20% of losing coalitions).

Voting coalitions crossing party lines appear in the middle section of the table. The first inter-party voting coalition includes several versions of the well known Conservative Coalition, here defined as Republicans and Democrats less the "liberal" Honey Bee - Boll Weevil coalition. All three Republican groups and the Boll Weevil Democrats voted together 21 times and never lost. However, the most frequently occurring, and winning (96 times), coalition combined the two most "conservative" Republican groups (i.e., all except Gypsy Moths) and the Boll Weevil Democrats. The least successful combination was Yellow Jacket Republicans and Boll Weevil Democrats, which formed 29 times but lost 11 times. Other combinations of Republicans and Boll Weevils occurred only 5 times. All together, variations of the Conservative coalition accounted for 140 or 24% of the winning coalitions in the 97th Senate.

The second subcategory focuses on what we tentatively call the Liberal Coalition (i.e., Democrats and Republicans less the "conservative" Yellow Jacket Republicans). Here the most frequently occurring pattern united Gypsy Moth Republicans and Honey Bee - Boll Weevil Democrats. This combination won 32 times and lost 19 times. The next most frequent pattern, which occurred 19 times, united the Boll Weevil Democrats joined the two previously mentioned groups. Other combinations occurred infrequently. All together the Liberal Coalition results in 59 winning coalitions and 19 losing coalitions.

Table 2

Voting Coalitions in the 97th Senate

	(YJ)	(YJ-GM)	(GM)	(BW)	(HB-BW)	WINNING	LOSING
			INTRAPARTY				
Republican	X	X	X	--	--	141	2
	X	X		--	--	77	21
		X	X	--	--	27	0
	X		X	--	--	4	0
Democrat	--	--	--	X	X	32	89
			INTERPARTY				
Conservative (Reps. & Dems. less HB-BW Dems.)							
	X	X		X	--	96	0
	X	X	X	X	--	21	0
	X			X	--	18	11
		X		X	--	3	0
		X	X	X	--	2	0
Liberal (Dems. & Reps. less YJ Reps.)							
	--		X		X	32	19
	--		X	X	X	19	0
	--	X	X		X	5	0
	--	X			X	2	0
	--	X	X	X	X	1	0
Opposites (Including YJ Reps. & HB-BW Dems.)							
	X			X	X	2	0
	X	X	X	X	X	2	0
			OTHER				
Lone Multi-Issue							
	X	--	--	--	--	9	51
	--	X	--	--	--	14	4
	--	--	X	--	--	15	51
	--	--	--	X	--	14	27
	--	--	--	--	X	24	133
No Multi-Issue							
	--	--	--	--	--	20	172
					Total	580	580

The third subcategory includes infrequently occurring voting coalitions that bring together the Yellow Jacket Republicans and Honey Bee - Boll Weevil Democrats. In two instances a coalition of these opposites lacked support from two of the three Republican groups. In another two instances we see examples of a "Hurrah" vote when all five coalitions vote together. All together, intraparty voting coalitions accounted for 203 (or 35%) of all winning coalitions and 30 (or 5%) of all losing coalitions.

Two additional patterns are shown at the bottom of the table. The first represents situations in which a single multi-issue coalition functioned as a voting coalition. Among these, losing coalitions appeared more frequently than winning ones, except in the case of the Yellow Jacket - Gypsy Moth coalition which won 14 times and lost only four times. The impressive record of this group might be explained by the fact that it included most of the Republican leaders in the 97th Senate. The final type of voting coalition, which appears to lack any association with multi-issue coalitions, occurred 192 times but won only 20 times.

What is striking in this analysis is how infrequently the polar opposite multi-issue coalitions formed voting coalitions. For example, Yellow Jackets and Honey Bee-Boll Weevils never joined to form a voting coalition of their own, and joined in combination with other multi-issue coalitions only four times. Similarly, the Boll Weevils and Gypsy Moths never formed a voting coalition by themselves, and when they otherwise joined (47 times) it was mainly as components of either the Conservative (23 times) or Liberal (20 times) coalition. This observation further reinforces earlier arguments that voting occurs across two dimensions rather than along a single liberal-conservative one, and that there are basically only four core multi-issue coalitions.

5. How does the association among coalitions we observe help to explain the Congress and American politics?

Since the essential aim of this study was to objectively test our thesis that multi-issue coalitions are the appropriate unit of Congressional analysis, we have focused on the basic structure of voting as opposed to the content of issues. However, in comparing our results with previous studies,[6] the following impressions emerge. The Senate is organized by four groups reflecting four distinct world views: Yellow Jacket conservatives are concerned about national security and are willing to spend to expand and maintain it, but they oppose economic intervention on domestic issues, especially aid to individuals. Honey Bee liberals have opposite priorities. Gypsy Moth Republicans and Boll Weevil Democrats display another opposite cross cut. Gypsy Moths favor legislation that advances the individual and tend to oppose government intervention in either domestic or foreign affairs. Boll Weevils favor a strong defense and government intervention in domestic affairs.

Our preliminary analysis of the 96th House of Representatives suggests that various combinations of the same four groups also organize that body. Also, a recent study by Mattox and Lilje [10] of election polls found a similar four-group pattern, which suggests that the multi-issue coalitions are

---

[6] See [14] for an analysis of issues and the background characteristics, constituency relationships and committee actions of multi-issue coalition members in the 96th and 97th Senates.

rooted in the electorate. In addition, Wildavsky [15] argued that political action derives from four subcultures: hierarchy, equality, competition or apathy. While apathy is no doubt more characteristic of the dispossessed and politically inactive than of groups within the Congress, the remaining three seem generally to fit our understanding of Yellow Jackets, Honey Bees, and Gypsy Moths, and some combination of equity and hierarchy may explain the Boll Weevils.

CONCLUSION

What this research has attempted to demonstrate is the significance of group behavior in the Senate below the level of party and above the level of the individual. Our basic hypothesis that voting in the Senate is structured by a small number of multi-issue coalitions was supported by our analysis of data from six Senates. This result opens the way to new approaches to research on Congress -- approaches that were not plausible with a focus on individual members or on parties.

Recognizing the importance of intermediate-level groupings can provide promising new opportunities for applying coalition theory in the American setting similar to recently productive applications that have evolved in studies of European parliaments [4]. More specifically, developing theory from studies employing multi-issue coalitions as the unit of analysis will call attention to how competition and cooperation among them leads to the formation of winning voting coalitions, how bargaining over the content of bills produces payoffs that enable such coalitions to form, how small groups become pivotal in the process of coalition formation, and how coalitions form positions on specific issues affecting education, welfare, and defense.

Finally, the identification of a small number of groups as the most significant political actors permits Congressional studies to be linked to the basic political tendencies in the American polity as a whole, a result, again, not as plausible when individuals or parties are the focus of the analysis. The promise of this approach goes beyond the explanation of contemporary politics, for there is evidence (not examined here) that the constellation of political forces identified in the group structure of the Senate has ancient roots in American politics. Thus, our approach can help to illuminate this history both within and outside the Congress.

REFERENCES

1) Baker, Frank and Lawrence Hubert. 1976. "A Graph-Theoretic Approach to Goodness-of-Fit in Complete-Link Hierarchical Clustering." Journal of the American Statistical Association 71, 870-878.

2) Browne, Eric C. and John Dreijmanis (Eds.). 1982. Government Coalitions in Western Democracies. New York: Longman Inc.

3) Clausen, Aage R. 1973. How Congressmen Decide: A Policy Focus. New York, N.Y.: St. Martin's Press.

4) Davidson, Roger H. and Walter J. Oleszek. 1984. "Changing the Guard in the U. S. Senate." Legislative Studies Quarterly 9, 635-663.

5) Hammond, Susan W., Arthur J. Stevens Jr. and Daniel P. Mulhollan. 1983. "Congressional Caucuses: Legislators as Lobbyists." In Allen J. Cigler and Burdett A. Loomis (Eds). Interest Group Politics. Washington, D.C.: CQ Press, 275-297.

6) Hinckley, Barbara. 1981. Coalitions and Politics. New York: Harcourt Brace Jovanovich, Inc.

7) Hoadley, John F. 1980. The Dimensions of Congressional Voting, 1971-1978: Some Preliminary Considerations. Paper delivered at the 1980 meeting of the Midwest Political Science Association, Chicago, IL.

8) Kingdon, John W. 1981. Congressmen's Voting Decisions. New York: Harper & Row.

9) Manley, John F. 1973. "The Conservative Coalition in the Congress." American Behavioral Scientist, 223-247.

10) Mattox, William S. and Stuart A. Lilje. 1984. Beyond Liberal and Conservative: Reassessing the Political Spectrum. Washington, DC: Cato Institute.

11) Poole, Keith T. and Howard Rosenthal. 1983. "Analysis of Congressional Coalition Patterns: A Unidimensional Spatial Model." Legislative Studies Quarterly 45, 55-77.

12) Schneider, Jerrold E. 1979. Ideological Coalitions in the Congress. Westport, Conn.: Greenwood Press.

13) Schneider, Jerrold E. 1984. Congressional Coalitions: Recent Findings and the Future of Ideological Coalitions. Paper presented at the annual meeting of the American Political Science Association, Washington, D.C.

14) Stampen, Jacob O. and Roxanne W. Reeves. 1986. "Coalitions in the Senates of the 96th and 97th Congresses." Congress and the Presidency 13, 187-208.

15) Wildavsky, Aaron (1987). "Choosing Preferences by Constructing Institutions: A Cultural Theory of Preference Formation." American Political Science Review 81, 3-22.

COMPLEMENTARY PROCESSING: A SUPERCOMPUTER/PERSONAL COMPUTER U. S. CENSUS DATABASE PROJECT

Orville Vernon Burton
History Department, University of Illinois. For 1989, Woodrow Wilson International Center for Scholars, Smithsonian Institution Building, Washington, DC 20560

Examples of how a Supercomputer could help satisfy the insatiable empirical needs of historians and other scholars are endless; the point is that super fast computing is useful not only for scientists but also for the thousands of humanistic scholars who have been locked out of the supercomputing revolution. If computer companies want students, researchers, and professors from all disciplines to use their products, then they must show them that a computer is more than just a word processor, number cruncher, or video game; and supercomputing in tandem with personal computers could attract a whole new generation of researchers to the powers of computing.

Historians work differently from scientists. Both use laboratories, but the historian's laboratory is the record of the past, and the historian's creation is the memory of civilization. Historians have traditionally relied on diaries, letters, newspapers, and other written sources that have been preserved. Yet, only a small group of elite and middle class generally left such written records, records which have greatly prejudiced the interpretations of history. Partly as a reaction to this bias, beginning in the 1960s and continuing today, some historians, working on diverse special topics and using new methods and approaches, developed a movement that came to be identified as the "new" social history. "New" social history employed what humanists considered at the time to be "sophisticated" quantitative techniques. Adapting theories and methods from other disciplines, especially sociology, economics, political science, and anthropology, these scholars tried to recover the historical experience of entire communities, of persons and groups not hitherto part of mainstream historical studies, of the plain people, Afro-Americans and other minorities, of women, of immigrants, working classes, and poor.

Given the scarcity of records for common folk, who are the lifeblood of a community, the federal census often remains the best source from which to reconstruct a picture of their lives. The printed volumes provide basic aggregate data, and the unpublished manuscript census returns (population, agriculture, slave, mortality, industry, and social statistics) provide information about individuals and their families, households, and communities. The United States has taken a federal census decennially since 1790 (a few earlier isolated censuses exist), and all up until 1910 (most of 1890 was destroyed) are now open to the public. Every local political district (county, city, etc.) has population schedules housed at the National Archives in Washington D.C.; these are available on microfilm. Once the federal government became interested in agriculture, mortality, slave, social statistics, and manufacturing, census enumerators also collected information on these subjects. These are generally located in state archives and are usually available on microfilm.[1] A number of state or local censuses are also available. The U.S. federal manuscript population census returns include at various decade intervals, the household head, and information on the members of the household, such as number of individuals in the household and gender of each person.

By 1850, the population census enumerates every person in a household with individual information on real property, and beginning in 1860 the occupations for all persons fifteen and older are listed. Other information in the population censuses are race or color, birthplace of each person, and also information on where people lived, their physical condition (deaf, blind, insane), marital status, literacy, whether children attended school, number of months employed, and other items provided in answer to questions asked by the census enumerator. In addition, the agricultural census provides information on livestock, crops, acreage, tenure, fences, home manufactures, and other related items (See appendix for the 1850 through 1880 population census schedules and examples of other schedules). Therefore, by linking separate census schedules, like the population and agricultural, slave, and social statistics, historians can construct rich data files from which to measure agricultural production, social structure, and change over time. Moreover, farms, individuals, families, and communities can be traced across censuses.[2]

This "new" history is no longer so new. It has had a profound effect on the profession, but it has also evoked tremendous criticism. Some of the attack is based on methodology, skeptics objecting that the most important questions are important precisely because they cannot be quantified. But today the issue is larger; it is an argument about the nature of history. Is the essence of history a sort of verstehen obtained by thinking as people in the past--in which case the use of computers in historical work may be quite limited. Or is history the discovery of social or economic or political "forces" that operated in part independently of what people thought--in which case computers may help to measure these forces? But this dichotomy is false. Unless one knows the past, one cannot think as those who lived it; thoughts are affected by social forces that often do not operate on the highest level of consciousness, and people may be unaware of all the reasons why they feel a certain way. And even though total knowledge is beyond human endeavor, historians must seek out the widest possible range of source materials to discover as much as possible about the past. This information cannot be obtained only from traditional sources but also needs to be uncovered through methods of the new social history, and in particular through systematic computer analysis of available records.

Ironically, at the very same time that the new history is coming under renewed assault, technological innovations applied to historical research can minimize problems. One such problem has been data entry. This once meant transcribing onto sheets of papers and then keypunching or entering data onto a mainframe computer (with all the problems associated with time-sharing). Now we have microcomputers, database management systems, and user-friendly revised statistical packages to alleviate the frustrations of entering and manipulating data. Users no longer have to numerically encode information for computer manipulation. For example, now gender or occupation can be encoded alphabetically instead of with some esoteric numeric code, reducing confusion and errors, as well as the gut reaction by humanists that somehow sex should not be reduced to numbers.

Another problem has been the sheer enormity of historical databases. Since the early 1970s I have been coding the U.S. manuscript census returns into machine-readable form for computer manipulation to ferret out a more accurate historical understanding of the rural South. My research has required a huge database (over 130,000 eighty-column computer-card images) that has caused countless computing frustrations. Whenever I needed to transfer data between mainframes to use a particular statistical package, I was banished to the graveyard shift because my files overwhelmed tielines. This very semester as my research assistant is trying to salvage fourteen years of data collection and analysis from the soon to be discarded CYBER at the University of Illinois, he has been reprimanded about the amount of time on the tieline. To many, indeed most, historians the technical complications seemed insurmountable. But now microcomputers in conjunction with a supercomputer, make these types of problem obsolete. A supercomputer easily handles huge data files, and could, quite literally (if data were in machine-readable form), handle those for the entire country. The speed of a supercomputer when combined with the versatility of a microcomputing environment allows historians to explore questions that were previously too complex (and too expensive) to answer.

With the support and encouragement of Larry Smarr, Director at the University of Illinois's National Center for Supercomputing Applications (NCSA), I have been working within this complementary computing environment over the last few years to develop an integrated system for analyzing manuscript level census data. We are constructing a large prototype to combine and analyze all manuscript U. S. census data for every available census, and I hope to establish a Center for the study of community and regional history built around a database containing all the manuscript census returns as they were originally recorded. The Center would use the Supercomputer for large file data manipulation and visualization of data and would use personal computers for data entry, access to the Supercomputer database, storage of results from Supercomputer research, and analysis and manipulation of smaller datasets. This distributed computing environment (between the Supercomputer and personal computers) will be a two-way system of communication that will provide a systematic basis for analyzing fragmented and scattered data wherever historians may locate the information--deposited in local archives, churches, courthouses, and attics throughout the United States.

Computers can help to democratize access to information throughout the world, and it is our intention to further this process through the Supercomputer history project. Problems of data storage, manipulation, and results display are answered by using personal computers as the crucial frontend machines, the most widely used and dispersed component of our overall plan. Kodak has recently solved the dilemma of massive data storage with the development of a laser disk that can store databases the size of what we are proposing. The data will be stored on these laser disks and headers will be developed to allow the Supercomputer to read the data on the disk. This is another example of the multivendor, distributed computing format that is underway at NCSA.

The research process involves the collection, analysis, and presentation of data. We have developed an efficient method of data entry that entails the use of microfilm in conjunction with personal computers. We have also tried to obtain all the datasets that various scholars have put together from the U. S. manuscript censuses. Generally, these researchers did not record all available information, and they usually only sampled for the heads of households instead of for every person in the census. We have written and tested a TURBO PASCAL data entry program which utilizes previously compiled datasets and allows data-entry operators to link persons already recorded with other members of their family or household. We have also written DBASEIII+ programs for IBM computers that build upon datasets compiled by others and adds all other information for each individual that was not originally recorded.

Most census data, however, has never been put into machine-readable form, so we have developed DBASEIII+ programs to enter data for the first time.[3] It is more straightforward and less complicated. In addition, we have developed a program in Microsoft Windows that is by far the easiest and most fool-proof data-entry program yet developed. Data-entry operators can use a mouse to simply click data into the dataset. Electronic notepads are handily available for recording problems or notes. In the future we hope that optical character scanners can be used to make the data entry process even more efficient. Existing scanners available at the University of Illinois can already read handwriting if it is consistently written, and continued development should soon make it possible to read census schedules directly from microfilm. In any event numerous published censuses can be read by the current generation of scanners, and we plan to convert them to machine readable form. Despite marvelous advances, data entry has been and continues to be the greatest hindrance for the historian's use of computer technology both in research and teaching. I am looking forward to the day when the researcher takes affordable hand-held scanning devices into archives and is able to digitize nineteenth century script for analysis.

The data entry for our prototype module (the analysis of

a region in South Carolina which contains five counties today) is near completion, and we are now running trial analysis programs. We are using DBASEIII+ files on the microcomputer because we plan to use INFORMIX as a data-management system on the CRAY Supercomputer. INFORMIX uses SQL, and the soon-to-be released DBASEIV will also be compatible with SQL. We are committed to a process that works both ways, from the personal computer to the Supercomputer and back. The memory and speed limitations of microcomputers and even most mainframes, makes a Supercomputer the only available means for collecting, storing, and manipulating the huge amounts of data we propose to collect in anything close to real time. Subsets for individual scholar's use, however, would be available for analysis, storage, and manipulation on microcomputers.

To encourage use of the database we will develop a user interface that will allow those unfamiliar with computing to extract data as easily as possible. We will also provide library routines and other software program tool kits to help researchers develop their own programs for analysis and/or data extraction. We hope to combine SQL, INFORMIX, SAS, SPSS, (which are available for use on the CRAY) and other software to make the census information as accessible and generic as possible. All of these packages (and others) are now available for the Supercomputer, and we hope that the use of standard data-management or statistical packages will encourage researchers to utilize the database. Users will be able to access the Supercomputer through frontend machines and modems. Patrons will be able to select sub-sets of data (county, city, town, or township level in most instances) for analysis on microcomputers using existing software packages. At the moment all our microcomputer programs are compatible with IBM machines, but as we move into the next phase we may need to change to a new environment. The proposed interface should help users download selected data from the Supercomputer for analysis at their remote location.

It is our intention to work with Larry Smarr, Director of NCSA, to attract scholars who are interested in using the database through the existing NCSA short term visitor program. Although not everyone can use the CRAY at NCSA, proposals that are accepted by the review committee (which already exists) will be allowed to explore all facets of the data. We envision that an approved client will be able to access the database via modem from any remote location. In addition, anyone interested in data, whether allowed to work on the CRAY or not, could request copies of specific data or some local subset on tape or disk. A graduate research assistant will handle requests for information. We are willing and anxious to share information with other Supercomputing centers to make the information as accessible as possible.[4]

The creation of the Supercomputer census database is not an end but a beginning. Researchers in every discipline that uses history as a laboratory or is interested in the development of American society will find the world-class database indispensable. Historians, genealogists, economists, sociologists, geographers, anthropologists, linguists, dialectologists, and medical researchers (who are interested in the patterns and history of disease and nutrition) will all benefit from this project. Of course, many laypeople will also be interested in compiling their own family or community database. With the entire U.S. manuscript census returns available for scholars, teachers, and their students, the potential for creative uses in scholarship and classroom are exciting.

Before researchers can use this incredible source of historical information, we need to pull together, or link, the various censuses and records into one coherent database. Our research team has developed programs to link persons across censuses and schedules. Not everyone in the population census appears in the agricultural or slave censuses of the same year, but every person who owned or rented slaves or who operated a farm should appear in the population manuscript. By following the order of the different censuses, researchers can link them. Decennial linkages are more difficult. Although the logical steps to link persons across censuses are straightforward, the number of possible matches and the means of confirming a match are not. Spellings were imprecise, names were sometimes sobriquets, age was not always reliable. Often names and ages of other household members are the key to linking families across different decades. Thus the time needed to run linkage programs on censuses was beyond the realm of possibility--without the Supercomputer.

Our research team is currently testing linkage algorithms, designed with linguist and team member Atsushi Fukada, against censuses that have been hand-linked to determine the accuracy of machine-linked data. Our linkage programs now run on PCs (although they take upwards of twenty-four hours to complete) and preliminary results indicate that we are matching seventy-five percent of all possible matches. We plan to improve upon these first-run programs, but considering how long it takes to hand-link the same data our linkage algorithms are a major accomplishment. Indeed, even if we did not improve on our linkage proportion, a scholar who used one of the counties we had machine-linked would have only 25 percent of the population to link by hand instead of the entire population.

The leading textbook on quantitative historical techniques claims that the major problem confronting quantitative researchers is that there are too many data for historians to use effectively. Although the author made the point that computers have made the analysis of large datasets more practicable, he argued that some historical datasets are so large that the historian has no choice but to base his/her conclusions on a sample. In conclusion, he meekly advised that "historians should not hesitate to use sampling methods rather than give up an analysis project because the bulk of the records."[5]

But we are asking quantitative investigators to change the scope of their research, to look at the complete record linkage rather than a sample. Scholars sample because it is too difficult and too expensive to work with populations, but new capabilities exist. Looking at the whole population data would solve the problem of outliers (small portions of the data which do not conform with patterns). The usual method of dealing with outliers has been either to ignore them or to take a larger sample. Yet historians are often as interested in explaining the exceptions as the rule; with all outliers available, historians are more likely to perceive previously undetected patterns and to understand why nonconforming cases are different. Then too, population data will assist historians in their quest for synthesis. For if one can analyze data on a regional or national scale, then more general and more accurate conclusions are likely to follow. Because a Supercomputer has such great speed and can handle so much data, historians can transcend county boundaries, which often obscure more refined patterns of migration, industrialization, mortality, religious affiliation etc., to develop and test new theories about almost every aspect of American life. Humanistic researchers need access to more information to make their conclusions more tenable, and the Supercomputer database project will provide the basis for more credible and insightful analysis among researchers in the humanities.

This has proven so in my own research. In my analysis of Edgefield County (In My Father's House are Many Mansions) I discovered with the use of a computer that a "black matriarchy" did not exist in rural Edgefield as other scholars, most notably Herbert Gutman, had shown for other areas.[6] For sixty years scholars believed that black men were not heading Afro-American families, but careful study of the different patterns of families in the countryside, small hinterland towns, and cities showed that in the countryside black families were overwhelmingly headed by men. In the cities and towns, however, both black and white families had a substantial number (but never a majority) of families headed by females. I was able to demonstrate how earlier scholars had erred because they analyzed samples which obscured the fact that different patterns existed in the towns and in the country. My typology, conversely, was developed only because I used the entire community for my study, which required systematic analysis on a computer.[7]

Sampling is not the only dilemma quantitative historians have had to face. Because we work with large historical datasets, we have had to develop a model or theory and decide before collecting the data which variables needed collecting. Moreover, if we failed to record a variable in our initial hypothesis, we could not easily go back and redo our coding. Social historians have generally encoded information for households or aggregated information to the head of the household. However, questions and problems may well require the analysis of a society's entire population, not just that of the household heads. For instance, in the initial construction of my Edgefield County database, for each household and/or family I counted the number of children between the ages of 5-17 to analyze different rates of school attendance for boys and girls. Later I realized that the poor used different strategies for sending children to school and I needed more information to explain school attendance. For example, one year a family would send boys 6-8 years of age to school, and then the following year boys aged 10-12. In other families some children worked so that others could attend school. The age breakdowns for black and white children, rich, poor, middle-class, boys and girls, needed to be analyzed more discreetly than an overall age category like 5-17 years of age. If my data had been recorded for each individual instead of summarized on the record of the family head, I could easily have tested various age groupings. Instead, I had to undertake a massive and time consuming addition to my database. (A lot of work for one table and a one paragraph explanation, yet the information is important and others can expand on it.)

For the most part the study of history has been a solitary occupation. I believe computers will bring about more team effort in research areas. As questions are refined by historians, we should consider what might be important for future investigations. We may have argued for "total history," that is, the inclusion of all the people from the census, but we have not used all variables in all the available records. If historians included all information in their databases, then future scholars will utilize not only a historian's conclusions but also the data the conclusions were based upon. We can more easily build upon each other's work.

More comprehensive analyses should uncover exciting new discoveries about the nature of our society and the way in which it operates. For example in Democracy in America, Alexis De Tocqueville argued that Americans were especially upwardly mobile.[8] The poor became middle class and the middle class became wealthy. With the complete U.S. manuscript census as a database we could finally test his thesis. Thus far, social history studies have been limited by the fact that 33 to 66 percent of all people in one census are not found in the next census at the same location. Did these people wander as poor all their lives or did they indeed move geographically and improve their lot? By having all of the U.S. Census available, we can better answer this major question concerning the meaning of American democracy.

The versatility and increased capacity of a Supercomputer in tandem with microcomputers will allow researchers to arrive at a fuller understanding of this mobility issue as well as other major issues in American history. Up until now historians have been able only to guess at the economic development of both blacks and whites after the Civil War. The 1870 and 1880 manuscript census returns for agriculture and population are crucial to our understanding of the development from slavery to freedom and the initial years of capitalism in the American South. These censuses hold the systematic data which are the key to explaining economic life after emancipation. Another burning issue involves the Civil War. By checking census and economic data for specific persons with the records of those who served in the Union and the Confederacy, we could learn who served and for how long and who served in safe positions behind lines. In other words, we could answer a question historians have been asking for a long time: Was the Civil War a rich man's war and a poor man's fight?

With census material available at the regional history center, a historian could download a census database for his/her region, have students in a class add church records which identify who belonged to which church and then correlate this information with wealth and status data from the census, and even see which church members volunteered, were drafted, or avoided military service from the American Revolution to 1910. The same could be done for litigation which might help explain who benefited the most from the court system.

Another area of interest, which a member of our research team is presently exploring, is patterns of violence in the United States. Despite years of effort and a wealth of studies, historians and other scholars have been unable to adequately explain why some areas of the country are more violent than others. Terence Finnegan proposes to study one of the most visible and heinous forms of southern violence--lynching. He utilizes census data from 1880 to 1930 (a period in which there were over 5000 reported lynchings). Finnegan believes that studying the entire South will allow him to uncover demographic, social, and economic patterns that will help explain why some areas of the South had high incidences of lynching and others did not. The Supercomputer is important to Finnegan's work because he is studying approximately a thousand counties and will need countless calculations to construct the appropriate indexes and color graphics. Finnegan used a personal computer to enter and massage his data in preparation for use on the Supercomputer. When his analysis is done on the Supercomputer, he will use mapping software and seek input from NCSA's experts on visualization and color graphics to display his results on microcomputer. Another issue needing a Supercomputer is the structure of antebellum slaveownership. Graduate student Karl Bridges plans to use color patterns to map slave ownership, wealth, land type, crops and other demographic/geographic characteristics. His work will be a major new contribution to one of the most studied aspects of American culture. If in the past cautious and conservative conclusions have made quantitative historical research anathema to some traditional historians, the scope of these research projects certainly answers that criticism.

Will and Ariel Durant termed geography the "matrix of history, its nourishing mother and disciplining home,"[9] but historians are just beginning to understand how powerful geography can be in historical analysis, and especially if used with a Supercomputer. Mapping and coloring patterns for visualization are, in fact, one of the most exciting capabilities of a Supercomputer. Color patterns and overlays can suggest relationships hitherto unexplored. NCSA has developed the best interdisciplinary environment for data-visualization in existence today. Artist Donna Cox, for example, has color coded everything from breast cancer to corn disease and genetic patterns with remarkable results. Data-visualization experts will provide a tremendous resource for scholars using the U.S. census database. Detailed maps like none ever digitized can be overlapped with actual agricultural, population, demographic, and occupation data to show changes over time from 1790! Political historians will be able to color code votes with demographic and other information with relative ease. Historians have prided themselves on a felicitous pen; they must now find elegant visual ways to display data, maps, color patterns, in addition to tables, graphs, and charts.

Once this database is compiled and available, its impact on historians and other researchers and how they formulate questions will be tremendous. This computing power fosters creativity and may engender a profound change in the discipline.[10] Historians have a rare opportunity to change the scale and magnitude of historical inquiry. Supercomputing in tandem with microcomputers offers immense opportunities to historians, for their combined power allows scholars to organize, analyze, and comprehend historical data, including all the census information for the entire United States, in ways that have never before been possible. Thus, with the new technology and hardware, we can preserve the record just as it was recorded, go back for more and different questions, and make it available for future scholars to ask diverse questions from a separate set of concerns. My research team is the first group of historians to use a Supercomputer, and we believe our experiences will benefit others interested in working with large historical databases. Our proposed regional history center will not only provide scholars with a great opportunity but it will also be encouraging humanistic researchers to develop new ways in which computers can help us to understand ourselves and the world in which we live.

APPENDIX

1850 Population Census

Schedule I. Free Inhbitants in ____________ in the County of ____________ State of____________ enumerated by me, on the ____ day of ____ 1850. ________ Assistant Marshall.

line number (1-40)

1. Dwelling-houses numbered in the order of visitation
2. Families numbered in the order of visitation
3. The Name of every person whose usual place of abode on the first day of June, 1850, was in this family.

Description: (heading for 4-6)

4. Age
5. Sex
6. Color, White, black, or mulatto
7. Profession, Occupation, or Trade of each Male Person over 15 years of age (occasionally females' occupation listed)
8. Value of Real Estate owned.
9. Place of Birth, Naming the State, Territory, or Country
10. Married within the year
11. Attended School within the year.
12. Persons over 20 years of age who cannot read & write
13. Whether deaf and dumb, blind, insane, idiotic, pauper, or convict.

NOTES

1. The slave censuses for 1850 and 1860 are available on microfilm from the National Archives.

2. For more detailed discussions of the manuscript censuses see Vernon Burton, "Using the Computer and the Federal Manuscript Census Returns to Teach an Interdisciplinary American Social History Course," The History Teacher 12 (November 1979): 71-88; and Vernon Burton, "The Development of Tenantry and the Post-Bellum Afro-American Social Structure in Edgefield County, South Carolina." In Presentations Paysannes, Dimes, Rente fonciere et Mouvement de la Production Agricole a l'epoque Preindustrielle: Actes du Colloque preparatoire (30 juin-let et 2 juillet 1977) au VIIe Congres international d'Histoire economique Section A3. Edimbourg 13-19 aout 1978, edited by E. LeRoy Ladurie and J. Goy, Vol. 2: 762-78. Paris: Editions De L'Ecole des Hautes Etudes En Sciences Sociales, 1982.

3 We have also experimented with and are considering using some of the Texas Census Data System (Madison: Wisc-Ware, 1988) Entry programs developed by Prof. Myron P. Gutmann and Amy E. Holmes.

4. I have already discussed joint ventures with John Connolly, Director of the Supercomputer Center at the University of Kentucky. Connolly is especially interested in obtaining and contributing data on Appalachia. I feel certain that other Supercomputer centers will also want to work together once the project is at a stage from which others can benefit.

5. Roderick Floud, An Introduction to Quantitative Methods for Historians, 2nd ed., (London: Methuen, 1979), pp. 165-166, 185.

6. Orville Vernon Burton, In My Father's House Are Many Mansions: Family and Community in Edgefield County, South Carolina (Chapel Hill: The University of North Carolina Press, 1985). See Herbert G. Gutman, The Black Family in Slavery and Freedom, 1750-1925 (New York: Pantheon, 1976).

7. This lead one physicist to comment on my work, "He is asking questions which have answers. That is the key to science. He is doing science."The Chronicle of Higher Education, May 6, 1987, p. 8.

8. Alexis De Tocqueville, Democracy in America orig. publd 1835 and 1840 in Paris. (2 vols. New York: Knopf, 1976).

9. Will and Ariel Durant, The Lessons of History (New York: Simon and Schuster, 1968), p. 15.

10. Larry Smarr has estimated that there are now roughly 100 installed supercomputers and over ten million installed PCs, which possess the computing power of over 10,000 Cray-1 supercomputers or equivalents. See Larry L. Smarr, "The Computational Science Revolution: Technology, Methodology, and Sociology," National Center for Supercomputing Applications, adapted from a review article appearing in High-Speed Computing: Scientific Applications and Algorithm Design, Robert B. Wihelmson editor, (Urbana: University of Illinois Press, 1987).

Structural Analysis

BENCHMARKING THE PERFORMANCE OF PHYSICAL IMPACT SIMULATION SOFTWARE ON VECTOR AND PARALLEL COMPUTERS

Myron Ginsberg
Computer Science Dept., GM Research Laboratories
General Motors Technical Center, Warren, MI 48090-9055

James P. Johnson
C-P-C Engineering Center, General Motors Corporation
30003 Van Dyke, Warren, MI 48090-9060

ABSTRACT: The cost of just one physical car crash experiment can range between $50,000 and $750,000 depending upon whether the test is performed on a production model car or on a prototype vehicle, respectively. The high expense of impact testing and the availability of a variety of vector and parallel computers have motivated the development of sophisticated software to model such complex physical phenomena. An investigation has recently been initiated to improve performance of such programs. The purpose of the research is to define and apply methodology to reduce execution time and improve transportability of physical impact simulation software for vector and parallel processors. This paper focuses upon the design and analysis of a set of relevant test problems for applicability in current and future computational environments with vector and/or parallel facilities. The attributes of each test problem are discussed along with performance data using the DYNA3D nonlinear physical impact simulation program on a CRAY X-MP/24 supercomputer.

1. INTRODUCTION

Structural crash analysis investigates the response of vehicle structural components to impact forces in order to achieve designs that maximize protection of vehicle occupants. The traditional approach to this problem has been to use lumped mass and stiffness parameter dynamic simulation codes to simulate whole vehicle structural response to a crash event. These codes, available since the early 1970's, handle small problems very well on conventional (scalar) mainframes [1]. In the early 1980's, successful use of the explicit integration finite element method was achieved for structural crash analysis. This method offers more fidelity to geometric shape and material behavior than the lumped parameter method but the computational requirement is significant when problem size is moderate to large [2]. For that reason, the finite element codes have been vectorized to perform efficiently on single processor vector computers [3].

Experience has shown that using an explicit integration finite element approach to analyze vehicle components or subassemblies can require 1 to 4 hours of execution time on a single processor of a CRAY X-MP supercomputer. Full car crash simulations have required up to 20 hours on one processor of an X-MP. While such analyses have provided valuable design guidance, the execution time and associated expense required to perform the computations are a legitimate concern in an industrial environment. Utilizing the parallel processing architecture of supercomputers and minisupers has the potential to provide more efficient and affordable computational capability for these programs.

The long-term goals of this investigation with respect to crashworthiness simulations are: (1) to reduce computer throughput time; (2) to utilize software tools to determine CPU bottlenecks and data dependencies as well as to improve vectorization; (3) to develop transportable vectorization and parallelization strategies which will enable such codes to run efficiently on a variety of small and large vector and parallel computers; (4) to create a set of practical guidelines to accomplish (1) through (3) above for a variety of crashworthiness codes of interest to GM Divisions and Staffs. The outgrowth of this project when completed is to improve the economic viability of crashworthiness simulations and thereby reduce the frequency of costly physical testing. During the course of the project, the research results will be applied to an existing crashworthiness code of interest to GM and will be tested on a series of increasingly difficult structural impact analyses.

There are many computer science research issues involved in this project which have not been thoroughly investigated by the engineering community that has created the existing crashworthiness codes. At present, most of the commercially available finite element programs have not been parallelized and few have been sufficiently vectorized to take full advantage of the new minisupers and supercomputers. Furthermore, many of these codes have not been analyzed to determine the effects of these new machine architectures on their performance nor have they effectively exploited both vectorization and parallelism.

In this paper, attention is focused on the initial analysis phase of the aforementioned project with a specific physical impact simulation code, DYNA3D. In Section 2, the hardware and software environments are defined. Section 3 contains descriptions of crashworthiness analysis software and the test problems used to evaluate program performance and serve as the focal points for vectorization and parallelism experiments. Performance attributes for the test problems with DYNA3D on a CRAY X-MP are given in Section 4. Section 5 provides discussion of vectorization and parallelization issues.

2. INITIAL COMPUTATIONAL ENVIRONMENT

The first computational environment investigated in this project is the General Motors Research Laboratories' CRAY X-MP/24 using the COS (Version 1.16BF1) Operating System with both the Cray CFT (Version 1.15BF2) and CFT77 (Version 2.0) Fortran compilers. Both of the compilers from Cray Research are Fortran 77 optimizing compilers. CFT77 is the newer of the two and is suppose to generate more efficient code for most applications. Details about both compilers can be found in [4,5].

The initial physical impact simulation code chosen for examination is DYNA3D from Lawrence Livermore National Laboratory [3,6]. This program, primarily developed by J. O. Hallquist, is an explicit finite element code for three-dimensional dynamic analysis and contains over 49,000 source lines and 610 subroutines. DYNA3D was selected because it and its commercial derivatives are of interest to several groups within GM.

A set of increasingly complex structural test problems has been defined ranging from small subassemblies to a full car crash simulation. CPU times for these problems range from approximately 15 minutes to twenty hours on a single processor of a CRAY X-MP. This set will be used to examine the effects of vectorization and parallelism.

3. TEST PROBLEMS

Nine test cases were chosen to represent typical structural analysis problems encountered by automotive crashworthiness engineers. Diversity of geometric shape, load and constraint conditions, and material types were sought in order to exercise a wide range of solution algorithms in the finite element program. Table 1 provides a qualitative comparison of these benchmarks. Table 2 summarizes quantitative attributes of the finite element models for these test cases.

Eight of the nine problems utilize contact algorithms which provide constraints to prevent inter-penetration of finite elements which model physical surfaces. Two distinct formulations were used, master-slave and single surface. The master-slave algorithm is typically applied when a priori knowledge of the collapse mechanism is available (often after an initial checkout run). The analyst then constrains a group of finite elements, designated a slave segment, to contact, slide along, stick to, or separate from but not penetrate another group of elements, designated the master segment. Single surface contact algorithms are applied in problems of severe structural collapse where a material surface may fold on itself and a priori knowledge of where contact will occur is lacking. This algorithm allows surface contact, sliding, sticking, or separating but prohibits penetration. See reference [7] for descriptions of these formulations.

Problems 1 and 2 simulate the collapse of a generic automotive structural component known as the "S" frame or torque box, illustrated in Figure 1. References [8,9] are historical examples of analyses of this type of structure. An "S" frame represents the locus of the axis of a horizontal frame/rail that lies at the full vehicle width along the passenger compartment and then narrows toward the vehicle centerline to lie inboard of the front tires. The bending collapse mechanism of this structure is well known. Problem 1 uses this knowledge by defining master-slave contact segments at the locations of the rail cross-sectional collapse. Problem 2 ignores this information, and a single surface contact algorithm is used. In each case, a single rail undergoes impact along its longitudinal axis.

Problem 3 focuses on the deformation of a rear frame subassembly, shown in Figure 2, which consists of two parallel longitudinal rails and lateral crossmembers subjected to a distributed, oblique impact load into one of the rails. This situation occurs in certain side impacts.

One possible interaction between vehicle occupants and the interior structure during a crash event is the impact of an unbelted occupant's knees into the lower surface of the instrument panel. Test cases 4 and 5 study this interaction. Knowledge gained from these analyses assist in the proper design of inflatable restraints, i.e., air bags. These problems model a luxury vehicle instrument panel with thick urethane foam padding molded to a steel backing

TABLE 1: Qualitative Comparison of Benchmark Problems

TEST CASE	STRUCTURAL CLASSIFICATION	DESCRIPTION	CONTACT ALGORITHM
1	COMPONENT	GENERIC FRONT RAIL	MASTER-SLAVE
2	COMPONENT	GENERIC FRONT RAIL	SINGLE SURFACE
3	SUBASSEMBLY	REAR FRAME ASSEMBLY	NONE
4	SUBASSEMBLY	INSTRUMENT PANEL	MASTER-SLAVE
5	SUBASSEMBLY	INSTRUMENT PANEL	MASTER-SLAVE
6	COMPONENT	REAR LONGITUDINAL RAIL	SINGLE SURFACE
7	COMPONENT	FRONT LONGITUDINAL RAIL	SINGLE SURFACE
8	SUBASSEMBLY	FRONT RAIL & BUMPER	SINGLE SURFACE
9	FULL VEHICLE	FULL VEHICLE STRUCTURE	MASTER-SLAVE & SINGLE SURFACE

TABLE 2: Attributes of Benchmark Problems

Test No.	1	2	3	4	5	6	7	8	9
Nodes	496	496	3583	243	941	3303	1237	2171	15564
Brick Elts	0	0	0	105	609	0	0	0	0
Shell Elts	440	440	3721	44	152	3045	1145	2000	16649
Beam Elts	0	0	0	26	26	0	0	0	122
Material Types	1	1	1	2	2	1	1	1	4
Master-Slave Contacts	2	0	0	1	1	0	0	0	4
Single Surface Contacts	0	1	0	0	0	1	4	4	12

plate being impacted by rigid hemispherical knees. Master-slave contacts are used. The problem 4 solution uses a coarse finite element mesh shown in Figure 3. Problem 5 uses the same solution algorithms for an eight times finer mesh density.

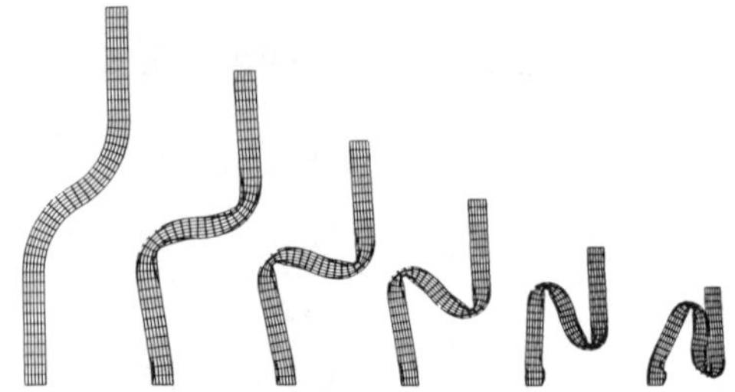

Fig. 1 S Frame Deformations over Time

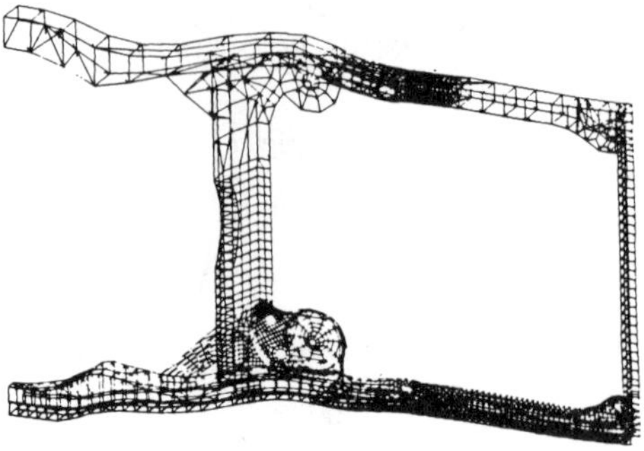

Fig. 2 Rear Frame Subassembly

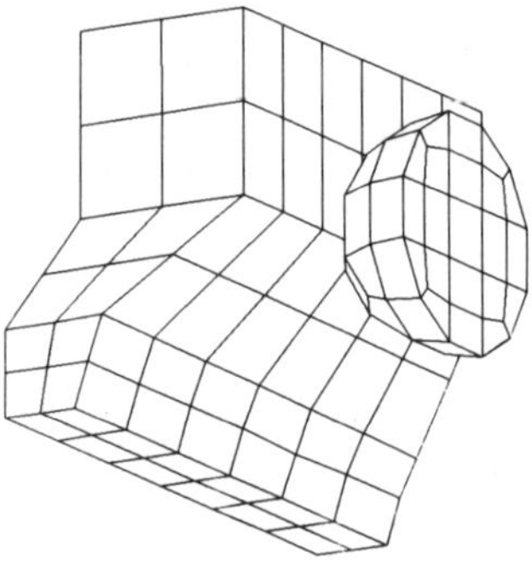

Fig. 3 Knee Bolster

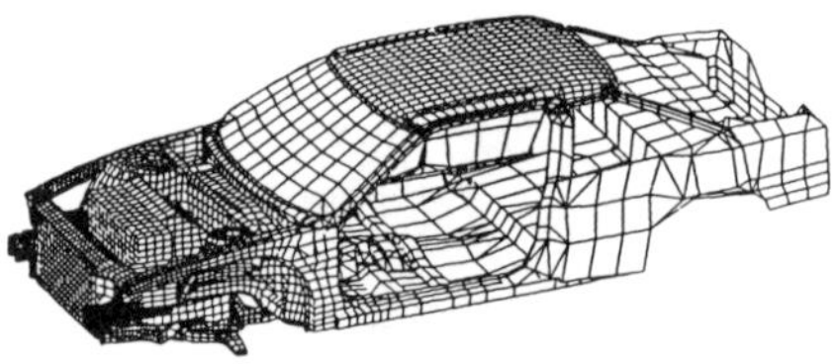

Fig. 4 Full Car Finite Element Model

Problem 6 analyzes the reaction of a straight, symmetric, thin-walled rail component to an axial impact loading. The geometry is clean, a straight hatsection rail that is typically located in the rear of vehicles. Such a structure will undergo a complex collapse (commonly called accordion folding) resulting in a series of folds beginning at the impact end, propagating axially along the rail and causing significant end-to-end shortening of the structure. A fine-grained finite element mesh is required to capture the wavelength of the folding mechanism. The integration time step is correspondingly small. A single surface contact algorithm must be used.

Test case 7 studies the axial impact of a straight, symmetric, thin-walled rail found in the front structure of a current GM vehicle. Significant geometric complexity is added in the form of a short wraparound collar spot welded to one end. Both the collar and rail have stamped indentations known as collapse initiators to insure that folding begins in a desired local area. As in problem 6, a fine-grained finite element mesh is necessary, and the single surface contact algorithm is required.

Test case 8 merges the structure of problem 7 into a subassembly including the front rail structure and the front bumper. This test problem simulates a 30 mph impact of the subassembly into a rigid barrier, a common component test. Additional contact elements are required to insure that the rail does not penetrate the rear face of the bumper.

Problem 9 is a simulation of the frontal 30 mph impact of a full vehicle structure into a rigid barrier. Reference [3] is an example of an earlier analysis of this type. All main load carrying members of the vehicle structure are modeled as well as its inertia properties. Extensive use of both types of contact algorithm is required to simulate the interaction of distinct vehicle components such as the radiator, engine, and rail structures. The finite element model, Figure 4, is very large and complex. The resulting CPU requirement to simulate 0.080 seconds of such a crash event using this model size is now approximately 25 CRAY X-MP hours for the single processor version of the finite element program.

4. PERFORMANCE ATTRIBUTES OF TEST PROBLEMS

Before any meaningful attempt can be made to improve the performance of a crashworthiness program, it is necessary to understand how each of the aforementioned test problems behaves on one or more vector and/or parallel computers. Here we focus on the environment described in Section 2. Performance data is gathered for the test problems using the initial version of a crashworthiness package. Such information helps to determine approaches for additional improvements in vectorization and suggests ways to define parallelism. Then as code modifications are made, performance results can be compared with the baseline data for the original version of the package. Several software and hardware facilities are available on the CRAY X-MP and other computers to assist in obtaining the baseline data; a few examples are given in this section.

Figures 5 through 9 provide results from applying FLOWTRACE on the CRAY X-MP to the test problems executed with DYNA3D. FLOWTRACE [10] enables the user to observer where the bulk of the CPU time is spent during execution of a program with a specific input test problem. This is very valuable information because crashworthiness codes tend to be large programs. Thus applying FLOWTRACE to each test problem run enables us to determine which routines are most active and then to focus on altering those routines in the hope of thereby maximizing the potential performance improvement. For simplification purposes, the routines are referenced as R1, R2, etc. rather than using the specific names given in DYNA3D.

There are several observations which can be made from a perusal of the results in Figures 5 through 9. We note than in some problems (see Figures 5 and 6) one or two routines can take on the order of 20% to 30% of the total CPU time whereas for other problems (see Figures 7 and 8) most of the dominant routines take only 5% to 10% of the total CPU time. It is interesting to note that across all the test results given, only 24 routines were used 5% or more of the time despite the fact that the DYNA3D package contains 610 routines. Thus to improve performance it will not be necessary to examine most of the routines in the package. A structural engineer would also note that similar types of routines are used in each test problem and are dependent upon the type of contact algorithm used and/or the type of material involved.

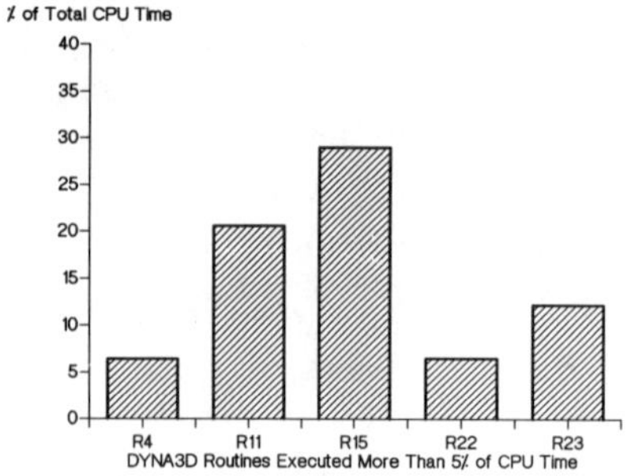

Fig. 5 FLOWTRACE for Problem 2

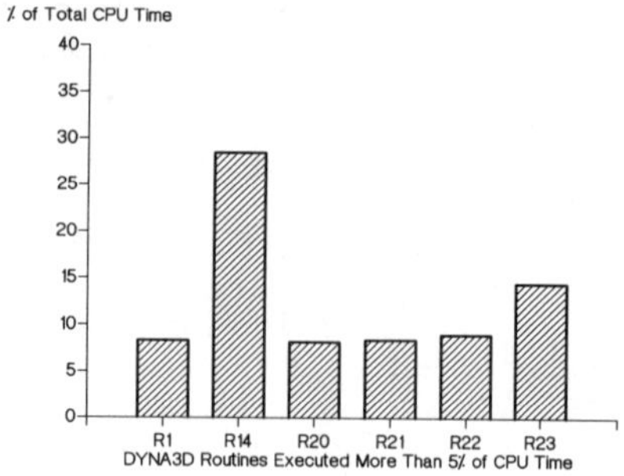

Fig. 6 FLOWTRACE for Problem 3

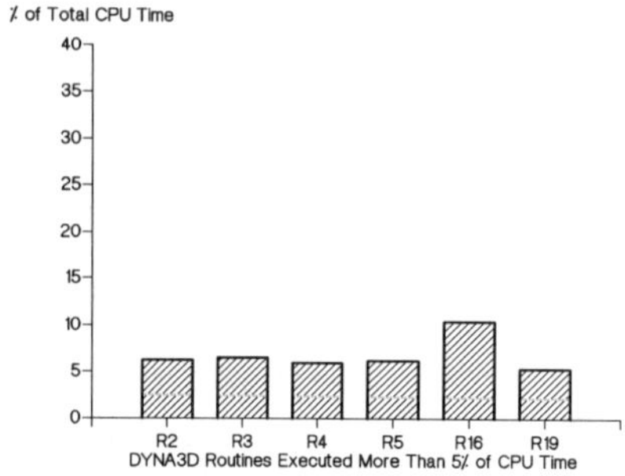

Fig. 7 FLOWTRACE for Problem 4

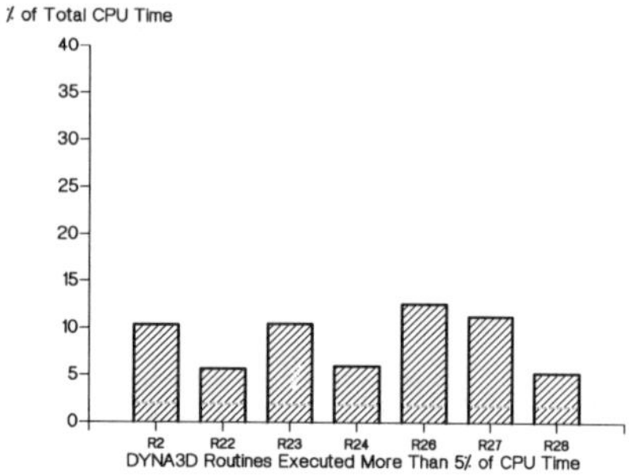

Fig. 8 FLOWTRACE for Problem 8

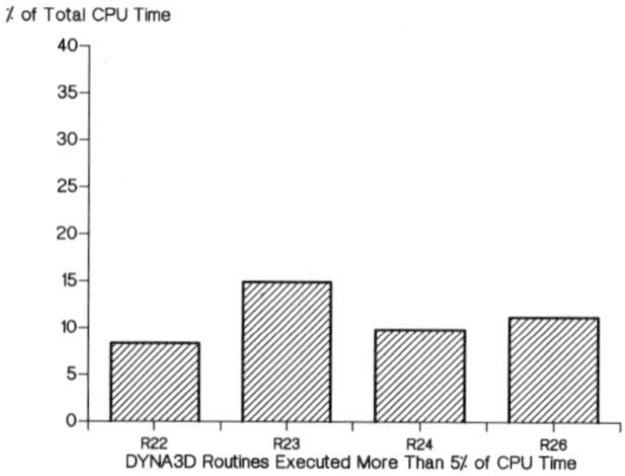

Fig. 9 FLOWTRACE for Problem 9

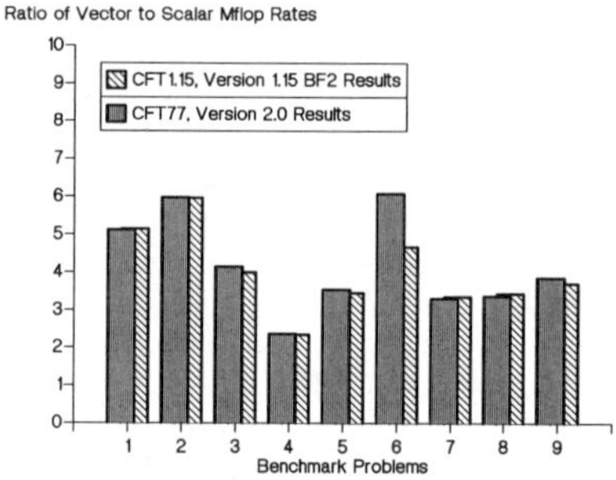

Fig. 10 Ratio of Vector to Scalar Speed

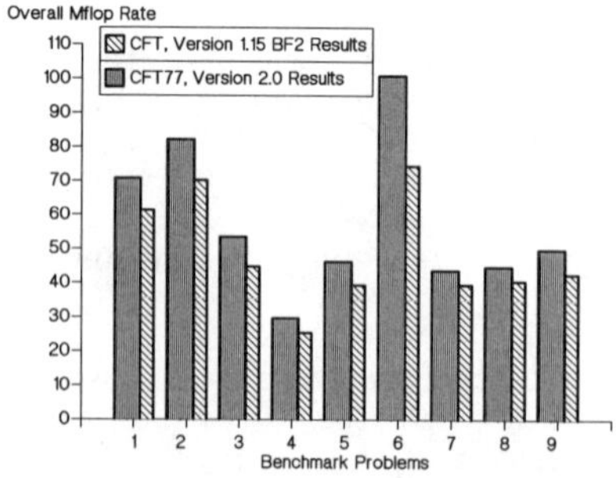

Fig. 11 MFLOP Performance

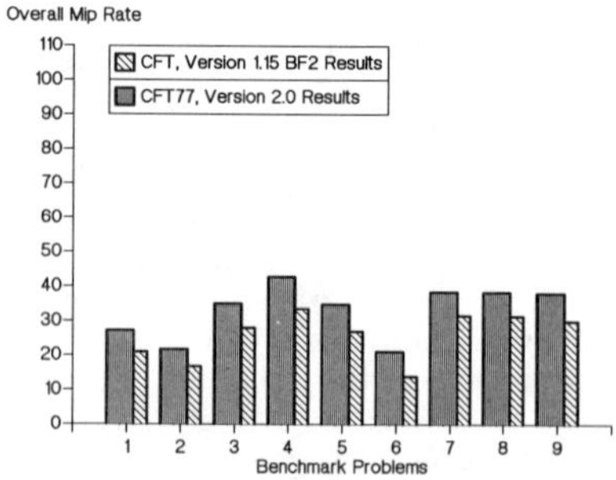

Fig. 12 MIP Performance

Additional examples of baseline data collected are illustrated in Figures 10, 11, and 12. Cray hardware monitors can be invoked by an interface called PERFMON [10] and permit the user to gather statistics about various aspects of program performance; this is how the results were obtained for those figures.

Several observations can be made from examination of those three figures. Note that the MFLOP (millions of floating-point operations executed per second) and MIP (millions of instructions per second) rates fluctuate both with respect to compiler used and with respect to test problem executed. Both the MFLOP and MIP rates are consistently higher when the CFT77 Fortran compiler rather than the CFT Fortran compiler is used with each test problem displayed here. Note also that none of these problems is executing at anywhere near the peak possible rates for a single processor of a CRAY X-MP, even though DYNA3D is generally recognized as being a highly vectorized code.

Further observe that for Problems 1, 2, 3, 5, 6, 7, 8, and 9 displayed in Figures 11 and 12 the MFLOP rates are greater than the MIP rates with both Fortran compilers. In contrast, for Problem 4, the MIP rates are greater than the MFLOP rates with both compilers; this would seem to suggest that few floating-point operations are being performed for each instruction executed and thus little vectorization occurs with the resulting performance mostly in scalar mode. Note this observation is, indeed, confirmed in Figure 10 in which the ratio of vector to scalar speeds for Problem 4 (with both compilers) is the lowest of all test cases and is approximately 2.

From the examples presented in this section it should be obvious that once benchmark test problem sets are defined, much insight can be obtained by performance analysis; thus the programmer is provided with directions in which to attempt to improve execution time and also has baseline data with which to measure performance modifications. Additional performance data are in [11].

5. STRATEGIES AND TRADEOFFS FOR VECTORIZATION AND PARALLELISM

Once the CPU bottlenecks are identified as indicated in the previous section, then attempts can be made to vectorize and/or parallelize the program segments which dominate execution time. The best strategy is to give first priority to vectorizing a program as much as possible and only then attempt to parallelize it. For the computational environment described in Section 2, the best vector speedup that can be expected on a CRAY X-MP is about 10 times scalar speed but the best speedup that can be expected via use of its multiple processors is a factor of 2 or 4, depending upon whether an X-MP/2 or X-MP/4, respectively, is used. We thus see in such circumstances that vectorization can potentially have a much greater impact than parallelism in this specific environment.

All 24 routines which accounted for 5% or more of CPU time for any of the nine benchmarks were examined to determine if the levels of vectorization could be increased. Many of these routines were already totally or mostly vectorized. This may seem somewhat surprising when noting that the overall MFLOP rates for all nine benchmarks (see Figure 11) are well below supervector speeds of 150 MFLOPS or more. There are several reasons which seem to account for this behavior: (1) many of the vectorized loops involve data movement, thus significant amounts of CPU time have a very low density of floating-point operations and hence contribute to lowering the overall MFLOP rate; (2) In simulations involving extensive use of contact algorithms, as the computations progress, more and more time is spent executing these algorithms which involve large amounts of dependencies which inhibit vectorization; (3) there are small amounts of computations involving indirect addressing and which do not run at vector speeds but are executed often as, for example, in the full-car crash (Problem 9) where one routine takes approximately 20% of the CPU time but 55% of that time is spent in two loops running at scalar speed.

Implementing parallelism for the environment defined in Section 2 requires the use of Cray multitasking facilities [12]. There are two alternative ways of implementing parallelism with the multitasking facilities: macrotasking and microtasking. Macrotasking defines parallelism at the subroutine level, i.e., two or more subroutines can be executed in parallel. Microtasking defines parallelism at the loop level within a subroutine, i.e., two or more loop iterations can be executed in parallel.

For DYNA3D we choose to use microtasking rather than macrotasking to implement parallelism [12]. The microtasked approach has the following advantages: (1) improves program performance even on a non-dedicated CRAY X-MP; (2) minimizes the amount of system overhead associated with execution of parallel segments; (3) minimizes the amount of code rewriting.

Our examination of the nature of the vectorization in DYNA3D gives us some insight as to what the tradeoffs should be between vectorization and parallelism. Unaltered scalar code can be run in scalar concurrent mode and thus lead to some speedup, although not as much as from vectorization. Probes can be inserted into the code to sample vector length. Then using this information dynamically with microtasking directives can help to determine when it is efficient to partition vector loops amongst multiple processors.

Another limitation with regard to parallelism should be mentioned. The cost to execute the program could be equal to or greater than that for single processor execution of the same job due to the amount of multitasking overhead! The primary motivation of parallelism is to reduce program throughput time. However, in an industrial environment where computer job costs are also important, many users may find it unacceptable to improve throughput time while increasing job costs.

Since job billing algorithms are usually defined by each computer installation rather than by the computer vendor, it is imperative that billing practices be adopted to encourage users to utilize multiple processors, otherwise it will not be economically feasible to attempt to parallelize a program. Some of the factors which should be considered to encourage the use of parallelism are: (1) adjust the CPU charges to favor jobs which use more than one CPU; (2) bill for wall clock usage of memory rather than for the number of CPU's which reference the same memory; (3) minimize charges for interprocessor communications.

6. SUMMARY AND CONCLUSIONS

A crashworthiness computational performance project has been initiated to investigate ways to improve throughput time on vector and parallel computers.

Initial efforts have focused on the definition of a relevant set of benchmark problems and establishing a performance baseline with them using DYNA3D on a CRAY X-MP with the CFT and CFT77 Fortran compilers. Hardware monitors and software tools have been used to examine performance including the determination of where the CPU bottlenecks occur with the given benchmarks. Some test results have been presented as examples. Initial results indicate that performance with DYNA3D and the given benchmarks consistently produces faster results with the CFT77 (Version 2.0) than with the CFT (Version 1.15 BF2) Fortran compiler. Current activities in this project are focusing on using the baseline data results to improve vector performance and to establish approaches to parallelize the code. Some of the specific vector and parallel issues have been discussed.

ACKNOWLEDGMENTS

We extend our deep appreciation to Paul Du Bois (consultant) and Mark Skynar of GM C-P-C Engineering for their efforts developing the finite element models for test cases 7, 8, and 9. We are very grateful for the assistance of Richard Katnik of GM C-P-C Engineering for helping us to better understand the computational behavior of crashworthiness codes. Thanks to Dr. Tawfik B. Khalil of the GMR Engineering Mechanics Department for providing us with the GM DYNA3D source code and for discussions about its use. We appreciate the efforts of Walt Wolf (Cray Research Analyst at GMR) for the innumerable assists in responding to software problems.

REFERENCES

1. M. M. Kamal, "Analysis and Simulation of Vehicle to Barrier Impact," SAE Paper 700414, Society of Automotive Engineers, Inc., Warrrendale, PA, May 1970.

2. J. F. Chedmail, P. Du Bois, and A. K. Pickett, "Numerical Techniques, Experimental Validation and Industrial Applications of Structural Impact and Crashworthiness Analysis with Supercomputers for the Automotive Industries," Proceedings of the International Conference on Supercomputer Applications in the Automobile Industry, edited by C. Marino, Cray Research, Inc., Minneapolis, MN, Oct. 1986.

3. D. J. Benson, J. O. Hallquist, M. Igaraski, K. Shimomaki, and M. Mizuno, The Application of DYNA3D in Large-Scale Crashworthiness Calculations, Report UCRL-94028, Lawrence Livermore National Laboratory, Livermore, CA, Apr. 1986.

4. Cray Research, Inc., FORTRAN (CFT) Reference Manual, SR-0009, Rev. L, Cray Research, Inc., Mendota Heights, MN, July 1986.

5. Cray Research Inc., CFT77 Reference Manual, SR-0018, Rev. A, Cray Research, Inc., Mendota Heights, MN, Sept. 1986.

6. J. O. Hallquist, DYNA3D User's Manual (Nonlinear Dynamic Analysis of Structures in Three Dimensions), Report UCID-19592, Rev. 4, Methods Development Group, Mech. Eng. Dept., Lawrence Livermore National Laboratory, Livermore, CA, Apr. 1988.

7. J. O. Hallquist et al., "Sliding Interfaces with Contact-Impact in Large-Scale Lagrangian Computations," Computer Methods Appl. Mech. Eng., Vol. 51, 1985, pp. 107-137.

8. Chi-Mou Ni,"Impact Response of Curved Box Beam-Columns with Large Global and Local Deformations," Proc.,ASME/AIAA/SAE,14th Structures, Structural Dynamics, and Materials Conf., Williamsburg, VA, March 1973.

9. J. Argyris et al., "Computer Simulation of Crash Phenomena," Intl. J. Num. Methods Eng., Vol. 22, 1986, pp. 497-519.

10. Cray Research, Inc., COS Performance Utilities Reference Manual, Reference Manual SR-0146, Cray Research, Inc., Mendota Heights, MN, Apr. 1987.

11. M. Ginsberg, Analyzing the Performance of Physical Impact Simulation Software on Vector and Parallel Processors, Research Publication GMR-6149, Computer Science Dept., General Motors Research Laboratories, Warren, MI, Feb. 9, 1988.

12. Cray Research, Multitasking User Guide, Technical Note SN-0222, Rev. B, Cray Research, Inc., Mendota Heights, MN, 1986.

Tuning the ANSYS Kernel LSOLVE for a Parallel Computer

Richard E. Hessel
Supercomputer Systems, Inc.
1414 W. Hamilton Ave.
Eau Claire, WI 54701

Mathew Myszewski **Giacomo Brussino**
Alliant Computer Systems Corporation
One Monarch Drive
Littleton, MA 01460

John A. Swanson **Lauralee Wagner**
Swanson Analysis Systems, Inc.
P.O. Box 65
Houston, PA 15342-0065

Abstract

A new solver kernel, `lsolve`*, has been added to ANSYS.* `lsolve` *is a rank-n update routine that can be implemented efficiently on parallel and vector machines with a hierarchical memory structure. An implementation of* `lsolve` *on a parallel computer is described by examining the Fortran code used on the Alliant parallel computer. The utility of* `lsolve` *is demonstrated by performance on standard ANSYS benchmarks.*

1 Introduction

ANSYS [1] is a finite element analysis code distributed by Swanson Analysis Systems, Inc. (SASI). In solving large structures problems, most of the time is spent in a linear equation solver. The standard solver kernel for ANSYS is `msolve`, which does a rank one update to a triangular matrix. John Swanson has defined an alternate solver kernel, `lsolve`, which does a rank-n update so that the work is partitioned into larger pieces. Using the summation convention, the rank one update in `msolve` is essentially $a_{ij} = a_{ij} + b_i * c_j$. The rank-n update in `lsolve` is essentially $a_{ij} = a_{ij} + b_{ik} * c_{kj}$.

The rank-n update is coded with a "block" algorithm. The calculations are arranged to make use of memory locality to minimize the number of memory references. The first references to block algorithms appeared in the mid 1950's when they were used to minimize tape I/O. More recently, the BLAS3 routines and FX/LINPACK [2] use block algorithms. Algorithms with data reuse are essential for good performance on modern supercomputers and minisupercomputers [2, 3, 5, 6, 8, 10].

[1] ANSYS is a trademark of Swanson Analysis Systems, Inc.

[2] Alliant, FX/8, FX/80, FX/LINPACK, and FX/Fortran are trademarks of Alliant Computer Systems Corporation

Figure 1: Data structures for lsolve

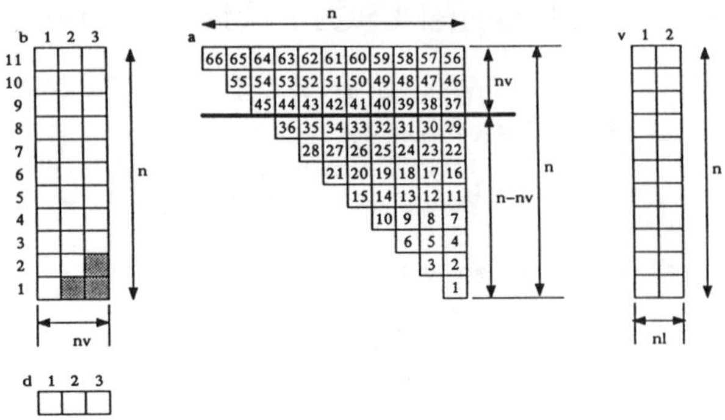

The algorithm will be described in detail by looking at the Fortran implementation on the Alliant computer. The details of loop splitting and rearrangement are the essence of block algorithms. The code presented in this paper is essentially the same as in the Alliant version of ANSYS 4.3. Compiler directives and special case code for short loops, etc. have been removed for clarity.

A programming language is a notation used to describe an algorithm to a computer. The computing literature on models of parallel computing is extensive. Yet, programming scientific applications require few of these concepts. Scientific parallel programming requires the study of the *application* to determine which operations can be done in parallel while avoiding problems of data dependencies.

Many applications require only a directive to "do it in parallel" and, perhaps, to lock around critical regions. The parallel implementation of `lsolve` requires only a single "do it in parallel" directive.

2 The `lsolve` Interface

Figure 1 shows the data structures used by `lsolve`.

The input data structures include the triangular matrix, `a`; the load vectors, `v`; and an error flag, `kerr`. On output, the variables corresponding to the first `nv` rows have been eliminated in both the matrix `a` and the load vectors `v`. The scaled versions of the first `nv` rows of the matrix have been placed in `b`, and the diagonals before scaling have been placed in `d`.

3 Functional Algorithm

The algorithm will be explained by examining the Fortran code for a simple, non-optimized version. First consider the declarations.

```
*      call lsolve(akv(1),nmrow,nvect,btemp(1,1),
*     &              nlvect,vload(1),kerr,tol,diag(1))

       subroutine lsolve(a,n,nv,b,nl,v,kerr,tol,d)
```

```
implicit real*8 (a-h,o-z)
dimension a(n*(n+1)/2),b(n,nv),v(n,nl),d(nv)
ix(i) = (i*(i-1))/2
```

Note that within the subroutine, the names have been simplified from those used outside, in the rest of ANSYS. **kerr**, **tol**, and the arguments shown in figure 1 are the only arguments. The routine is double precision throughout. A statement function, **ix**, defines an index function that gives the number of cells in a triangle of the next smaller size. Thus, **ix(n+1)** is the number of cells in a triangular matrix of size **n**.

The code itself is in two major parts. The first part computes exclusively in the first **nv** rows; the second with the last **n-nv** rows. In each case, indexing is done with a row count **i**, a row length **in**, and a row offset, **ir**. Here is the code that deals with the indexing:

```
in = n
ir = ix(in+1)
do i = 1, nv
     ...
    ir = ir - in
     ...
```

Here, **in** is the number of elements in the row and **ir** is the row offset. That is, the row consists of elements **a(ir+1:ir+in)** with the diagonal element being **a(ir+in)**.

```
      ...
    in = in - 1
end do
```

For each of the first **nv** rows, there are three steps: move the diagonal element to **d(i)**, scale the row by the reciprocal of the diagonal, and eliminate the variable in the remaining rows **i+1** to **nv**. Here is the code that moves the diagonal element and tests it for error conditions. The variable **ke** is a copy of the input value of the error flag **kerr**.

```
in = n
ir = ix(in+1)
do i = 1,nv
    d(i) = a(ir)
    ir = ir - in
    if ( d(i).lt.tol ) then
        if( ke.eq.0 .and. d(i).lt. -tol ) then
            kerr = 1
            p = 0.0d0
        else if ( d(i).gt.-tol ) then
            p = 0.0d0
        else
            p = 1.0d0/d(i)
        end if
    else
        p = 1.0d0/d(i)
```

```
        end if
        do j = 1, in
            b(j,i) = a(ir+j)*p
        end do
```

Rows i+1 to nv are indexed by j, jn, and jr in much the same way that i, in, and ir are used.

```
        jn = in
        jr = ir
        do j = i+1, nv
            jn = jn - 1
            jr = jr - jn
```

The processing in the loop subtracts a multiple of row i from row j in both the matrix a, and the load vectors v:

```
            do k = 1, jn
                a(jr+k) = a(jr+k) - b(jn,i)*a(ir+k)
            end do
            do k = 1, nl
                v(jn,k) = v(jn,k) - b(jn,i)*v(in,k)
            end do
        end do
        in = in -1
    end do
```

That is all there is to processing the first nv rows. The remaining rows are processed by a rank-n update using the first nv rows of the matrix and the nv columns of b.

```
    in = n-nv
    ir = ix(in+1)
    do i = n-nv,1,-1
        ir = ir - in
        do k = 1,min(n-nv,in)
            jn = n
            jr = ix(jn+1)
            do j = 1, nv
                jr = jr - jn
                a(ir+k) = a(ir+k) - b(i,j)*a(jr+k)
                jn = jn - 1
            end do
        end do
        in = in - 1
    end do
*............process the load vector(s) - typically nl=1, nv=7
    do k = 1, nl
        do j = 1, nv
            do i = nv+1, n
```

```
                    v(n-i+1,k) = v(n-i+1,k) - b(n-i+1,j)*v(n-j+1,k)
                end do
            end do
        end do
*............zero the eliminated rows of a
        istart = ix(n) - n*(nv-1) + ix(nv) + 1
        istop  = ix(n) + n
        do i = istart, istop
            a(i) = 0.0d0
        end do
        return
        end
```

4 The Alliant Architecture

The optimized implementation of **lsolve** is tailored to the Alliant architecture. However, any parallel computer or computer with a hierarchical memory structure would benefit from similar code. A brief description of the Alliant architecture will provide a basis for understanding the optimal algorithm presented in the next section.

The Alliant FX/8 minisupercomputer is a shared memory parallel computer with up to 8 processors. Each processor is a vector computer with 8 vector registers of 32 double precision floating point numbers. The processors share a common global memory through a 512k byte cache and a crossbar switch. The memory system of the Alliant appears to be "flat" to an application program. However, performance can be improved if a program organizes its data to make efficient use of virtual memory, main memory, cache, and registers. "Blocked" algorithms use data locality to optimize performance on such a hierarchical memory system.

The Alliant Fortran compiler does a good job of automatically detecting loop level parallelism. Parallel performance can be further improved by using blocked algorithms at a low level or tasking at a high level. Shared memory and low concurrency overhead allow the programmer to ignore the costs of interprocessor communication [7].

5 Optimal Algorithm

The functional algorithm is a good description of the work to be done, but it does not take advantage of the rank-n update to get memory locality. This section presents the processing of the last n-nv rows in a way that takes advantage of locality. Processing the first nv rows is the same as before.

In ANSYS today, there is most often one load vector and sometimes none. Since this is the case, the processing of the load vectors has been split into its own loop and special cased. First consider the processing of the matrix:

```
*.....process the remaining n-nv rows with a rank nv update
         np = lib_number_of_processors()
         nstrip = max( 8, min( 32, (n-nv)/(np*2)+1 ) )
cvd$ cncall
         do ka = nv+1, n, nstrip
             kb = min(ka+nstrip-1,n-nv)
```

Figure 2: Matrix striping for concurrent processing

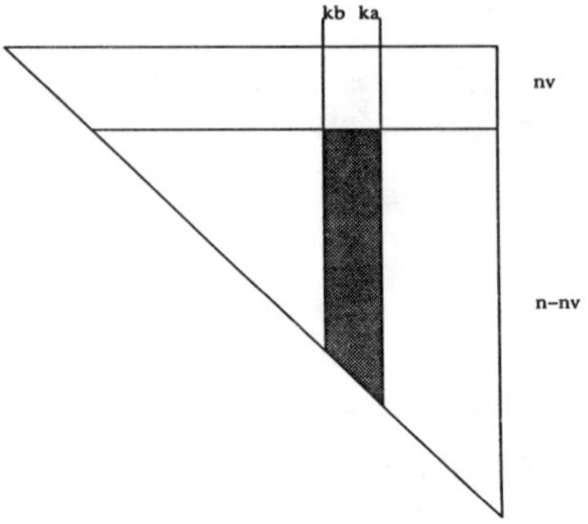


```
        call rankn(a,n,b,nv,ka,kb)
    end do
```

Notice that the matrix is being processed in several strips. Figure 2 shows that each strip consists of columns **ka** to **kb**.

The processing itself consists of calling a reentrant subroutine, **rankn**, concurrently.[3] In short, each strip is executed by a different processor in turn. The size and number of strips are chosen to optimize the algorithm on a particular machine. On the Alliant, each strip is allowed to be up to 32 elements long, the size of an Alliant vector register. However, if the matrix is small, say 100 rows with an 8 processor system, processing should not be limited to only a few processors, nor should the first processor, that takes the rightmost, longest strip, dominate the running time. So, the strip size is reduced so there are at least twice as many strips as processors. However, a vector length of at least 8, an arbitrary cutoff, is maintained. For the case just mentioned, the strips would be max(8,min(32,100/16+1)), or 8 long. There will be 12 of these and one remnant of length 4. The timing diagram appears in Figure 3.

```
*........process the remaining n-nv rows with a rank nv update
      np = lib_number_of_processors()
      nstrip = max( 8, min( 32, (n-nv)/(np*2)+1 ) )
cvd$ cncall
      do ka = nv+1, n, nstrip
          kb = min(ka+nstrip-1,n-nv)
          call rankn(a,n,b,nv,ka,kb)
      end do
*........process the load vector(s) with a rank nv update
      if ( nl.ge.1 ) then
          do i = nv+1, n
              do k = 1, nl
                  do j = 1, nv
                      v(j,k) = v(j,k) - b(i,j)*v(i,k)
```

[3]The compiler directive, cvd$ cncall, directs the Alliant FX/Fortran compiler to generate code for the concurrent call.

Figure 3: Timing Diagram

```
                end do
            end do
        end do
    end if
    return
    end
```

6 Blocked Kernel

The key to high performance is the use of a "block" algorithm in the implementation of the kernel, **rankn**. The basic idea is to split the **nv** updates into blocks of seven,[4] move the seven updates to the inner loop, and unroll them. The resulting code can be easily implemented to keep the updates in vector registers. On machines that support chaining of operation, e.g., CRAY X-MP, some of the vector registers will be need to hold intermediate results. The following code will illustrate these ideas.

First the **rankn** routine:

```
      recursive subroutine rankn(a,n,b,nv,ka,kb)
      implicit real*8 (a-h,o-z)
      dimension a(n*(n+1)/2),b(n,nv)
      do ja = 1, nv-6, 7
          call rank7(a,n,b,nv,ka,kb,ja)
      end do
      jresid = mod(nv,7)
      ja = nv-jresid+1
      go to (1,2,3,4,5,6,ja), jresid
      return
1         call rank1(a,n,b,nv,ka,kb,ja)
      return
2         call rank2(a,n,b,nv,ka,kb,ja)
```

[4]Each Alliant processor has 8 vector registers and does not require registers for intermediate results.

```
      return
 3        call rank3(a,n,b,nv,ka,kb,ja)
      return
 4        call rank4(a,n,b,nv,ka,kb,ja)
      return
 5        call rank5(a,n,b,nv,ka,kb,ja)
      return
 6        call rank6(a,n,b,nv,ka,kb,ja)
      return
      end
```

Now look at the routine rank7. The other routines are similar.

```
      recursive subroutine rank7(a,n,b,nv,ka,kb,ja)
* ...........lowest level routine in ANSYS lsolve
* ...........This version works for rank1, rank2, .. rank7
*............as it is coded in Fortran with 'do j=ja,min(nv,ja+6)'.
      implicit real*8 (a-h,o-z)
      dimension a(*),b(n,nv)
      ix(i) = (i*(i-1))/2
      in = n-nv
      ir = ix(in+1)
      do i = n-nv,1,-1
          ir = ir - in
          do k = ka, min(in,kb)
              jn = n - ja + 1
              jr = ix(n+1)
*.....................Note: nv=7
              do j = ja, min(nv,ja+6)
                  jr = jr - jn
                  a(ir+k) = a(ir+k) - b(i,j)*a(jr+k)
                  jn = jn - 1
              end do
          end do
          in = in - 1
      end do
      end
```

Note that the innermost loop, `do j = ja,min(nv,ja+6)`, can be explicitly unrolled since `nv` = 7 and `ja` = 1. The length of the `do k` loop is less than or equal to 32 by the way `ka` and `kb` were chosen. Vector registers can be used to store the section of the `a` array on the left hand side and the seven sections of `a` that appear on the right hand side.

This code will have to be written in assembly language on most machines to properly allocate the vector registers. The resulting assembly code is verbose but straightforward. To illustrate, here is a pseudo-code version of the rank2 routine:

```
      recursive subroutine rank2(a,n,b,nv,ka,kb,ja)
*............lowest level routine in ANSYS lsolve
      implicit real*8 (a-h,o-z)
```

```
      dimension a(*),b(n,nv)
      dimension v0(32),v1(32),v2(32)   ! vector registers
      integer v_len
      ix(i) = (i*(i-1))/2
      v1 = a(ix(n)+ka : ix(n)+kb)
      v2 = a(ix(n-1)+ka : ix(n-1)+kb)
      in = n-nv
      ir = ix(in+1)
      do i = n-nv,1,-1
          ir = ir - in
*.............set vector length for operations
          v_len = min(in,kb)-ka+1
          v0(1:v_len) = a(ir+ka : ir+min(in,kb))
          v0(1:v_len) = v0(1:v_len) - b(i,1) * v1(1:v_len)
          v0(1:v_len) = v0(1:v_len) - b(i,2) * v2(1:v_len)
          a(ir+ka : ir+min(in,kb)) = v0(1:v_len)
          in = in - 1
      end do
      end
```

7 Performance

The performance improvement of **lsolve** over **msolve** is dramatic on an Alliant minisupercomputer. The combination of optimal parallel partitioning, vector register allocation, and reduced memory traffic result in an overall rating of 28 MFLOPS on the ANSYS S4 benchmark with an FX/80. That number is the sustained rate over the entire S4 benchmark. The FX/80 uses Alliant's new ACE processors; the FX/8 uses the older CE processors. Figure 4 illustrates the how the performance improves as the number of processors increased from 1 to 8 on the Alliant. Note that the performance of **lsolve** is superior to **msolve** even on a single processor[1].

In summary, the advantages of **lsolve** are:

- scalable parallel performance,
- reduced memory traffic, and
- reduced number of instructions. (due to data reuse)

A relevant question is how well does S4 represent applications of ANSYS to the real world. S4 is a very large linear statics problem with an artificially large wavefront[5]. As a result, the percent of time spent in the solver is well over 90%. This figure is probably high even for large linear statics problems. Amdahl's Law is harsh—if 75% of the time is spent in the solver and the solver is tuned to run infinitely fast then there is only a 4x speedup. An even smaller percentage of the execution time is spent in the solver for nonlinear problems.

The solution is clear: more of the code must execute in parallel. Fortunately, this is conceptually easy. The foundations of finite elements make it a natural for parallel processing.

[5]If the nodes are reordered by adding 2 cards to the input deck the problem runs in 1688 seconds on a single processor FX/8-1

Figure 4: Performance of `lsolve` on ANSYS S4

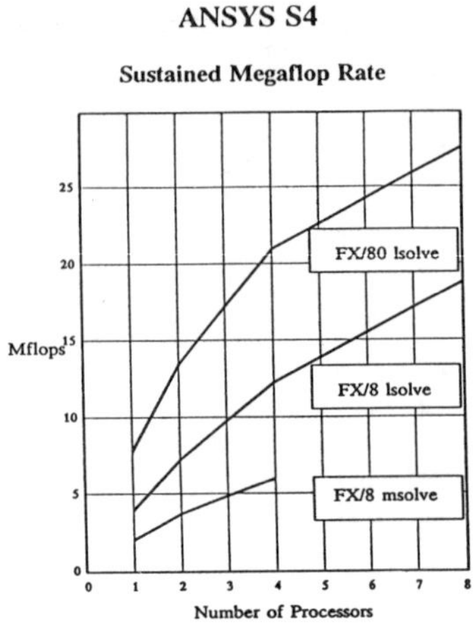

Most of the loops outside the solver, such as element formulation and stress recovery should be easy to run in parallel.

Unfortunately, this is not so trivial with real codes.. The memory systems of state-of-the-art computers are a bottle neck when faced with state-of-the-art sized applications. Large finite element codes tend to be very I/O intensive to overcome memory size limitations. This dependence on external storage often means that the data is not available in main memory for parallel processing. A careful rewritting of these codes is required to allow a maximum of parallel processing and still deal with the limitations of memory systems [4, 9].

8 Conclusions

The `lsolve` project illustrates that low level kernels are not large enough to allow modern parallel computers to perform optimally. Increasing the amount of work in the kernel from a rank one update to a rank-n update permits the use of a blocked algorithm and a dramatic improvement in performance.

This code also illustrates that real applications require very simple parallel constructions. The work of parallel programming is in understanding the data structures and access patterns of the application.

In the 1970's many codes and algorithms were revisited to take advantage of the vector facilities that were introduced on the supercomputers of the day. Parallel computing will become an important technology in much the same way. The opportunities for parallel computing are obvious in the formulation of many problems in computational mechanics. The challenge is to uncover this parallelism in existing codes and to write new codes that are designed explicitly to run in parallel. We look forward to the pleasures and challenges of helping to bring parallel computing to the users of finite element codes.

References

[1] "Ansys Large Scale Benchmark Timing Results," Swanson Analysis Systems, Inc., Houston, PA, 1988.

[2] M. Berry, K. Gallivan, W. Harrod, W. Jalby, S. Lo, U. Meier, B. Phillipe, and A. Sameh, "Parallel Numerical Algorithms on the CEDAR system," CSRD Report 581, University of Illinois at Urbana-Champaign, 1986.

[3] D. Calahan, "Block-Oriented, Local-memory-based Linear Equation Solution on the CRAY-2: Uniprocessor Algorithms," in *Proceedings of ICPP 1986*, IEEE Computer Society Press, pp. 375-378.

[4] G. F. Carey, "Parallelism in Finite Element Modeling," *Communications in Applied Numerical Methods,* Vol. 2, pp 281-287, 1986.

[5] J. Dongarra, J. Du Croz, I. Duff, and S. Hammarling, "A Proposal for a Set of Level 3 Basic Linear Algebra Subprograms," Argonne National Laboratory, Technical Memorandum No. 88, April 1987.

[6] J. Dongarra and I. Duff, "Advanced Architecture Computers," Argonne National Laboratory Report, ANL-MCS-TM-57 (revision 1), January 1987.

[7] "FX/Fortran Programmer's Handbook," Alliant Computer Systems Corporation, Littleton, MA, 1987.

[8] K. Gallivan, W. Jalby, U. Meier, and A. H. Sameh, "Impact of Hierarchical Memory Systems on Linear Algebra Algorithm Design," *The International Journal of Supercomputer Applications,* Volume 2, No. 1, Spring 1988, pp. 12-48.

[9] R. E. Hessel, "Finite Element Analysis on the Alliant Minisupercomputer," *Finite Element News,* 1988 Issue No. 1 (February), pp. 5-9.

[10] B. Liu and N. Strother, "Programming in VS Fortran on the IBM 3090 for Maximum Vector Performance," *Computer,* June 1988, pp. 65-76.

THREE DIMENSIONAL DELAUNAY TRIANGULATION ON A CRAY X-MP

David A. Field (presenting author)
Mathematics Department
General Motors Research Laboratories
30500 Mound Road
Warren, MI 48090-9055

Kenneth Yarnall
Mathematics Department
University of South Carolina
Columbia, SC 29208

ABSTRACT: A tetrahedral finite element mesh generation software package whose kernel is a robust three dimensional Delaunay triangulation algorithm was ported to a CRAY X-MP for vector processing. The total execution time for the critical subroutines of the kernel decreased by a factor of 6 over scalar mode on the CRAY X-MP. The kernel is characterized by simple data structures and $O(N^2)$ arithmetic operation counts, N being the number of finite element nodes. Although the kernel is essentially a sequential algorithm, its simple data structures allowed for key uses of vector processing and for streamlining sequential processing.

1. INTRODUCTION

The problems of triangulating N planar points and of identifying nearest neighbors are intimately related. The nearest neighbor problem can be solved by constructing Voronoi diagrams, also known as Dirichlet or Theissen tesselations, which are the duals of Delaunay triangulations. With the aid of modern computers much effort has been made to efficiently compute both Voronoi diagrams and Delaunay triangulations. Yet, few published algorithms for constructing Voronoi diagrams and Delaunay triangulations have been favored for practical implementation [7]. These algorithms generally emphasize search techniques and data structures whereas geometric considerations can cause numerical difficulties which undermine techniques as well as structures. Reasons for the lack of practical interest vary from complexity of algorithms, to imprecise specification and their improper handling of degenerate cases.

Degeneracies are easier to handle with Delaunay triangulations. Since triangulations are often the final product, a simpler and less efficient algorithm due Boyer [1] and to Watson [10] has been implemented in two and three dimensions for generating finite element meshes [2,5,6]. It will be seen in this paper that implementing this algorithm with simple data structures rather than with more efficient data structures for scalar machines will be crucial to a remarkable speedup through vectorizing an essentially sequential algorithm.

Vector processing has been singularly effective for large numerical calculations involving matrices. Computational geometry, on the other hand, has developed efficient algorithms for computationally intensive geometric calculations by emphasizing sophisticated data structures and elegant geometric

 TH0237-8/89/0000/0202$01.00

techniques. These data structures and techniques usually inhibit the advantages of vector processing. This paper deals with the optimization of the kernel in an automatic three dimensional finite element mesh generator developed by the first author. Optimizing the kernel for vector processing is significant because it represents one of the few instances where vectorization of code for computational geometry has been undertaken.

The kernel of the mesh generator creates a Delaunay triangulation of points in 3 dimensions using Watson's algorithm and a one-at-a-time insertion strategy. At each stage, the program finds tetrahedra in the existing mesh that must be removed, creates new tetrahedra, and updates data structures. Since geometric problems can occur due to inaccurate computations, the use of extra tests insures that these problems are avoided. For a detailed discussion of the algorithm and its numerical difficulties, see [5].

The original kernel is a robust and reliable code and has been very cost effective in scalar mode for relatively small problems. For much larger problems, such as generating finite element meshes with tens of thousands of finite elements, accurate execution times were lacking. We took the opportunity not only to determine accurate execution times for small and large problems but also to optimize the code. We went one step further, and optimized the kernel for vector processing on the CRAY X-MP at General Motors Research Laboratories (GMR).

Since the original code in the kernel was already executing quickly (see the tables in section 7), and since the CRAY X-MP is a vector processor, our initial focus was on vectorizing the code. Unfortunately, the mesh generator, like most triangulation algorithms, is inherently sequential but has the advantage of accepting triangulation points in arbitrary order. No preordering of points is required. Nevertheless, considerable performance gains were made through streamlining the code, rewriting portions of code, and forcing vector processing where possible. In all, execution time was reduced by nearly one half in addition to the reduction of one third gained by letting the CRAY compiler vector process the original scalar code.

The next section of this paper outlines the Delaunay triangulation algorithm which comprises the kernel and highlights the impediments to vectorization. Sections 3, 4 and 5 present the modifications made to each subroutine and the subsequent gains in speed. Section 6 reviews the attempts made to use FORGE, software designed to aid in vectorizing FORTRAN code for CRAY computers [8]. The final section, Section 7, summarizes our work and comments on the CRAY compilers that were available.

2. DESCRIPTION OF KERNEL

The mesh generator is designed to produce finite element decompositions of complex three dimensional geometries with well proportioned tetrahedra. The mesh generator is automatic to relieve the tedium of human interaction in creating finite element meshes and its kernel is a robust three dimensional version of a Delaunay triangulation algorithm originally proposed by Watson.

An examination of the assumptions of Watson's algorithm reveals why the algorithm's implementation to generate finite element meshes is not straightforward. Watson's algorithm is based upon the following characteristic of Delaunay triangulations [9].

Given N random points in three dimensions, there exists a unique decomposition of their convex hull into tetrahedra where each tetrahedron enjoys the property that its 4 vertices also define a sphere those interior and surface contain none of the remaining N-4 points.

When creating Delaunay triangulations for finite element meshes the triangulation points are the finite element nodes and their locations often cause degeneracies. Not only are triangulations no longer unique, but a unique number of tetrahedra cannot be guaranteed, see Figure 2.1. Most importantly, the locations of finite element nodes tend to create geometric situations whose numerical difficulties must be taken into account in order to preserve the integrity of the finite element mesh. The following algorithm is the kernel of the mesh generator and it addresses the numerical difficulties of degenerate cases. The term circumball will be used to mean the interior and the surface of the sphere which passes through the vertices of a tetrahedron. The radius of a circumball will be called its circumradius. Two dimensional illustrations follow the statement of the algorithm.

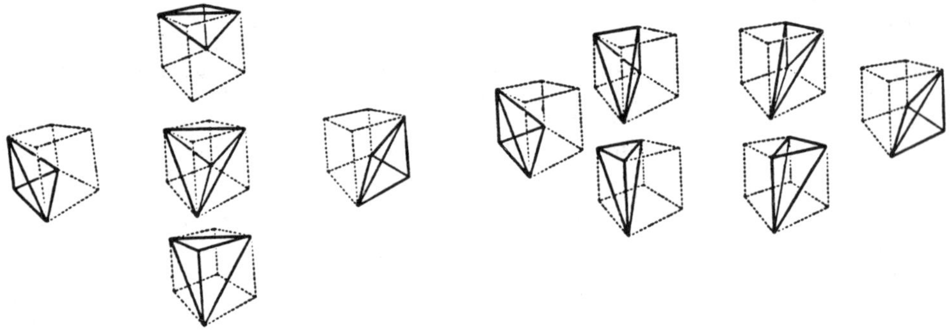

Figure 2.1 The decomposition of a cube into five and six tetrahedra.

STEP1. Create a tetrahedron which encloses all the finite element nodes.

STEP2. Construct the Delaunay triangulation of the vertices of the enclosing tetrahedron and one of the finite element nodes by connecting the node to each vertex. Maintain a master list of the tetrahedra and their associated circumballs.

STEP3. Insert the other finite element nodes into the triangulation one at a time as follows:

a) Determine which existing circumballs contain the new node.
b) If the new node lies within an epsilon of the surface of a circumball go to STEP4.
c) Create a list of the tetrahedra associated with the circumballs determined in STEP3a. The union of these tetrahedra is called an <u>insertion polyhedron</u>.
d) Create a list of surface triangles of the insertion polyhedron.
e) Create new tetrahedra filling the insertion polyhedron by connecting the new node to the surface triangles of the insertion polyhedron.

f) If the volume of the insertion polyhedron does not equal the volume of the union of new tetrahedra or if the volume of a new tetrahedron is too small proceed to STEP4.

g) Delete from the master list the tetrahedra and circumballs determined in STEP3a and STEP3c.

h) Add to the master list all tetrahedra and their associated circumballs created in STEP3e.

STEP4. Append the new node to the list of nodes and proceed to STEP3 until the list contains only nodes which cannot pass STEP3b or STEP3f. If the triangulation list consists of nodes which fail STEP3b or STEP3f proceed to STEP3 while omitting STEP3b. If the list of nodes consists of nodes that will fail STEP3f while omitting STEP3b, proceed to STEP5.

STEP5. Remove from the master list all tetrahedra which share a vertex with the enclosing tetrahedron. The union of the remaining tetrahedra in the master list is a Delaunay triangulation of the given finite element nodes.

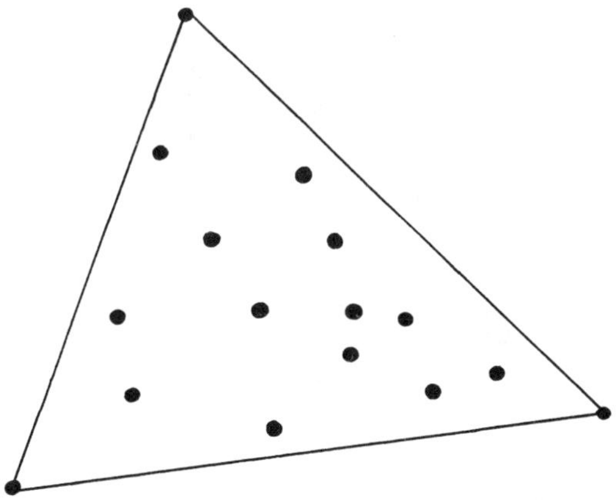

Figure 2.2 The triangulation points and an enclosing triangle.

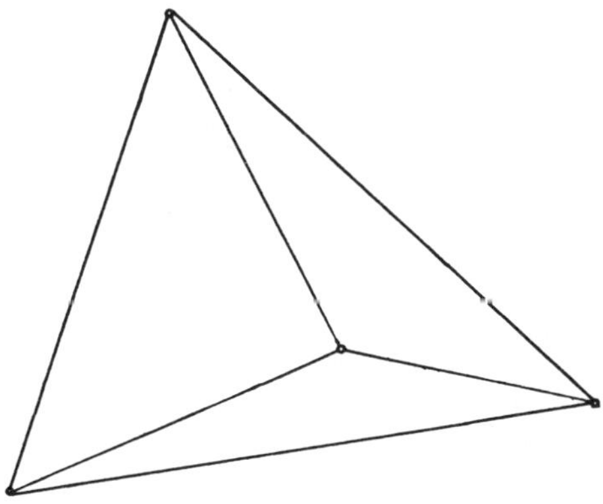

Figure 2.3 The Delaunay triangulation after inserting the first point.

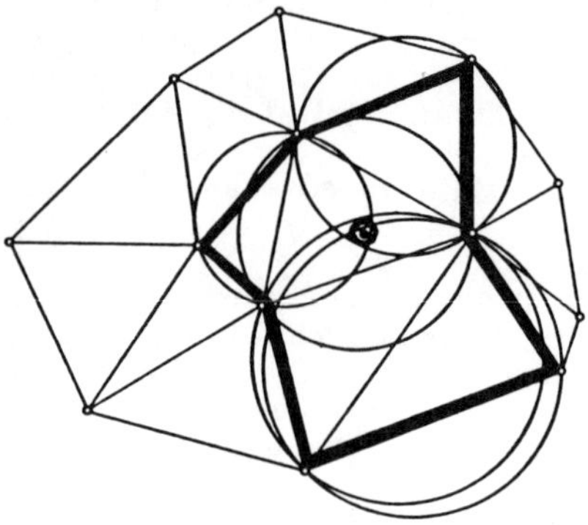

Figure 2.4 A new triangulation point and the nonempty circumcircles.

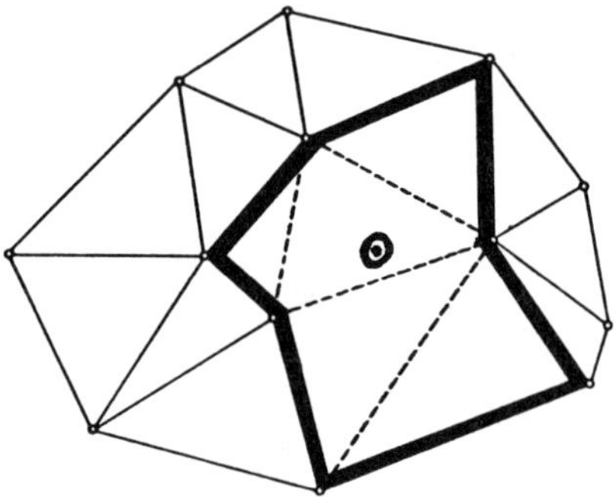

Figure 2.5 The insertion polygon.

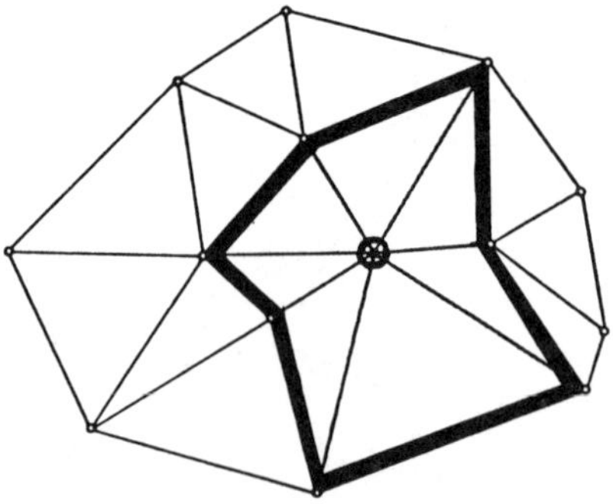

Figure 2.6 The retriangulation of the insertion polygon.

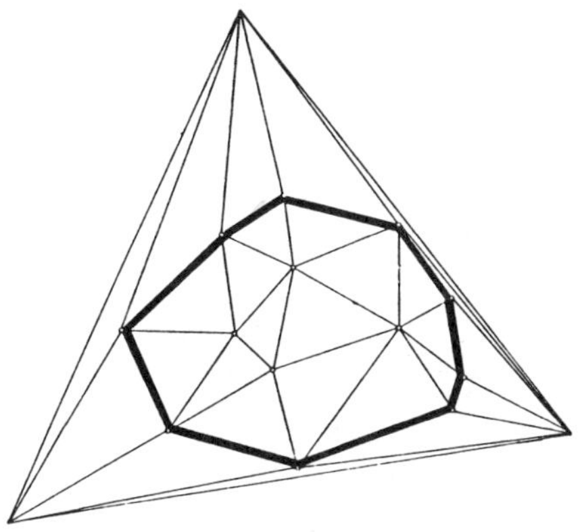

Figure 2.7 Triangles sharing a vertex with the enclosing triangle must be removed.

The above algorithm uses a volume test whereas tests of normalized shape ratios have been included in later versions of the kernel. The addition of normalized shape ratio tests would have little or no effect on the work reported in this paper. Step4 is essentially a consequence of avoiding degenerate geometric situations which may arise from the combination of numerical procedures and nonrandomness of finite element nodes. For further information on degeneracies and their circumvention see [5]. The sequential nature of the algorithm, the fact that the algorithm takes place in only three dimensions, and especially the circumvention of these degeneracies inhibit intensive vector processing of the algorithm. The circumvention of degenerate geometric situations requires conditional branching which severely taxes attempts to produce code suitable for vector processing.

Step3a turns out to be a crucial step in an efficient and fast implementation of the above algorithm. STEP3a requires a search for nonempty circumballs. This search can, with appropriate data structures, have O(logM) arithmetic operation counts where M is the number of tetrahedra. To produce this efficient sequential search requires sophisticated data structures which must be updated. The search also relies on following sequences of conditional branches, which are very effective in scalar mode but are inhibitors to vector processing. Consequently, we kept the data structures simple not only for enhancing the possibilities of vectorizing but also for ease in programming.

Code for the above algorithm separates into two major subroutines. The main program calls subroutine MESH which takes care of STEP1, STEP2, STEP3a, STEP3b, STEP3g, STEP3h, STEP4 and STEP5. MESH calls subroutine INSIDE which executes STEP3c, STEP3d, STEP3e and STEP3f. Subroutines MESH and INSIDE call subroutines CIRCEN and VOLUME to calculate circumcenters, circumradii and volumes and call LINEQ to solve 3x3 system of linear equations. All parts of the program contain special numerical and geometric tests specifically designed to ensure that suitable finite element meshes are produced.

3. SUBROUTINE MESH

MESH is the main subroutine in the program. MESH controls the entire algorithm and calls all other subroutines. The tasks of subroutine MESH are:

1) Initialize the data structure--the list of elements, the list of inserted nodes, the list of circumcenters and circumradii and the list of nodes which failed insertion.
2) As each node is inserted, determine which existing elements have nonempty circumballs.
3) Call subroutine INSIDE to create the new elements, and subroutine VOLUME to check them for possible errors.
4) Update the data structures.
5) Attempt to reinsert any nodes that failed to get into the mesh.

Of these tasks, the second task, (2) provides the largest gain in execution time through vector processing. Execution of the task involves a dot product, computed once for each tetrahedron in the current triangulation, and incrementing counters and vectors which identify nonempty circumballs. The obstacles inhibiting vectorization are a conditional branch out of a loop when a new node is inserted within epsilon of the surface of a circumsphere and the conditionally incremented scalar and vector which identify how many and which circumspheres are no longer empty. In order to enhance vector processing, the work in (2) is partitioned so that the dot products and the testing of distances to circumballs are isolated from one another. Vector processing requires that these distances be stored in vectors not only for vectorizing numerical computations but also for vectorizing tests for branching.

The determination of the distances of a new node to the current circumballs is necessary to identify the nonempty circumballs. To prevent geometric degeneracies and to produce suitable finite elements, however, it is necessary to avoid conditions which cause degeneracies and create unsuitable elements. Since these conditions cannot always be anticipated, it is inefficient to calculate all of the distances before performing any tests for these conditions. The amount of wasted work may be substantially reduced when the loop which calculates distances is broken into segments of short length and the vectors produced by each segment are immediately used to test for degenerate geometric situations and to identify nonempty circumballs. The potential amount of wasted work may be small if the resultant vector lengths can in some way be optimal. Since the CRAY has vector registers of length 64, the length of these segments should be some multiple of 64, [3]. Experimentation with several vector lengths led to 512 as the best vector length. The major overhead of segmenting the processing of the second task is the start up times of the vector processing for each segment.

The technique used in task (2) is not optimal for scalar computers. There are several data structures that make the search for empty circumballs very efficient on scalar machines, see [7] for example. However, these methods use search methods that are inherently not vectorizable. The simple method used here does have the advantage of vectorizability.

The remainder of the original subroutine MESH contained additional code that would benefit directly from vector processing. In fact, some of this code inhibited proper vector processing. Since the CRAY CFT 1.15 vector compiler vectorizes innermost DO loops, it is advantageous that the innermost loops in the code have the longest vector lengths. Loops with short vectors may actually run slower in vector mode than in scalar mode. Since the Delaunay triangulation algorithm produced three dimensional tetrahedra, many loops depended upon the dimensionality of the geometry so that there were many loops with vectors of lengths two to four. The most helpful modification in this case was to unroll these short loops [4]. Unrolling these loops turned outer loops into longer and more efficient inner loops. An added benefit was that not as many vector processes were initialized, thus saving start up times required for each vector process. This strategy was used repeatedly, not only in MESH, but in every subroutine in the program.

Maintenance of data structures offered a final opportunity for optimizing subroutine MESH. After the short inner loops had been unrolled, several loops became good candidates for vector processing. The CRAY compiler, however, did not recognize this fact. In these loops the compiler was confused by indirect addressing and the compiler would not invoke vector processing even though no recursive references actually occurred in these loops. Our solution to this impasse was to insert compiler directives into the source code and force the compiler to ignore any potential dependencies and to invoke vector processing for these loops. This directive, CDIR$ IVDEP, was issued immediately before these loops. Since this CRAY directive contains a 'C' in column one, other compilers will ignore the directive so portability of FORTRAN code is preserved

Table 3.1 presents a comparison of the execution time required by the original and the optimized versions of subroutine MESH. The programs were submitted as batch jobs to GMR's CRAY X-MP/24 computer with the optimizing FORTRAN compiler, CFT 1.15, and with double precision switched off. The timings, in seconds, were provided in both vector and scalar modes by the FLOWTRACE facility, [3]. Note that the timings for the new code in scalar mode were performed without segmenting the search for empty circumballs. Also, branching out of the search was done immediately when conditions for possible geometric degeneracies were identified. Two datasets were used; the first produced 4664 elements from 753 nodes, and the second produced 23,431 elements from 3897 nodes. All subsequent tables refer to the same data.

Table 3.1

Times in seconds for Subroutine MESH

	Dataset 1		Dataset 2	
	Vector	Scalar	Vector	Scalar
Original	0.748	2.283	20.278	70.238
Optimized	0.401	*2.051	11.098	*64.751

4. SUBROUTINE INSIDE

Subroutine INSIDE creates new elements to be inserted into the mesh. Basically, INSIDE performs the following tasks:

1) Find the boundary faces of the insertion polygon in STEP3c.
2) Create new tetrahedra by connecting the new node to these faces.
3) Call subroutine CIRCEN to calculate the new circumcenters and circumradii and return the new data to subroutine MESH.

Since INSIDE used more CPU time than any other subroutine called by MESH (see Tables 7.1 and 7.2), it was essential to concentrate on improving the execution of this part of the algorithm. Initial attempts at improving the performance of subroutine INSIDE through vector processing resulted in meager gains because the first task, the major task of INSIDE, was to identify the surface triangles of the insertion polyhedron by comparing the faces of all tetrahedra which comprise the insertion polyhedron. Since each tetrahedron has only four faces, the comparisons of faces doomed anticipated improvements in execution time through vector processing of the first task.

The attempts to minimize execution time in this case forced a complete revision of subroutine INSIDE. While the nature of the problem is unattractive for vector processing, the original code eliminated some but not all redundant comparisons. A detailed analysis of the possible ways that the face of one tetrahedron might match the face of another tetrahedron showed that, by numbering their respective vertices with increasing node numbers, at most six comparisons of node numbers can determine when two tetrahedra have a common face. Since the original code did list the node numbers of vertices of a tetrahedron in increasing order, a nearly eight fold improvement in execution time was obtained. Table 4.1 gives the execution times for the two versions of subroutine INSIDE.

Table 4.1

Times in seconds for Subroutine INSIDE

	Dataset 1		Dataset 2	
	Vector	Scalar	Vector	Scalar
Original	1.697	1.744	8.695	8.962
Optimized	0.206	0.239	1.090	1.253

5. SUBROUTINES CIRCEN, VOLUME AND LINEQ

As the subroutine names indicate, CIRCEN calculates circumcenters and circumradii of tetrahedra, VOLUME calculates volumes of tetrahedra and LINEQ solves the 3x3 systems of equations that arise in geometric calculations. The execution times for subroutines CIRCEN, VOLUME and LINEQ were not substantial when compared to execution times for subroutines MESH and INSIDE. Their optimization was therefore relatively unimportant. Nevertheless, the basic strategies of unrolling short loops and restructuring code were applied. The speedups of execution times, although considerable in terms of percentage of subroutine time saved, are of secondary importance when the entire program is considered. Tables 5.1 - 5.3 present the time comparisons for these three routines.

Table 5.1

Times in seconds for Subroutine CIRCEN

	Dataset 1		Dataset 2	
	Vector	Scalar	Vector	Scalar
Original	0.094	0.088	0.489	0.476
Optimized	0.058	0.061	0.313	0.321

Table 5.2

Times in Seconds for Subroutine VOLUME

	Dataset 1		Dataset 2	
	Vector	Scalar	Vector	Scalar
Original	0.090	0.125	0.519	0.722
Optimized	0.043	0.052	0.254	0.302

Table 5.3

Times in seconds for Subroutine LINEQ

	Dataset 1		Dataset 2	
	Vector	Scalar	Vector	Scalar
Original	0.349	0.355	1.853	1.880
Optimized	0.136	0.219	0.726	1.166

6. FORGE

FORGE is software tool that is intended to extensively automate the process of restructuring FORTRAN programs to improve vector processing on CRAY computers. Initial results with a test version of FORGE indicated that it would be a useful tool, but errors were encountered. For example, when FORGE was asked to modify a loop in subroutine INSIDE (unmodified version), FORGE's analysis incorrectly indicated that the IF statements were independent of the loop, and FORGE extracted the IF statements from the loop to produce executable but incorrect code. Other errors in analysis, coupled with some annoying quirks of the installation (e.g., choosing the reformatting option caused the system to crash) made FORGE difficult to use, and its use was abandoned.

Although this particular experience with FORGE was not ideal FORGE did suggest good places to restructure our code. Very good results have been obtained for other codes written at GMR and the errors we encountered should be eliminated in future versions of the FORGE. Further use of FORGE is encouraged since FORGE did direct attention to potential reductions of execution times through vector processing.

7. CONCLUSIONS

The execution times of the original Delaunay triangulation code in the kernel were improved by vector processing. Recoding to take advantage of vector processing improved execution time by a factor of 5.4 and 6.1 for 753 and 3897 triangulation points, respectively. Times and percentages of total execution times for each subroutine are given in Tables 7.1 and 7.2.

Note that for subroutine MESH, the percentage of total execution time of the optimized code in vector mode increased dramatically from 47.5% to 82.3% when using 753 and 3897 triangulation points, respectively. This increase reflects the $O(n^2)$ asymptotic time bound that is characteristic of our search method for nonempty circumballs. The asterisk in each table indicates taking advantage of branching immediately out of the search for nonempty circumdisks when potential geometric difficulties are detected. The total execution, compile, and system management time for generating 23,431 tetrahedra was approximately 20 seconds.

CRAY compiler directives were extremely useful and we highly recommend their use. Unrolling loops, a standard technique of optimizing code for vector processing, was also a frequently used strategy. Because problems and solutions involving computational geometry generally encompass combinatorics, lower dimensional geometry and sophisticated data structures, it appears that parallel processing offers more opportunities for improving computation times. While rewriting code for vector processing, opportunities to invoke parallel computations and maintenance of data structures would have been very welcome.

Our use of FORGE was a disappointing experience. A disappointing outcome was our use of the CFT77 version compiler. The new compiler increased execution time by approximately 70% for 3897 triangulation points.

Table 7.1

Execution times and percentage of total execution times of subroutines for 753 triangulation points

	VECTOR			SCALAR	
	Seconds	% Total	Subroutines	Seconds	% Total
Original	0.748	25.12	MESH	2.283	49.68
	1.697	56.99	INSIDE	1.744	37.95
	0.094	3.16	CIRCEN	0.088	1.92
	0.09	3.02	VOLUME	0.125	2.72
	0.349	11.71	LINEQ	0.355	7.73
Total	**2.978**	**100**		**4.595**	**100**
Optimized	0.401	47.51	MESH	*2.051	78.22
	0.206	24.41	INSIDE	0.239	9.12
	0.058	6.87	CIRCEN	0.061	2.33
	0.043	5.09	VOLUME	0.052	1.98
	0.136	16.11	LINEQ	0.219	8.35
Total	**0.844**	**100**		**2.622**	**100**

Table 7.2

Execution times and percentage of total execution times of subroutines for 3897 triangulation points

	VECTOR Seconds	VECTOR % Total	Subroutines	SCALAR Seconds	SCALAR % Total
Original	20.278	63.7	MESH	70.258	85.37
	8.695	27.31	INSIDE	8.962	10.89
	0.489	1.54	CIRCEN	0.476	0.58
	0.519	1.63	VOLUME	0.722	0.88
	1.853	5.82	LINEQ	1.88	2.28
Total	**31.834**	**100**		**82.298**	**100**
Optimized	11.098	82.32	MESH	64.751	95.51
	1.09	8.09	INSIDE	1.253	1.85
	0.313	2.32	CIRCEN	0.321	0.47
	0.254	1.88	VOLUME	0.302	0.45
	0.726	5.39	LINEQ	1.166	1.72
Total	**13.481**	**100**		**67.793**	**100**

REFERENCES

1. Boyer, A., "Computing Dirichlet tesselations," The Computer Journal, Vol. 24, pp. 162-166 (1981).
2. Cavendish, J. C., Field, D. A. and Frey, W. H., "An approach to automatic three-dimensional mesh generation," International Journal for Numerical Methods in Engineering, Vol. 21, pp. 329-347 (1985).
3. CRAY Research Corporation, Cray X-MP and Cray-1 Computer Systems Fortran(CFT) Reference Manual, Cray Research, Mendota Heights, MN, 1986.
4. Dongarra, J. J. and Eisenstat, S. C., "Squeezing the most out of an algorithm in CRAY FORTRAN," ACM Trans. Math. Software, Vol. 10, pp. 219-230 (1984).
5. Field, D. A., "Implementing Watson's algorithm in three dimensions," Proc. Second Annual ACM Symp. on Comp. Geom., pp. 246-259 (1986).
6. Frey, W. H., "Selective refinement: an new strategy for automatic node placement in graded triangular meshes," International Journal for Numerical Methods in Engineering, Vol. 24, pp. 2183-2200 (1987).
7. Guibas, L. J. and Stolfi, J., "Primitives for the manipulation of general subdivisions and the computations of Voronoi diagrams", ACM Trans. on Graphics, Vol. 2, pp. 74-123 (1985).
8. Pacific-Sierra Research Corporation FORGE™ A Fortran Expert Workstation User's Handbook, Placerville, CA, 1986.
9. Rogers, C. A., Packing and Covering, Cambridge Mathematical Tracts, No. 54, Cambridge University Press 1964.
10. Watson, D. F., "Computing the n-dimensional Delaunay tesselation with applications to Voronoi polytopes," The Computer Journal, Vol. 24, pp. 167-172 (1981).

The ARGOT Strategy III: The BBN Butterfly Multiprocessor

Elizabeth J. O'Neil
Bolt, Beranek, and Newman, Inc., 10 Moulton St., Cambridge, MA (eoneil@bbn.com) and
Dept. of Math and Computer Science, Univ. of Massachusetts, Boston, MA
Craig G. Shaefer
Rowland Institute for Science, 100 Cambridge Pkwy, Cambridge, MA (shaefer@bbn.com)

ABSTRACT: Genetic algorithms offer massively parallelizable algorithms for optimization problems. They, however, have certain inefficiencies and disadvantages, such as premature convergence of the chromosome population, that may cause them to fail. The ARGOT strategy combines genetic algorithms with a mechanism providing a dynamically adaptive representation to form a robust optimization tool, as previously shown in the uniprocessor environment. For implementation of ARGOT on the BBN Butterfly multiprocessor, a parallel selection algorithm and a method of incremental payoff update was developed. These lead to enhanced parallelism and reduced the amount of computation needed by any genetic algorithm, including ARGOT. Experimental results on two matrix problems are presented, one a linear system from a FEM problem, and another a nonlinear problem not well-behaved enough for consistent conjugate gradient results.

GENETIC ALGORITHMS

A recent innovation in search strategies is the genetic algorithm (GA) optimization procedures [1]. Current research is demonstrating not only wide applicability but also search efficiencies surpassing the more traditional approaches [2]. A GA is a stochastic search technique, but instead of having a single trial that is perturbed to yield the next trial, as in simulated annealing (SA), a GA employs a population of trials, represented by bit-strings, that 'evolve' much like biological species. Thus population genetics and biological evolution serve as the paradigms for genetic algorithms. Analogous to biology, the population of trials as a whole (and not individual members) solves problems through its ability to combine beneficial partial solutions found by different members. This combination is possible because the information embodied in these adaptations is encoded in the structure of the chromosomes of its members. The process of sexual reproduction then provides the mechanism whereby distinct beneficial adaptations from two members' chromosomes are united in a single offspring. This often leads to a symbiotic effect of the two partial solutions. For instance, two parents, each having undergone distinct but beneficial mutations, can mate and thereby efficiently pass along both mutations to their offspring. It would be much less likely for both mutations to occur in a single individual. Since parents having beneficial mutations reproduce more often than those without, the probability of combination is greatly enhanced. This recombination explores a space very efficiently, in fact, it can be shown that this leads to an 'implicitly parallel' search of the chromosome space. In the next section we discuss a hypothetical problem that not only distinguishes the methodology and goals of traditional search methods from those of genetic algorithms but also provides an analogy to help illustrate the origins of the search power of GAs.

A wide variety of problems have been solved with genetic algorithms, including multidimensional function optimizations, nonlinear systems, job shop scheduling, combinatorial optimizations, and bin packing [2]. These applications provide empirical evidence that GAs perform well when searching complex spaces and also help to define the scope of the problems that might profit from a GA approach. In addition, GAs can be parallelized easily since the genetic operators can be applied to the individual members of the chromosome population in parallel to produce the next generation. The evaluation of the members of the new generation can also be performed in parallel, as we note later.

Many practical problems have search domains that are extremely complex, being both multimodal as well as epistatic and thus often confound traditional approaches. GA techniques, on the other hand, address just these issues but have their own disadvantages and inefficiencies when applied to complex searches [3,4,5]. Many of the disadvantages stem from problems arising in the representation of the trial solutions. These representational issues are likewise often encountered by the traditional search algorithms. Recently, an advanced GA approach has demonstrated successes at searching complicated spaces for both nonlinear function optimizations [4,5] as well as combinatorial optimizations [5,6]. This method, called the Adaptive Representation Genetic Optimizer Technique (ARGOT) [4,5], is a search system that adjusts its internal representation of the trial solutions by inserting an intermediate, dynamically adjusted, mapping between the chromosome space and the solution search space. This dynamic adaptation enables ARGOT to develop a representation appropriate to the problem being solved and thus leads to both enhanced search capabilities as well as reducing or eliminating the problems associated with high epistasis and irregularity in the domain.

An Example: Traditional Methods *vs* GAs

Let us consider the following hypothetical problem: "Find the location of the summit of Mt. Washington". We have at our disposal the 100 New Hampshire paratroopers and we equip each with a radio, a sextant, a watch, and an altimeter. We don't know where Mt. Washington is located, but we do know it is somewhere in the state of New Hampshire, we know the location of the state, and we know the summit of Mt. Washington is the highest point in the state. We first attempt to find the summit by flying, with a random flight plan, over the state and at random times dropping a paratrooper. After all paratroopers have landed, each takes latitude and longitude readings and measures his/her altitude. All locations and altitudes are transmitted to our command post. We simply choose the location of the paratrooper with the highest altitude as our current best approximation for the summit. We have, in essence, employed a Monte Carlo random sampling technique to approximate the solution. Our accuracy can be increased by collecting our paratroopers and making a second pass over the state. It is well known that the accuracy increases slowly with respect to the number of passes we make; consequently this is a time consuming, *albeit* robust, search strategy. This Monte Carlo search can easily be extended to a simulated annealing approach simply by having each paratrooper take random steps from their landing points and accept their new locations based upon a Metropolis sampling technique over their height differentials. This sampling introduces a 'temperature' parameter which is adjusted according to an annealing schedule.

Let us next consider an alternative strategy: a homotopy approach. Each paratrooper is instructed to determine the trajectory of steepest ascent and to follow it uphill. Each eventually converges onto a summit. This method would appear to be

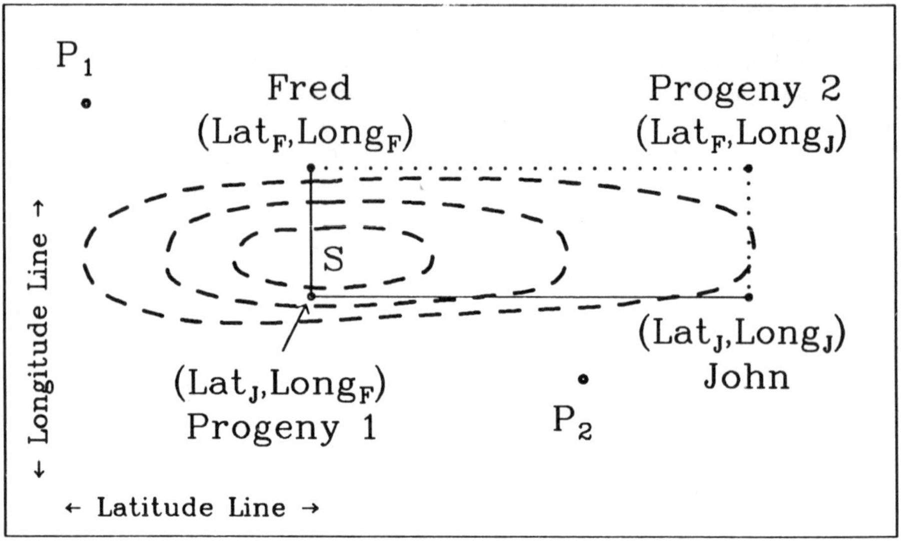

Figure 1

Why are genetic algorithms powerful search methods? See the text for an explanation.

much more accurate and have a much greater chance of finding the summit of Mt. Washington. This, of course, depends upon the particular details of the search space. If the 'basin of attraction' surrounding Mt. Washington is large in comparison to the basins surrounding all local maxima, then this strategy will be very good indeed since it is then likely that a paratrooper landed in the basin of attraction of the summit and consequently will necessarily locate the peak. Many complex, practical problems, however, do not have this 'nice' property and thus this method fails by becoming 'stuck' at a local maximum. We recognize that this method is simply some form of a homotopy or Newton-like technique. For certain special search domains, these methods and their extensions are very fast and accurate, but for many complex problems homotopy methods are not as robust as the Monte Carlo and simulated annealing algorithms.

It is important at this point to notice that in each of the above scenarios, the altitudes measured by the paratroopers impart information to us only about the precise locations of the paratroopers. It is true that for this particular problem we may then assume the 'nice' property of relative smoothness of the topography of the search space and extend, in an approximate fashion, this information concerning single points in the state to small neighborhoods surrounding those points. But the size of this extension is based upon a *priori* knowledge of the search domain. Next we see what is possible if one samples *via* an alternative technique: a recombination algorithm.

Consider the two paratroopers, John and Fred, of Figure 1. These two paratroopers have the highest altitudes of the population of 100 paratroopers that we have randomly dropped. What if we now consider two new locations, one has John's latitude and Fred's longitude and the other has John's longitude and Fred's latitude. Notice on this figure that one of these new points, the one labelled Progeny 1, is actually much closer to the summit than either John or Fred or the other new combination point. There is a reason for this occurrence. To be specific, the altitudes of John and Fred provide more information, through the operation of this recombination algorithm, than just the heights in the vacinities of their locations. In particular, John's altitude is very good because he happened to land at approximately the latitude of the summit while Fred's altitude is good because he landed at approximately the proper longitude. Thus by choosing a location with John's good latitude and Fred's good longitude combines in a symbiotic fashion the information contained within the representations of their locations in 2-space. In other words, this algorithm of selecting the paratroopers with the better altitudes and recombining the information contained within their latitude and longitude positions is a way to discover 'good' building blocks for the composition of even better locations. Notice that the original 100 paratroopers provides helpful information on something approaching 100 different latitudes and 100 different longitudes. In other words, among the 100 paratroopers it is likely that a few will be in locations similar to John's where their latitude values are close to being correct. Note that since the 100 paratroopers should be roughly evenly distributed along the possible latitudes, finding a few good latitudes is much more likely than for a few of the paratroopers to actually be near the summit. Likewise, these same hundred paratroopers are evenly distributed along the possible longitudes and hence a few will likely have longitudes close to being correct. Through the selection and recombination mechanism we see that the same 100 paratroopers effectively search both the space of latitudes and the space of longitudes simultaneously and in parallel. This implicitly parallel search ability leads to the power of the recombination method.

In effect, we have just described a pseudo-GA approach to this problem. The reason we say 'pseudo-' is because we have limited our algorithm to recombinations of latitude and longitude values. A true GA performs even a deeper recombination which we explain below. But before doing so, you may be complaining that we have cheated in our original positioning of John and Fred. In fact, you are correct; we did take care in choosing the locations of Fred and John, but that was only for the argument's sake: the real genetic algorithm does not rely on this type of special choices. Rather, the GA employs a finite representation for both the latitude and longitude values (finite-length bit strings). And a similar algorithm that now is allowed to form recombinations between any two bits, including between bits internal to either the latitude or longitude values, will form building blocks at the bit level instead of at the latitude/longitude level. Hence the algorithm endeavors to find good bit values rather than simply good values of the latitude and longitude. Returning to our figure, we could therefore make the identical argument given above for any two positions of John and Fred, say at P_1 and P_2, since now wherever they reside some hyperplane (bit position) will be properly valued in each of them (chances are the good bits are in different bit positions in each) and thus the recombination process stands a good chance of composing a new trial location containing both good bits.

While this process of recombining good information from different individual trials in a symbiotic fashion to find much better solutions is very powerful, it does suffer from its own forms of inefficiencies and disadvantages. Many of these result from the fact that a particular fixed choice for the representation is picked. This choice almost always has biases build into it. For example, if too few bits are used to represent the latitude and longitude values, then the distances between potential trial latitudes and longitudes will be so large that the summit of Mt. Washington will escape through the cracks of our sampling grid. In addition, there are other problems related to the representation but stemming more from the operation of the algorithm. These include the so-called 'Hamming cliff' problems and premature convergence. Fortunately, the ARGOT algorithm, through its ability to appropriately and dynamically adjust the representation, alleviates or eliminates most of these issues. An important consequence of the elimination of these representational biases is that the ARGOT Strategy allows the GA to remain maximally efficient and effective at searching the solution space. Therefore the GA becomes a very effective discovery method when employed within the ARGOT Strategy.

In recapitulation, for traditional algorithms the altitude values provide information concerning points in 2-space (and perhaps small local neighborhoods of those points in 2-space by assuming certain nice properties of the search space). Simulated annealing, homotopy, and clustering methods utilize this type of local information for the computation of their next trial solutions to be evaluated. On the other hand, the GA implements a recombination method for 'spreading' this altitude information over components of the representation (the latitude and longitude from above) thereby hunting for good building blocks rather than just good points in 2-space.

Adaptive Representation Genetic Optimizer Technique (ARGOT)

The ARGOT method [4] is a search system designed in a manner flexible enough to allow it to "learn" its own strategies for searching solution spaces. This system employs a Standard Genetic Algorithm Optimizer (SGAO) [7] as its basis and hence utilizes chromosomes composed of bit strings to represent, in some fashion, the trial solutions of the search space. ARGOT differs from the SGAO through insertion of an intermediate Translation Mapping and associated ARGOT Operators between the chromosome space and the solution space (see Figure 2). It is this mapping that interprets the chromosomes to give their proper trial solutions, and instead of this mapping being a fixed one, it dynamically changes based upon internal statistical measurements over the populations of chromosomes and trial solutions.

Referring to Figure 2, the SGAO can be separated into three major components (drawn with the thinner lines). One component, common to all optimizers, is the Solution Space: the space of potential trial solutions being searched. A set of these trials, represented by bit strings, form the Chromosome Space. Various standard Genetic Operators are employed to manipulate the individual bit strings, or chromosomes, in order to generate new trials. These trials are evaluated to yield Payoffs to the individual chromosomes that are then employed to control the genetic operators. These components may thus be viewed as performing a pseudo-Darwinian evolution of the trial solutions, *i.e.*, trials are generated or perturbed at random with reproduction dependent upon the payoff of the individual. In Darwinian terms, the genetic material of the 'fittest' individuals survives through mating and reproduction. From a cognitive viewpoint, information is passed from the chromosomes (genotype) to the solution space (phenotype) where it is evaluated. Since this transfer does not entail abstraction of information contained in the trial solutions nor concomitant concept formulation, we label the SGAO evolutionary to distinguish it from a learning algorithm. Besides the SGAO components, the ARGOT strategy also includes the dynamically adjusted Translation Mapping, the ARGOT operators which allow this mapping to generalize and store information, and the various statistical measurements over the Chromosome and Solution Spaces that control the ARGOT operators (drawn in thicker lines). Only the Convergence measurement

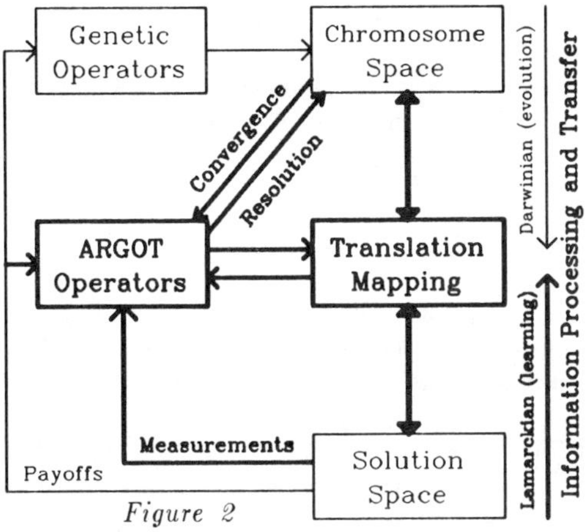

Figure 2

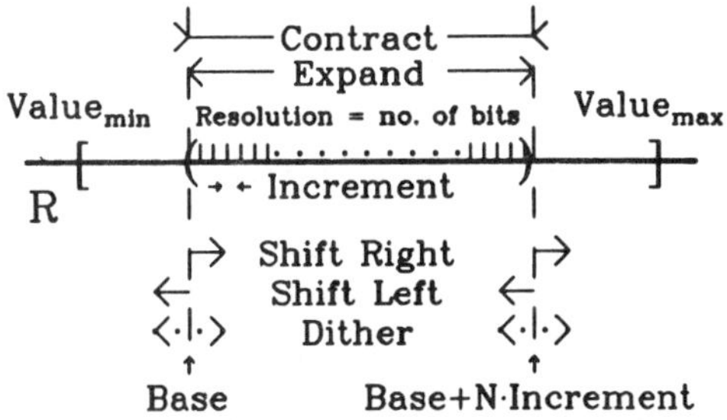

Figure 3

The components linked with the thinner arrows plus a static representation (in effect, a static Translation Mapping) constitute the standard genetic algorithm method. The ARGOT Strategy (includes the thicker lines) allows a dynamic mapping regulated by the ARGOT operators, themselves driven by statistical population measurements in the Chromosome and Solution Spaces. In Figure 3, the ARGOT operations on the Translation Mapping of a single parameter are indicated.

and Resolution operator are labeled on this diagram, but numerous other operators are employed to manipulate the translation mapping. These new components allow for a pseudo-Lamarckian evolution to occur, *i.e.*, information is processed and transferred from the Solution Space into the Translation Mapping and Chromosome Space. This abstraction of information from the phenotype, along with concept formulation and retrograde transfer into the genotype, is what distinguishes Lamarckian from Darwinian evolution. Because of this generalization of information contained in the current trial solutions, the ARGOT strategy is a learning algorithm which distinguishes it from the evolutionary SGAO.

A number of advantages accrue from ARGOT's learning capability. For one, ARGOT discovers interesting and appropriate strategies for searching various different solution spaces, as demonstrated for the Travelling Salesman Problem [5,6]. For another, the ARGOT adaptation alleviates many of the biases inherent within individual discovery components or representations. For example, ARGOT overcomes the 'Hamming Cliffs' of binary representations for the genetic algorithm discovery component by continually adapting the Mapping [8].

The ARGOT Mapping values are calculated *via* the Translation Mapping of Figure 2 and illustrated in Figure 3. Figure 3 illustrates the components of the mapping and the operators affecting those components. To summarize, the ARGOT Mapping translates the binary number represented in a gene's bits into a value on the real number line, $\Re$. The translated value lies between what are termed the Roving Boundaries given by the $Base$ and $Base + N \cdot Increment$. The Mapping constrains the Roving Boundaries to lie within the Brick-wall Boundaries given by the interval: $[Value_{min}, Value_{max}]$. Within the Roving Boundary interval, the mapping can have any one of the $N_{max} = 2^{Resolution}$ discrete values, where $Resolution$ is the number of bits of the gene. For instance, a possible ARGOT Mapping value is $Value = Base + 23 \cdot Increment$ where 23 is the Gene allele value provided by the binary number represented in the gene. The ARGOT Operators, triggered through statistical measurements over both the trial solutions and the chromosome population, adjust the Roving Boundaries and Resolution appropriately. Indications of the Roving Boundary adjustment operators are provided in this Figure, *e.g.*, the Expand, Contract, Shifts, and Dither operators.

INCREMENTAL UPDATES OF PAYOFFS

Some problem domains have a special type of separability, or near separability, that allows for the Payoffs to be updated in an incremental fashion. In particular, if the Payoff calculation can be divided into individual portions where the full Payoff is simply the sum of the partial payoffs and each sub-calculation only depends upon a subset of the parameters making up $\vec{x}$, then the full Payoff can be calculated incrementally. This means that once a sub-calculation yields a partial payoff for a particular instantiation of one of the subsets of parameters, then this partial payoff need not be recalculated but simply copied for all trials that include this parameter instance. If the subsets of parameters are nonintersecting, that is, each parameter is assigned to a unique subset, then a single parameter change means that only one partial payoff needs to be recalculated. On the other hand, if there is overlap of the parameter subsets, then more than one sub-calculation will be required by a parameter changed. Obviously, the amount of re-calculation depends upon the quantity of overlap.

GAs are especially suited to this type of incremental payoff calculations because of the nature of the operators they employ for creating new trials. For instance, the mutation operator typically alters the value of a single parameter and hence the new trial has almost an identical set of parameters as the original. Thus all but one partial payoff may be copied from the original parent and only a single sub-calculation need be performed in order to evaluate the new trial. Whenever the evaluation of trials is computationally expensive, then this incremental evaluation can save a tremendous amount of time. Likewise, the GA crossover operator, which recombines the trial solutions from two parents to yield two new progeny solutions in much the same way that biological crossover produces recombinations of the DNA from two parental chromosomes, typically alters the values of only two parameters while the others are simply copied appropriately from the parents. All but two partial payoffs for each offspring may be copied from the parents again saving most of the effort of re-evaluation. In addition, when the ARGOT Mapping is adapted by means of the ARGOT operators, typically only a small number of parameters are actually affected and therefore re-evaluation of the trial population can also be performed incrementally. To give a numerical example, say that a hypothetical problem can be separated into 100 sub-calculations of equal size, then partial updating saves about 95-99% of the evaluation computation for new trials created by mutation, crossover, and the ARGOT operators.

To illustrate the nature of problems that display partial separability under the ARGOT system, we consider several specific examples of linear systems of equations to be solved: $\mathbf{A}\vec{x} = \vec{y}$ with matrices $\mathbf{A}$ being banded, symmetric, and positive definite (further details of these problems are provided in a later section). These banded matrices may be blocked at a number of alternate block sizes. The nature of the crossover, mutation, and ARGOT operations upon these blocked matrices and the manners in which we choose to evaluate and store the block partial payoffs lead to different degrees of separability

Incremental Update of Payoffs					
Matrix Problem	Number of Parameters	Block Size	Band Width	Percent of Payoffs Copied	
				Expected	Empirical
Test	4	2	3	5-15%	27%
$3 \times 3 \times 3$	144	18	57	8-14%	16%
$3 \times 3 \times 3$	144	6	57	18-25%	31%
$4 \times 4 \times 4$	300	5	85	32-38%	40%

Table 1

This table lists the expected and empirical percentages of copied versus recalculated partial payoffs for applications stemming from finite element method $n \times n \times n$ Boussinesq problems. The expected percentages of copied partial payoffs are calculated based upon the probabilities of the crossover, mutation, and ARGOT operators. The empirical percentages are the values recorded during actual ARGOT solutions of these problems. Since the dynamically adapted Mapping alters the effective probabilities of these operators during the course of a solution, the expected percentages are given as a range of values based upon the typical range of these effective probabilities.

for both different block sizes as well as alternate evaluation metrics and storage methods. Based upon the above considerations, approximate expected percentages of copied versus recalculated partial payoffs are computed. Experiments using different matrices and different block sizes have recorded the actual payoff copy percentages during typical ARGOT solutions. These results are provided in Table 1. Note that empirically more partials payoffs were copied than expected. There are two main reasons for this, the first is that our expected calculations do not take into account the overlap of the various operators, that is, crossover, mutation, and the ARGOT operators may all require that a certain partial payoff be recalculated. Instead of recalculating it for each operator, the payoff is recalculated only once. In addition, the ARGOT adaptations to the Mapping tend to minimize the effects of the operators. This both reduces the number of bits in the representation and thus over time limits the effects of mutation as well as lowers the number of times the ARGOT operators are used as the solution progresses. This makes the actual number of copied versus recalculated payoffs dependent upon the difficulty of the problem; simpler problems require fewer ARGOT operations and thus more partial payoffs will be copied than recalculated. This is especially obvious for the simple Test problem where many more payoffs were copied than expected. Of course, the actual time saved by copying rather than recomputing partial payoffs is dependent upon the computational time for recalculation. When the payoff recalculations are computationally expensive, incremental updates can save significant amounts of time. If recalculation is not very expensive, then little time savings are observed since the overhead of storing and retrieving the partial payoffs then competes with the recalculation times.

PARALLEL SELECTION OPERATOR

The commonly-used selection method, the "standard selection operator", entails a serial access to the whole set of payoffs to construct a rating system from which parents are chosen. This rating and selection thus necessitates global memory access and consequently form a parallel bottleneck. Nature does not do it this way: biological selection occurs within small subsets of the full population. With this as a model, we have devised a correspondingly simple parallel selection scheme: randomly pick a fractionally small subset of the population and choose the chromosomes with the highest two payoffs as candidates for crossover [9]. We have studied the statistical properties of various selection methods, both by means of a mathematical model and empirically. Our empirical studies have shown that the above easily parallelized selection operator is satisfactory for the ARGOT strategy to successfully locate optima of nonlinear function optimization problems. Of course, the time saved by employing a parallel selection procedure depends upon the relative number of chromosomes in the population and the expense of the payoff evaluations. For very expensive evaluations and populations numbering in the hundreds, parallel selection will not save an immense amount of computational time.

It is interesting to note that even an entirely random choice of the two parental chromosomes from the population, without replacement, slightly biases those selected towards the better ones. Although this bias is not, in general, large enough for standard GAs to operate properly when solving complicated problems, ARGOT, on the other hand, is able to extract enough information from the slowly evolving population to work, but at a slower learning rate.

THE BUTTERFLY MULTIPROCESSOR

Like most learning techniques, ARGOT requires significant machine resources to do its work, in memory and CPU and to a lesser extent, stable storage. The advent of multiprocessors based on inexpensive microprocessors, such as the BBN Butterfly, make such general-purpose techniques more attractive as the real cost of computation falls, assuming they can be parallelized. The goal of our work is to show that ARGOT can be parallelized, and further, that ARGOT will do the multiprocessing management, so that the application can be cast in the simpler uniprocessor-like setting. With cheap processing power, we tend to treat larger problems, so it is important to show that ARGOT can handle practically-sized problems.

The ARGOT algorithm is a highly parallelizable search method. Besides the obvious parallelization stemming from the genetic algorithm discovery component (it is based upon the inherently parallel evolution of individual trials in a population), the ARGOT Operators themselves perform independent operations upon the application's parameters and thus may also be computed in parallel. This basic independence of operations in the ARGOT algorithm make it parallelizable on a wide variety of multiprocessors. Currently, ARGOT is running on two extremely different architectures, the Thinking Machines Connection Machine [5,6] (SIMD) and the BBN Butterfly Plus Multiprocessor (MIMD). Since, for most practical problems, the most important unit of work in the ARGOT method is a chromosome evaluation in a generation, and empirically it is often found that more than 200 chromosomes are not generally useful, it can be argued that a medium-grained multiprocessor with up to 200 processors is best for this technique. Under these circumstances and on the BBN Butterfly Multiprocessor the applications-level code itself does not need to have explicit multiprocessing constructs. The ARGOT program handles all multiprocessing requirements and allows the user to quickly code an application as if for an uniprocessor. We have several applications coded for uniprocessors that show multiprocessor speedups when simply executed on the Butterfly computer.

The Butterfly Plus multiprocessor is a MIMD system with up to 256 nodes, each with a MC68020 CPU, MC68882 floating-point coprocessor, 4 megabytes of memory, and Butterfly switch interface. The memory can be used as local memory or mapped over the Butterfly switch for access by any node. The switch also implements the necessary atomic operations. The Uniform System, a system library, provides applications with task generators, lock facilities, and means to scatter data across nodes while maintaining normal array access to the data. Butterfly FORTRAN has been extended to allow "allocatable" arrays so that runtime bindings to shared memory can be used, both to simple arrays on one node and to scattered arrays.

Parallelization

The most computationally intensive portion of the algorithm has been fully parallelized, that is, the work of the generations performing selection, crossover, mutation, conjugate gradient or other homotopy operator, and payoff evaluation. Figure 4 shows the speedup curve for this portion of the computation for the linear matrix application described below. Here 100 chromosomes are encoding 144 optimization parameters each. Each parameter uses from 3 to 6 bits in its representation; the number of bits is dynamically adjusted as the solution proceeds. Significant speedup is shown here for up to 60 processors. The irregularities (plateaus) in the curve are caused by the packing problem of tasks to processors. Here there are from 55-60 tasks (35-45 are of roughly equal size with the remainder requiring slightly less computation) to be assigned to P processors. For $P = 30$, these tasks schedule nicely into 2 timesteps, but for $P = 40$, two timesteps are still required since those 20 tasks left over from the first population of the 40 processors with tasks must now execute in the second timestep on 40 processors in effect idling 20 processors. Similarly there is a shelf in the speedup curve from 60-100 processors where tasks pack into one timestep thus idling all processors beyond the 60 needed for the tasks. In our speedup studies we choose to always employ 100 chromosomes which results in these Speedup Curve plateaus. For the greatest utilization of the multiprocessor, however, one would choose the chromosome population size such that the resulting number of ARGOT tasks would be an integral multiple of the number of processors. This then assures the minimum number of idle processors. An important aspect of the ARGOT approach is the wide flexibility in choosing the population size so as to optimize the processor utilization without resulting in significant degradation of the solution speed or accuracy. In other words, ARGOT can compensate for widely different population sizes through its adaptation of the representation.

The importance of memory contention inside the ARGOT program is shown by Figure 4, which compares the same problem before and after the gene data was scattered across the memories: in both cases the gene data was in shared memory, but in the first case each array was wholly contained in a single memory, while in the second it was distributed round-robin by elements to all memories. After taking the task-to-processor packing into account, the scattered case shows nearly linear speedup to 60 processors.

Results for the nonlinear matrix problem show less impressive speedups. Because this problem is smaller, the tasks are smaller and the memory contention resides pri-

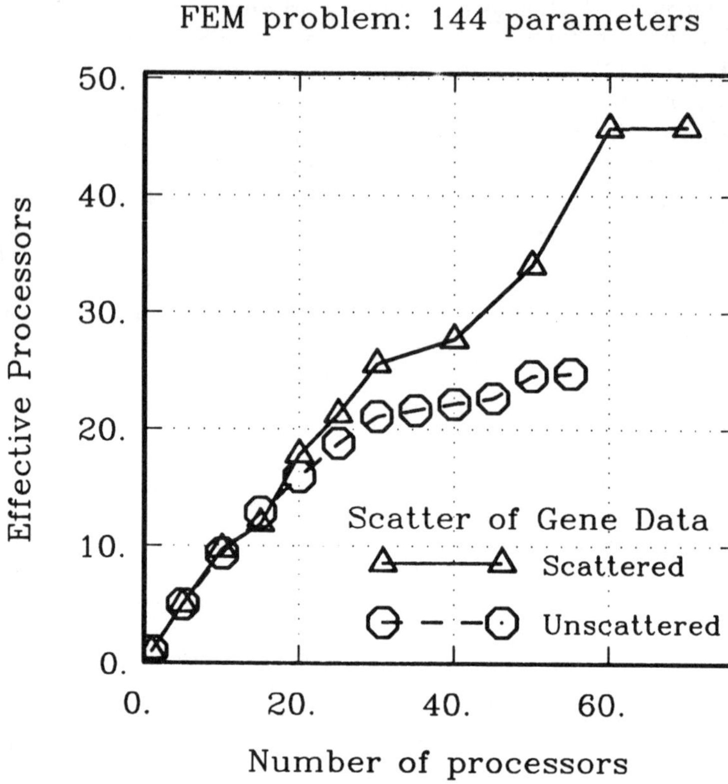

Figure 4

This figure graphs the Speedup Curves for the Linear Matrix Problem with 144 parameters. Note the generally good speedup to 60 processors. The scalloped plateau appearance derives from the packing problem of 55-60 tasks to the number of processors. When the Gene Data are scattered across the entire memory of the Butterfly thereby reducing switch contention, approximate linear speedup is observed (taking into account the task/processor plateaus). When the data are unscattered, switch contention intervenes to reduce the speedup as shown in the lower curve.

marily in the ARGOT Gene Data. Therefore, the larger the application task the better the speedup.

After the generations calculations, the next most computationally intensive portion of the algorithm is the learning step. Although we have not yet fully parallelized this computation, it is clearly feasible since the ARGOT operators on different genes are independent of one another, and the gene data is already scattered across all memories. When the number of parameters is very large or little *a priori* information is known about the search space so that ARGOT is required to learn a considerable amount about this space and adapt the Mapping extensively, then parallelization of these computations will lead to significant speedups. We are presently parallelizing these computations.

THE MATRIX APPLICATION

Solution methods for large linear systems have been studied in some depth on the Butterfly [10,11,12,13], in large part for the case of interest in finite element analysis (FEM): banded, symmetric, positive-definite systems. The bandedness limits the parallelism attainable with Gaussian elimination, and contention over the pivot rows further degrades performance [11]. Blocking of the matrix helps, both because of reduced communications costs and bundling of active pivots, so that more work is currently applicable at each point in time [12]. But the blocked method soon reaches its own parallelism limit. The conjugate gradient method speeds up comparably. [13] Thus, as a first experiment with the parallelized ARGOT program, we are trying these FEM problems. ARGOT has the edge with parallelism, but of course the classical methods are very good when the matrices are so well behaved.

The problem is to find the vector $\vec{x} = (x_1, x_2, \ldots, x_n)$ satisfying $\mathbf{A}\vec{x} = \vec{y}$, with matrix $\mathbf{A}$ and vector $\vec{y}$ given. For ARGOT, we use the energy formulation just as in the conjugate gradient method: the energy provides the payoff metric, $F(\vec{x}) = \frac{1}{2}\vec{x}^T\mathbf{A}\vec{x} - \vec{x}^T\vec{y}$, to be minimized and the solution components $x_1, x_2, \ldots, x_n$ are the optimization parameters. For the FEM problems, physical estimates give the search space limits; these can be greatly overestimated for ARGOT without much computational penalty since ARGOT quickly adjusts its limits to appropriate sizes. Hence the *a priori* physical information is not required by the ARGOT method.

When ARGOT presents a new $\vec{x}$ to the matrix application, the latter could do the full energy computation for it, but this is easily seen to be expensive. By blocking the matrix, the energy is partitioned into block-contributions, or 'partial energies', that satisfy the conditions for incremental update presented earlier. Thus only a fraction of the energy data must be recalculated on each generation as discussed earlier.

The multiprocessor ARGOT results show convergence to expected solutions. In fact, *via* the task-based random number scheme, identical runs (vs. uniprocessor ARGOT) with 50 chromosomes for 50 generations on up to 50 processors have been made. The ARGOT program adapts the Mapping for these matrix applications in a manner displaying the typical convergence onto solutions [4,5,6].

Results

We chose test matrices from static finite element problems involving banded, symmetric, positive definite matrices (specifically, a $3 \times 3 \times 3$ element Boussinesq problem with a 144×144 matrix of band 57 and a $4 \times 4 \times 4$ element Boussinesq problem with a 300×300 matrix of band 85). ARGOT converged to known solutions in less than 25 generations, and subsequently provided increasing accuracies with further generations. It must be emphasized that this is not a competitive method for such well-behaved matrices: it takes minutes on the multiprocessor to solve what can be done in seconds on a uniprocessor by traditional methods. This, of course, is a somewhat unfair comparison since the traditional methods are specifically designed for the special form of these matrices and are not directly applicable to less well-behaved ones while ARGOT, being a learning algorithm, is required to learn characteristics about the search space and does not depend upon any special features of the problem. As such, ARGOT, without change, is applicable to nonlinear matrix problems where the tradition methods either are not applicable or have severe limitations. On the other hand, these linear matrices are practically-sized problems and show the generality of the ARGOT method. In addition, ARGOT is capable of combining a conjugate gradient discovery component with the genetic algorithm for problems only locally well-behaved and for which conjugate gradient techniques alone become 'stuck' at local optima. In the next section we describe problems for which the traditional methods have not provided reliable solutions.

A Nonlinear Matrix Problem

Consider an $m \times n$ matrix $\mathbf{A}$, where $m > n$ in the interesting case, and a real nonlinear function $\vec{f}$ to be applied to each component of a vector to map it to a target vector. Then, given a target vector $\vec{y}$, the general problem is to find $\vec{x}$ as the "best" approximation solving $\vec{f}(\mathbf{A}\vec{x}) = \vec{y}$ using the usual metric of minimal square residual or some other appropriate measure. If the function $\vec{f}$ is invertible and $m = n$, these problems reduce to the linear matrix problem discussed in the previous section. When $m > n$, however, there are more components of $\vec{y}$ than $\vec{x}$, so no exact solution is expected for non-degenerate $\mathbf{A}$. Also, if $\vec{f}$ is singular anywhere within its domain of interest, these problems do not reduce to the linear matrix case.

We have tested three problems of this type, a small 5×4 test problem, a 25×15 problem, and a 70×50 problem using several nonlinear $\vec{f}$s and randomly initialized $\mathbf{A}$ and $\vec{y}$. Conjugate gradient, conjugate direction (Powell's), and ARGOT all found the same solution for the 5×4 test problem. For the two larger cases, however, conjugate gradient and conjugate direction methods located several suboptimal solutions starting from different initial points. In addition, the conjugate gradient technique often diverged instead of converging to a solution. ARGOT, for both of these larger problems, and starting with exactly the same initial points, always converged to superior solutions.

It is interesting to note that when a single iteration of a conjugate gradient or conjugate direction discovery step is included in addition to the normal genetic algorithm component, ARGOT converged faster to its superior solutions. Thus, while the homotopy techniques alone often diverge or lead to local solutions, they do provide enhanced learning rates when combined with the genetic algorithm serving as the discovery component of ARGOT. In addition, we found that the greatest speeds were obtained by employing the homotopy techniques at relatively low probabilities (for less than 10% of the trial solutions) and for only a single iteration. Thus, instead of allowing the homotopy methods to take each current trial and traverse to the optimum of its local basin, qualitatively the same information is obtained much earlier by stopping the homotopy iteration after its first step. In other words, this first iteration provides the greatest gain in information about the local basin and ARGOT is entirely capable of utilizing this information to adapt the Mapping appropriately. By not allowing the homotopy methods to iterate to the local optima greatly reduces the amount of computation without hindering the learning by ARGOT nor the quality of the solutions discovered.

Because of the relatively small amount of application data associated with the problem, we simply replicated the data on all nodes. The Butterfly has currently 4 megabytes of memory per node, so most problems amenable to this approach should be able to have private copies of the problem data. The speedup curves indicate that up to about 20 processors can be used effectively for the 25×15 problem: larger problems, or ones with more difficult $\vec{f}$ evaluations, would of course be able to utilize more processors. We are presently extending these studies to other nonlinear $\vec{f}$ functions in addition to problems where there is noisy access to the **A** matrix elements (*i.e.*, whenever an element of **A** is required its value is returned with random noise added) or where the rows of the **A** matrix are slowly varying thus requiring the solutions to 'track' the varying **A** matrix.

Acknowledgements

We would like to thank Lawrence Davis for his penetrating insights into the properties of genetic algorithms; and we owe a special thanks to BBN Advanced Computers, Inc. not only for Butterfly computer time but also for cheerful and capable support during the implementation of ARGOT on the Butterfly. We also would like to thank Sandip Sen for his programming of the conjugate gradient technique as an additional discovery component for the ARGOT method.

REFERENCES

[1] Holland, J.H. *Adaptation in Natural and Artificial Systems*, University of MichiganPress, Ann Arbor, **1975**.

[2] Grefenstette, J.J. ed. *Genetic Algorithms and Their Applications: Proceedings of the Second International Conference on Genetic Algorithms*, Lawrence Erlbaum Associates, New Jersey, **1987**.

[3] Baker, J.E. "Reducing Bias and Inefficiency in the Selection Algorithm" in *Genetic Algorithms and Their Applications: Proceedings of the Second International Conference on Genetic Algorithms*, p 14, Lawrence Erlbaum Associates, New Jersey, **1987**.

[4] Shaefer, C.G. "The ARGOT Strategy: Adaptive Representation GeneticOptimizer Technique," in *Genetic Algorithms and Their Applications:Proceedings of the Second International Conference on Genetic Algorithms*,Grefenstette, J.J. ed., p. 50, Lawrence Erlbaum Associates, New Jersey,**1987**.

[5] Shaefer, C.G. "The ARGOT Strategy: Adaptive Genetic Optimization," Reported at TIMS/ORSA National Meeting, April 25-27, **1988**,Washington, D.C., abstract MC22.2.

[6] Presented at the International Workshop on Change of Representation and Inductive Bias, June 8-10, 1988, Briarcliff, NY. and to be published in a hardbound volume resulting from this workshop, expected in 1989. Craig G. Shaefer, Smith, S.J.

[7] DeJong, K.A. *Analysis of the Behavior of a Class of Genetic Adaptive Systems*. Ph.D. dissertation, University of Michigan, Ann Arbor, **1975**.

[8] A manuscript describing several emergent properties of the ARGOT Strategy including alleviation of representational biases is in preparation for submission elsewhere.

[9] There have been a number of similar proposed parallel implementations of selection operators and GAs, for instance see Grefenstette, J.J. "Parallel Adaptive Algorithm for Function Optimization" Technical Report CS-81-9 Computer Science Dept. Vanderbilt University, November 1981; and Suh, J.Y., Van Gucht, D. "Distributed Genetic Algorithms" Technical Report No. 225 Computer Science Dept. Indiana University, Bloomington, July 1987.

[10] Crowther, W., Goodhue, J., Starr, E., Thomas, R., Milliken, W., Blackadar,T.; "Performance Measurements on a 128-Node Butterfly Parallel Processor",International Conference on Parallel Processing, **1985**.

[11] Allik, H., Moore, S., O'Neil, E., Tenenbaum, E. *Computers and Structures* **1987**, *27(1)*, 13. "Finite Element Analysis on the BBN ButterflyMultiprocessor"

[12] O'Neil, E., Allik, H., Moore, S., Tenenbaum, E.; "Finite ElementAnalysis on the BBN Butterfly Multiprocessor" in *Proceedings of the Second International Conference on Supercomputing*, **1987**.

[13] Tenebaum, E., O'Neil, E., Allik, H., Moore, S.; "Parallelizing Conjugate Gradient for Finite Element Analysis" in *Proceedings of the 1987 Summer Computer Simulation Conference*, Montreal, **1987**.

Global Change

BREAKTHROUGHS IN OCEAN AND CLIMATE MODELING MADE POSSIBLE BY SUPERCOMPUTERS OF TODAY AND TOMORROW

Albert J. Semtner, Jr.
Naval Postgraduate School, Monterey CA 93943

Robert M. Chervin
National Center for Atmospheric Research, Boulder CO 80307

ABSTRACT

A three-dimensional hydrodynamic model has been constructed for the purpose of simulating ocean circulation on modern supercomputing architectures. The model is designed to take advantage of faster clock speeds, increased numbers of processors, and enlarged memories of machines expected to be available over the next decade. The model allows realistic global simulations to be conducted in support of the Global Change Program. This involves resolving the energetic scales of motion, usually referred to as 'eddies'. Such global ocean modeling is essential for proper representation of the full range of oceanic and climatic phenomena. The first-ever global eddy-resolving ocean calculation is reported here as a genuine breakthrough made possible by today's supercomputers. More definitive results on global dynamics and global change will be forthcoming, as coupled atmosphere-ocean models having very high resolution and improved physical and biogeochemical processes accomplish future breakthroughs with the help of the supercomputers of tomorrow.

1. INTRODUCTION

There has been considerable concern of late over the possibility of climatic change and its consequences for the nations of the world. Climatic change can occur either in the form of interannual variations, generally thought to be attributable to natural multi-year fluctuations of the tropical ocean and global atmosphere system, or in the form of secular climatic drift, now seriously believed to be occuring as a result of anthropogenic sources of carbon dioxide and other trace gases, which modify the earth's radiation budget. In the latter situation, the global ocean acts as a buffer for climatic change by absorbing and redistributing both heat and carbon dioxide. In either case, the ocean plays a significant role, but its contribution is poorly understood.

During the mid-1980's the international scientific community formulated a two-prong approach to understanding climatic change. The ongoing TOGA program (Tropical Ocean, Global Atmosphere) seeks understanding and prediction of interannual climate variability, whereas the planned WOCE program (World Ocean Circulation Experiment) seeks a global understanding of ocean circulation to allow prediction of long-term climatic change. Both of these programs emphasize the joint use of observations and numerical models of the ocean-atmosphere system to attain their objectives. However, as we approach the decade of the 1990's, a growing perception of the strong global linkages of a multitude of physical and biogeochemical processes has exposed the need for an even broader program to study global change. Thus the Global Change Program has been initiated, within which climate programs such as WOCE and TOGA can be expected to be central components.

The world ocean is being increasingly regarded as a tightly connected system of varied phenomena which influence each other on many time scales, some of them as short as months to years, over the vast distances which separate individual ocean basins. It becomes imperative in trying to understand the role of the ocean in climate not to leave out the interconnectivity of the ocean basins, whereby changes in wind forcing in one part of the world ocean may profoundly influence heat transport and atmosphere-ocean interaction in a distant region. A particularly important example of such ocean basin interconnectivity involves the cycle for formation and replenishment of North Atlantic Deep Water (cf. Gordon. 1986), with associated climatic effects of truly global proportions. Another important global ocean phenomenon is the Antarctic Circumpolar Current, the instabilities of which strongly influence the amount of heat available to melt the West Antarctic Ice Sheet from below, with the potential to change sea level by tens of meters on time scales of centuries. Thus global ocean modeling is essential for proper representation of the full scope of climatic possibilities.

Modeling of the atmosphere has been carried out for over 40 years and has achieved considerable realism in both deterministic prediction and in simulating the statistical properties of the atmosphere. Similar progress in oceanography has been impossible because of the lack of observed data and because of the lack of computer power for running ocean models. Now the promised availability of global synoptic data from ocean-sensing satellites and the anticipated speedup of computing power by one to two orders of magnitude in the next five years make global ocean modeling and climate prediction attainable goals. The present paper describes an ocean model recently constructed with those objectives in mind; and it describes the first global ocean simulation with resolution barely fine enough to allow the spontaneous formation of mesoscale eddies, which are the oceanic analogues of synoptic weather systems. Resolving mesoscale eddies is thought to be crucial to understanding the global ocean circulation because the eddies redistribute momentum, heat, and salt in complex ways which have never been adequately parameterized in either an oceanic or atmospheric context. Higher resolution can greatly improve climatic and oceanic studies in support of the Global Change Program; and this will require the enhanced power of supercomputers of the next decade, accompanied by advanced modeling techniques to use those machines.

2. STATEMENT OF THE SCIENTIFIC PROBLEM

To isolate the essentials in what has been discussed so far, we set forth the following elements of the scientific problem at hand:

(i) The capability to simulate the earth's climate is a central requirement for the *Global Change Program.*

(ii) A proper representation of various climatic states (both in equilibrium or in transition, and for conditions representative of past, present, and future biogeochemical situations) requires proper modeling of both the atmosphere and the ocean.

(iii) Both the atmosphere and ocean are turbulent fluids which transport momentum, heat, water, chemicals, and biological species in very complex ways. The turbulent motions need to be explicitly included in model studies to assure proper representation of their net effects.

(iv) Unfortunately, the turbulent length scale of the ocean is one tenth that of the atmosphere (a few tenths of a degree versus a few degrees of latitude and longitude). Furthermore, the time scale for the coupled ocean-atmosphere system is at least ten times as long as that for the atmosphere alone. A net thousandfold computational increase results.

(v) Fortunately, supercomputers expected in the next decade make ocean and climate studies tractable, if proper planning allows the high performances of the machines to be fully exploited. Real 'breakthroughs' can then be realized in support of the *Global Change Program.*

3. SUPERCOMPUTING PROSPECTS

To give some estimate of supercomputing developments of the 1990's, Table 1 (from Semtner and Luther, 1988) has been assembled from numerous sources of information. It is not intended to be an exhaustive list of anticipated products or to provide definitive technical information. (In particular machines of masssively parallel architecture are not included although they may come into widespread use in the mid-1990's, because their applicability to complex climate modeling problems is still a matter of discussion.) Nevertheless, there are some very clear trends visible in supercomputing. These fall into three classes: (i) decreasing cycle time of basic machine operations to the likely technological limit; (ii) increasing number of processors; and (iii) larger amounts of high-speed memory. To exploit the capabilities of these machines to the fullest, climate and ocean models must be able to take advantage of each of these categories of improvement, so that the indicated machine speeds can in fact be approached.

If we confine our attention to the computationally very demanding oceanic component of any coupled climate model, we can estimate what kinds of calculations will be possible on machines of today and tomorrow. Table 2 gives an estimate of the wall-clock hours required to run a progression of increasingly more realistic ocean simulations for a period of 25 years. These estimates are based on extrapolating memory requirements and model performance from an existing model configured as in the first line of the table. Full utilization of features (i) through (iii) listed in the previous paragraph is required.

Some of the simulations listed in Table 2 are 'reasonable and feasible', and some are not. For the latter situation, coarser resolution calculations can be envisioned as a way of decreasing the computing time requirement or increasing the length of the integration. The usual rule of thumb is that a two-fold decrease in horizontal resolution leads to an eight-fold decrease in computing requirement. In actuality, one can expect that on any given machine a number of ocean and climate simulations could be carried out, for different time and space scales of importance to the Global Change Program.

TABLE 1: SUPERCOMPUTERS FOR TODAY AND TOMORROW

Machine/ Availability	No. Processors/ (Cycle Time in nanoseconds)	Peak Multitasked Vectorized Speed (gigaflops)	High-Speed Memory (Main/Secondary in megawords)
CRAY X-MP/48 (1986)	4/8.5	0.94	8/256
ETA 10 8/256E (1988)	8/10.5	3.3	256
CRAY Y-MP/832 (1988)	8/6.0	2.7	32/512
ETA 10 8/256G (1989)	8/7.0	5.0	256
CRAY 3 (1990)	16/2.0	16.	512
ETA 30 (1991)	16/4.0	30.	4096
SS,Inc.–SS1 (1992)	64/2.0	64.	1024/4096
CRAY 4 (1994)	64/0.7	180	2048

TABLE 2: CLOCK HOURS FOR PARALLEL, VECTOR 25-YEAR RUNS

Machine/ Availability	Horizontal Grid Spacing (degrees)	Number of Levels	N. Atlantic Basin	Global Ocean
CRAY X-MP/48 (1986)	1/2 x 1/2 1/3 x 2/5	20 20	125 290	1250 2900
ETA 10 8/256E (1988)	1/3 x 1/3	30	90	900
CRAY Y-MP/832 (1988)	1/4 x 1/4	40	707	7070
ETA 10 8/256G (1989)	1/3 x 1/3	30	60	600
CRAY 3 (1990)	1/4 x 1/4	40	120	1200
ETA 30 (1991)	1/6 x 1/6	40	125	1250
SS,Inc.–SS1 (1992)	1/6 x 1/6	40	100	1000
CRAY 4 (1994)	1/8 x 1/8	40	83	830

4. AN OCEAN-CLIMATE MODEL FOR THE 1990'S

To take advantage of the machines listed in Table 1, a new ocean model has been contructed with near total vectorization, a parallel architecture that can exploit up to 100 processors, and a memory structure that allows the global configurations of Table 2 to run in the (non-disk) memories of the listed machines. The model took some five person-years to develop from an earlier version of an ocean model first formulated by Bryan (1969). The modernization effort is described in Chervin and Semtner (1989). A similar restructuring effort has also been carried out for an atmospheric model at the National Center for Atmospheric Research (NCAR), and this is described in Chervin (1988). The two models, when coupled together, constitute a powerful climate model for studies of global change.

We briefly enumerate some features of the new ocean model, the results of which will be described in a following section:

- Designed for CRAY X–MP and anticipated other supercomputers.
- 98% vectorized in longitude across individual ocean basins.
- 99.64% parallel processed in latitude for 4–64 processors.
- Straightforward treatment of vertical processes.
- Energetic consistency checked independently.
- 450 megaflops sustained performance on NCAR's CRAY X–MP/48.
- Negligible (4%) loss of time in I/O transfers with SSD.
- Global, 1/3 x 2/5 degree, 20 level model possible on NCAR's X–MP/48.
- Global, 1/6 degree, 20 level model possible on Cray's X–MP/464.

To give an indication of the applicability of the ocean model to other supercomputers, the global code was recently run without modification on a prototype CRAY Y–MP and found to run 2.7 times faster than on an X-MP48. That is exactly what would be expected from considerations of a doubling of the number of processors and a reduction in cycle time from 8.5 to 6.3 nanoseconds. Even including the I/O overhead of 200 Mbytes/sec, the sustained model performance (with the 6.3 clock) was 1100 megaflops.

5. A 1988 'BREAKTHROUGH' EXPERIMENT

We now describe in brief the configuration and results of a 1988 ocean simulation which is the first such undertaking to be both global in scope and eddy-resolving in physical realism. More detail can be found in the December 1988 color issue of Journal of Geophysical Research (Oceans).

The configuration of the model run was as follows:

- o 1/2 degree grid spacing in latitude and longitude, for (marginal) resolution of turbulent eddies.
- o 20 vertical levels maximum, consistent with coastlines and bottom topography.
- o Observed annual-mean wind stress, as well as heat and moisture fluxes at the sea surface.
- o Initialization of the abyssal ocean with observed temperature and salinity.
- o Integration for a simulated period of 22 years, sufficient to develop the turbulent equilibrium of the upper ocean (requiring 500 wall-clock hours at 450 megaflops).
- o Archiving of 50 gigabytes of model data over the final two years.

Much of the visual output from the global 22-year simulation is in the form of color raster prints and 16 mm film animations of global and regional ocean phenomena. The reader is referred to Semtner and Chervin (1988) for more information, including some of the color results. It is hoped that the readers of this article were able to see some of the 16 mm film ouput at the SUPERCOMPUTING '88 Conference. To give some idea here of the nature of two key fields, Figure 1 shows instantaneous maps of the global temperature field at 160 m depth and of the streamlines of the volume transport by ocean currents. Each panel is 720 by 280 gridpoints in size; and the coutour intervals are 1° C and 10^7 m^3 sec^{-1}, for upper and lower panels, respectively. The incredibly small detail is a result of the fundamental ten-fold difference in length scale relative to that of the atmosphere. Ocean currents and eddies appear to be miniscule relative to atmospheric jets and storms. Nevertheless, the depicted features are realistic; and the net effects of the strong currents, waves, and eddies in the ocean are of primary importance in the context of global change issues.

The results of the 1988 global ocean simulation are being analyzed and compared against global observations taken from satellites. Satellites provide measurements for approximately the same time and space scales as the model, giving an opportunity to 'validate' model performance in a way which was previously impossible with conventional oceanographic observations. So far, very favorable comparisons have been obtained between a number of measurable quantities related to the intrinsic variability of unstable currents. An example of one such comparison is shown in Figure 2, which shows the

Figure 1. (upper) Temperature at 160m depth and (lower) streamlines of volume transport by currents. More explanation on these instantaneous model fields is given in Section 5.

'mesoscale variability' in both SESAT altimeter data (Cheney et al., 1983) and model transport for the Southern Hemisphere south of 30° S. The areas of maximal variability are very nearly coincident in both panels, indicating a successful simulation of the unstable parts of the greatest of the oceanic currents of the world—the Antarctic Circumpolar Current. Comparison of satellite and model variability on a global basis, showing matching instabilities in northern hemisphere currents as well, can be found in the November 1988 issue of Oceanography Magazine.

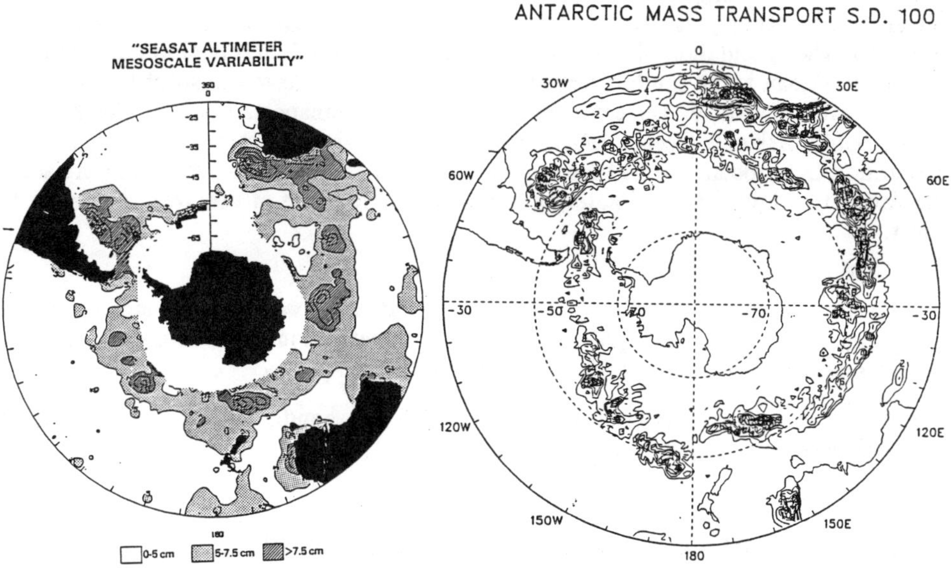

Figure 2. (left) Observed ocean variability and (right) modeled variability, both of which derive from instabilities of strong currents.

6. SUMMARY AND CONCLUSIONS

It would appear that the 1988 simulation has been moderately sucessful in modeling the global ocean circulation with resolved eddies. Although the grid resolution is marginal, the relative realism of the results give an optimistic outlook for future modeling efforts with better resolution. A large number of oceanic regions of mesoscale variability have been identified, and these correspond in general to those identified in satellite altimeter data by Cheney et al. (1983).

In the more detailed paper of Semtner and Chervin (1988), a number of western boundary currents have been subjected to a first-order examination and found to exhibit a variety of behaviors. This gives hope that this model and future modeling at higher resolution can be judged on performance in simulating a suite of western boundary currents rather than just one. An examination of inter-ocean basin connectivity seems to confirm the speculation of observational oceanographers (notably Gordon, 1986) that the Indian Ocean is the conduit for completing the cycle of heat transport to the surface of the North Atlantic, by the coupling of upper-ocean transports from the North Pacific to the South Atlantic Ocean. Furthermore, some regions of strong variability in the Antarctic Circumpolar Current have been found, which affect the heat transport across the Antarctic Circle and ultimately govern the melting rate of the West Antarctic Ice Sheet.

Looking at the ocean/climate simulations that are possible on supercomputers of today and knowing the anticipated structures of supercomputers of tomorrow (i.e. into the next decade), we can draw the following conclusions:

(1) An ocean modeling system now exists which can handle large ocean and climate problems on anticipated supercomputers of the 1990's.

(2) A 'breakthrough' experiment in 1988 on the CRAY X–MP/48 at NCAR represents the first global ocean simulation which resolves the turbulence inherent in the real ocean. Statistical comparisons with upper ocean global datasets are very encouraging.

(3) Using supercomputers available in the early 1990's, additional 'breakthrough' experiments with coupled ocean atmosphere models can be anticipated in support of the *Global Change Program.* These include:

   (a) Simulation of the equilibrium climate of the present day, requiring multi-century integrations;

   (b) Simulations of the equilibrium climate and of transient climatic change caused by the anthropogenic increase in atmospheric trace gases;

(c) Studies of ice-age climates and of paleocirculations of the atmosphere-ocean system;

(d) Studies of the effect of biogeochemical processes on the partitioning of carbon among the ocean, the atmosphere, and the biosphere.

ACKNOWLEGMENTS.

The first author of this paper is supported by NSF Grants ATM-8705980 and OCE-8812472, and the second author is partially supported by a Department of Energy grant from their Carbon Dioxide Research Program to NCAR. Computing resources were provided by the Scientific Computing Division of the National Center for Atmospheric Research. NCAR is sponsored by the National Science Foundation.

REFERENCES

Bryan, K., 1969: A Numerical Model for the Study of the World Ocean. J. Computat. Phys., 4, 347–376.

Cheney, R.E., J.G. Marsh, and B.D. Beckley, 1983: Global Mesoscale Variability from SEASAT collinear altimeter data. J. Geophys. Res., 88, 4343–4354.

Chervin, R.M., 1988: On the relationship between computer technology and climate modelling. In: Physically-Based Modelling and Simulation of Climate and Climatic Change – Part II (M. Schlesinger, ed.), Kluwer Academic Publishers, Dordrecht, 1053–1068.

Chervin, R.M., and A.J. Semtner, 1989: An ocean modeling system for supercomputer architectures of the 1990's. In: Proceedings of the 1988 NATO Advanced Research Workshop on Ocean-Climate Interaction (M. Schlesinger, ed.), in press.

Gordon, A., 1986: Interocean Exchange of Thermocline Water. J. Geophys. Res., 91, 5037–5046.

Semtner, A.J., and R.M. Chervin, 1988: A Simulation of the Global Ocean Circulation with Resolved Eddies. J. Geophys. Res,, 93, in press.

Semtner, A.J., and M.E. Luther, 1988: Computational Resource Considerations for the World Ocean Circulation Experiment. In: WoceNotes (D. Mayes, ed.), U.S. WOCE Office, Texas A&M Univ., College Station, Vol.1, No.2, 4–5.

GLOBAL CHANGE: THE SOLAR INFLUENCE

R. G. Roble
High Altitude Observatory
National Center for Atmospheric Research*
P.O. Box 3000
Boulder, CO 80307

The variable outputs of the sun that influence the Earth's atmosphere include electromagnetic radiation, the solar wind and energetic particles emitted by flares and other disturbances. Irregularities in the solar wind can also modulate galactic cosmic rays that impact the Earth. In addition, there are variations in the solar energy at the top of the atmosphere caused by long-term changes in the Earth's orbital elements. All of these variations are currently being imposed upon an atmosphere whose composition and thermal structure is changing as a result of trace gas increases from man's activities. There is need for a next generation climate model that extends from the ground to the thermosphere that can be used to study the effects of solar variability on a changing atmosphere. Such a model will probably require an increase in our present day computational power by factors of 10 to 100.

INTRODUCTION

The sun and Earth's atmosphere are evolving constantly with time. Stellar theory suggests that the early sun was only about 70 percent as luminous as it is today [1]. Climate theory indicates that if the early Earth's atmosphere had its present composition, the Earth would have existed in permanent glaciation since its beginning and would not yet have thawed out. It was, therefore, suggested that the early terrestrial atmosphere was poor in oxygen and rich in infrared-opaque gases so that an enhanced greenhouse could keep the mean surface temperature above freezing [2].

Fluctuations in greenhouse gases (CO_2 and CH_4) have been measured in deep ice cores extracted from Antarctica [3]. These ice cores provide a record of atmospheric climate and CO_2 that is representative of global changes over the last glacial-interglacial cycle (160,000 years). CO_2 concentrations as low as 180 ppmv have been derived during the height of the glacial advances about 18,000 years ago. At the present time CO_2 (345 ppmv) is changing rapidly, but this time in response to man's increasing activities. A doubling of the CO_2 concentration is expected to occur by the end of the 21st century [4]. The greenhouse radiative effect on climate from CO_2 is also being enhanced by increasing concentrations of CH_4, O_3, N_2O and chlorofluorocarbons CFC's [5, 6]. The Global Change and the International Geosphere/Biosphere Programs will pursue extensive theoretical, numerical and experimental research to better understand the projected weather and climate changes that are expected to occur from both natural variability and from trace gas increases as a result of man's activities.

In this paper, I present a brief review of our current understanding of solar variability and the effect of that variability on different atmospheric regions from the troposphere to the thermosphere (Fig. 1). The projected changes in the atmosphere composition and temperature structure as a result of trace gas increases will also be reviewed. Finally, the need for a climate model that extends from the ground to the thermosphere and includes ocean coupling to study the effects of solar variability on a changing atmosphere will be discussed.

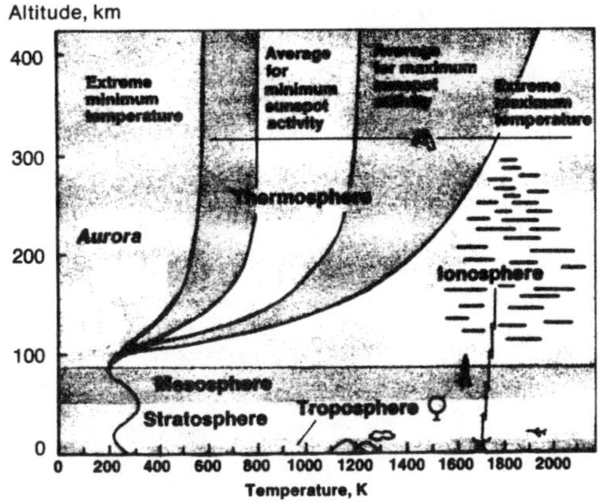

Figure 1

Schematic of the atmospheric temperature structure that is used to define atmospheric regions.

SOLAR VARIABILITY

The search for solar luminosity variations in measurements made from the ground has generally been unsuccessful because of turbulent distortions of the overlying atmosphere. More accurate measurements had to await the development of rockets and satellites that were able to measure the total and spectral solar irradiance from outside of the Earth's atmosphere. The satellite record of solar spectral irradiance measurements is relatively short yet significant variations have been detected. An example of the spectral distribution of the solar irradiance and its variation with solar activity is shown in Figure 2.

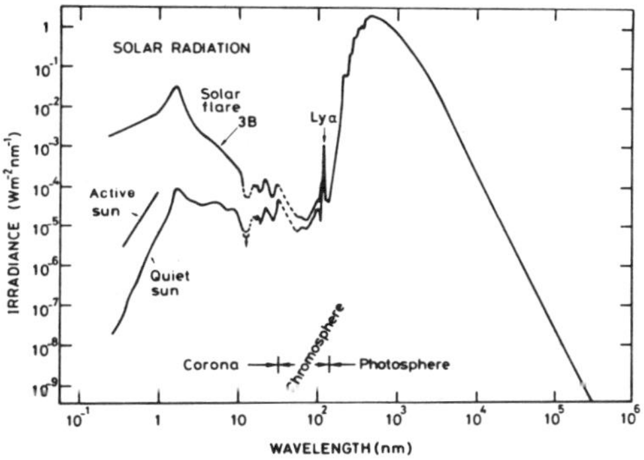

Figure 2

Spectral distribution of the solar irradiance, and its variation with solar activity. The logarithmic representation emphasizes the contribution of X-rays and extreme ultraviolet radiation [32].

The visible and infrared portions of the solar spectrum are essentially a continuum and they are emitted from the sun's photosphere (Fig. 3). At wavelengths less than 300 nm absorption lines are superimposed on the ultraviolet continuum that basically originate from the sun's chromosphere. For wavelength's less than 200 nm emissions by chromospheric and coronal lines begin to dominate the continuum, and the emissions become highly variable depending on solar activity that is characterized by such physical phenomena as flares, sunspots, faculae, plages etc.

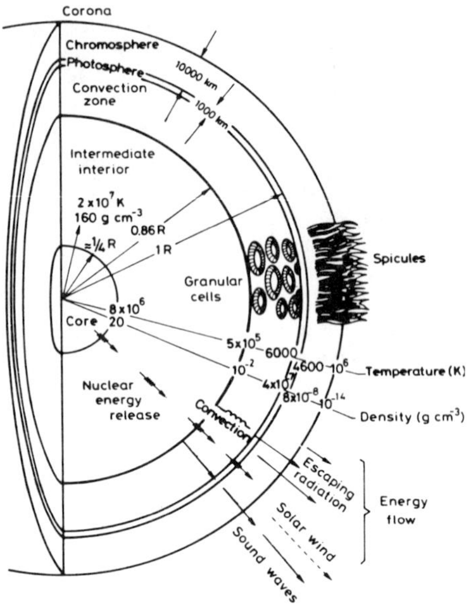

Figure 3

Schematic of the solar atmosphere [32].

Solar X-ray, EUV and UV ($\lambda < 400$ nm) variability

Absorption of solar radiation at wavelengths less than 200 nm primarily affect the Earth's thermosphere and ionosphere. Knowledge of variations in these regions is important for predictions of satellite drag and radio communication.

The Atmosphere Explorer satellites (AE-C, D and E) launched between December 1973 and November 1975 each carried an extreme ultraviolet spectrometer to measure the full-disk solar EUV and UV flux over the wavelength range 15 to 200 nm. These measurements during solar cycle 21 showed that there was a considerable change in the solar EUV and UV flux from July 13-26, 1976, a period of spotless conditions at minimum levels of solar activity, to the 1979-1980 period near the maximum levels of the sunspot cycle [7]. At short wavelengths less than 30 nm, the EUV emissions that emanate from the corona are highly variable increasing by factors of 10 to 100 between solar minimum and maximum. For wavelengths between 30 and 120 nm the emissions that emanate more from the chromosphere are much less variable; factors of 2-3. The variability then decreases from a factor of 2 near 100 nm to about 1.1 near 200 nm. In addition to the overall change in solar radiation between solar minimum and maximum, there are also shorter term fluctuations on a daily basis with the coronal emissions being much more variable than the chromospheric emissions. The measured solar UV irradiance beyond 200 nm has variations on daily, 27 day solar rotation period and 13.5 half-day solar rotation period (from two widely separated active regions) as well as a general variation over a solar cycle [8]. The overall 11-year variation is approximately a factor of two at the Lyman-α wavelength, 121.6 nm, and less than 1% at longer wavelengths near 300 nm.

Total solar radiative output variability

The satellite record of total solar irradiance extends only a few years. Discoveries from two data sets spanning the late 1978 to present time period (solar cycle 21 and the beginning of solar cycle 22) have provided substantive new information on total solar irradiance variability on time scales ranging from minutes to the duration of the record. A systematic long-term decrease in solar luminosity was noted between 1980 to mid-1985 [9]. It remained constant from mid-1985 until mid-1987 and has recently begun to increase as we begin the new solar cycle 22. A long-term variation of 0.09% in total solar irradiance occurred over this time period. Both the total radiative output and the UV emission from the sun reach their peak values at times near the maximum of solar magnetic activity. There are two main components to the total radiative output variation. The first is associated with sunspot blocking of total radiation and the second is associated total radiation enhancements from active region phenomena (faculae, plages). Sunspots are regions in the photosphere where the heat flow is inhibited, with a reduction in emission corresponding to a reduced temperature. Faculae are those magnetic regions in the sun's photosphere where the visible continuum emission is enhanced above that from the surrounding quiet sun. These same sites of enhanced photospheric emissions, when viewed at UV wavelengths which are formed in the chromosphere, are called plages. Faculae and plages typically identify regions of enhanced visible and UV emission. Figure 4 shows the time behaviour of the daily sunspot blocking function, the daily facular irradiance excess and the daily total solar irradiance as reconstructed from various data [10].

The direct correlation of solar luminosity with magnetic active regions is a major discovery. It agrees in sense with the low solar luminosity that would be predicted to occur in association with the prolonged low sunspot period during the Maunder Minimum that extended from 1645 to 1715 (Fig. 5) and with the "Little Ice Age" climate anomaly that occurred at the same time [11, 12].

This connection of the sun with climate has been used to infer solar luminosity variations over the last 10,000 years [13]. There is a statistically significant correspondence between the cold periods, indicated by the glacier record, with positive anomalies in the ^{14}C record. Positive anomalies in the ^{14}C record are associated with periods of low sunspot number. A simple climate model has been used to speculate that if the Little Ice Age/Maunder Minimum period represents a cooling of 0.4 °C, this could correspond to a change of

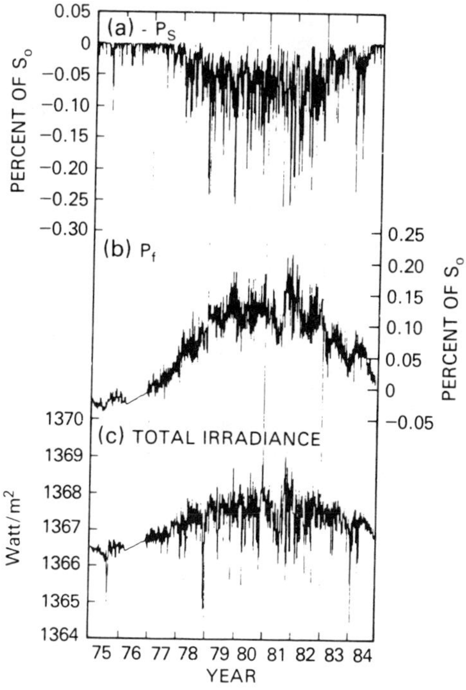

Figure 4

Solar cycle 21 behavior of (a) the percent reduction of total solar irradiance by the daily sunspot blocking function, P_s, (b) the percent daily facular irradiance excess calculated from the He I index, and (c) the reconstructed total solar irradiance [10].

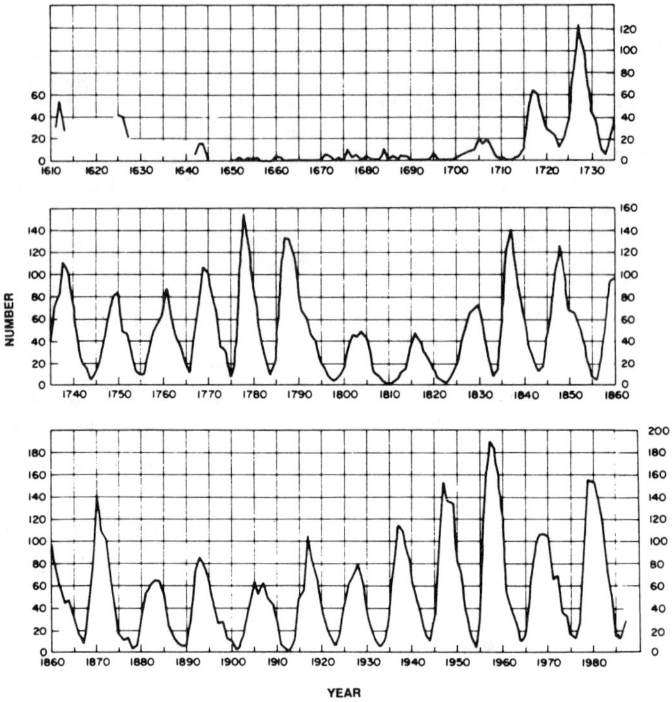

Figure 5

Annual mean sunspot numbers, 1610-1987. Cycle 19 (peak year 1958) exhibited the highest sunspot number on record [11].

solar output of between 0.2% and 0.5%.

Sea surface temperature measurements made by ships since 1854 were used to compile global average sea surface temperature variations over the 1854-present time period [14]. A simple advective-diffusive model of the response of the ocean to thermal forcing has also been used to estimate the amplitude of the solar variation needed to explain the observed temperature variability. A modulation of the sun's luminosity with a period of about 80 years and an amplitude of about 0.5% has been found to be consistent with variations in the globally averaged sea surface temperature measurements.

Solar wind, energetic particles and galactic cosmic ray variations

The outermost atmosphere of the sun is composed of the corona and a solar wind, which expands into interplanetary space at an average speed of about 400 km/s^{-1}. Because the corona is a plasma which is an excellent electrical conductor, the solar wind is guided by solar magnetic fields. The average bulk properties of the solar wind, that include density, velocity and magnetic field, do not vary greatly over a solar cycle. High speed streams that are associated with coronal holes on the sun do, however, and occur more frequently during the declining and minimum phases of solar activity. The high speed solar wind streams also have much more variability at solar maximum. It appears that the variability in magnetic field direction is an ingredient for coupling solar wind energy into the Earth's atmosphere. When the interplanetary magnetic field is southward there is a much more efficient coupling mechanism with the Earth's magnetic field that operates to transfer solar wind plasma into the Earth's magnetosphere than when the interplanetary magnetic field is northward. The solar wind energy that impinges upon the Earth's atmosphere is channeled by complex processes into the high latitude thermosphere and ionosphere. Much of the enhanced energy transfers occur in the aurora during geomagnetic storms and substorms. The inputs from aurora particle precipitation and the Joule dissipation of ionospheric currents can vary by about three orders of magnitude; $10^{10} W$ for very quiet geomagnetic activity, $10^{11} W$ for moderate geomagnetic activity and $10^{12} W$ for brief periods during geomagnetic storms. The heat and momentum transferred to the neutral gas of the thermosphere causes a large dynamic response of this region to auroral variability.

The output of high-energy particles from the sun in the MeV range is determined by the production and successful escape of such particles from solar flares that occur sporadically. A solar energetic particle event displays a flux of particles at the Earth that has a rapid rise and slow exponential decline caused by the initial transfer of particles directly from the sun, followed by particles diffusing from other directions. The energetic solar particles are mostly protons that are effectively guided by the Earth's magnetic field into magnetic conjugate polar caps. The particles have a variety of fluxes and energies and they are sufficiently energetic to produce ionization below 100 km and cause polar cap radiowave absorption events or PCA's [15]. The interaction of these particles with the middle atmosphere can perturb the normal chemistry of the region producing chemicals that can catalytically destroy O_3. These events are easily identified by satellite measurements of ozone depletions. The very energetic high flux solar proton event on August 4, 1972 produced sufficient NO in the middle atmosphere to cause a significant high latitude total ozone depletion above the 4mb (40 km) level [16].

In another event that occurred on July 13, 1982, a flux of lower energy solar protons initiated an ion chemical chain that produced copius amounts of odd hydrogen (H, OH, HO_2) that catalytically destroyed ozone near the 75 km level in the mesosphere [17]. These events clearly illustrate that energetic particle precipitation can have an important overall role in the sporadic production of chemicals that can affect the O_3 balance of the middle atmosphere.

Although not a solar output, galactic cosmic rays reaching the Earth display an anticorrelation with solar activity. The exact mechanism causing this modulation is not understood although it appears that inhomogeneities in the solar wind over a solar cycle are responsible. More inhomogeneties occur during solar maximum that lead to a greater scattering of galactic cosmic rays with a lower flux incident on Earth. It has been speculated that the solar cycle modulation of this galactic cosmic ray flux of particles, that are energetic enough to penetrate deep into the atmosphere, may play an important role in modulating the electrification of the atmosphere and thereby affect the Earth's global electric circuit [18]. Galactic cosmic rays also produce the radioactive element Carbon-14 which are produced in tree rings. The deposited isotope thus produces an identifiable record of solar activity that has been used for climate studies in the geological record [11, 12].

ATMOSPHERIC RESPONSE TO SOLAR VARIABILITY

The different regions of the atmosphere absorb different portions of the solar spectrum and have different radiational, chemical and dynamic responses to solar variability.

Thermosphere response to solar variability

Solar EUV and UV radiation ($\lambda < 200$ nm) are absorbed in the thermosphere above 80 km. Virtually all solar photons at wavelengths less than 102.5 nm are absorbed by the major neutral constituents of the thermosphere - N_2, O_2 and O leading to ionization of the absorbing species and the formation of the ionosphere. There is a large variability in the temperature and density of the thermosphere and ionosphere because of the large variability of the solar EUV and UV radiation. The global mean temperature variation of the thermosphere as a function of the solar activity is shown in Figure 1. The atmosphere also expands in response to temperature increases and the density at 500 km can vary by almost three orders of magnitude over a solar cycle. These density variations can have an important influence on the drag experienced by satellites.

In addition, to the absorption of solar EUV and UV radiation, the high-latitude thermosphere and ionosphere are affected by energy and momentum addition from auroral processes that are driven by the interaction of the solar wind with the Earth's magnetic field. At times, the energy deposited at high latitudes in the aurora can locally exceed the energy deposition from solar EUV radiation. As a result, the thermosphere is a dynamically active region with large variations about its basic state and large responses to solar and auroral variability [19, 20].

Middle atmosphere response to solar variability

Solar UV radiation (200 nm $\leq \lambda \leq$ 400 nm) affects a variety of physical and chemical processes in the middle atmosphere (stratosphere and mesosphere). The depth of penetration of solar UV radiation is governed by absorption from several chemical constituents as shown in Figure 6. The response of ozone to solar UV variability has been

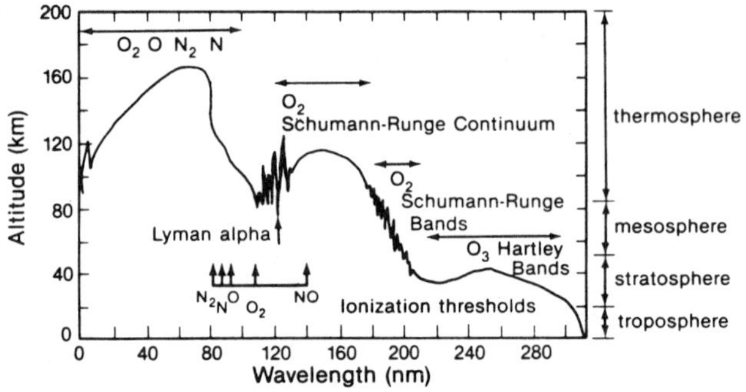

Figure 6

The altitude in the Earth's atmosphere where the solar radiation is altenuated by 1/e of its incident value for vertical incidence. The wavelength regions of absorption by the primary atmospheric species and their ionization thresholds are identified.

detected by satellites. Near 70 km, it is found that ozone is immediately depleted by short term increases in solar UV radiation. An apparent mechanism for the ozone depletion is increased odd hydrogen production as a result of increased photodissociation of H_2O vapor by solar Lyman-α radiation. The odd hydrogen catalytically destroys O_3. The response of mesospheric temperature to short term solar UV variability has also been identified in the data sets. There is a 0.3 K increase for a 1% increase in solar UV radiation centered near 205 nm with a small phase lag [21].

Temperature and ozone are oppositely correlated throughout the lower mesosphere and upper stratosphere because of temperature sensitive rate coefficients that control the O_3 density [22]. Ozone can be destroyed by both increased solar UV radiation and by a temperature increase. In the stratosphere, ozone responds directly to changes in solar UV radiation with a phase lag of about 0.5 days. Deeper in the atmosphere near 20 km it has a 2 day phase lag.

Zonally averaged models of middle atmosphere have also been used to demonstrate the response of the middle atmosphere chemistry and dynamics to solar variability over an 11 year solar cycle [23].

Lower atmosphere response to solar variability

The lower atmosphere is a highly complex nonlinear system that is subject to a large component of random variability due to its internal dynamics. Even under conditions of constant external solar forcing, weather and climate will vary. Weather variability arises primarily as a result of instability of the mean flow of the atmosphere and it is determined by the day-to-day evolution of the large-scale synoptic pressure systems that dominate the atmospheric circulation. Climate is simply the statistical result of averaging the weather over a period of time.

There have been many attempts to correlate the weather with various properties of the sun [24]. Most correlations have involved sunspots, but others have considered solar sector boundary crossings, flares, plages etc. Generally, these correlations have a tendency to break down after a period of time. Recently, it has been discovered that there is a strong correlation between the solar cycle and high-latitude stratospheric temperature and geopotential height data when the data are categorized according to the east or west phase of the quasi-biennial-oscillation (QBO) in the equatorial stratosphere [25]. When the QBO is in the west phase the polar data are positively correlated with the solar cycle while those in middle and low latitudes were negatively correlated. The converse holds for the east phase of the QBO. These effects were found to hold throughout the troposphere and in the mesosphere. No physical mechanism linking the solar variability with the observations has yet been found.

The troposphere has a large natural variability that can exist without any change in external forcing. The energy associated with known solar variability is too small, by about three orders of magnitude, to perturb the enormous energy contained in the basic flow of the troposphere. Realizing this enormous energy imbalance most studies seeking sun-weather relationships have usually involved some trigger mechanism that somehow could tap the basic energy of the flow [26].

There appears to be more evidence suggesting possible sun-climate relationships. The climate energy balance models [13, 14, 27] all show that the sensitivity of the global climate response to solar variations is an important function of the period of forcing, because of the couplings between the atmosphere and oceans. The thermal lag in the models suggest that any climate response to total solar irradiance variability on an 11-year sunspot cycle time period is small but the response increases on longer-time scales. A more effective response is obtained on Gleissberg cycle time scales of sunspot activity ($\sim$ 80-90 years), and during the prolonged Maunder Minimum.

GLOBAL ATMOSPHERIC CHANGE

The problems of increasing atmospheric trace gas concentrations, as a result of human activity, and possible future climate changes have attracted considerable attention in recent years. Trace gases such as CO_2, CH_4, tropospheric O_3, N_2O and the chlorofluorocarbons (CFC's) are steadily increasing in the atmosphere. A doubling of the present day concentration of several of these gases is predicted to occur by the end of the next century [4].

According to the greenhouse theory of climate change, the radiative imbalance caused by trace gas increases will be restored to equilibrium by a warming of the surface-troposphere system. There are many uncertainties concerning the rate of trace gas increases and also with modeling the climate response but, it is generally agreed that the global mean equilibrium surface temperature, due to increases of CO_2 and other greenhouse gases, is likely to be in the range of 1.5 - 5.5 °C [3, 4, 5]. This is about the same magnitude as the change of global temperature from the last glacial period to the present interglacial. Three-dimensional climate models also predict a general change in the climate and weather patterns in response to trace gas increases [28]. There have been no reported studies of the effects of solar variability on the troposphere under the changed conditions caused by trace gas increases.

The stratosphere is expected to cool by about 10K in response to a doubling of the CO_2 concentration because of enhanced infrared cooling to space. But the stratospheric concentration of other trace gases, such as CH_4, N_2O and CFC's, are also increasing at a rapid rate, and these gases are predicted to have an additional influence on the temperature structure, not only because of effect on blocking thermal infrared radiation, but also because of their ability to destroy ozone through catalytic chemical reactions. Recent calculations have shown that the stratopause will cool from present day values by -16 to -22K and ozone will be depleted by -5 to -30% near 40 km by the end of the 21st century as a result of trace gas increases [29]. The combined effects of trace gas increases and decreases in solar UV radiation, over the declining phase of solar cycle 21 from 1979 to 1986, indicate that total ozone has decreased on the order of 2 percent and the ozone density near 40km has decreased 7 to 12% over the period as shown in Figure 7 [30].

A self-consistent global average model of the coupled thermosphere, ionosphere and mesosphere have been used to examine the structure of these regions and their response to solar and auroral variability [31]. It has also been used to examine the effect of trace gas increases, primarily doublings of CO_2 and CH_4, on the global mean structure of these regions. The results show that the mesopause region will cool approximately 10K and the thermosphere 50K in response to these trace gas doublings. The compositional, heating and cooling structure of these regions will also be altered by the changed thermal structure. Since these regions respond strongly to solar EUV and UV

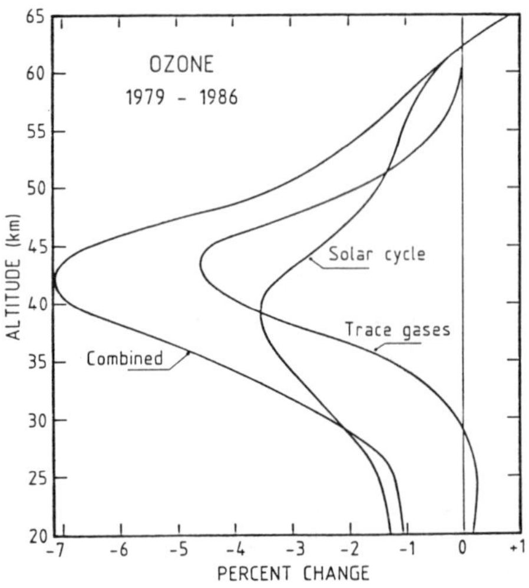

Figure 7

Relative ozone change between 1979 and 1986 (expressed in percent) averaged over all latitudes and seasons. The contributions of the trace gas and solar effects are shown together with the combined results [30].

variability and auroral variability, it is expected that there will be a changed response to these forcings from the restructuring of the thermal and compositional profiles caused by trace gas increases. These effects have not yet been studied in detail.

DISCUSSION

There is an important need for the development of a next generation climate model that can be used to examine the effect of solar variability on the atmosphere. Such a climate model should include coupling of the atmosphere and ocean, since the role of sea surface temperature appears to be important for long term climate changes. The model should also include sufficient vertical layers to cover the entire atmosphere from the troposphere to the thermosphere (0-500 km) and also model interactions with the ionosphere, magnetosphere and solar wind. Currently, lower atmosphere general circulation models have a lid at some atmospheric height, usually in the middle atmosphere below 80 km, and they do not describe the effects of solar variability adequately. The model should also include detailed chemistry, radiation and electrodynamics to examine coupling between regions. These couplings include the upward transport of trace gases from the troposphere, the downward transport of chemicals, such as nitric oxide, produced by the aurora and thermospheric processes and electrical interactions in the Earth's global circuit. Finally, the physical processes responsible for solar spectral irradiance variability need to be adequately described as well as the transfer of solar wind energy through the magnetosphere and into the thermosphere. Such a complete solar variability/climate model, when developed, will probably exceed the computer prower of today's computers. It will probably require an increase in current-day computational power by factors of 10 to 100 to perform effective simulations. It is important to pursue such model development to better understand the coming global change and the modified forcings from solar variability.

* The National Center for Atmospheric Research is sponsored by the National Science Foundation.

References

[1] G. A. Newkirk, Jr., *Ann. Rev. Astron. Astrophys.* **21,** 429 (1983).

[2] C. Sagan and G. Muller, *Science* **177,** 52 (1972).

[3] C. Lorius *et al.*, *EOS* **69,** 681 (1988).

[4] B. Bolin, B. R. Döös, J. Jäger and R. A. Warrick, Eds., *The Greenhouse Effect, Climate Change and Ecosystems,* (Wiley, New York, 1986).

[5] R. E. Dickinson and R. J. Cicerone, *Nature* **319,** 109 (1986).

[6] V. Ramanathan, *Science* **240,** 293 (1988).

[7] H. E. Hinteregger, *Adv. Space Res.* **1,** 39 (1981).

[8] J. Lean, *J. Geophys. Res.* **92,** 839 (1987).

[9] R. C. Willson *et al.*, *Science* **234,** 1114 (1986).

[10] P. Foukal and J. Lean, *Astrophys. J.* **328,** 347 (1988).

[11] J. A. Eddy, *Science* **192,** 1189 (1976).

[12] J. A. Eddy, *Climate Change* **1,** 173 (1977).

[13] T. M. L. Wigley, *Secular Solar and Geomagnetic Variations in the Last 10,000 Years,* pp. 209, Kluwer Academic Pub. (1988).

[14] G. C. Reid and K. S. Gage, *ibid.*, pp. 225.

[15] G. C. Reid, *Fundam. Cosmic Phys.* **1,** 167 (1974).

[16] D. F. Heath *et al.*, *Science* **197,** 886 (1977).

[17] S. Solomon *et al.*, *Geophys. Res. Lett.* **10,** 257, (1983).

[18] R. G. Roble, *J. Geophys. Res.* **90,** 6000 (1985).

[19] A. E. Hedin and H. G. Mayr, *J. Geophys. Res.* **92,** 869 (1987).

[20] T. L. Killeen and R. G. Roble, *Rev. Geophys.* **26,** 329 (1988).

[21] G. M. Keating *et al.*, *J. Geophys. Res.* **92,** 889 (1987).

[22] J. C. Gille *et al.*, *Science* **225,** 315 (1984).

[23] R. R. Garcia *et al.*, *Planet. Space Sci.* **32,** 411 (1984).

[24] J. R. Herman and R. A. Goldberg, *Sun, Weather and Climate,* NASA SP-426 (1978).

[25] K. Labitzke and H. van Loon, *J. Atmos. Terr. Phys.* **50,** 197 (1988).

[26] Solar Variability, Weather and Climate, *Studies in Geophysics,* National Academy Press, Wash. D.C. (1982).

[27] R. E. Dickinson, *Solar Radiative Output Variation,* (P. Foukal, ed.), 49 (1987).

[28] J. Hansen *et al.*, *J. Geophys. Res.* **93,** 9341 (1988).

[29] G. Brasseur and M. H. Hitchman, *Science* **240,** 634 (1988).

[30] G. Brasseur *et al.*, *Geophys. Res. Lett.* **15,** 1361 (1988).

[31] R. Roble *et al.*, *J. Geophys. Res., in press, (1988).*

[32] G. Brasseur and S. Solomon, *Aeronomy of the Middle Atmosphere,* D. Reidel Pub. (1986).

GLOBAL CHANGE—HUMAN INTERACTIONS
A MULTIVARIATE ASSESSMENT FRAMEWORK

Robert S. Chen
Alan Shawn Feinstein World Hunger Program, Brown University
Box 1831, Providence, Rhode Island 02912 USA

Myron B Fiering
Gordon McKay Professor of Engineering and Applied Mathematics, Harvard University
Pierce Hall, Cambridge, Massachusetts 02138 USA

Research in the area of human interactions with the environment has not in general utilized supercomputing technologies. However, the research community is increasingly being called upon not just to diagnose environmental problems but also to explore policy options and other management issues. This will necessitate more widespread application of methods from systems analysis, operations research, risk assessment, and related fields to find optimal policies for managing complex systems. Computing demands will likely grow dramatically as a result. In this paper, we present a basic multivariate framework for assessing the interactions between human activities and environmental processes that illustrates the range of potential nonlinearities, feedbacks, and synergisms and some of the possible analytic complexities.

INTRODUCTION

Our planet has been changing throughout the billions of years of its existence. What is thought to be unique to this century, however, is that its surface is now covered with billions of people whose activities already have begun to cause changes in the global environment that are noticeably different from—and faster than—the natural changes. And as the current population of five billion grows to ten billion or more by the middle of the 21st century, the adverse consequences of natural and anthropogenic environmental changes are likely to grow in prevalence and severity. The important issue is the certainty of, and consequent strategy for, the range of anticipated changes.

These concerns have led to several major research initiatives in the natural and social sciences.

On the natural-science side, the U.S. National Academy of Sciences (NAS) has proposed the development of the International Geosphere-Biosphere Program (IGBP), a long-term international research program based primarily in the geophysical and biological sciences and modeled to some degree after previous large-scale research programs such as the International Geophysical Year and the Global Atmospheric Research Program [1,2]. These early proposals were refined and adopted at the international level under the auspices of the International Council of Scientific Unions, which agreed that the primary goal of the IGBP would be:

> To describe and understand the interactive physical, chemical, and biological processes that regulate the total earth system, the unique environment that it provides for life, the changes that are occurring in this system, and the manner in which they are influenced by human actions [3].

More recently, this goal has been expanded to include explicit consideration of the consequences of global change for resource availability [4,5], but nowhere in the statement is there any serious reference to *management* of the environment.

National and international efforts are also under way to develop parallel research activities focused on the *interface* between human activities and the environment. These include an international program on the "Human Response to Global Change" being planned by the International Federation of Institutes for Advanced Study, the International Social Sciences

Council, and the U.N. University. In the U.S., the Social Science Research Council is working to identify some key interdisciplinary research areas in which interactions between human and environmental systems are likely to be especially important, and the NAS plans to work to encourage and coordinate social-science research in conjunction with IGBP activities.

It now appears that the *human interactions* component of the IGBP will focus on the *direct* implications of human activities for environmental systems and environmental change for human systems over the next century. Specific proposals for research include the development of a detailed historical data base on land use patterns and associated vegetative changes, assessment of flows of materials and energy that affect key biogeochemical pathways, and analysis of how human perceptions and social institutions affect environmental management [6,7]. Although the data and computing requirements for these sorts of research are growing, to date there has been little need for the computational power embodied in supercomputers.

More generally, however, the issue of human interactions with the global environment can be viewed from the broad perspective of human occupance and use of the planet. As Barbara Ward wrote more than two decades ago,

> Modern science and technology have created so close a network of communication, transport, economic interdependence—and potential nuclear destruction—that planet earth, on its journey through infinity, has acquired the intimacy, the fellowship, and the vulnerability of a spaceship [8].

The "spaceship" analogy suggests that we may increasingly have the responsibility to *manage* the life-support systems of our planet. In practice, this means that we may find it increasingly necessary not just to predict, but also to influence or *control* changes in the environment. It will not therefore be sufficient *only* to diagnose and predict environmental change, as implied by the IGBP objective quoted above, but also to develop *control* and *optimization* strategies that are likely to involve numerous players, multiple objectives, large stochastic variations, diverse feedbacks, and many seemingly non-environmental considerations. This broadening of the problem implies the need to consider a much wider range of variables in human and environmental systems and to apply state-of-the-art methods from systems analysis, operations research, decision and game theory, risk assessment, and other fields to find optimal policies for managing complex systems. It therefore is likely that computing demands will grow dramatically as research activities move increasingly from diagnosis and prediction to optimization and policy applications and as our mechanistic understanding is enhanced.

In this paper, we develop a multivariate assessment framework that begins to account for some of the expected increases in complexity and that hints at the extent to which computing demands could grow.

A MULTIVARIATE ASSESSMENT FRAMEWORK

Every profession, every institution, every trade, and every academic discipline has its own version of Murphy's Law. In the environmental sciences, one manifestation of this famous but gloomy forecast is that undesirable consequences always seem to occur despite the fact that the probability of such undesirable consequences due to each of several possible causes, when taken individually, can be shown with reasonable confidence to be negligible. Somehow, the several causes interact so as to enhance their individual effects, with synergisms potent enough to initiate significant, worrisome, or even catastrophic results. The whole is greater (i.e., worse) than the sum of its parts!

Why does the conventional wisdom appear to break down? Why are we so frequently faced with the observation that yet another system has failed, even though the best available analyses of its individual components clearly show such a small risk of failure that the prospect could readily be ignored by a prudent designer or planner?

One possible explanation lies in how we think about, formulate, and utilize models of complex systems. We often start with "box-and-arrow" models that represent simplified versions of what we know or can estimate about a system's dynamics. Typically, the material flux from Box A to Box B depends on the levels stored in A and B at time **t** and is calculated according to some set of relationships with fitted or estimated parameters. In some cases, the resulting set of coupled equations can be solved analytically as a simultaneous system, whereas in the more general and complicated models some form of system simulation is required to generate numerical solutions for the various time series that constitute the model output.

In symbolic form, an action or decision **X** causes an intermediate response **Y** which exerts an impact **Z**. We adjust **X** so that **Z** remains in the "acceptable" portion of its range; if we succeed, there is no catastrophe and no surprise.

A simplistic model of this process typically formalizes the causal structure by connecting **X** to **Y** and then **Y** to **Z**. If the system contains more elements, then $\mathbf{X_i}$ causes $\mathbf{Y_i}$ which causes $\mathbf{Z_i}$, for $\mathbf{i} = 1, 2, \ldots$ elements. In a more realistic model, any $\mathbf{X_i}$ might induce any response $\mathbf{Y_j}$, which can then cause any impact $\mathbf{Z_k}$. The relationships among these are now arrayed as a network, but even here the typical analyses do not account for synergism between or among the elements. In an even more complete model, the $\mathbf{X_i}$ might induce a direct impact on any $\mathbf{Z_k}$, thereby bypassing all the intermediate responses $\mathbf{Y_j}$. And, finally, the effects of any of the $\mathbf{X_i}$ and any of the $\mathbf{Y_j}$ on the several $\mathbf{Z_k}$ might depend on the current values of any or all of the state variables $\mathbf{X_i}$, $\mathbf{Y_j}$, and $\mathbf{Z_k}$.

Such problems in multivariate estimation are often cast in one or another form of multivariate analysis, e.g., multivariate regression, principal component analysis, factor analysis, canonical correlation, and time series analysis. Most of the theoretical work and numerical applications involving these techniques are based on the assumption of normality among the data and the imposition of plausible linear relationships among the variables. Even if they do not hold strictly, these assumptions can be safely used in a vast number of applications, whereupon the results are generally considered reasonable.

However, in the case of possible human interactions with environmental change, many of the basic human and environmental data appear to be highly skewed and, for some variables, constrained to be non-negative, thereby precluding or at least questioning the straightforward utilization of the multivariate normal density function. Moreover, many of the system relationships between activity and response, and between response and impact, are not linear, thereby rendering the multivariate linear formulation too simplistic.

We therefore need a more general modeling technique to accommodate these cases, even if it turns out to be a less powerful one. In this paper, we employ standard operations from multivariate differential calculus to express some of the covariances and statistical interactions that typically are omitted from the simpler matrix formulations of linear multivariate analysis.

We postulate that the time series of impacts **Z** and the total derivative taken with respect to time $\frac{d\mathbf{Z}}{dt}$ are the interesting output variables for policy analysis and/or decision-making. The time derivative is important because its magnitude and sign indicate when the system is changing so rapidly in a particular direction that system failure is likely to occur. If a plausible system objective function can be imposed and if $\frac{d\mathbf{Z}}{dt}$ can be monitored reliably enough to serve as a basis for action, then the selection of policy can be affected by choosing a set of activities $\mathbf{X_i}$ such that the derivatives $\frac{d\mathbf{Z_k}}{dt}$ and the time series of impacts $\mathbf{Z_k}$ meet specified constraints while attaining optimal values. In particular, we compute the sensitivity of the time derivative to the activities $\mathbf{X_i}$; in our formulation, this appears as the total derivative $\frac{d\left(\frac{d\mathbf{Z}}{dt}\right)}{d\mathbf{X_i}}$ or $\frac{d^2\mathbf{Z}}{dt\,d\mathbf{X_i}}$.

The next three sections give some of the basic mathematics by which these derivatives can be calculated, and the following section shows an example for a simple three-variable model. We then point out some of the computational difficulties inherent in making the model more realistic and more useful in a decision or policy framework. It is here that the use of new computing technologies may contribute to making this approach more feasible.

Basic Mathematical Formulation

The total time derivative $\frac{dZ}{dt}$ can be written as

$$\frac{dZ}{dt} = \frac{\partial Z}{\partial t} + \frac{\partial Z}{\partial X}\frac{dX}{dt} + \frac{\partial Z}{\partial Y}\frac{dY}{dt} \qquad [1]$$

by routine application of the chain rule. Note that, for the partial derivatives, we have not listed the state variables for which specific values must be assigned (i.e., which are held constant), but a useful rule is that the "intermediate" variables are prescribed. Thus, **X** and **Y** are functionally intermediate between **t** and **Z**, so that the partial derivative $\frac{\partial Z}{\partial t}$ is evaluated for constant values of **X** and **Y**. Similar arguments hold for all the partial derivatives.

Eqn. 1 contains three segments. The first, $\frac{\partial Z}{\partial t}$, is the time-dependent change in response **Z** due to time *alone*, such as might be due to cycles, trends, or periodicities in **Z** without regard to human influences. The second, the product $\frac{\partial Z}{\partial X}\frac{dX}{dt}$, is the change in **Z** due to a unit change in **X**, as processed through the fixed level of the intermediate variable **Y**, multiplied by the total extent of the time-dependent change in **X** itself. This segment accounts for the direct effect of **X** on **Z**, without regard to changes in **Y**. Finally, the third segment of eqn. 1 reflects the effect of changing **Y**, or $\frac{\partial Z}{\partial Y}\frac{dY}{dt}$, by taking account of the fact that **Y** can change because of its own inherent cycles, trends, or periodicities *and* because of the effect of changing **X**. We again apply the chain rule, this time to the total derivative $\frac{dY}{dt} = \frac{\partial Y}{\partial t} + \frac{\partial Y}{\partial X}\frac{dX}{dt}$, to obtain:

$$\frac{dZ}{dt} = \frac{\partial Z}{\partial t} + \frac{\partial Z}{\partial X}\frac{dX}{dt} + \frac{\partial Z}{\partial Y}\frac{\partial Y}{\partial t} + \frac{\partial Z}{\partial Y}\frac{\partial Y}{\partial X}\frac{dX}{dt} \qquad [2]$$

Eqn. 2 contains four terms. It is our contention that analysts often ignore one or more of these terms, depending in part on their interest and disciplinary background. For example, analysts concerned with the causal chain of events **X**→**Y**→**Z** tend to focus on the last term \F(∂**Z**,∂**Y**) \F(∂**Y**,∂**X**) \F(d**X**,dt), perhaps utilizing comparisons with the direct influence of variations in **Y** itself, $\frac{\partial Z}{\partial Y}\frac{dY}{dt}$. The direct influence of **X** on **Z** (without passing through **Y**) and the natural variations of **Z** tend to be unintentionally overlooked or intentionally ignored because the resulting error is thought to be tolerably small. In contrast, analysts concerned with the effects of **X** on **Z** often appear to ignore the natural effects of **Y** on **Z**, i.e., $\frac{\partial Z}{\partial Y}\frac{dY}{dt}$. Finally, analysts concerned with "the rate of change of **Z**" appear to us to focus primarily on the first two terms of eqn. 2, the "natural" variation in **Z** and the variation induced directly through activity **X**. They tend to ignore the last two terms, which constitute the incremental portion of the total derivative that can be attributed to "natural" and "induced" variations in **Y**. All of these omitted terms contribute to the empirical verification of Murphy's Law.

Two important points may be made here. The first concerns the stability of the derivative $\frac{dZ}{dt}$. It should be noted that differentiation, or its finite-difference approximation, is inherently an unstable process. If a random error is encountered among the data subject to numerical differentiation or differencing, the inevitable consequence is a large error in the numerical assessment of the derivative. By the same argument, the error in numerical integration or quadrature tends to be much smaller, so it is generally taken as a canon of numerical calculus that integration is stabilizing whereas differentiation is destabilizing. Thus, eqn. 2 is likely to contain errors which might conveniently be collected into an aggregate error term and, on the basis of statistical arguments, carried through the subsequent computations.

The second point is that it is tempting to ignore some of the pathways specified in eqn. 2 because we anticipate that the error introduced by not including all the terms is small enough to be ignored. In other words, the potential random error is large enough to accommodate faulty or incomplete models and therefore to prevent us from clearly discriminating between errors due to ordinary, anticipated stochastic variation and those due to incomplete formulation.

However, if we expand the model to consider the more realistic cases in which there are several actions $\mathbf{X_i}$, several intermediate responses $\mathbf{Y_j}$, and several impacts $\mathbf{Z_k}$, then the number of terms in the full expansion for $\frac{dZ}{dt}$ might be large, and, more significantly, their sum might be too important (i.e., large in absolute value) to ignore. Yet most analyses of the independent effects of the several activities $\mathbf{X_i}$ do not account for these small, subtle interactions and dependencies. In small systems, with few elements and hence relatively few interactions, this might be acceptable—but as the complexity of systems and models increases, such combinations can become quite important.

Sensitivity of the Time Derivative with Respect to Decisions

We compute the sensitivity of the time derivative to changes in **X** by applying the chain rule a second time. The result is two groups of terms, one that reflects the effects of the change in **X** on the system and the other that reflects the effects of the change in **Y** *induced by the change in* ***X*** on the system:

$$\begin{aligned}\frac{d^2Z}{dtdX} &= \frac{\partial^2 Z}{\partial X \partial t} + \frac{\partial^2 Z}{\partial X^2}\frac{dX}{dt} + \frac{\partial^2 Z}{\partial X \partial Y}\left(\frac{\partial Y}{\partial t} + \frac{\partial Y}{\partial X}\frac{dX}{dt}\right) + \frac{\partial Z}{\partial Y}\frac{\partial^2 Y}{\partial X \partial t} \\ &+ \frac{\partial Z}{\partial Y}\frac{\partial^2 Y}{\partial X^2}\frac{dX}{dt} + \left(\frac{\partial Z}{\partial X} + \frac{\partial Z}{\partial Y}\frac{\partial Y}{\partial X}\right)\frac{\partial\left(\frac{dX}{dt}\right)}{\partial X} \\ &+ \frac{dY}{dX}\Big[\frac{\partial^2 Z}{\partial Y \partial t} + \frac{\partial^2 Z}{\partial Y \partial X}\frac{dX}{dt} + \frac{\partial^2 Z}{\partial Y^2}\left(\frac{\partial Y}{\partial t} + \frac{\partial Y}{\partial X}\frac{dX}{dt}\right) + \frac{\partial Z}{\partial Y}\frac{\partial\left(\frac{\partial Y}{\partial t}\right)}{\partial Y} \\ &+ \frac{\partial Z}{\partial Y}\frac{\partial\left(\frac{\partial Y}{\partial X}\right)}{\partial Y}\frac{dX}{dt} + \left(\frac{\partial Z}{\partial X} + \frac{\partial Z}{\partial Y}\frac{\partial Y}{\partial X}\right)\frac{\partial\left(\frac{dX}{dt}\right)}{\partial Y}\Big] \qquad [3]\end{aligned}$$

We interpret the first 6 terms of eqn. 3 as the effect of changing **X** on: *1)* the rate of change in **Z** at the current levels of all other variables; *2)* **Z**'s current sensitivity to **X** (given the total rate of change in **X**); *3)* **Z**'s current sensitivity to **Y** (given the current and induced rate of change in **Y**); *4)* the current rate of change in **Y** (given the current sensitivity of **Z** to **Y**); *5)* **Y**'s current sensitivity to **X** (given **Z**'s current sensitivity to **Y** and the total change in **X**); and *6)* the total rate of change in **X** (given **Z**'s direct and induced sensitivity to **X**). The second set of 6 terms—those in the brackets of eqn. 3 that are multiplied by $\frac{dY}{dX}$—may be interpreted analogously as the effects of the net **X**-induced changes in **Y** on each aspect of the system given by the first 6 terms. We note, however, that the two partial derivatives $\frac{\partial\left(\frac{\partial Y}{\partial t}\right)}{\partial Y}$ and $\frac{\partial\left(\frac{\partial Y}{\partial X}\right)}{\partial Y}$ are meaningful only when **Y** is a non-linear function of its own past values and **t** or **X** (or both), respectively.

In general, then, any change in **X** may affect the rate of change in **Z** not only directly or via a direct induced change in **Y**, but also by directly or indirectly altering the sensitivities of **Z** to **X**, **Z** to **Y**, and **Y** to **X** or by altering the rates of change of **X** and **Y** themselves.

Six-Variable Case

If the problem is expanded to include two actions ($\mathbf{X_1}, \mathbf{X_2}$), two intermediate responses ($\mathbf{Y_1}, \mathbf{Y_2}$), and two impacts ($\mathbf{Z_1}, \mathbf{Z_2}$), we find 12 terms in each total derivative, $\frac{dZ_1}{dt}$ and $\frac{dZ_2}{dt}$. The derivation of this result is a little tedious, but is worthy of inclusion as an indicator of the general methodology. We write

$$\frac{dZ_1}{dt} = \frac{\partial Z_1}{\partial t} + \frac{\partial Z_1}{\partial X_1}\frac{dX_1}{dt} + \frac{\partial Z_1}{\partial X_2}\frac{dX_2}{dt} + \frac{\partial Z_1}{\partial Y_1}\frac{dY_1}{dt} + \frac{\partial Z_1}{\partial Y_2}\frac{dY_2}{dt} + \frac{\partial Z_1}{\partial Z_2}\frac{dZ_2}{dt} \qquad [4]$$

and then expand most of the total derivatives on the right-hand side:

$$\frac{dX_1}{dt} = \frac{\partial X_1}{\partial t} + \frac{\partial X_1}{\partial X_2}\frac{dX_2}{dt} \qquad [5]$$

$$\frac{dX_2}{dt} = \frac{\partial X_2}{\partial t} + \frac{\partial X_2}{\partial X_1}\frac{dX_1}{dt} \qquad [6]$$

$$\frac{dY_1}{dt} = \frac{\partial Y_1}{\partial t} + \frac{\partial Y_1}{\partial X_1}\frac{dX_1}{dt} + \frac{\partial Y_1}{\partial X_2}\frac{dX_2}{dt} \qquad [7]$$

$$\frac{dY_2}{dt} = \frac{\partial Y_2}{\partial t} + \frac{\partial Y_2}{\partial X_1}\frac{dX_1}{dt} + \frac{\partial Y_2}{\partial X_2}\frac{dX_2}{dt} \qquad [8]$$

We rearrange these terms as follows:

$$\begin{aligned}\frac{dZ_1}{dt} = {} & \frac{\partial Z_1}{\partial t} \\ & + \left(\frac{\partial Z_1}{\partial X_1} + \frac{\partial Z_1}{\partial X_2}\frac{\partial X_2}{\partial X_1} + \frac{\partial Z_1}{\partial Y_1}\frac{\partial Y_1}{\partial X_1} + \frac{\partial Z_1}{\partial Y_2}\frac{\partial Y_2}{\partial X_1}\right)\frac{dX_1}{dt} \\ & + \left(\frac{\partial Z_1}{\partial X_2} + \frac{\partial Z_1}{\partial X_1}\frac{\partial X_1}{\partial X_2} + \frac{\partial Z_1}{\partial Y_1}\frac{\partial Y_1}{\partial X_2} + \frac{\partial Z_1}{\partial Y_2}\frac{\partial Y_2}{\partial X_2}\right)\frac{dX_2}{dt} \\ & + \frac{\partial Z_1}{\partial Y_1}\frac{\partial Y_1}{\partial t} + \frac{\partial Z_1}{\partial Y_2}\frac{\partial Y_2}{\partial t} \\ & + \frac{\partial Z_1}{\partial Z_2}\frac{dZ_2}{dt}\end{aligned} \qquad [9]$$

We interpret each of the five lines of eqn. 9 as *1)* the "natural" change in $\mathbf{Z_1}$, holding other influences constant; *2)* the change in $\mathbf{Z_1}$ due to the total change in $\mathbf{X_1}$, operating either directly or indirectly via $\mathbf{X_2}$, $\mathbf{Y_1}$, and $\mathbf{Y_2}$; *3)* the (symmetric) change in $\mathbf{Z_1}$ due to the total change in $\mathbf{X_2}$, operating either directly or indirectly via $\mathbf{X_1}$, $\mathbf{Y_1}$, and $\mathbf{Y_2}$; *4)* the change in $\mathbf{Z_1}$ due to the "natural" changes in $\mathbf{Y_1}$ and $\mathbf{Y_2}$, holding other influences constant; and *5)* the change in $\mathbf{Z_1}$ due to the total change in $\mathbf{Z_2}$.

The last term is the product $\frac{\partial Z_1}{\partial Z_2}\frac{dZ_2}{dt}$, and by symmetry the last term in the expression for $\frac{dZ_2}{dt}$ contains the same product with subscripts permuted: $\frac{\partial Z_2}{\partial Z_1}\frac{dZ_1}{dt}$. Each time derivative contains a product which utilizes the other time derivative(s), whereupon the two linear expressions define a system of equations which can be solved simultaneously.

The above argument generalizes readily to more than two actions, responses, and impacts, although no general expression for the number of terms typically ignored was obtained. In most applications, it is convenient and appropriate to assert that the impacts $\mathbf{Z_1}$ and $\mathbf{Z_2}$ are functionally and statistically independent, whereupon the sixth (last) term on the right-hand side in each version of eqn. 3 is identically zero (i.e., $\frac{\partial Z_2}{\partial Z_1} = \frac{\partial Z_1}{\partial Z_2} = 0$).

It is interesting and informative to speculate on the similarities between the structure of this problem with its total and partial derivatives and the utilization and structure of a multivariate statistical formulation involving total and partial correlation coefficients. Although there are many powerful analogies to be drawn, it is imprudent to seek too much agreement in results obtained from both models. Most multivariate models are based on multi-collinearity among the variables which, in turn, generally are taken to be normally distributed. The correlation and regression coefficients thus derived share rich graphical and analytical interpretations with the results presented here, but are perhaps not as informative and flexible as the derivatives developed in eqns. 4-8.

The important point to note is that an analyst interested in the effects, say, of a specific human activity X_1 on Z_1 operating through a particular threat Y_1 will likely look only at a small subset of the 12 terms in eqn. 9, e.g., the natural change in Z_1 and the induced change in Z_1 operating only through Y_1. Sometimes the induced changes are compared with the changes resulting from natural variations in Y_1, i.e., $\frac{\partial Z_1}{\partial Y_1}\frac{\partial Y_1}{\partial t}$. However, in general it is clear that because the other terms could be very influential, to ignore them in small models is probably unwise and in more complex models potentially catastrophic. If the signs of the neglected terms are by and large the same so that they tend not to cancel, then with high likelihood these terms, in the aggregate, can importantly influence assessment of the time derivatives. This can lead to significant errors, especially in optimization analyses of such systems.

The foregoing work can be extended to compute the sensitivity of the time derivatives to the actions X_i. These are the total derivatives or $\frac{d^2Z_k}{dtdX_i}$, and as usual the trick in interpreting them resides in the notion that we can reliably assess the correlation among the actions $X_1, X_2, \ldots, X_n$, taken two at a time. Second-order derivatives occur here, but these need not increase the complexity of the results because there might be more opportunities for terms to vanish; for example, further differentiation of polynomial functions can drive terms to zero. In any case, the structure allows the cross-product derivative terms to exert their influence on the impacts, confirming that there are several paths through which actions X_i affect impacts Z_k. These include *1)* the direct causal links between the X_i and the Z_k; *2)* the indirect links through any or all of the Y_j; *3)* the modifications of existing links among the X_i, Y_j, and Z_k consequent to changes in any or all of the X_i; *4)* the indirect links through some other actions X_q (where $q \neq i$) which are correlated with the occurrence and magnitude of X_i; and *5)* the remote indirect links due to influences of X_i on Z_r and of Z_r on Z_k (where $r \neq k$). The influences listed as items 1 and 2 are what most analysts mean when they refer to the effects of activities or decisions; those under 3-5 tend to be ignored, but should not be.

SUSTAINABLE YIELD: AN EXAMPLE

This section utilizes some of these mathematical manipulations in a particularly simple model of the long-term agricultural impact of a single activity. The driving variable is time, which initiates changes in the production, emission, and atmospheric concentration of carbon dioxide (CO_2), written as X in this model. We postulate a linear relationship between time and CO_2 concentration, so that

$$X = a_0 + a_1 t \qquad [10]$$

Of course, this simplified formulation is a hopelessly inadequate representation of the mechanisms that relate time, population, fossil-fuel consumption, CO_2 production, and the concentration of CO_2 in the atmosphere, but we do not claim here to provide a precise estimator of any element of the "system" or its dynamics. So long as the model is reasonably plausible, it serves our purposes in this example.

The CO_2 level, written X, induces a change in the ambient atmospheric surface temperature, written Y. We assume that appropriate spatial and temporal averaging windows are imposed, and that the parameters $\mathbf{a_i}$ are expressed in appropriate units so that the model equations are dimensionally homogeneous. We postulate a polynomial relationship for $\mathbf{Y}$:

$$\mathbf{Y} = \mathbf{a_2} + \mathbf{a_3X} + \mathbf{a_4X^2} + \mathbf{a_5t} + \mathbf{a_6tX} \qquad [11]$$

The atmospheric temperature is taken to be quadratic in the CO_2 concentration, and to include linear dependence on time and on the product of concentration and time.

The impact $\mathbf{Z}$ measures agricultural production and is assumed to be of the form

$$\mathbf{Z} = \mathbf{a_7} + \mathbf{a_8Y} + \mathbf{a_9Y^2} + \mathbf{a_{10}X} + \mathbf{a_{11}t} + \mathbf{a_{12}XY} + \mathbf{a_{13}Yt} + \mathbf{a_{14}Xt} + \mathbf{a_{15}XYt} \qquad [12]$$

Note that $\mathbf{Y}$ is quadratic in $\mathbf{X}$ and hence is quadratic in $\mathbf{t}$, whereupon $\mathbf{Z}$ is quartic in $\mathbf{t}$ because it is quadratic in $\mathbf{Y}$. The model as contained in eqns. 10-12 is completely deterministic, but even with this shortcoming it can yield important methodological results and interesting numerical insights if plausible values are assigned to its 16 coefficients. Thus, if the total derivative $\frac{\mathbf{dZ}}{\mathbf{dt}}$ is negative and large, the agricultural output in that year (or whatever time period is imposed) is decreasing sharply. If the total derivative with respect to $\mathbf{X}$ is large, the system is keenly sensitive to changes in the level of $\mathbf{X}$ (or the CO_2 concentration in the atmosphere).

Another function served by the time derivative $\frac{\mathbf{dZ}}{\mathbf{dt}}$ is that of anticipating *when* impacts might be expected to affect system production adversely. For example, it might be determined that "system collapse" occurs when $\frac{\mathbf{dZ}}{\mathbf{dt}}$ attains some specified negative value. If $\frac{\mathbf{dZ}}{\mathbf{dt}}$ for the next period of years is seen to be comfortably high with respect to this threshold value (and the second derivative of $\mathbf{Z}$ with respect to $\mathbf{t}$, not calculated here, is also small), then system planners and managers might not need to be overly concerned about system perfor-mance for the remainder of the period. Moreover, if the system is projected to migrate toward the boundary which separates satisfactory performance from collapse, application of control measures (e.g., optimally changing $\mathbf{X}$ in accordance with its dependence on $\mathbf{t}$ and its influence on $\mathbf{Z}$) could deflect the system to a more acceptable level of performance. The anticipated trajectories of $\mathbf{Z}$ and its higher derivatives can be used to generate an optimal control strategy.

The various derivatives can be estimated in at least two ways. First, and more clumsily, $\mathbf{Y}$ can be expressed as a function of $\mathbf{t}$ by substituting eqns. 10 and 11 into eqn. 12; this is, at least in principle, easily differentiable, despite the fact that the algebra is inelegant. The use of the chain rule of differential calculus is more direct and more instructive in terms of identifying types of interactions among the variables. We thus apply eqn. 2 to eqns. 10-12, which, upon performing the indicated differentiations and gathering like terms, can be written as the sum of products of various combinations of the coefficients $\mathbf{a_i}$ and eleven distinct terms: $\mathbf{X}$, $\mathbf{Y}$, $\mathbf{t}$, $\mathbf{XY}$, $\mathbf{Xt}$, $\mathbf{Yt}$, $\mathbf{X^2}$, $\mathbf{X^2t}$, $\mathbf{Xt^2}$, $\mathbf{t^2}$, and a constant. The details are:

$$\begin{aligned}
\frac{\mathbf{dZ}}{\mathbf{dt}} &= (\mathbf{a_{11}} + \mathbf{a_1a_{10}} + \mathbf{a_5a_8} + \mathbf{a_1a_3a_8}) \\
&+ (\mathbf{a_{14}} + \mathbf{a_5a_{12}} + \mathbf{a_1a_3a_{12}} + \mathbf{a_6a_8} + 2\mathbf{a_1a_4a_8})\ \mathbf{X} \\
&+ (\mathbf{a_{13}} + \mathbf{a_1a_{12}} + 2\mathbf{a_5a_9} + 2\mathbf{a_1a_3a_9})\ \mathbf{Y} \\
&+ (\mathbf{a_1a_{14}} + \mathbf{a_5a_{13}} + \mathbf{a_1a_3a_{13}} + \mathbf{a_1a_6a_8})\ \mathbf{t} \\
&+ (\mathbf{a_{15}} + 2\mathbf{a_6a_9} + 4\mathbf{a_1a_4a_9})\ \mathbf{XY} \\
&+ (\mathbf{a_1a_6a_{12}} + \mathbf{a_6a_{13}} + 2\mathbf{a_1a_4a_{13}} + \mathbf{a_5a_{15}} + \mathbf{a_1a_3a_{15}})\ \mathbf{Xt} \\
&+ (\mathbf{a_1a_{15}} + 2\mathbf{a_1a_6a_9})\ \mathbf{Yt} \\
&+ (\mathbf{a_6a_9} + 2\mathbf{a_1a_4a_{12}})\ \mathbf{X^2} \\
&+ (\mathbf{a_6a_{15}} + 2\mathbf{a_1a_4a_{15}})\ \mathbf{X^2t} \\
&+ (\mathbf{a_1a_6a_{15}})\ \mathbf{Xt^2} \\
&+ (\mathbf{a_1a_6a_{13}})\ \mathbf{t^2}
\end{aligned} \qquad [14]$$

Labeling each of the expressions in parentheses in eqn. 14 as $\mathbf{b_0}...\mathbf{b_{10}}$, respectively, we then take the total derivative of this expression with respect to $\mathbf{X}$ and gather like terms, yielding:

$$\frac{d^2Z}{dtdX_i} = (b_1 + b_5t + b_9t^2) + 2(b_7 + b_8t)\,X + b_4Y + (b_2 + b_4X + b_6t)\,\frac{dY}{dX} \qquad [15]$$

where **Y** is defined in eqn. 11 and $\frac{dY}{dX} = a_3 + 2a_4X + a_6t$. Making these substitutions and rearranging terms, we obtain

$$\begin{aligned}\frac{d^2Z}{dtdX} = {} & (b_1 + b_4a_2 + b_2a_3) + (b_5 + b_4a_5 + a_3b_6 + b_2a_6)\,t + (b_9 + b_6a_6)\,t^2 \\ & + 2[(b_7 + b_4a_3 + a_4b_2) + (b_8 + b_4a_6 + a_4b_6)\,t]\,X \\ & + (3b_4a_4)\,X^2 \end{aligned} \qquad [16]$$

The effect on $\frac{dZ}{dt}$ of a change in **X** in this model varies both as a quadratic in **X** and in time. Note that, of the original 16 parameters $a_0 \ldots a_{15}$, only two—a_{10} and a_{11}—are not found in eqn. 16. These two parameters represent the direct linear variation in **Z** due to **X** and **t**, respectively, as shown in eqn. 12, and therefore drop out when the second derivative of **Z** is taken with respect to both **Z** and **t**. The other 14 parameters all contribute to eqn. 16 in various combinations, demonstrating the *potential* sensitivity of this simple 3-variable system to the specification of its parameters. A simple computer program can be written to calculate values of the state variables **X(t)**, **Y(X,t)**, and **Z(X,Y,t)** and of the derivatives $\frac{dZ}{dt}$ and $\frac{d^2Z}{dtdX}$, given alternative sets of parameters $a_0 \ldots a_{15}$. A potential use of such a program is to determine whether realistic values of the parameters $a_0 \ldots a_{15}$ can produce a model system that exhibits highly nonlinear—and hence potentially dangerous—behavior under certain conditions.

IMPLICATIONS FOR COMPUTING NEEDS

In our example, the system dynamics are particularly simple: the relationship between **X** and **t** is a combined demographic and agricultural production model, the relationship between **Y** and its arguments **X** and **t** is a combined climatological and environmental model, and the relationship between **Z** and its arguments **X**, **Y**, and **t** is an environmental impact model. However, all the system dynamics in these component models is embedded within three simple polynomial equations, so the derivatives are easy to calculate analytically. Clearly, this level of simplicity is not a general property of such systems, whereupon the multi-dimensional calculations are likely to be much more cumbersome. It certainly is possible, for example, that the parameters a_i would have time or other dependencies, that some relationships might be exponential, logarithmic, or even discontinuous, and that there might be important lagged relationships among key variables. It is noteworthy indeed that atmospheric general circulation models (GCM's) currently used to study the effects of trace-gas increases on global temperature and precipitation—and which themselves are typically implemented on supercomputers—essentially apply only to the relationship between **Y** and **X** and **t**. However, GCM results have not yet been linked realistically with models of **X** and **t** and of **Z**, **X**, **Y**, and **t** (or, for that matter, with other possible Y_j).

Model complexity also increases with the number of variables. Each new variable requires specification of additional mathematical relationships between it and every other variable. If such relationships are not reversible, or if they are conditional on particular pathways or system states, information requirements can grow even faster. Thus, for example, in a system with only 3 activities (X_i's), 3 environmental variables (Y_j's), and 3 impact variables (Z_k's), at least 36 relationships between pairs of elements must be specified. In the context of the IGBP, there are dozens of human activities, environmental changes, and impacts of concern, many of which are known to have significant interactions and synergisms among them.

Computational requirements are likely to grow in other ways as well. Three aspects of the problem immediately come to mind as requiring substantially increased computational power to address effectively: stochastic influences, surprise, and management and optimization.

Stochastic Influences

The deterministic solution for the trajectory of $\mathbf{Z}$ and for its several derivatives does not account for inherent statistical error or imperfections in the model, for systematic or random error in fitting the parameters $\mathbf{a}_i$, or for any other flaws in the coupled equations which together define the model. As the complexity of the model is increased, the opportunity for cumulative error increases markedly. If even a few of the parameters $\mathbf{a}_i$ are subject to statistical error, the instabilities in the $\mathbf{Z}$ and the derivatives can become enormous, overwhelming any "signal" with "noise." In this case, the optimal strategy (or scheme for controlling $\mathbf{X}$) becomes strongly dependent on the analyst's (or decision makers') willingness to accept or avoid risks, and hedging strategies become an attractive option.

To account for the possibility of stochastic variation, we can add a random component, additive or multiplicative, to each of the equations of our simple model, thereby allowing for Monte Carlo analysis of the coupled set. However, it will be recalled that none of our equations contains any "memory" whatsoever; there is no autoregressive or moving average component in the model, so $\mathbf{X}$ is independent of earlier $\mathbf{X}$'s, $\mathbf{Y}$ is independent of earlier $\mathbf{Y}$'s, and $\mathbf{Z}$ is independent of earlier $\mathbf{Z}$'s. Thus the error encountered in any time period is estimated anew each time and does *not* include all previous errors plus the current incremental error. This is clearly unrealistic.

Nonetheless, this example shows how the analysis could progress with an improved formulation and provides some insight into the generation of an optimal strategy for releasing CO_2, as reflected in the time series $\mathbf{X(t)}$, subject to economic and social constraints. The use of the derivatives in the objective function and constraint functions of this model renders an optimal strategy sensitive to the range of technological, economic, and institutional realities.

Surprise

Much has been written about the identification of *robust* designs, those that minimize the "surprise" inherent in any plan of action which interferes with the natural world. When a designed system fails because the actual load imposed on it is larger than the so-called design load, we should not be surprised—saddened, perhaps, by our rotten luck, but not surprised. However, when a system fails because new and heretofore unknown combinations of destructive stresses are brought to bear, then we are not merely overwhelmed by having lost on a calculated risk but are genuinely surprised. It is fruitful to think of those terms typically ignored in the expansions as being one source of the surprises possible in a complex system.

As the planet becomes increasingly subject to change, it will be even more important to anticipate possible sources of surprise by taking into account more of the "missing terms" of the model. Among other things, it will be necessary to model explicitly the interaction terms (e.g., $\mathbf{XY}$ in eqn. 15) and any error terms. The present practice of running each component model separately, thereby constraining potentially important interactions with other components, is probably inadequate. At the least, methods of synchronous and asynchronous coupling now being developed for linking atmospheric, oceanic, and glacial models with their diverse time and space scales will need to be extended to linkages with other models—e.g., of atmospheric chemistry, land-surface processes, land use, and agriculture—with even more diverse time and space scales.

Management and Optimization

Finally, it may be increasingly necessary to use models of the kind outlined here to explore *optimal* or *robust* strategies for managing human activities that affect the environment. This could require numerous model simulations not only to assess the relative effects of alternative emission control policies, but also to ascertain the potential effectiveness of different strategies for preventing, responding to, or mitigating environmental changes should they occur.

For example, we note that a long-standing assumption in atmospheric GCMs has been to consider only aggregate global changes in the concentrations of CO_2 and other radiatively active trace gases. However, to the extent that these emissions are tied closely with other human activities that stress the environment—e.g., acid rain, air and water pollution, and deforestation—more detailed consideration of the time and space distribution of emissions and associated changes in boundary conditions will be required. In particular, a key task will be to develop models that treat feedbacks between climatic changes (including climatic variability) and land-surface processes consistently. For instance, significant changes in precipitation and soil moisture in mid-continental regions could well alter the vegetative cover and associated land use sufficiently on decadal time scales to have major regional climatic and other environmental effects. The ability of human institutions to deal with such effects by adaptation or mitigation is an important variable that is presumably subject to conscious alteration. Explicit inclusion of variables of this type in model runs will be necessary for realistic prediction of net risks and benefits as the basis for management and optimization decisions.

SUMMARY

Research in the area of human interactions with the natural environment has not utilized supercomputing technologies to a great degree, in part because most social-science models do not simulate human systems with the level of detail that is more typical of natural-science models. One major constraint is certainly that the data needed to implement more detailed models often do not exist.

However, as the scientific community is increasingly called upon not just to diagnose specific environmental problems but also to explore policy options and other management issues, it seems likely that much greater emphasis will be placed on quantitative assessment of the *larger* question of management of the global environment. It is in this relatively unexplored arena that we foresee many new opportunities for multidisciplinary, multivariate assessments that would undoubtedly benefit from advances in supercomputing technologies.

REFERENCES

[1] National Research Council. 1983. *Toward an International Geosphere-Biosphere Program: A Study of Global Change.* (Washington DC: National Academy Press).

[2] National Research Council. 1986. *Global Change in the Geosphere-Biosphere: Initial Priorities for an IGBP.* (Washington DC: National Academy Press).

[3] ICSU (International Council of Scientific Unions), Ad Hoc planning group on global change. 1986. *The International Geosphere-Biosphere Programme: A Study of Global Change.* (Paris: ICSU).

[4] ICSU (International Council of Scientific Unions), Special Committee for the IGBP. 1987. *Report of the First Meeting of the Special Committee, July 1987, Paris.* (Paris: ICSU).

[5] National Research Council. 1988. *Preliminary Plan for U.S. Participation in the International Geosphere-Biosphere Program.* (Washington DC: National Academy Press), in press.

[6] Clark, W.C. 1988. The human dimensions of global environmental change. In *Preliminary Plan for U.S. Participation in the International Geosphere-Biosphere Program,* National Research Council (Washington DC: National Academy Press), in press.

[7] Jacobson, H.K., and C. Shanks. 1987. Report of the Ann Arbor Workshop on an International Social Science Research Program on Global Change. Institute for Social Research, Univ. of Michigan, Ann Arbor MI.

[8] Ward, B. 1966. *Spaceship Earth.* (New York: Columbia Univ. Press).

Author Index